You don't have to read too much about the American West to realize that you're dealing with a myth.

The legend of the frontier is a frayed tapestry at best. The wilderness itself was the biggest killer, full of venomous critters, teeming with disease. A cowboy was more likely to be kicked to death by his ornery steed than shot by an outlaw. Gunfights and gunfighters were rare; if your trusty old .44 didn't jam or blow up in your hand then it probably missed completely, and most such disputes were settled when one protagonist snuck up and blew the other's head off with a shotgun.

The various personalities that populate the legends are also somewhat dubious, an odd collection of drunkards, liars and sociopaths who couldn't stay out of trouble, simply because there was so much of it to get into. Billy the Kid didn't shoot twenty-one men any more than Jesse James robbed from the rich to give to the poor. General Custer's reputation as an Indian fighter—prior to the spectacular piece of military incompetence that was the Little Bighorn—was based on a massacre of women and children.

Scalping was introduced by the U.S. cavalry. The settling and civilization of the Indian territories was essentially an act of genocide. The noble savage, in touch with his ancestors and the spirit of his mother the Earth, would be only too happy to leave you raped and castrated, desperately trying to pull your genitals out of your throat. It was a time when one tribe was outbutchered by a much bigger one, when right was asserted by nothing more than might. It was a time for killers. And they refuse to be forgotten.

The American myth originally intended to disguise this rather feisty past is, of course, the Western. In the beginning these stories were childishly simple morality tales, bearing only a minimal resemblance to the vicious reality described above. Today, at their very best, they can be so very much more. The modern western does not flinch from the horrors of the frontier. Its makers seek to understand what went before, to portray the men and women who made history, warts and all. What began as a whitewash of the past has become a tool to interrogate it.

And yet, for all that, the western remains a form of legend. The stories happen long ago and far away, in a land so wild and brutal we cannot imagine it. The characters who ride its streets and canyons are giants, the words they speak echo forever, and when the tale is told the sun goes down on a country as big as the world. I can honestly say, with my hand on my heart, that westerns are my favorite. I fervently hope they always will be.

I grew up a long, long way from America. I suppose I would have been about four when I got my first glimpse of it, watching Sunday afternoon movies on my grandparents' TV. It was always a western and it always starred John Wayne (my memory has long ago edited out the others). The Duke was just the greatest, a vast rock of a man hewn from the deserts and mountains and prairies that he strode across. *Stagecoach, Red River, She Wore A Yellow Ribbon*...I saw him stick the reins in his teeth and charge the bad guys, two guns blazing—"Fill your hand, you son of a bitch"—in *True Grit*, watched him walk away from that doorway at the end of *The Searchers*, and I saw him fall—shot in the back by Bruce Dern in *The Cowboys*, an act that lives in infamy. John Wayne, you see, was always right: because he was John Wayne. It couldn't have been simpler.

I got older. I saw Lee Marvin, Burt Lancaster, Gary Cooper, Gregory Peck. Eyes a-popping, I watched *The Wild Bunch* perish in a holocaust of lead, old men out of time who couldn't think beyond their guns. Most of all, I saw the figure who would become my greatest hero: Clint Eastwood. Because he was cool. And because he always seemed to know exactly what he was doing.

From the moment I saw the poncho-clad stranger blast these three—my mistake, four— scumbags to death at the start of *A Fistful of Dollars*, I knew I was watching something new. There was a big difference here, a sense of laid-back, self-assured cynicism. It sat well with the brutal world the stranger lived in, and for all the theatrics and superhuman gunplay of the *Dollar* trilogy, perhaps it was the first nod toward capturing the reality of the frontier. From the quiet farmer forced to vengeance in *The Outlaw Josey Wales*, to the stone killer of *Unforgiven*, Clint Eastwood shows us an Old West we would be both foolish and dishonest to deny.

It was *Unforgiven*, in fact, which led most directly to the creation of the story you're about to start reading, if you can ever get through this damned introduction. Something about the film touched me like nothing I'd ever seen before—touched me, Christ, it pinned me to my bloody seat. The story of a man who tried and tried and tried to deny his true nature, finally succumbing to the darkness inside him, damning himself completely. The last twenty-odd minutes, culminating in William Munny's ground-out, hate-filled warnings to the township, the Stars and Stripes flapping behind him in the driving rain, were nothing short of apocalyptic. He was tragic, invincible, terrifying: Clint Eastwood as the Angel of Death.

Three or four years ago I was getting ready to begin writing my own take on the western. It would be called PREACHER, I'd decided, and though set in modern-day Texas it would have all the hallmarks of the stories I grew up on. The hero would stand four-square for what was right and just, the girl would be beautiful, the sidekick a rogue, the villains a bunch of shits, the comic relief an annoying little bastard. But I felt one more character was needed to round out the cast: someone who would directly represent the Old West, who had walked straight out of history, and who brought with him the horror and terror of those times. He would be a figure of ultimate, inescapable doom. And the world would tremble at the thunder of his guns.

The artist of PREACHER was, and is—and could only ever have been—my good friend Steve Dillon, and he captured exactly what it was I wanted. Steve threw Lee Marvin into the mix, being a big fan, and what we got was a figure who moved and spoke like Eastwood, had his heartstopping glare, but also possessed the surly, carved-from-sandstone looks of Marvin. Thus was born the Saint of Killers.

We got lucky with PREACHER. Its modest success in a slumping industry gave me a chance to tell some dark little tales I'd always wanted to tell, one of those being the story of the Saint. It was his origin, I knew, that would set him apart; it was the things he'd been through as a man, both alive and dead, that would make him more than the sum of his parts. All of which brings me, by a long old trail, I know, back to the place I began. Myth.

The Saint of Killers story is a genuine western, in that its setting is that of the West, but it is told as a myth. It is a legend whispered from killer to killer down the years. The west portrayed is the real one taken to extremes, a cold, dread place where the sun rises only briefly, and then succumbs to night. Larry McMurtry's *Lonesome Dove* was an influence, and its melancholy adaptation so brilliantly brought to life by Robert Duvall and Tommy Lee Jones; so was the appalling frontier savagery depicted in *Blood Meridian*, by Cormac McCarthy. But above all I was remembering the vision of cinematic terror I'd seen in *Unforgiven*, a hundred times more awful than any vampire, alien or killer robot: the horror that one man held inside himself, finally and dreadfully let loose. Books and movies...SAINT OF KILLERS is a myth inspired by myths.

With Mr. Dillon busy on the monthly PREACHER, another Steve was brought in to illustrate SAINT OF KILLERS. Steve Pugh's finely textured pages caught the feeling I was after with uncanny grace. Here was a black, brooding world inhabited by trash and vermin, where a man who stood tall with unbowed head was practically unique. Vile things crawled from the shadows. Wretched little men committed wretched little acts. The land itself was a frozen, hostile foe; perhaps my favorite sequence of Steve's is the Stranger's ride through the forest, the wolf pack watching from the darkness. Then again, the hacking, blasting gun-and-sword affray that ends part two must be seen to be believed. Old master Carlos Ezquerra stepped in when time grew tight, illustrating the most arduous, macabre sequences with ease. Carlos, mind you, has been making the murderously difficult look simple for over twenty years.

Of all the stories I've written to date, this one is perhaps my favorite. I filled it full of all that good stuff I'd seen and loved in the movies: the hard-bitten, silent stranger, the lowdown, no-good skunks, the little town of frightened souls on the endless empty plain; the challenge, the killing, the long, long ride on the vengeance trail; the lone figure at story's end, never once looking back, stepping boldly into legend. The Saint casts his grim shadow over PREACHER to this day, and will continue to do so right up to the end. It's only right he should.

His story is a myth. All westerns are.

Writing my own was the joy I always knew it would be.

—Garth Ennis
SIPPIN' REDEYE, OCTOBER 1997

PREACHER
ANCIENT
HISTORY

Garth Ennis
WRITER

Steve Pugh
Carlos Ezquerra
Richard Case
ARTISTS

Pamela Rambo
Matt Hollingsworth
Nathan Eyring
COLORISTS

Clem Robins
LETTERER

PREACHER, SAINT OF KILLERS, ARSEFACE, and other
related characters created by Garth Ennis and Steve Dillon

TABLE OF CONTENTS

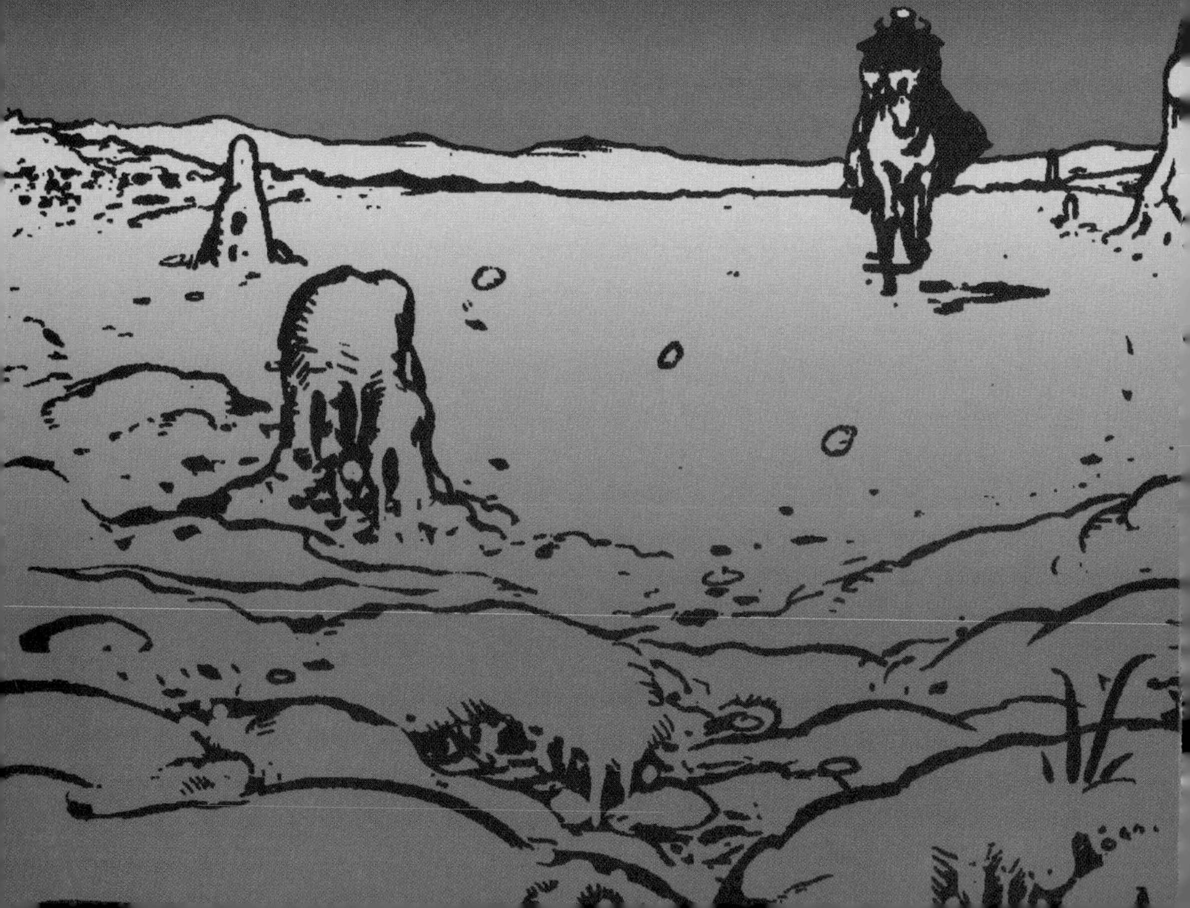

SAINT OF KILLERS

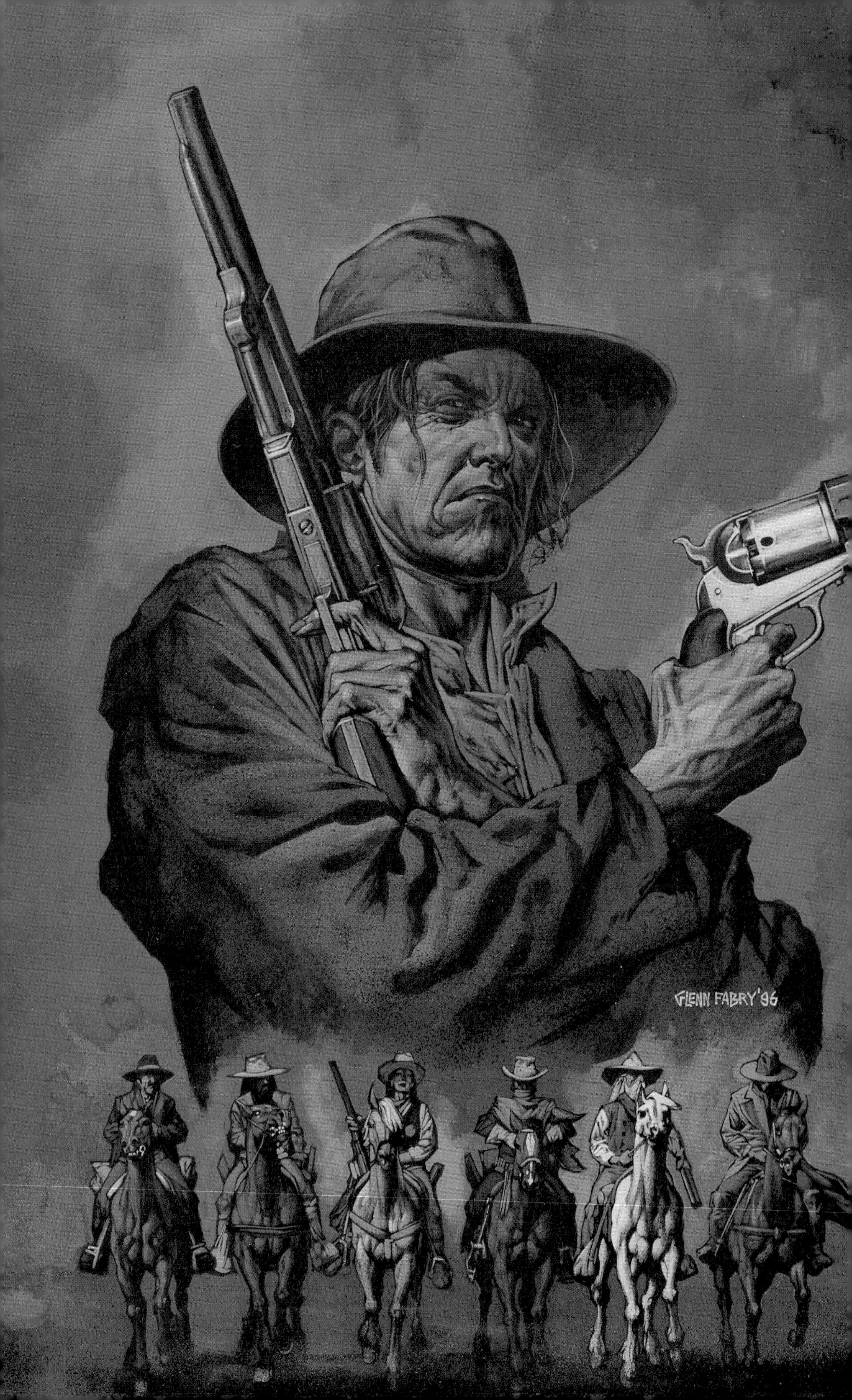
GLENN FABRY '96

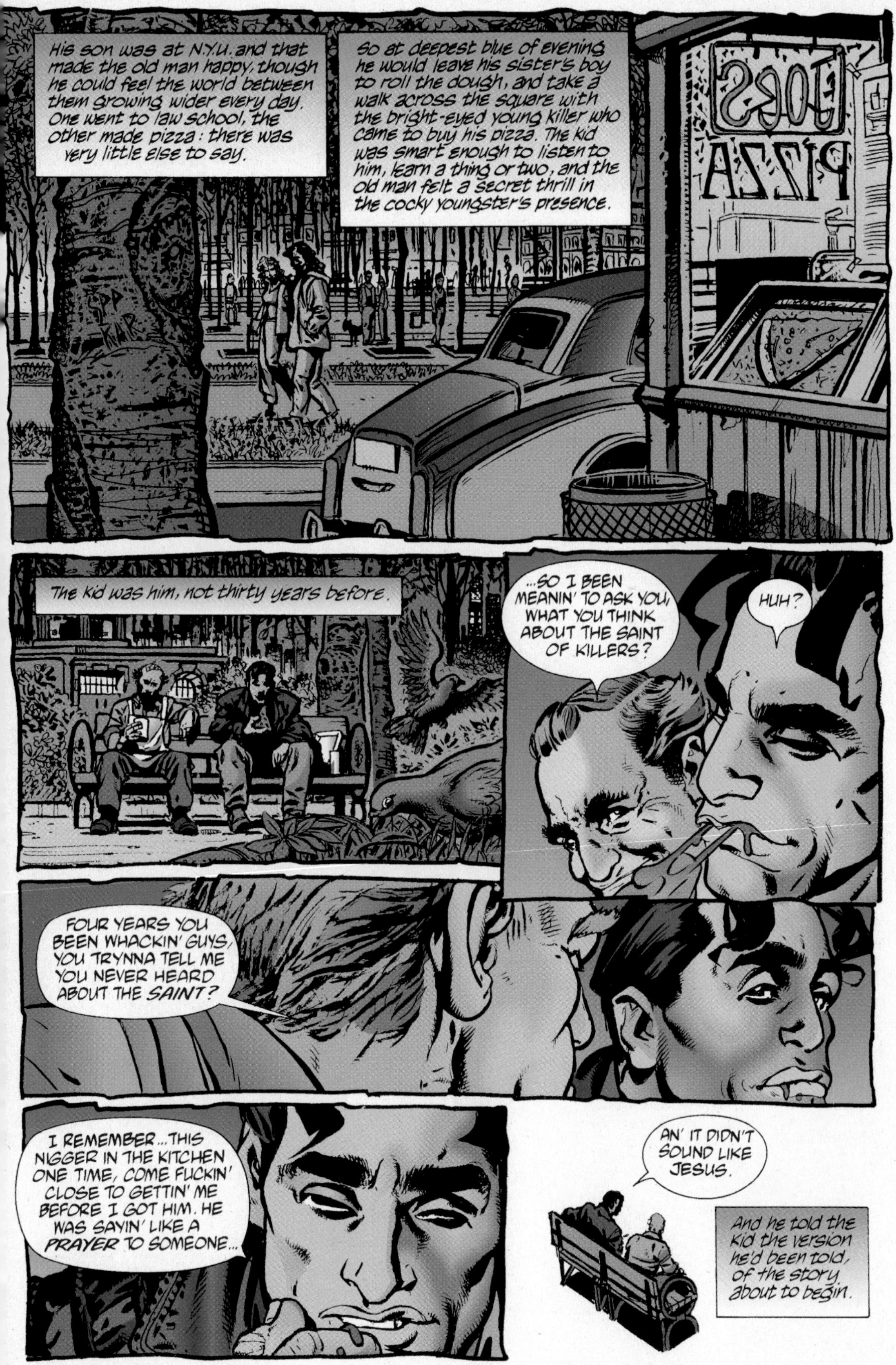
His son was at N.Y.U. and that made the old man happy, though he could feel the world between them growing wider every day. One went to law school, the other made pizza: there was very little else to say.
So at deepest blue of evening he would leave his sister's boy to roll the dough, and take a walk across the square with the bright-eyed young killer who came to buy his pizza. The kid was smart enough to listen to him, learn a thing or two, and the old man felt a secret thrill in the cocky youngster's presence.
PIZZA
The kid was him, not thirty years before.
...SO I BEEN MEANIN' TO ASK YOU, WHAT YOU THINK ABOUT THE SAINT OF KILLERS?
HUH?
FOUR YEARS YOU BEEN WHACKIN' GUYS, YOU TRYNNA TELL ME YOU NEVER HEARD ABOUT THE SAINT?
I REMEMBER... THIS NIGGER IN THE KITCHEN ONE TIME, COME FUCKIN' CLOSE TO GETTIN' ME BEFORE I GOT HIM. HE WAS SAYIN' LIKE A PRAYER TO SOMEONE...
AN' IT DIDN'T SOUND LIKE JESUS.
And he told the kid the version he'd been told, of the story about to begin.

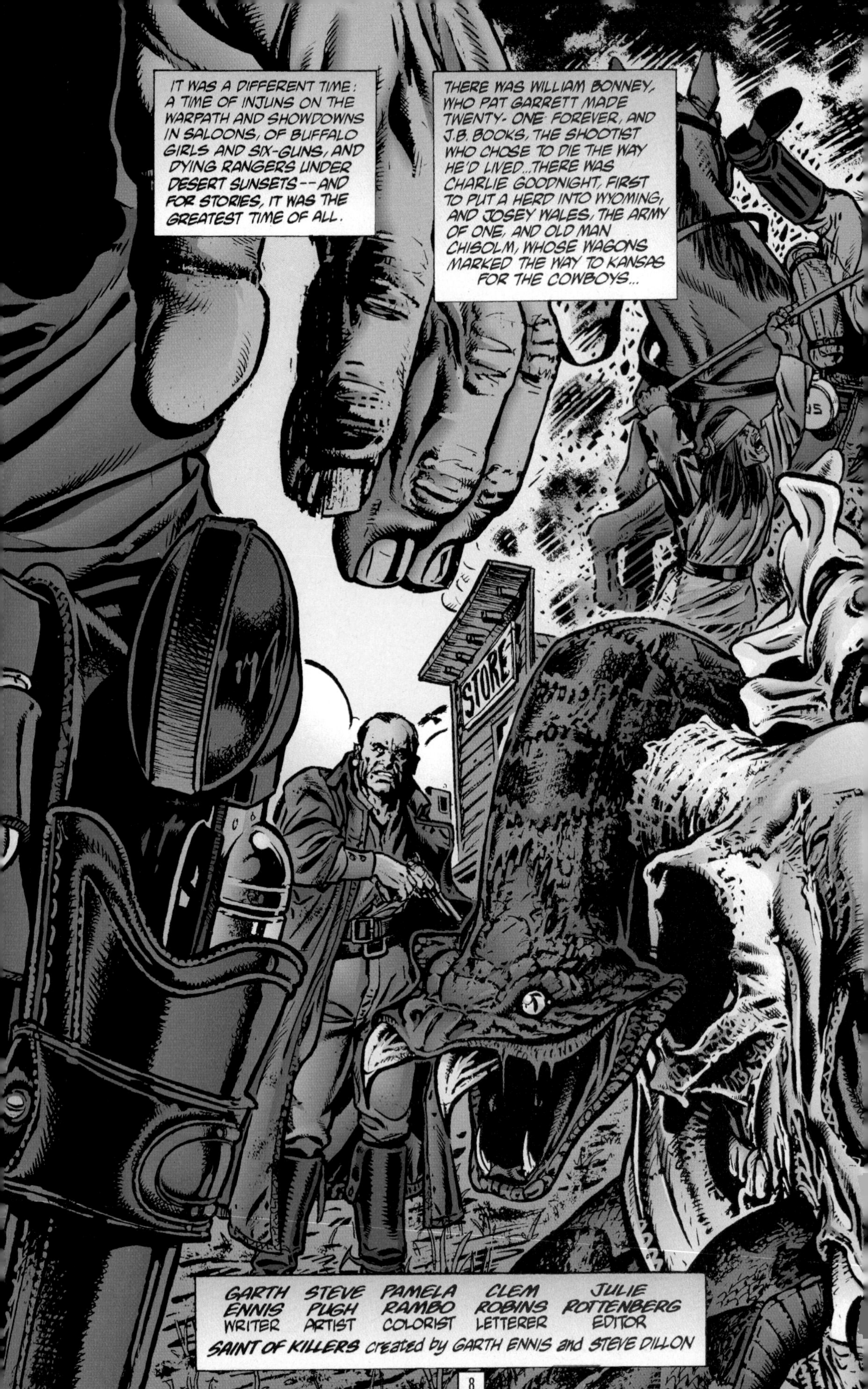
IT WAS A DIFFERENT TIME: A TIME OF INJUNS ON THE WARPATH AND SHOWDOWNS IN SALOONS, OF BUFFALO GIRLS AND SIX-GUNS, AND DYING RANGERS UNDER DESERT SUNSETS-- AND FOR STORIES, IT WAS THE GREATEST TIME OF ALL.
THERE WAS WILLIAM BONNEY, WHO PAT GARRETT MADE TWENTY-ONE FOREVER, AND J.B. BOOKS, THE SHOOTIST WHO CHOSE TO DIE THE WAY HE'D LIVED...THERE WAS CHARLIE GOODNIGHT, FIRST TO PUT A HERD INTO WYOMING, AND JOSEY WALES, THE ARMY OF ONE, AND OLD MAN CHISOLM, WHOSE WAGONS MARKED THE WAY TO KANSAS FOR THE COWBOYS...
STORE
GARTH ENNIS WRITER
STEVE PUGH ARTIST
PAMELA RAMBO COLORIST
CLEM ROBINS LETTERER
JULIE ROTTENBERG EDITOR
SAINT OF KILLERS created by GARTH ENNIS and STEVE DILLON

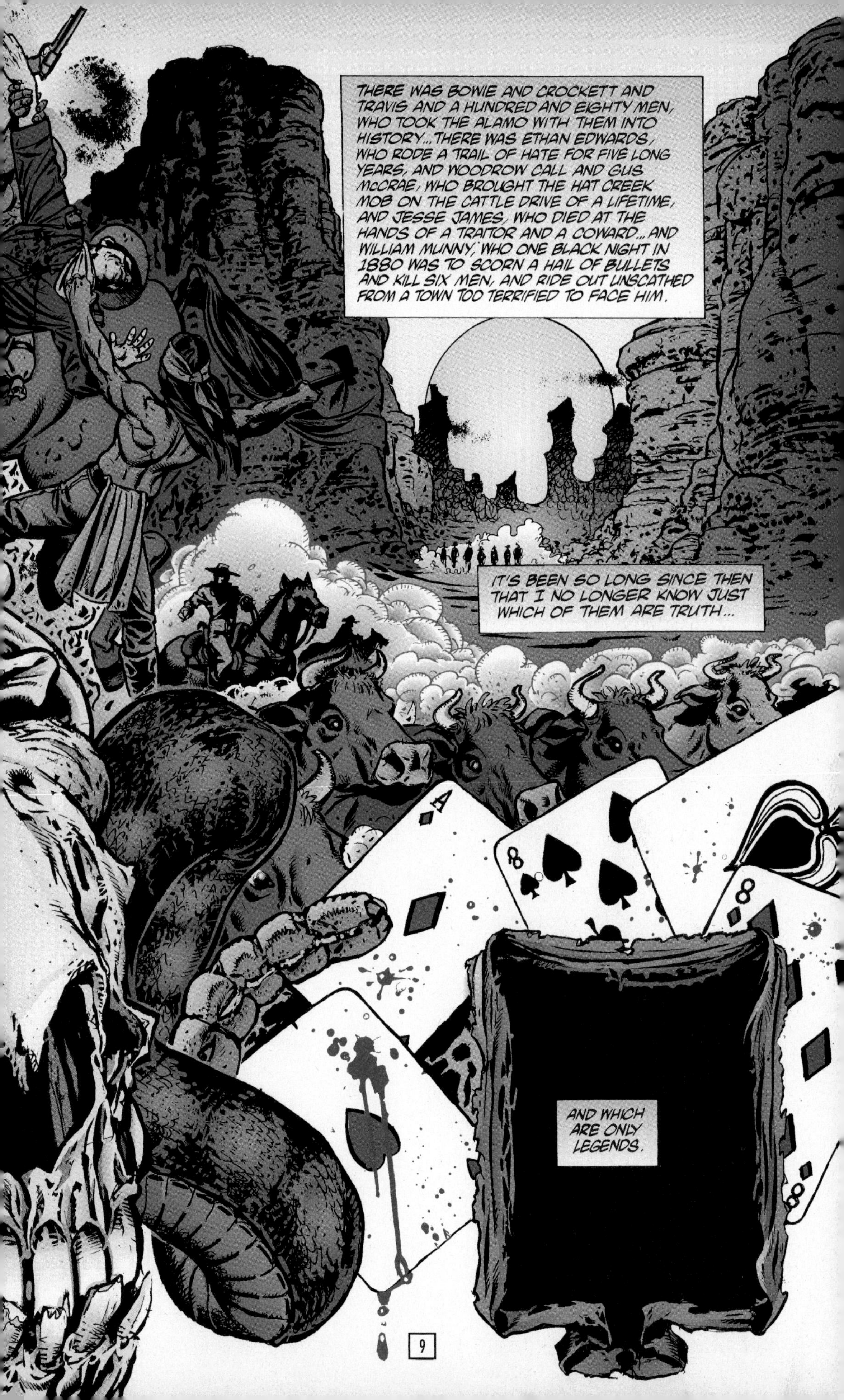
THERE WAS BOWIE AND CROCKETT AND TRAVIS AND A HUNDRED AND EIGHTY MEN, WHO TOOK THE ALAMO WITH THEM INTO HISTORY... THERE WAS ETHAN EDWARDS, WHO RODE A TRAIL OF HATE FOR FIVE LONG YEARS, AND WOODROW CALL AND GUS McCRAE, WHO BROUGHT THE HAT CREEK MOB ON THE CATTLE DRIVE OF A LIFETIME, AND JESSE JAMES, WHO DIED AT THE HANDS OF A TRAITOR AND A COWARD... AND WILLIAM MUNNY, WHO ONE BLACK NIGHT IN 1880 WAS TO SCORN A HAIL OF BULLETS AND KILL SIX MEN, AND RIDE OUT UNSCATHED FROM A TOWN TOO TERRIFIED TO FACE HIM.
IT'S BEEN SO LONG SINCE THEN THAT I NO LONGER KNOW JUST WHICH OF THEM ARE TRUTH...
AND WHICH ARE ONLY LEGENDS.

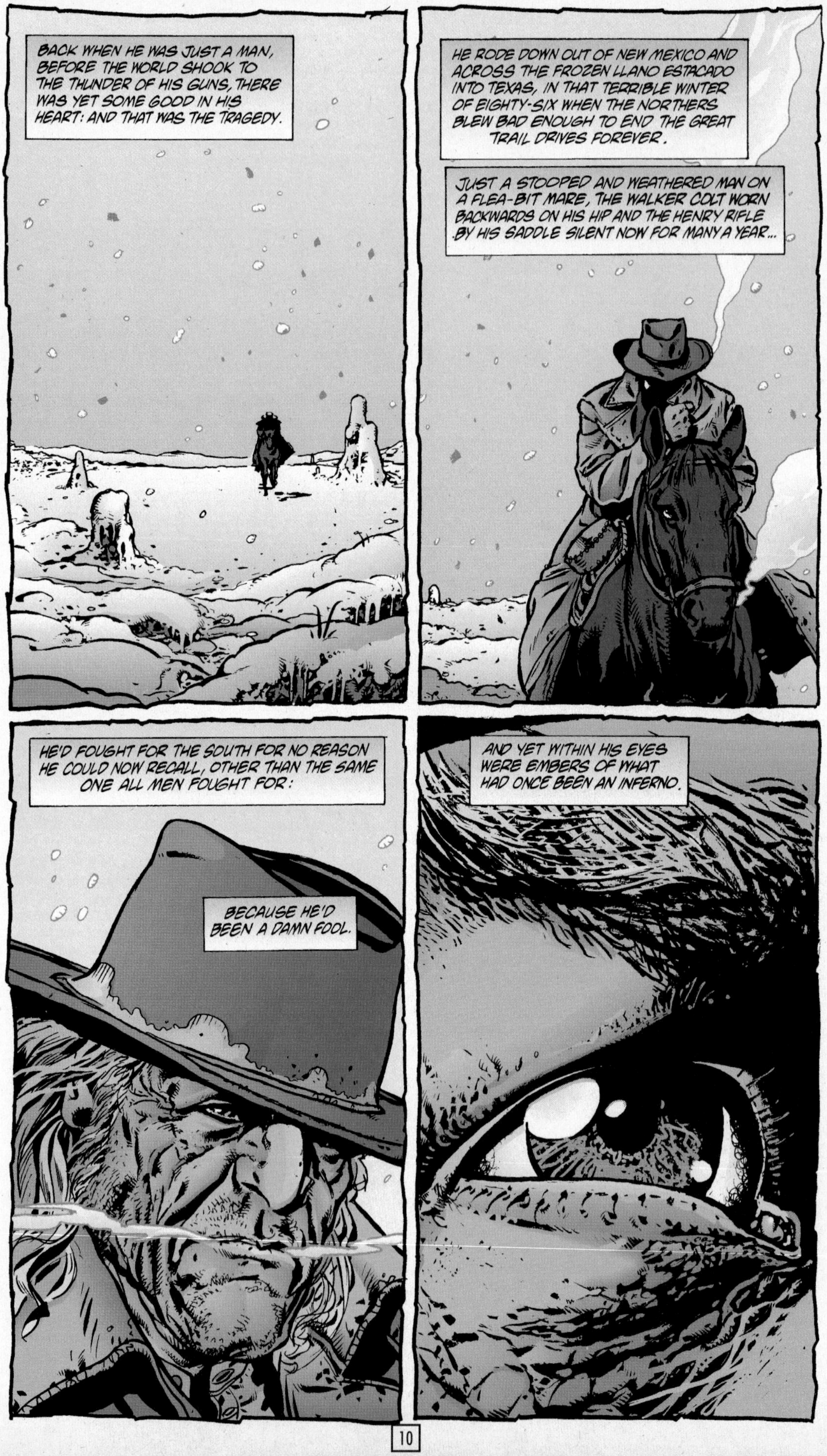
BACK WHEN HE WAS JUST A MAN, BEFORE THE WORLD SHOOK TO THE THUNDER OF HIS GUNS, THERE WAS YET SOME GOOD IN HIS HEART: AND THAT WAS THE TRAGEDY.
HE RODE DOWN OUT OF NEW MEXICO AND ACROSS THE FROZEN LLANO ESTACADO INTO TEXAS, IN THAT TERRIBLE WINTER OF EIGHTY-SIX WHEN THE NORTHERS BLEW BAD ENOUGH TO END THE GREAT TRAIL DRIVES FOREVER.
JUST A STOOPED AND WEATHERED MAN ON A FLEA-BIT MARE, THE WALKER COLT WORN BACKWARDS ON HIS HIP AND THE HENRY RIFLE BY HIS SADDLE SILENT NOW FOR MANY A YEAR...
HE'D FOUGHT FOR THE SOUTH FOR NO REASON HE COULD NOW RECALL, OTHER THAN THE SAME ONE ALL MEN FOUGHT FOR:
BECAUSE HE'D BEEN A DAMN FOOL.
AND YET WITHIN HIS EYES WERE EMBERS OF WHAT HAD ONCE BEEN AN INFERNO.

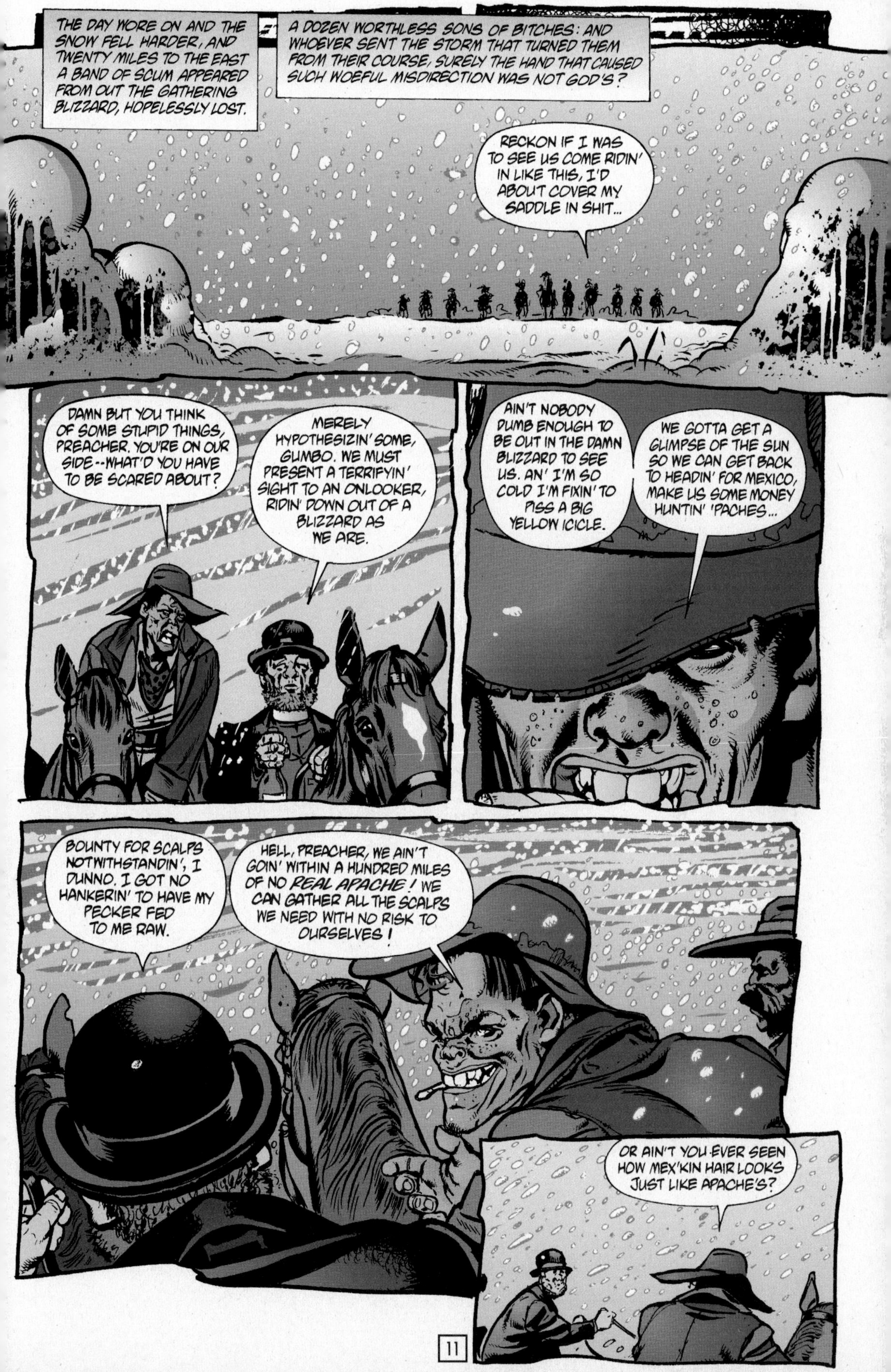

THE DAY WORE ON AND THE SNOW FELL HARDER, AND TWENTY MILES TO THE EAST A BAND OF SCUM APPEARED FROM OUT THE GATHERING BLIZZARD, HOPELESSLY LOST.
A DOZEN WORTHLESS SONS OF BITCHES: AND WHOEVER SENT THE STORM THAT TURNED THEM FROM THEIR COURSE, SURELY THE HAND THAT CAUSED SUCH WOEFUL MISDIRECTION WAS NOT GOD'S?
RECKON IF I WAS TO SEE US COME RIDIN' IN LIKE THIS, I'D ABOUT COVER MY SADDLE IN SHIT...
DAMN BUT YOU THINK OF SOME STUPID THINGS, PREACHER. YOU'RE ON OUR SIDE--WHAT'D YOU HAVE TO BE SCARED ABOUT?
MERELY HYPOTHESIZIN' SOME, GUMBO. WE MUST PRESENT A TERRIFYIN' SIGHT TO AN ONLOOKER, RIDIN' DOWN OUT OF A BLIZZARD AS WE ARE.
AIN'T NOBODY DUMB ENOUGH TO BE OUT IN THE DAMN BLIZZARD TO SEE US. AN' I'M SO COLD I'M FIXIN' TO PISS A BIG YELLOW ICICLE.
WE GOTTA GET A GLIMPSE OF THE SUN SO WE CAN GET BACK TO HEADIN' FOR MEXICO, MAKE US SOME MONEY HUNTIN' 'PACHES...
BOUNTY FOR SCALPS NOTWITHSTANDIN', I DUNNO. I GOT NO HANKERIN' TO HAVE MY PECKER FED TO ME RAW.
HELL, PREACHER, WE AIN'T GOIN' WITHIN A HUNDRED MILES OF NO *REAL APACHE!* WE CAN GATHER ALL THE SCALPS WE NEED WITH NO RISK TO OURSELVES!
OR AIN'T YOU EVER SEEN HOW MEX'KIN HAIR LOOKS JUST LIKE APACHE'S?

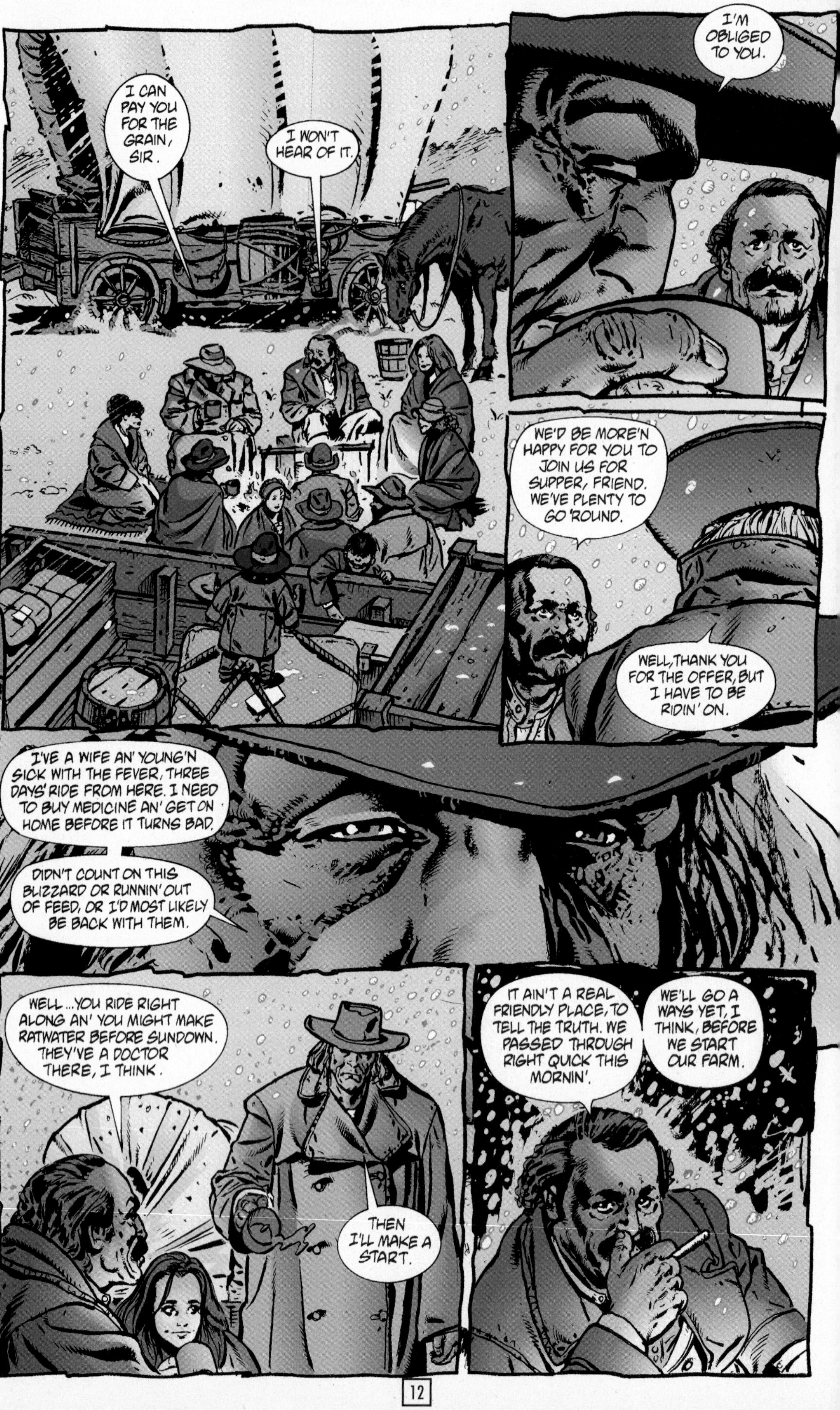
I CAN PAY YOU FOR THE GRAIN, SIR.
I WON'T HEAR OF IT.
I'M OBLIGED TO YOU.
WE'D BE MORE'N HAPPY FOR YOU TO JOIN US FOR SUPPER, FRIEND. WE'VE PLENTY TO GO 'ROUND.
WELL, THANK YOU FOR THE OFFER, BUT I HAVE TO BE RIDIN' ON.
I'VE A WIFE AN' YOUNG'N SICK WITH THE FEVER, THREE DAYS' RIDE FROM HERE. I NEED TO BUY MEDICINE AN' GET ON HOME BEFORE IT TURNS BAD.
DIDN'T COUNT ON THIS BLIZZARD OR RUNNIN' OUT OF FEED, OR I'D MOST LIKELY BE BACK WITH THEM.
WELL... YOU RIDE RIGHT ALONG AN' YOU MIGHT MAKE RATWATER BEFORE SUNDOWN. THEY'VE A DOCTOR THERE, I THINK.
THEN I'LL MAKE A START.
IT AIN'T A REAL FRIENDLY PLACE, TO TELL THE TRUTH. WE PASSED THROUGH RIGHT QUICK THIS MORNIN'.
WE'LL GO A WAYS YET, I THINK, BEFORE WE START OUR FARM.

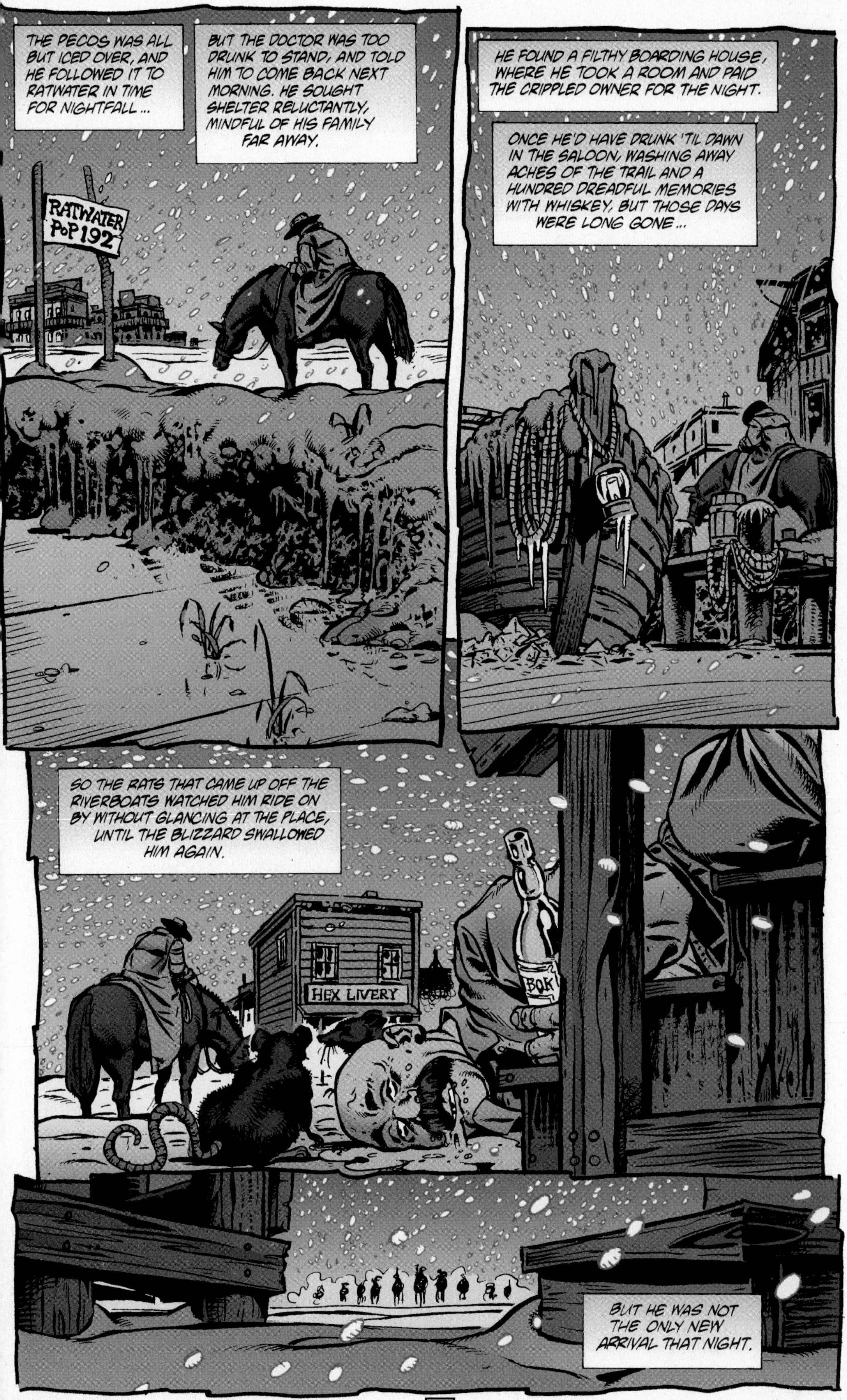
THE PECOS WAS ALL BUT ICED OVER, AND HE FOLLOWED IT TO RATWATER IN TIME FOR NIGHTFALL...
BUT THE DOCTOR WAS TOO DRUNK TO STAND, AND TOLD HIM TO COME BACK NEXT MORNING. HE SOUGHT SHELTER RELUCTANTLY, MINDFUL OF HIS FAMILY FAR AWAY.
RATWATER POP 192
HE FOUND A FILTHY BOARDING HOUSE, WHERE HE TOOK A ROOM AND PAID THE CRIPPLED OWNER FOR THE NIGHT.
ONCE HE'D HAVE DRUNK 'TIL DAWN IN THE SALOON, WASHING AWAY ACHES OF THE TRAIL AND A HUNDRED DREADFUL MEMORIES WITH WHISKEY, BUT THOSE DAYS WERE LONG GONE...
SO THE RATS THAT CAME UP OFF THE RIVERBOATS WATCHED HIM RIDE ON BY WITHOUT GLANCING AT THE PLACE, UNTIL THE BLIZZARD SWALLOWED HIM AGAIN.
HEX LIVERY
BOK
BUT HE WAS NOT THE ONLY NEW ARRIVAL THAT NIGHT.

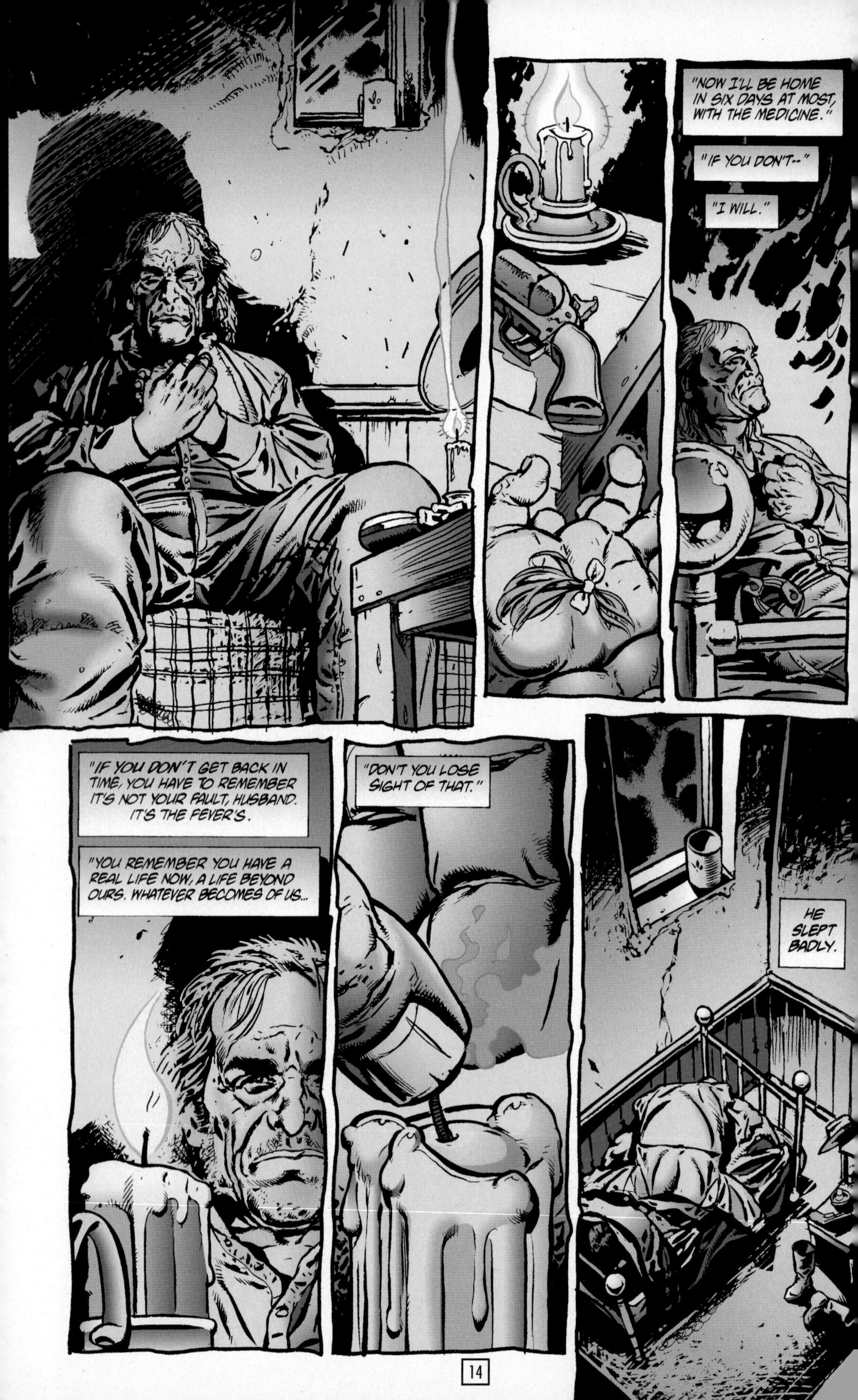
"NOW I'LL BE HOME IN SIX DAYS AT MOST, WITH THE MEDICINE."
"IF YOU DON'T--"
"I WILL."
"IF YOU DON'T GET BACK IN TIME, YOU HAVE TO REMEMBER IT'S NOT YOUR FAULT, HUSBAND. IT'S THE FEVER'S.
"YOU REMEMBER YOU HAVE A REAL LIFE NOW, A LIFE BEYOND OURS. WHATEVER BECOMES OF US...
"DON'T YOU LOSE SIGHT OF THAT."
HE SLEPT BADLY.

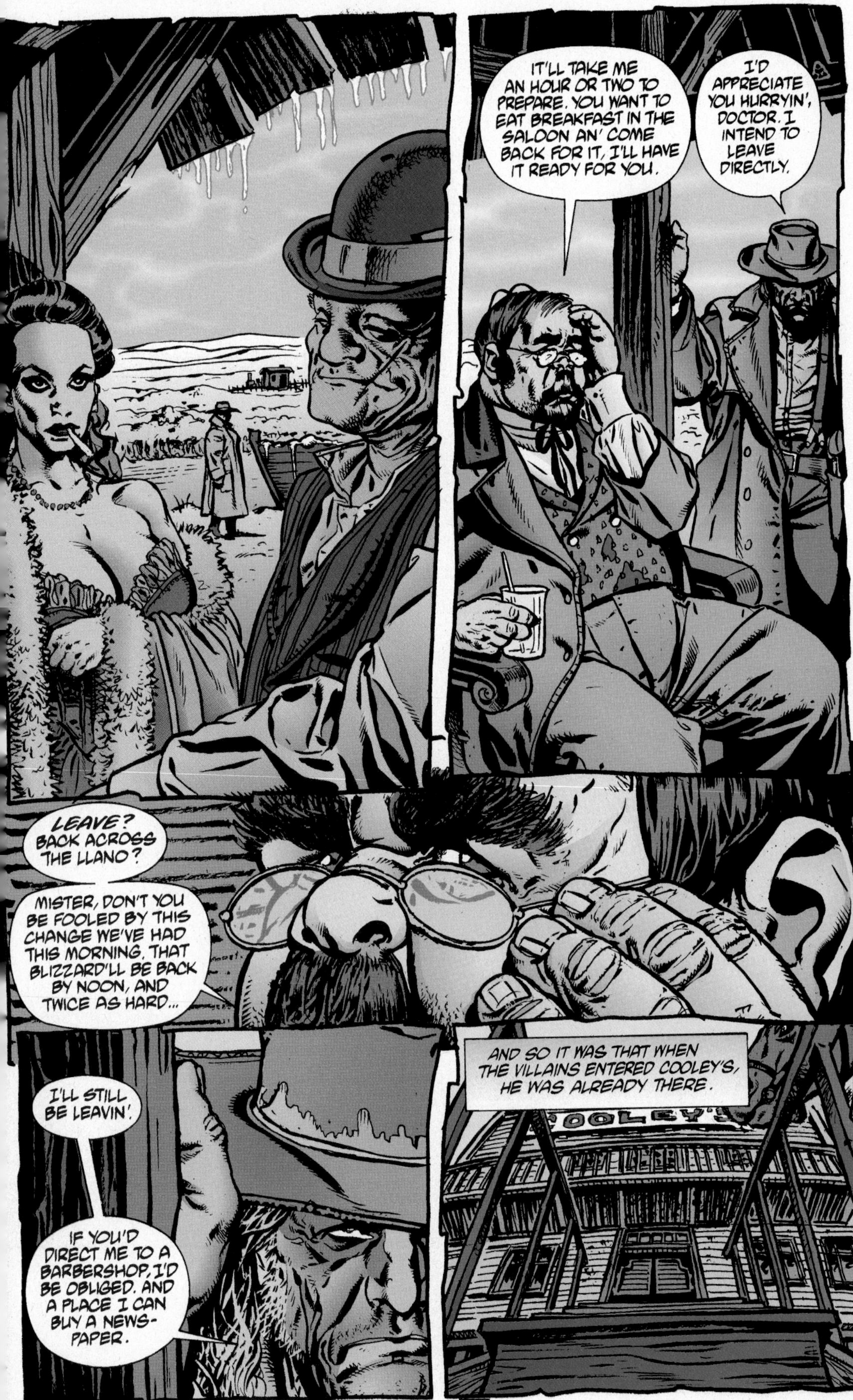
IT'LL TAKE ME AN HOUR OR TWO TO PREPARE. YOU WANT TO EAT BREAKFAST IN THE SALOON AN' COME BACK FOR IT, I'LL HAVE IT READY FOR YOU.
I'D APPRECIATE YOU HURRYIN', DOCTOR. I INTEND TO LEAVE DIRECTLY.
LEAVE? BACK ACROSS THE LLANO?
MISTER, DON'T YOU BE FOOLED BY THIS CHANGE WE'VE HAD THIS MORNING. THAT BLIZZARD'LL BE BACK BY NOON, AND TWICE AS HARD...
I'LL STILL BE LEAVIN'.
IF YOU'D DIRECT ME TO A BARBERSHOP, I'D BE OBLIGED. AND A PLACE I CAN BUY A NEWS-PAPER.
AND SO IT WAS THAT WHEN THE VILLAINS ENTERED COOLEY'S, HE WAS ALREADY THERE.

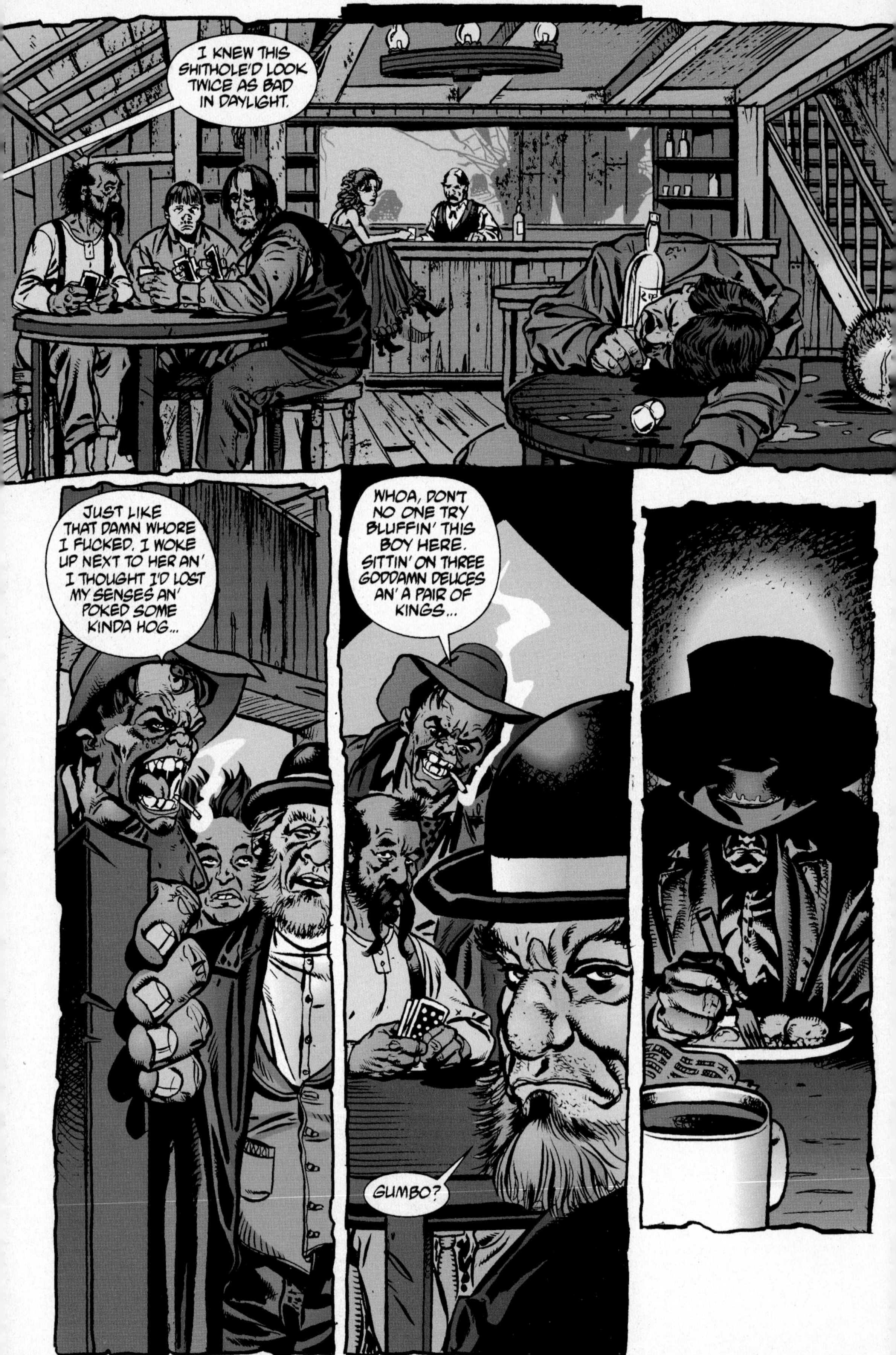
I KNEW THIS SHITHOLE'D LOOK TWICE AS BAD IN DAYLIGHT.
JUST LIKE THAT DAMN WHORE I FUCKED. I WOKE UP NEXT TO HER AN' I THOUGHT I'D LOST MY SENSES AN' POKED SOME KINDA HOG...
WHOA, DON'T NO ONE TRY BLUFFIN' THIS BOY HERE. SITTIN' ON THREE GODDAMN DEUCES AN' A PAIR OF KINGS...
GUMBO?

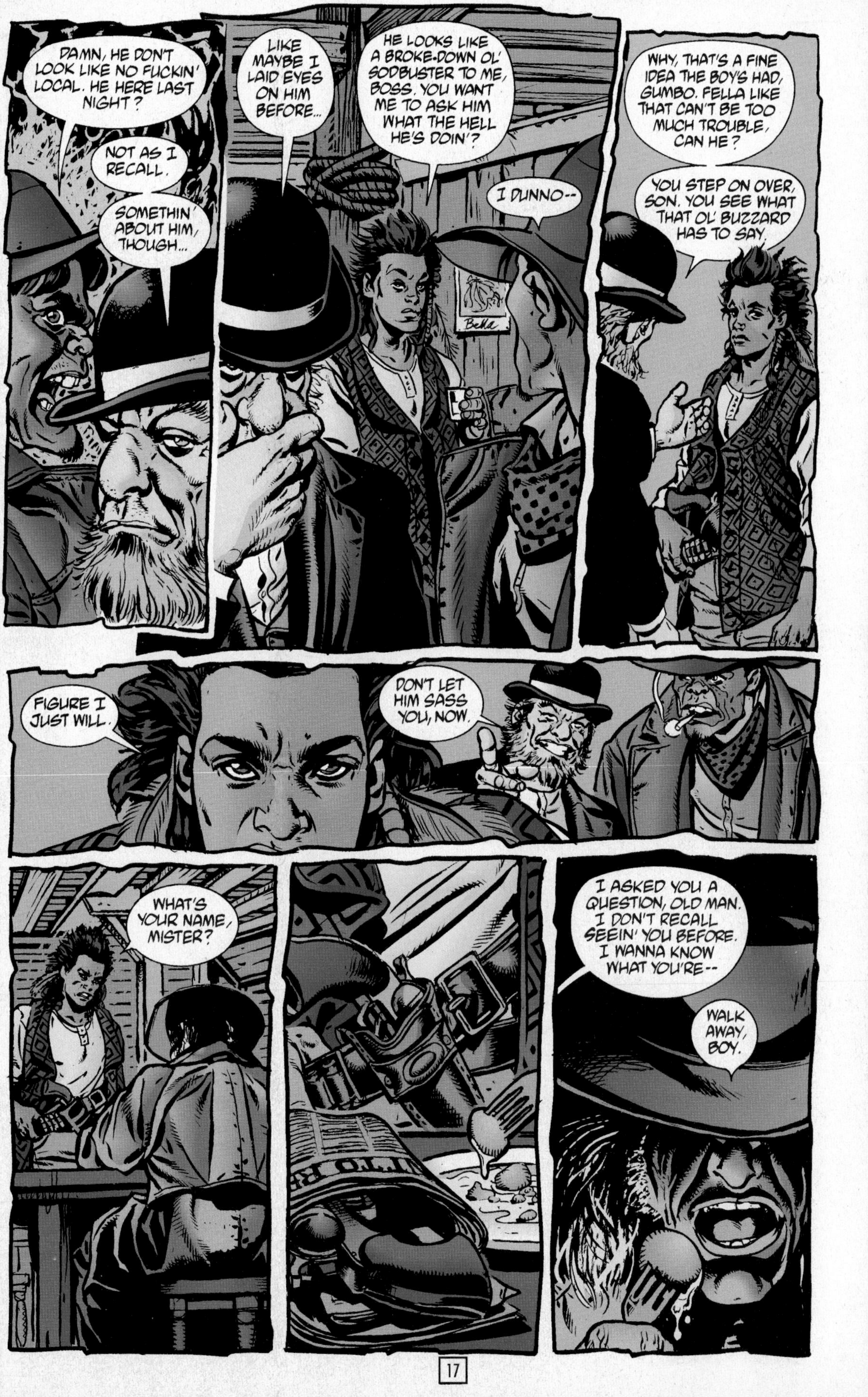
DAMN, HE DON'T LOOK LIKE NO FUCKIN' LOCAL. HE HERE LAST NIGHT?
NOT AS I RECALL.
SOMETHIN' ABOUT HIM, THOUGH...
LIKE MAYBE I LAID EYES ON HIM BEFORE...
HE LOOKS LIKE A BROKE-DOWN OL' SODBUSTER TO ME, BOSS. YOU WANT ME TO ASK HIM WHAT THE HELL HE'S DOIN'?
I DUNNO--
WHY, THAT'S A FINE IDEA THE BOY'S HAD, GUMBO. FELLA LIKE THAT CAN'T BE TOO MUCH TROUBLE, CAN HE?
YOU STEP ON OVER, SON. YOU SEE WHAT THAT OL' BUZZARD HAS TO SAY.
FIGURE I JUST WILL.
DON'T LET HIM SASS YOU, NOW.
WHAT'S YOUR NAME, MISTER?
I ASKED YOU A QUESTION, OLD MAN. I DON'T RECALL SEEIN' YOU BEFORE. I WANNA KNOW WHAT YOU'RE--
WALK AWAY, BOY.

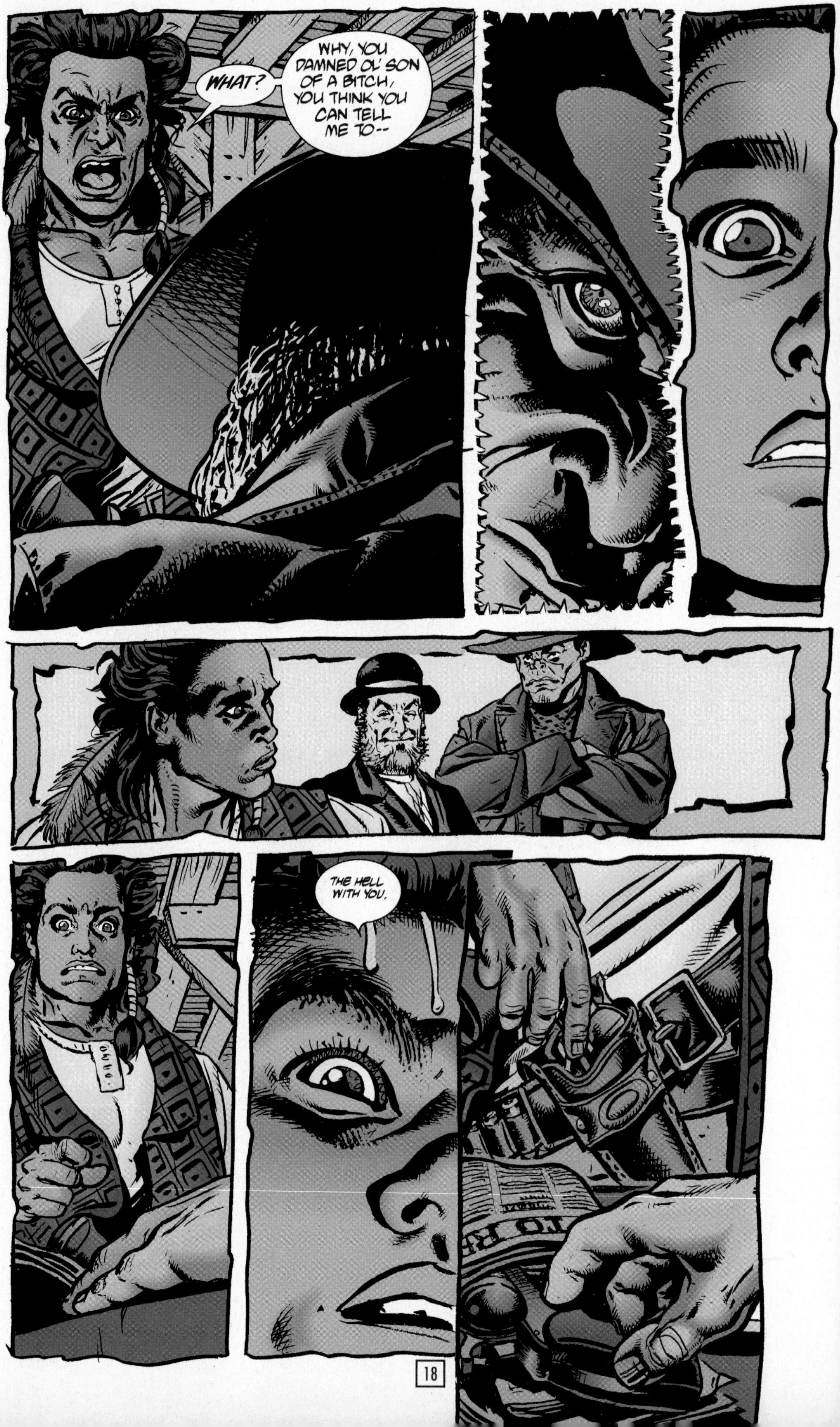
WHAT?
WHY, YOU DAMNED OL' SON OF A BITCH, YOU THINK YOU CAN TELL ME TO--
THE HELL WITH YOU.

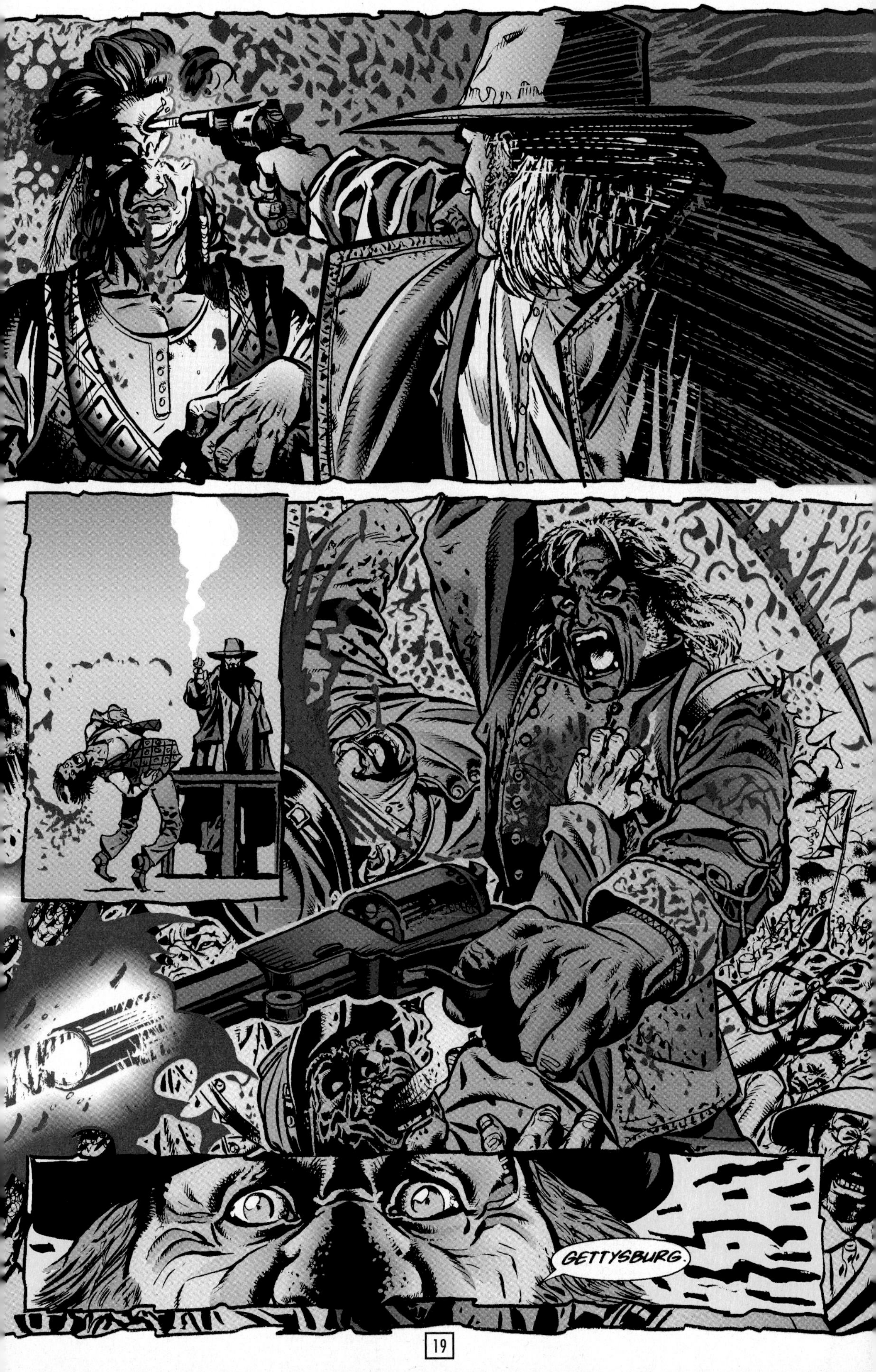
GETTYSBURG.

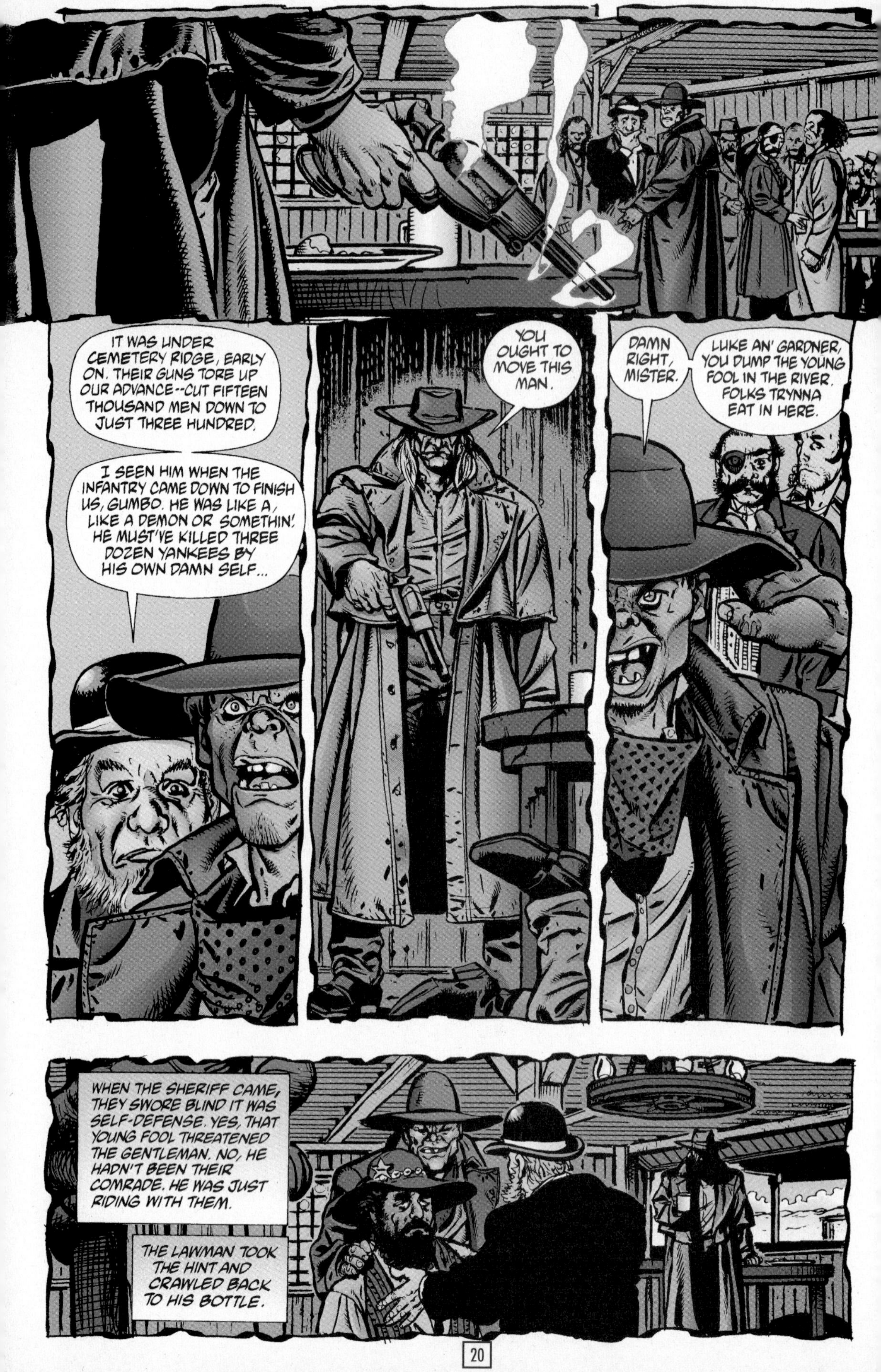
IT WAS UNDER CEMETERY RIDGE, EARLY ON. THEIR GUNS TORE UP OUR ADVANCE--CUT FIFTEEN THOUSAND MEN DOWN TO JUST THREE HUNDRED.
I SEEN HIM WHEN THE INFANTRY CAME DOWN TO FINISH US, GUMBO. HE WAS LIKE A, LIKE A DEMON OR SOMETHIN'. HE MUST'VE KILLED THREE DOZEN YANKEES BY HIS OWN DAMN SELF...
YOU OUGHT TO MOVE THIS MAN.
DAMN RIGHT, MISTER.
LUKE AN' GARDNER, YOU DUMP THE YOUNG FOOL IN THE RIVER. FOLKS TRYNNA EAT IN HERE.
WHEN THE SHERIFF CAME, THEY SWORE BLIND IT WAS SELF-DEFENSE. YES, THAT YOUNG FOOL THREATENED THE GENTLEMAN. NO, HE HADN'T BEEN THEIR COMRADE. HE WAS JUST RIDING WITH THEM.
THE LAWMAN TOOK THE HINT AND CRAWLED BACK TO HIS BOTTLE.

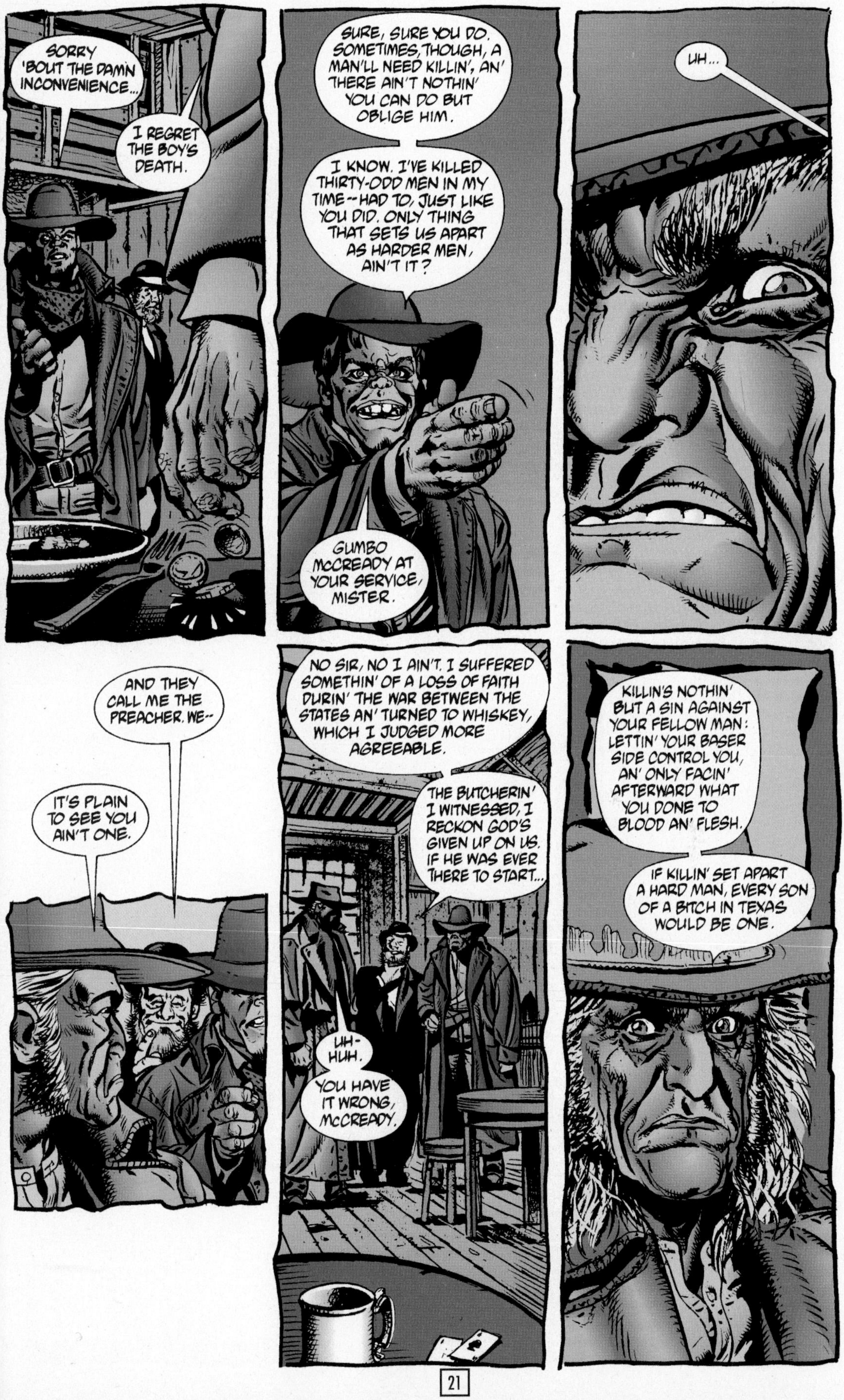
SORRY 'BOUT THE DAMN INCONVENIENCE...
I REGRET THE BOY'S DEATH.
SURE, SURE YOU DO. SOMETIMES, THOUGH, A MAN'LL NEED KILLIN', AN' THERE AIN'T NOTHIN' YOU CAN DO BUT OBLIGE HIM.
I KNOW. I'VE KILLED THIRTY-ODD MEN IN MY TIME--HAD TO, JUST LIKE YOU DID. ONLY THING THAT SETS US APART AS HARDER MEN, AIN'T IT?
GUMBO McCREADY AT YOUR SERVICE, MISTER.
UH...
AND THEY CALL ME THE PREACHER. WE--
IT'S PLAIN TO SEE YOU AIN'T ONE.
NO SIR, NO I AIN'T. I SUFFERED SOMETHIN' OF A LOSS OF FAITH DURIN' THE WAR BETWEEN THE STATES AN' TURNED TO WHISKEY, WHICH I JUDGED MORE AGREEABLE.
THE BUTCHERIN' I WITNESSED, I RECKON GOD'S GIVEN UP ON US. IF HE WAS EVER THERE TO START...
UH-HUH.
YOU HAVE IT WRONG, McCREADY.
KILLIN'S NOTHIN' BUT A SIN AGAINST YOUR FELLOW MAN: LETTIN' YOUR BASER SIDE CONTROL YOU, AN' ONLY FACIN' AFTERWARD WHAT YOU DONE TO BLOOD AN' FLESH.
IF KILLIN' SET APART A HARD MAN, EVERY SON OF A BITCH IN TEXAS WOULD BE ONE.

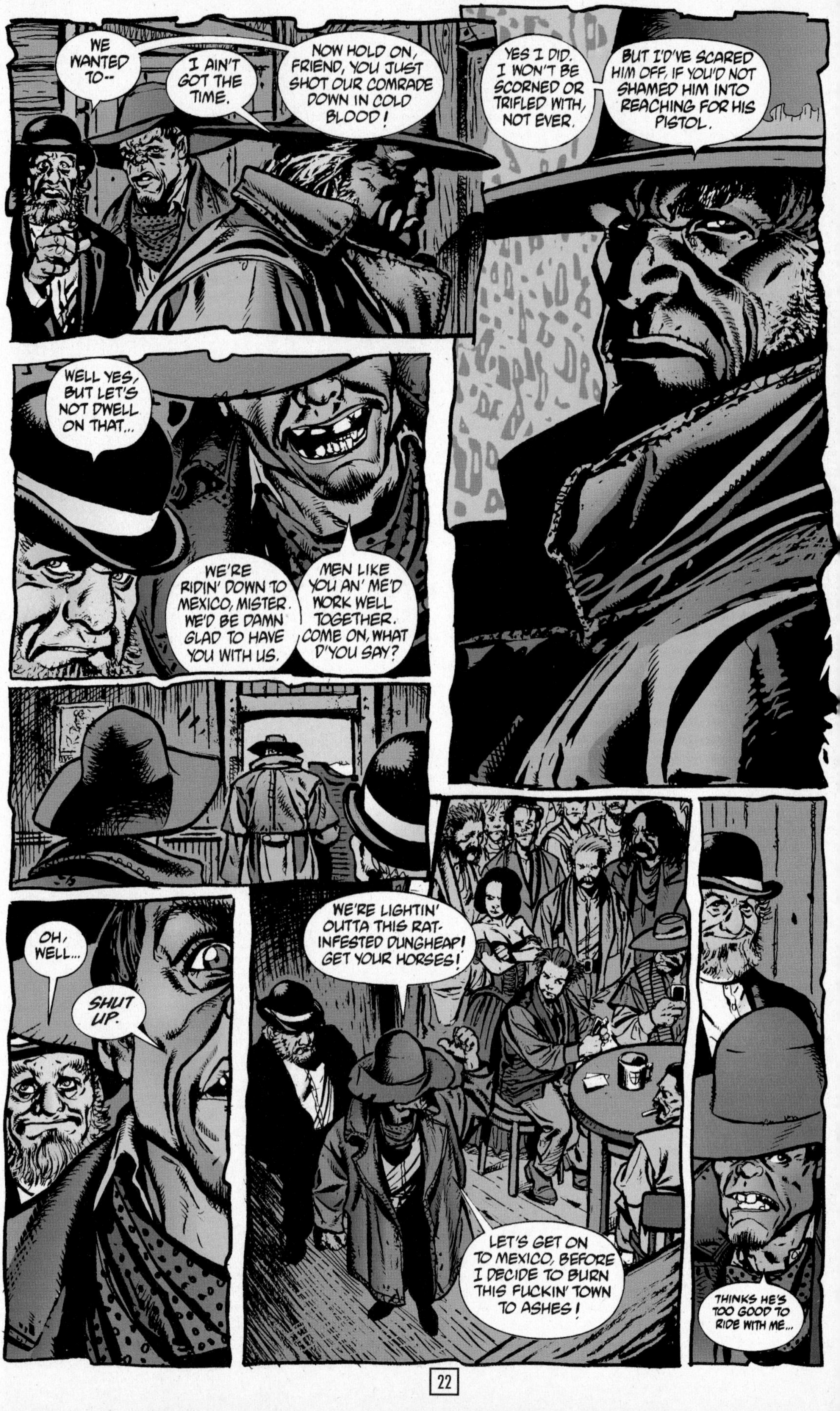

WE WANTED TO--
I AIN'T GOT THE TIME.
NOW HOLD ON, FRIEND, YOU JUST SHOT OUR COMRADE DOWN IN COLD BLOOD!
YES I DID. I WON'T BE SCORNED OR TRIFLED WITH, NOT EVER.
BUT I'D'VE SCARED HIM OFF, IF YOU'D NOT SHAMED HIM INTO REACHING FOR HIS PISTOL.
WELL YES, BUT LET'S NOT DWELL ON THAT...
MEN LIKE YOU AN' ME'D WORK WELL TOGETHER. COME ON, WHAT D'YOU SAY?
WE'RE RIDIN' DOWN TO MEXICO, MISTER. WE'D BE DAMN GLAD TO HAVE YOU WITH US.
OH, WELL...
SHUT UP.
WE'RE LIGHTIN' OUTTA THIS RAT-INFESTED DUNGHEAP! GET YOUR HORSES!
LET'S GET ON TO MEXICO, BEFORE I DECIDE TO BURN THIS FUCKIN' TOWN TO ASHES!
THINKS HE'S TOO GOOD TO RIDE WITH ME...

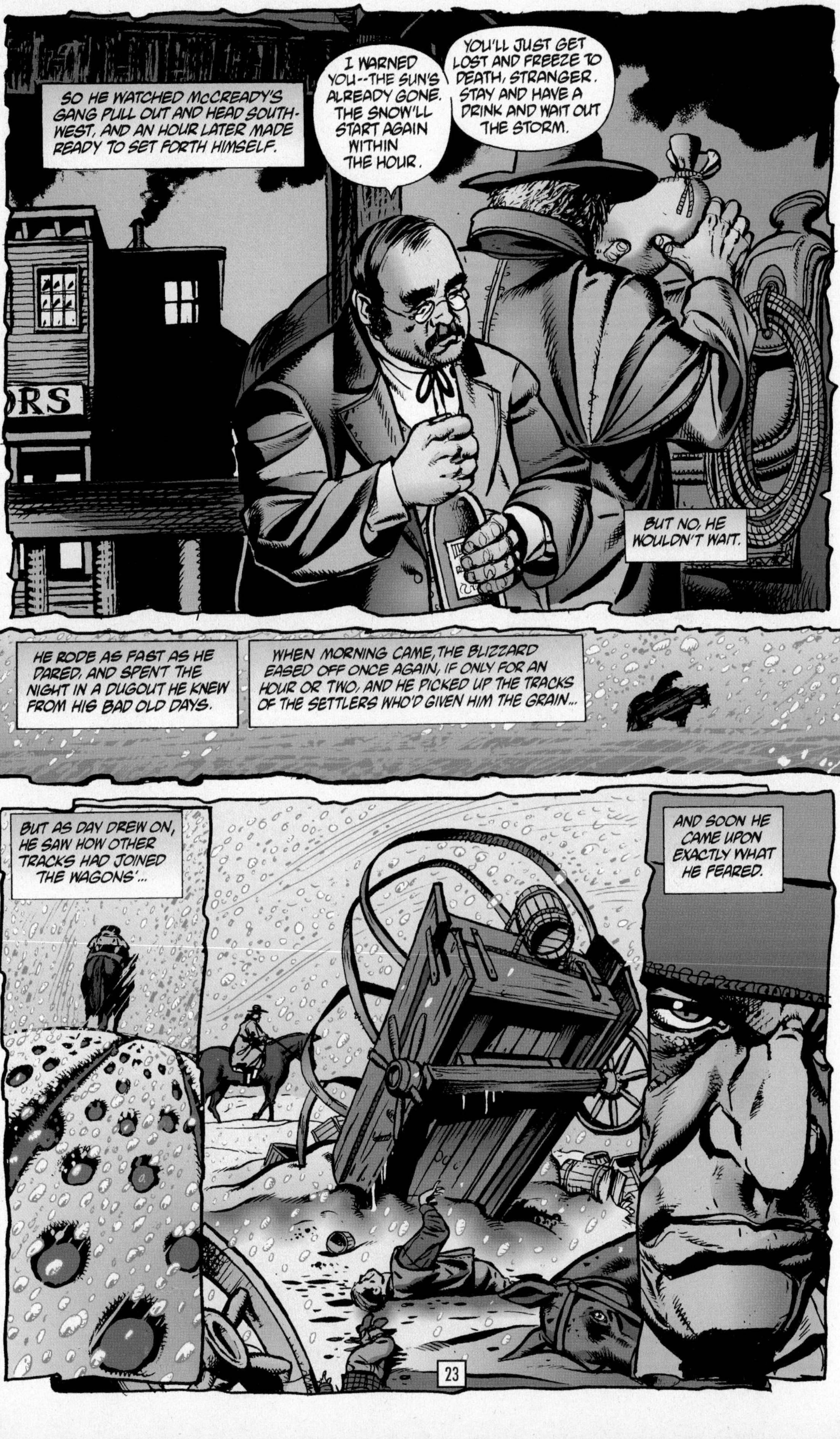
SO HE WATCHED McCREADY'S GANG PULL OUT AND HEAD SOUTH-WEST, AND AN HOUR LATER MADE READY TO SET FORTH HIMSELF.
I WARNED YOU--THE SUN'S ALREADY GONE. THE SNOW'LL START AGAIN WITHIN THE HOUR.
YOU'LL JUST GET LOST AND FREEZE TO DEATH, STRANGER. STAY AND HAVE A DRINK AND WAIT OUT THE STORM.
ORS
BUT NO, HE WOULDN'T WAIT.
HE RODE AS FAST AS HE DARED, AND SPENT THE NIGHT IN A DUGOUT HE KNEW FROM HIS BAD OLD DAYS.
WHEN MORNING CAME, THE BLIZZARD EASED OFF ONCE AGAIN, IF ONLY FOR AN HOUR OR TWO, AND HE PICKED UP THE TRACKS OF THE SETTLERS WHO'D GIVEN HIM THE GRAIN...
BUT AS DAY DREW ON, HE SAW HOW OTHER TRACKS HAD JOINED THE WAGONS'...
AND SOON HE CAME UPON EXACTLY WHAT HE FEARED.

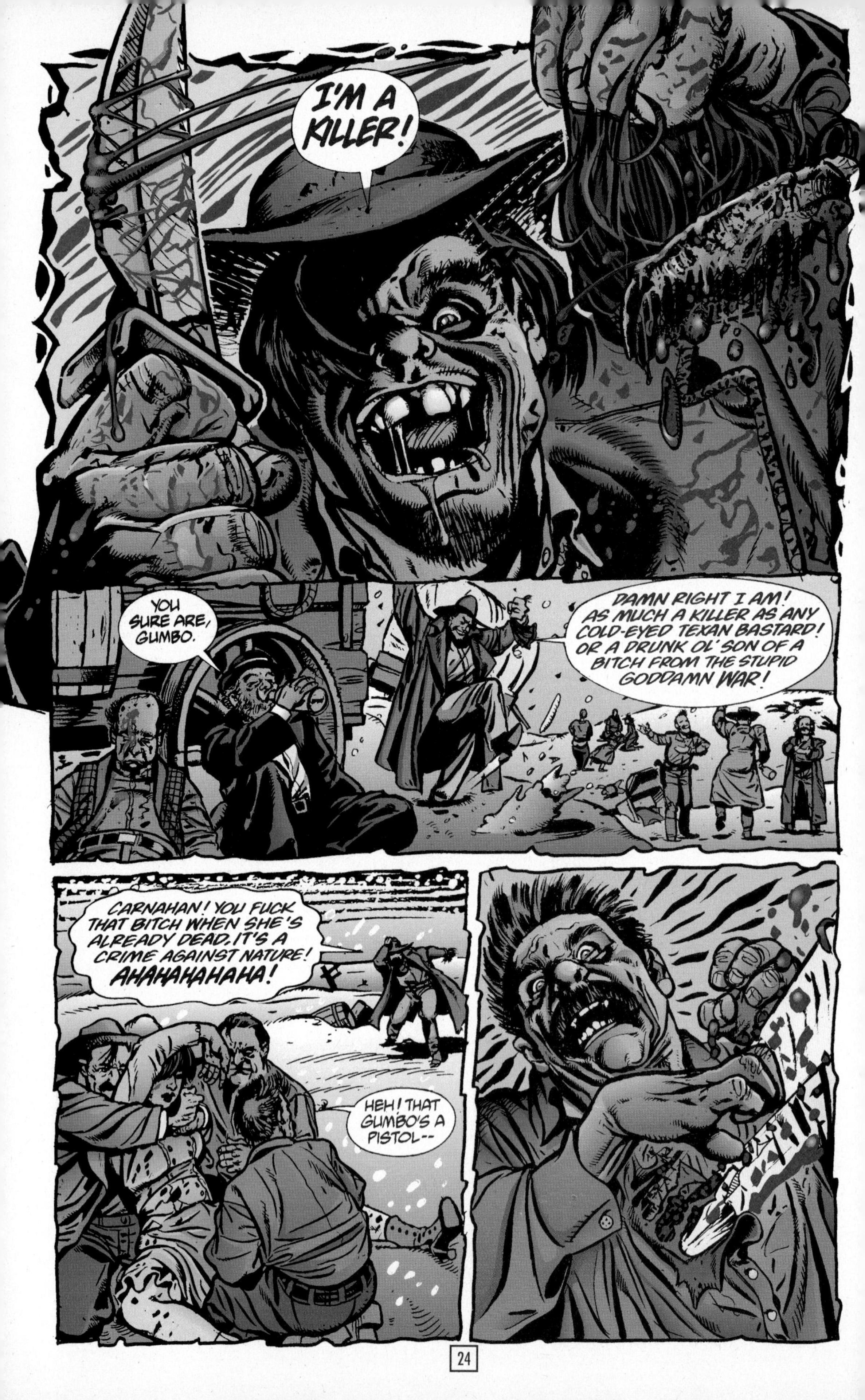
I'M A KILLER!
YOU SURE ARE, GUMBO.
DAMN RIGHT I AM! AS MUCH A KILLER AS ANY COLD-EYED TEXAN BASTARD! OR A DRUNK OL' SON OF A BITCH FROM THE STUPID GODDAMN WAR!
CARNAHAN! YOU FUCK THAT BITCH WHEN SHE'S ALREADY DEAD, IT'S A CRIME AGAINST NATURE! AHAHAHAHAHA!
HEH! THAT GUMBO'S A PISTOL--

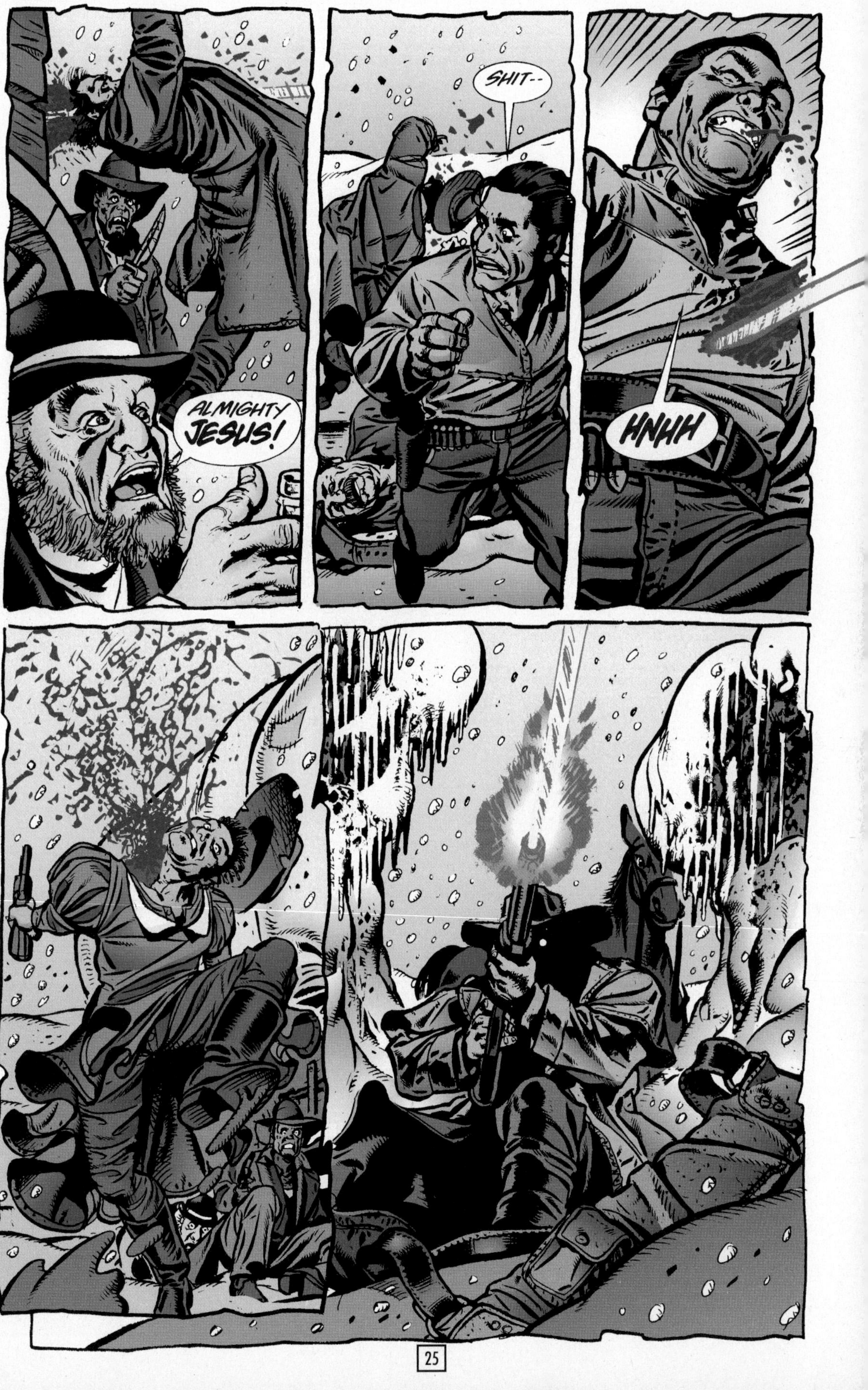
ALMIGHTY JESUS!
SHIT--
HNUH

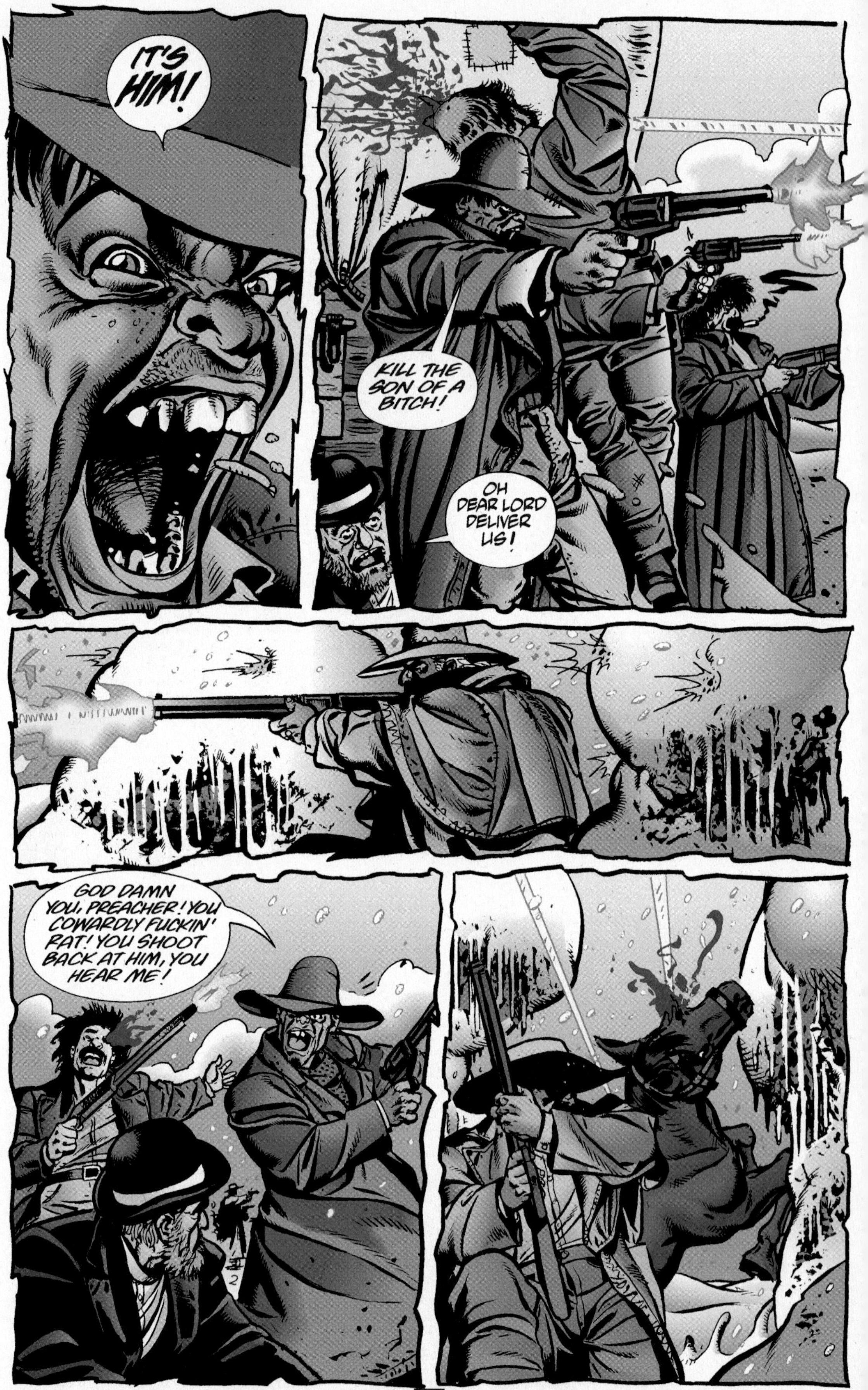
IT'S HIM!
KILL THE SON OF A BITCH!
OH DEAR LORD DELIVER US!
GOD DAMN YOU, PREACHER! YOU COWARDLY FUCKIN' RAT! YOU SHOOT BACK AT HIM, YOU HEAR ME!

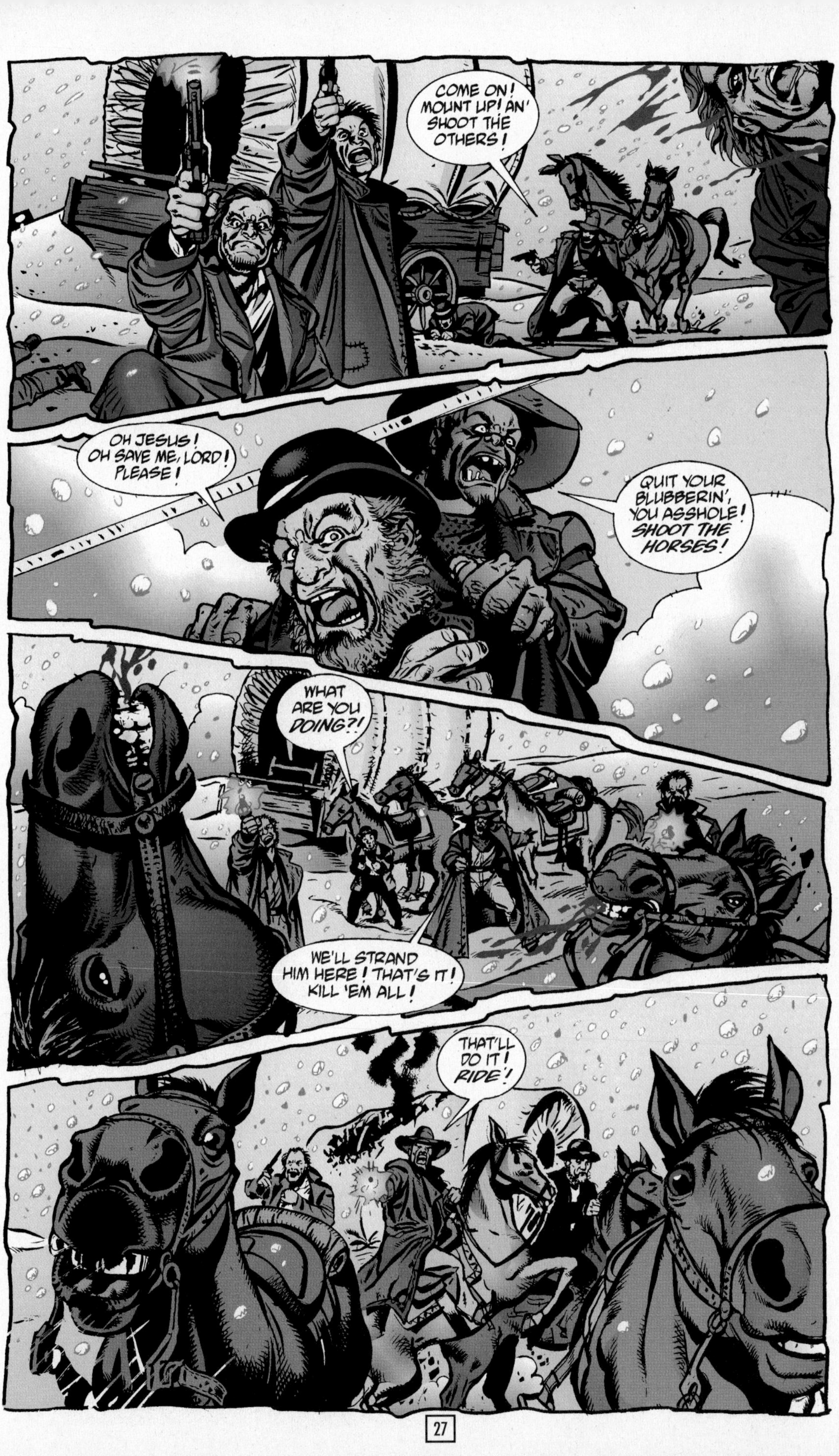
COME ON! MOUNT UP! AN' SHOOT THE OTHERS!
OH JESUS! OH SAVE ME, LORD! PLEASE!
QUIT YOUR BLUBBERIN', YOU ASSHOLE! SHOOT THE HORSES!
WHAT ARE YOU DOING?!
WE'LL STRAND HIM HERE! THAT'S IT! KILL 'EM ALL!
THAT'LL DO IT! RIDE!

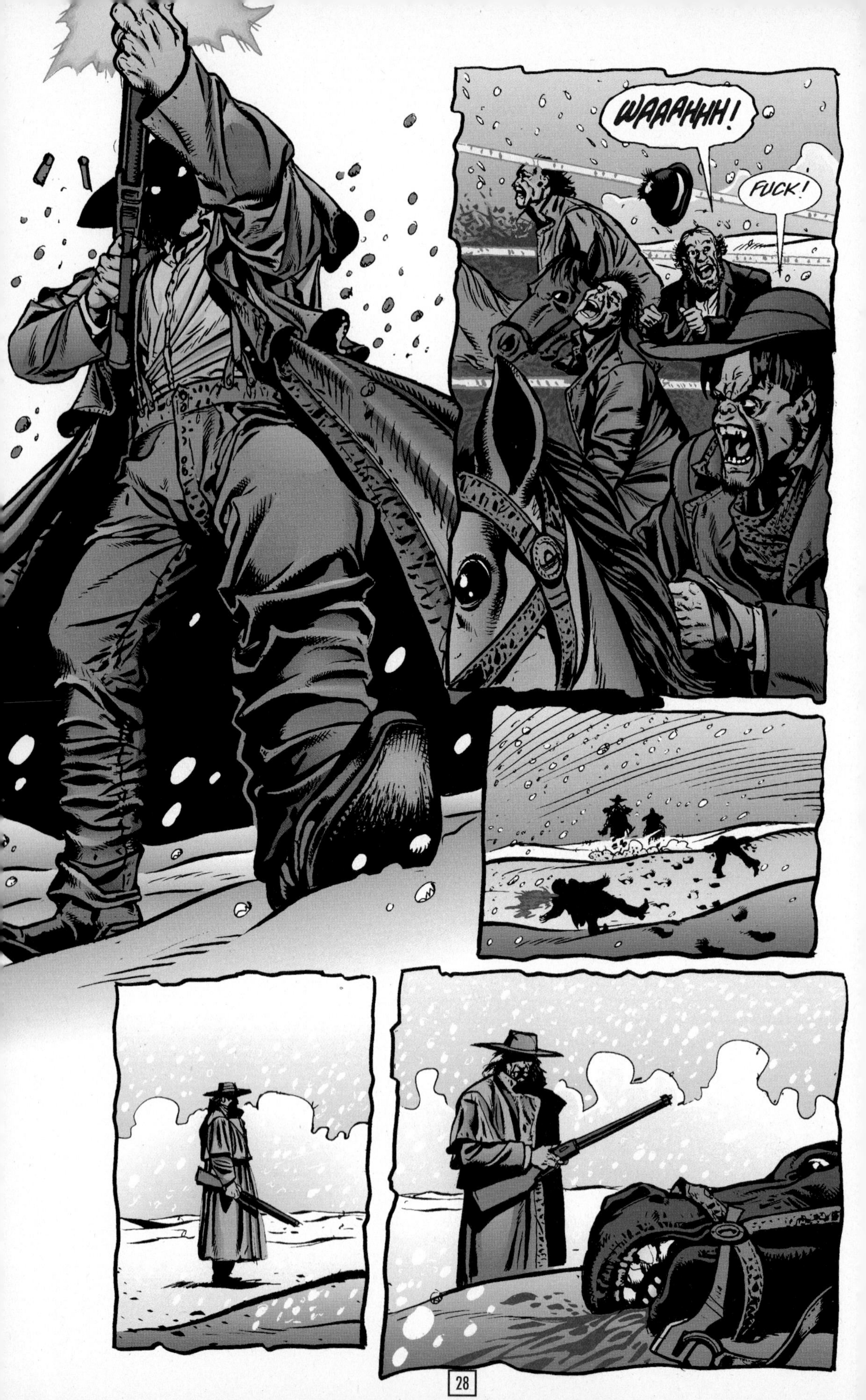
WAAAHHH!
FUCK!

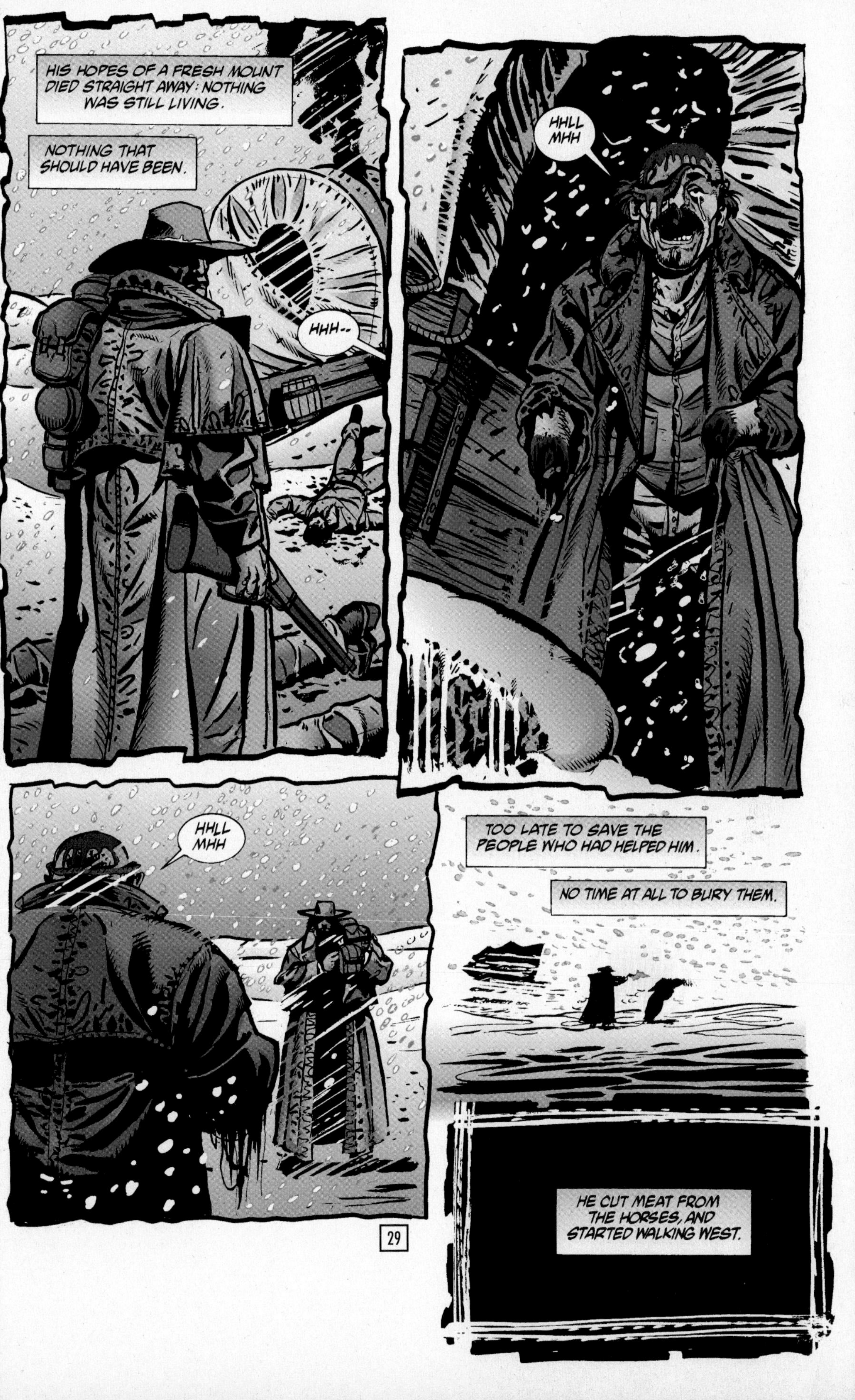
HIS HOPES OF A FRESH MOUNT DIED STRAIGHT AWAY: NOTHING WAS STILL LIVING.
NOTHING THAT SHOULD HAVE BEEN.
HHH--
HHLL MHH
HHLL MHH
TOO LATE TO SAVE THE PEOPLE WHO HAD HELPED HIM.
NO TIME AT ALL TO BURY THEM.
HE CUT MEAT FROM THE HORSES, AND STARTED WALKING WEST.

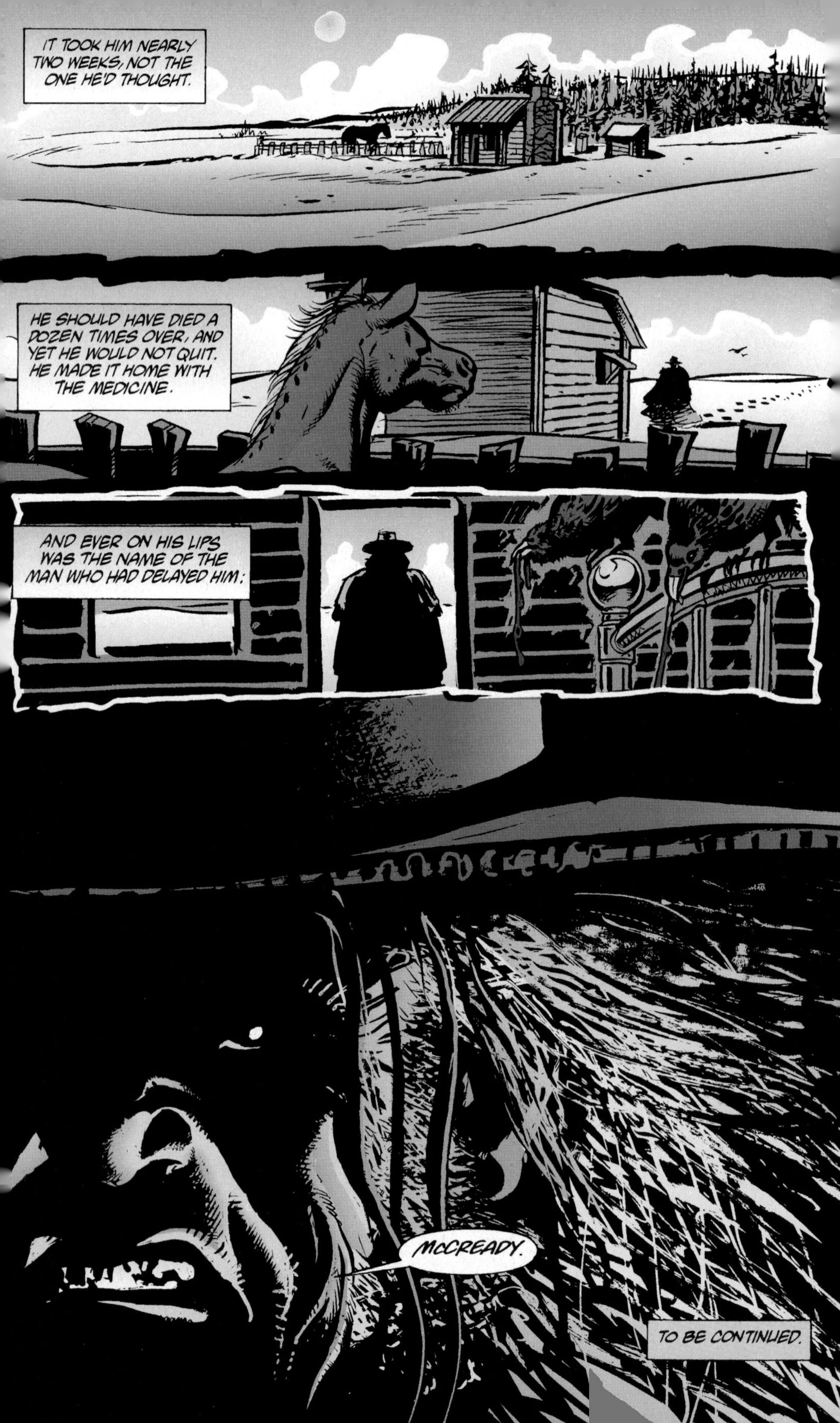
IT TOOK HIM NEARLY TWO WEEKS, NOT THE ONE HE'D THOUGHT.
HE SHOULD HAVE DIED A DOZEN TIMES OVER, AND YET HE WOULD NOT QUIT. HE MADE IT HOME WITH THE MEDICINE.
AND EVER ON HIS LIPS WAS THE NAME OF THE MAN WHO HAD DELAYED HIM:
McCREADY.
TO BE CONTINUED.

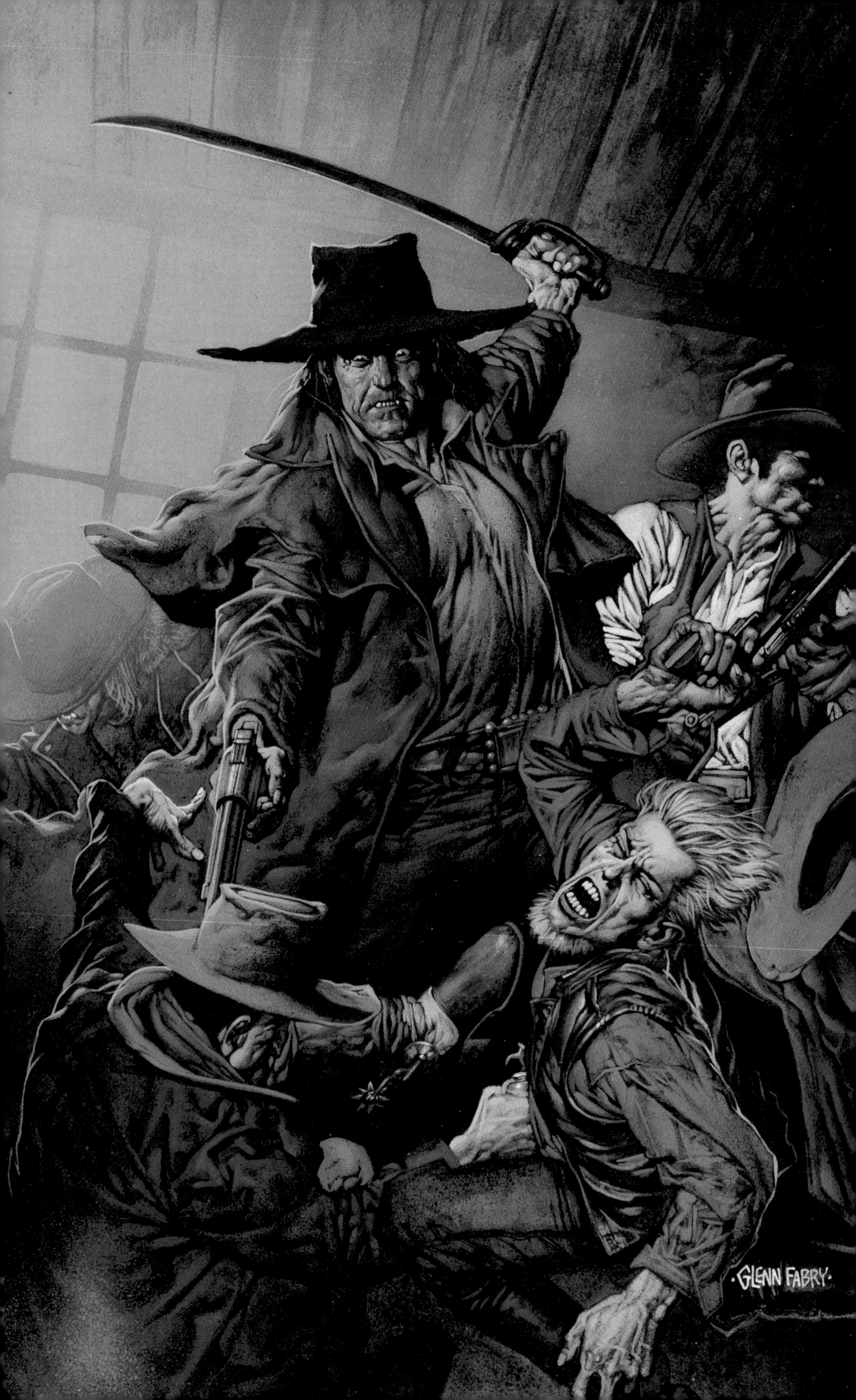
GLENN FABRY

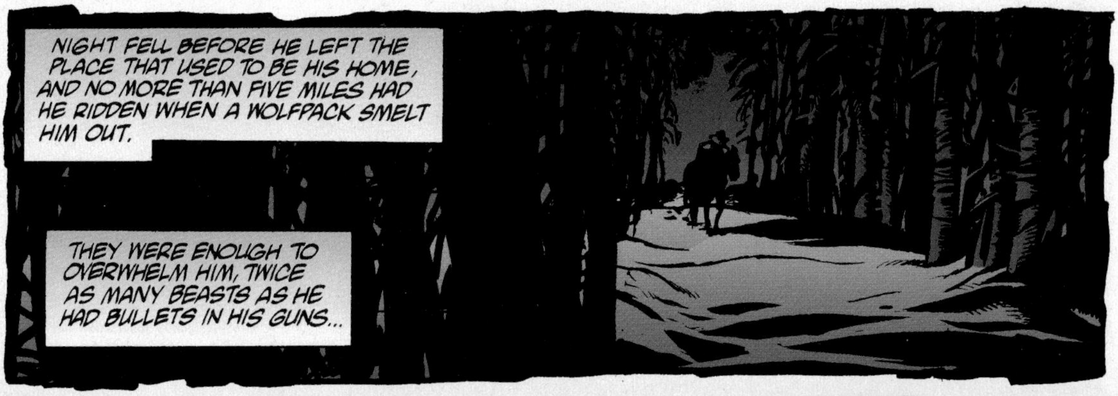
NIGHT FELL BEFORE HE LEFT THE PLACE THAT USED TO BE HIS HOME, AND NO MORE THAN FIVE MILES HAD HE RIDDEN WHEN A WOLFPACK SMELT HIM OUT.
THEY WERE ENOUGH TO OVERWHELM HIM, TWICE AS MANY BEASTS AS HE HAD BULLETS IN HIS GUNS...

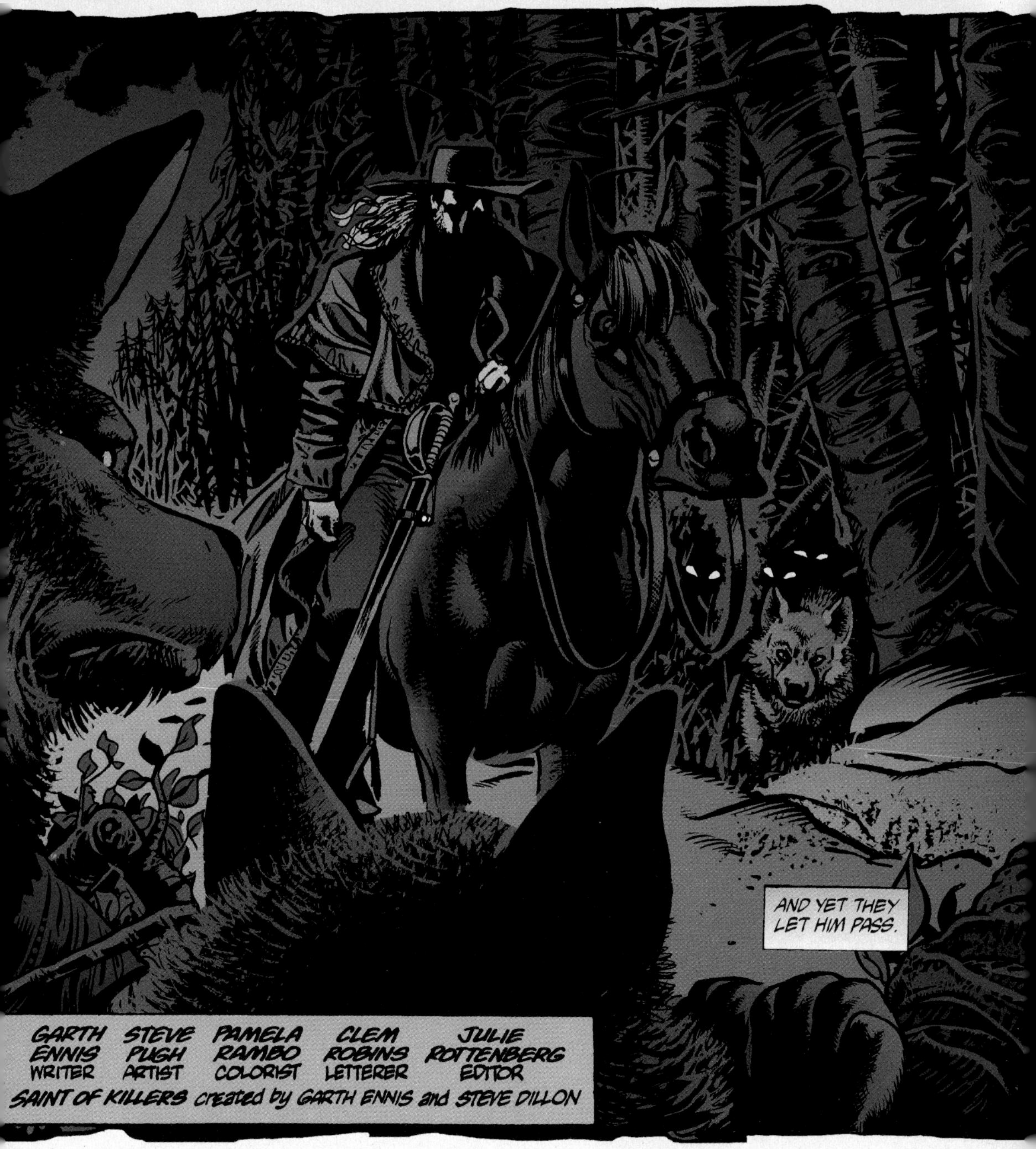
AND YET THEY LET HIM PASS.
GARTH ENNIS WRITER
STEVE PUGH ARTIST
PAMELA RAMBO COLORIST
CLEM ROBINS LETTERER
JULIE ROTTENBERG EDITOR
SAINT OF KILLERS created by GARTH ENNIS and STEVE DILLON

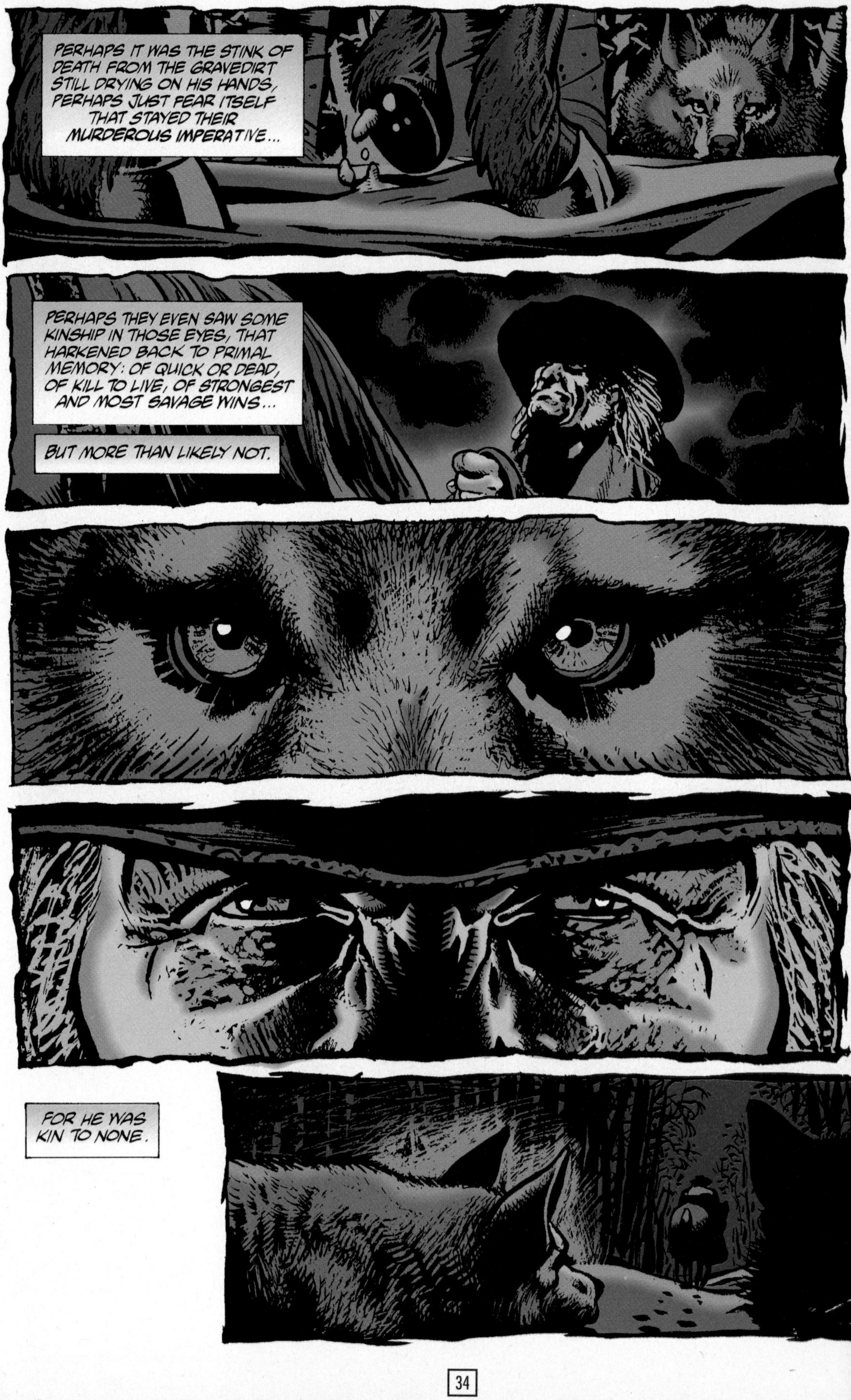

PERHAPS IT WAS THE STINK OF DEATH FROM THE GRAVEDIRT STILL DRYING ON HIS HANDS, PERHAPS JUST FEAR ITSELF THAT STAYED THEIR MURDEROUS IMPERATIVE...
PERHAPS THEY EVEN SAW SOME KINSHIP IN THOSE EYES, THAT HARKENED BACK TO PRIMAL MEMORY: OF QUICK OR DEAD, OF KILL TO LIVE, OF STRONGEST AND MOST SAVAGE WINS...
BUT MORE THAN LIKELY NOT.
FOR HE WAS KIN TO NONE.

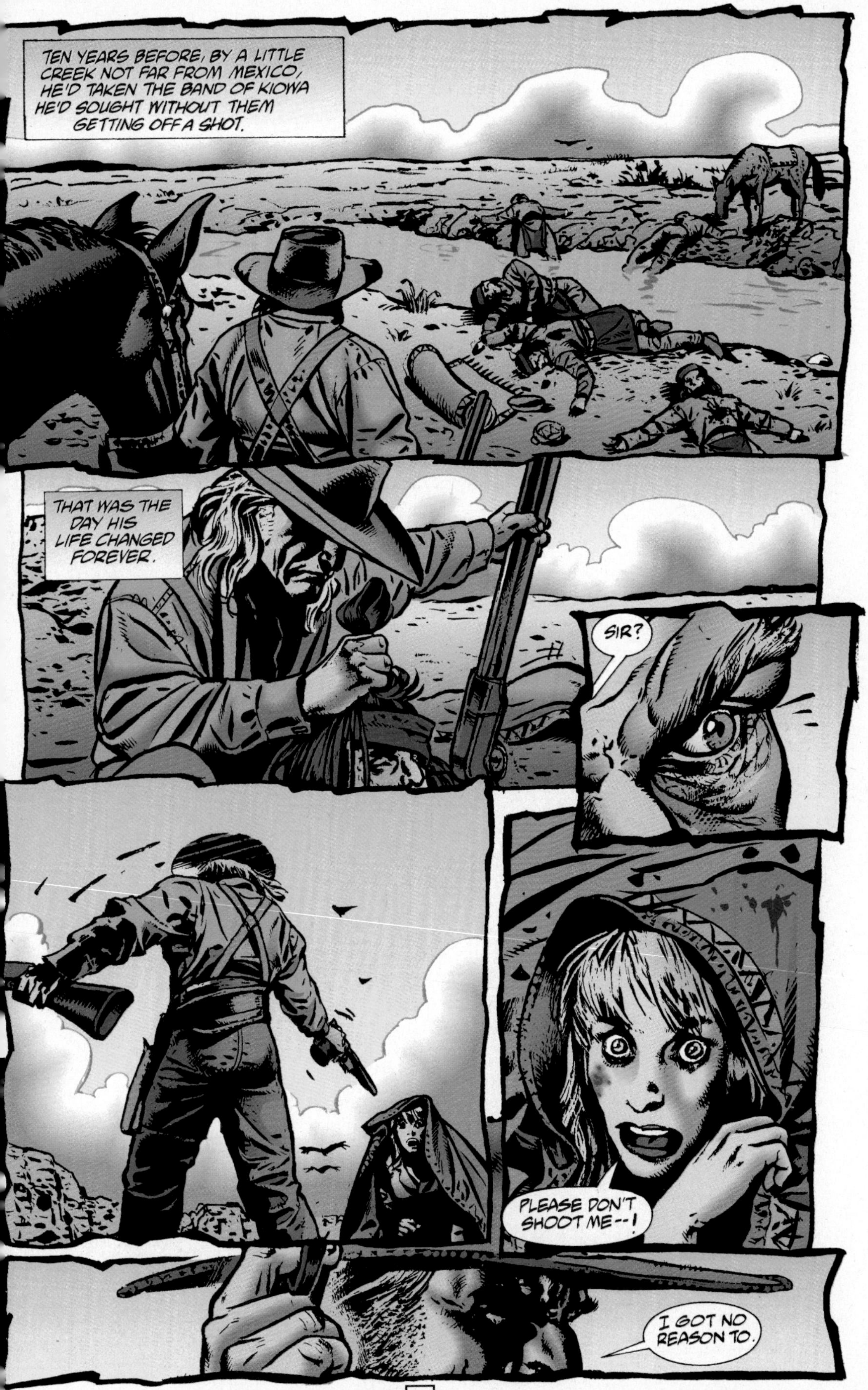
TEN YEARS BEFORE, BY A LITTLE CREEK NOT FAR FROM MEXICO, HE'D TAKEN THE BAND OF KIOWA HE'D SOUGHT WITHOUT THEM GETTING OFF A SHOT.
THAT WAS THE DAY HIS LIFE CHANGED FOREVER.
SIR?
PLEASE DON'T SHOOT ME--!
I GOT NO REASON TO.

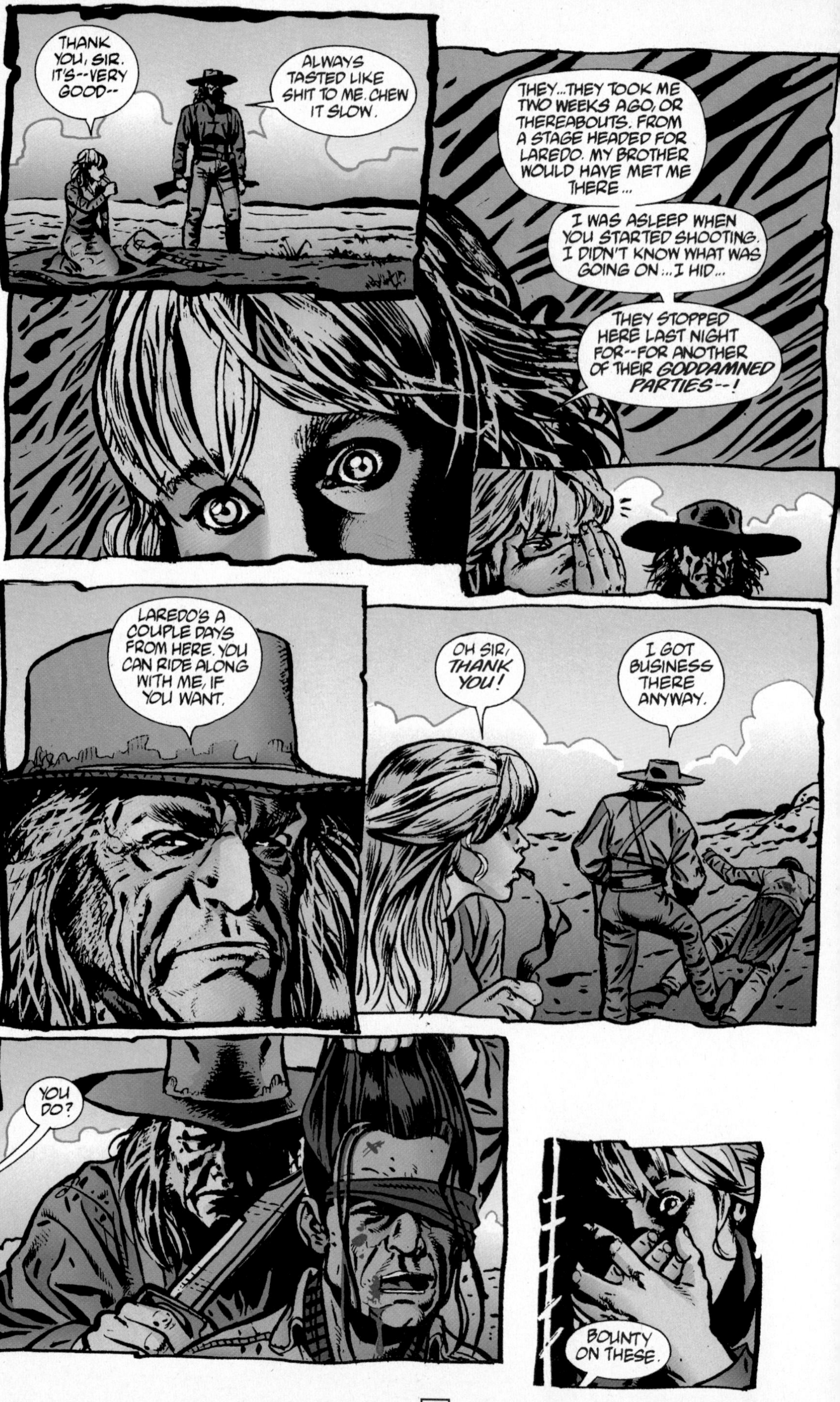
THANK YOU, SIR. IT'S--VERY GOOD--
ALWAYS TASTED LIKE SHIT TO ME. CHEW IT SLOW.
THEY...THEY TOOK ME TWO WEEKS AGO, OR THEREABOUTS. FROM A STAGE HEADED FOR LAREDO. MY BROTHER WOULD HAVE MET ME THERE...
I WAS ASLEEP WHEN YOU STARTED SHOOTING. I DIDN'T KNOW WHAT WAS GOING ON...I HID...
THEY STOPPED HERE LAST NIGHT FOR--FOR ANOTHER OF THEIR *GODDAMNED PARTIES*--!
LAREDO'S A COUPLE DAYS FROM HERE. YOU CAN RIDE ALONG WITH ME, IF YOU WANT.
OH SIR, *THANK YOU*!
I GOT BUSINESS THERE ANYWAY.
YOU DO?
BOUNTY ON THESE.

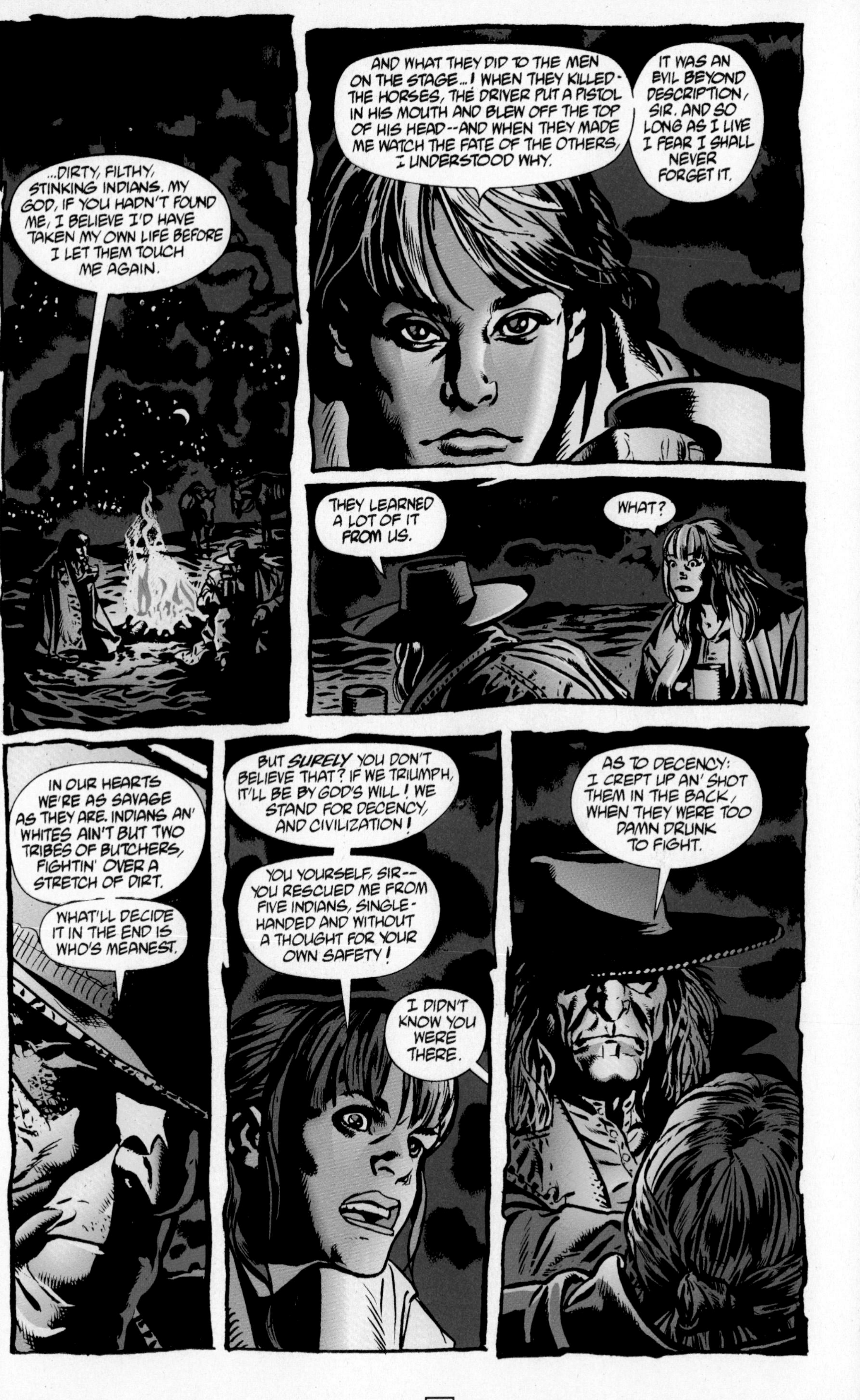
...DIRTY, FILTHY, STINKING INDIANS. MY GOD, IF YOU HADN'T FOUND ME, I BELIEVE I'D HAVE TAKEN MY OWN LIFE BEFORE I LET THEM TOUCH ME AGAIN.
AND WHAT THEY DID TO THE MEN ON THE STAGE...! WHEN THEY KILLED THE HORSES, THE DRIVER PUT A PISTOL IN HIS MOUTH AND BLEW OFF THE TOP OF HIS HEAD--AND WHEN THEY MADE ME WATCH THE FATE OF THE OTHERS, I UNDERSTOOD WHY.
IT WAS AN EVIL BEYOND DESCRIPTION, SIR. AND SO LONG AS I LIVE I FEAR I SHALL NEVER FORGET IT.
THEY LEARNED A LOT OF IT FROM US.
WHAT?
IN OUR HEARTS WE'RE AS SAVAGE AS THEY ARE. INDIANS AN' WHITES AIN'T BUT TWO TRIBES OF BUTCHERS, FIGHTIN' OVER A STRETCH OF DIRT.
WHAT'LL DECIDE IT IN THE END IS WHO'S MEANEST.
BUT SURELY YOU DON'T BELIEVE THAT? IF WE TRIUMPH, IT'LL BE BY GOD'S WILL! WE STAND FOR DECENCY, AND CIVILIZATION!
YOU YOURSELF, SIR-- YOU RESCUED ME FROM FIVE INDIANS, SINGLE-HANDED AND WITHOUT A THOUGHT FOR YOUR OWN SAFETY!
I DIDN'T KNOW YOU WERE THERE.
AS TO DECENCY: I CREPT UP AN' SHOT THEM IN THE BACK, WHEN THEY WERE TOO DAMN DRUNK TO FIGHT.

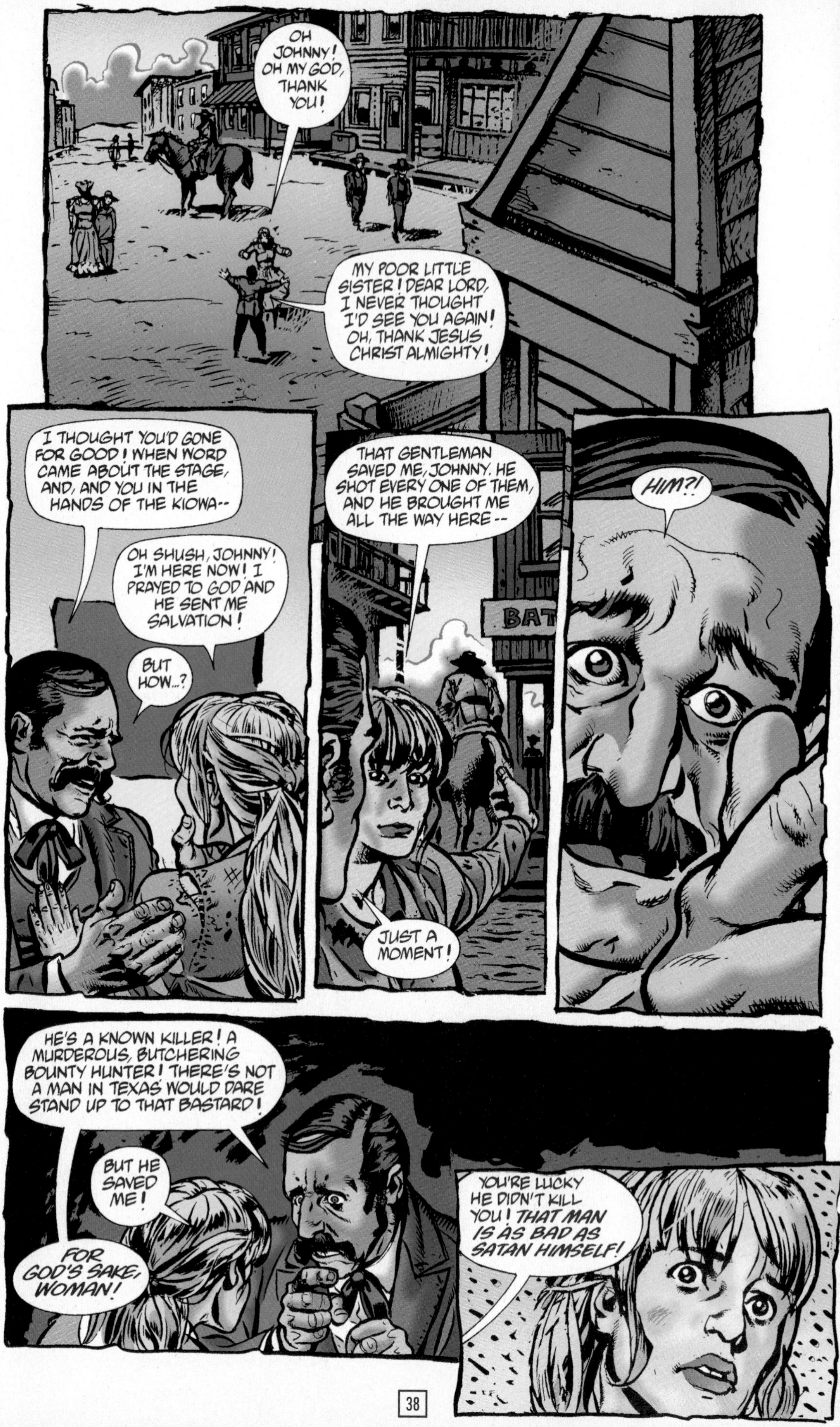
OH JOHNNY! OH MY GOD, THANK YOU!
MY POOR LITTLE SISTER! DEAR LORD, I NEVER THOUGHT I'D SEE YOU AGAIN! OH, THANK JESUS CHRIST ALMIGHTY!
I THOUGHT YOU'D GONE FOR GOOD! WHEN WORD CAME ABOUT THE STAGE, AND, AND YOU IN THE HANDS OF THE KIOWA--
OH SHUSH, JOHNNY! I'M HERE NOW! I PRAYED TO GOD AND HE SENT ME SALVATION!
BUT HOW...?
THAT GENTLEMAN SAVED ME, JOHNNY. HE SHOT EVERY ONE OF THEM, AND HE BROUGHT ME ALL THE WAY HERE --
JUST A MOMENT!
HIM?!
HE'S A KNOWN KILLER! A MURDEROUS, BUTCHERING BOUNTY HUNTER! THERE'S NOT A MAN IN TEXAS WOULD DARE STAND UP TO THAT BASTARD!
BUT HE SAVED ME!
FOR GOD'S SAKE, WOMAN!
YOU'RE LUCKY HE DIDN'T KILL YOU! THAT MAN IS AS BAD AS SATAN HIMSELF!

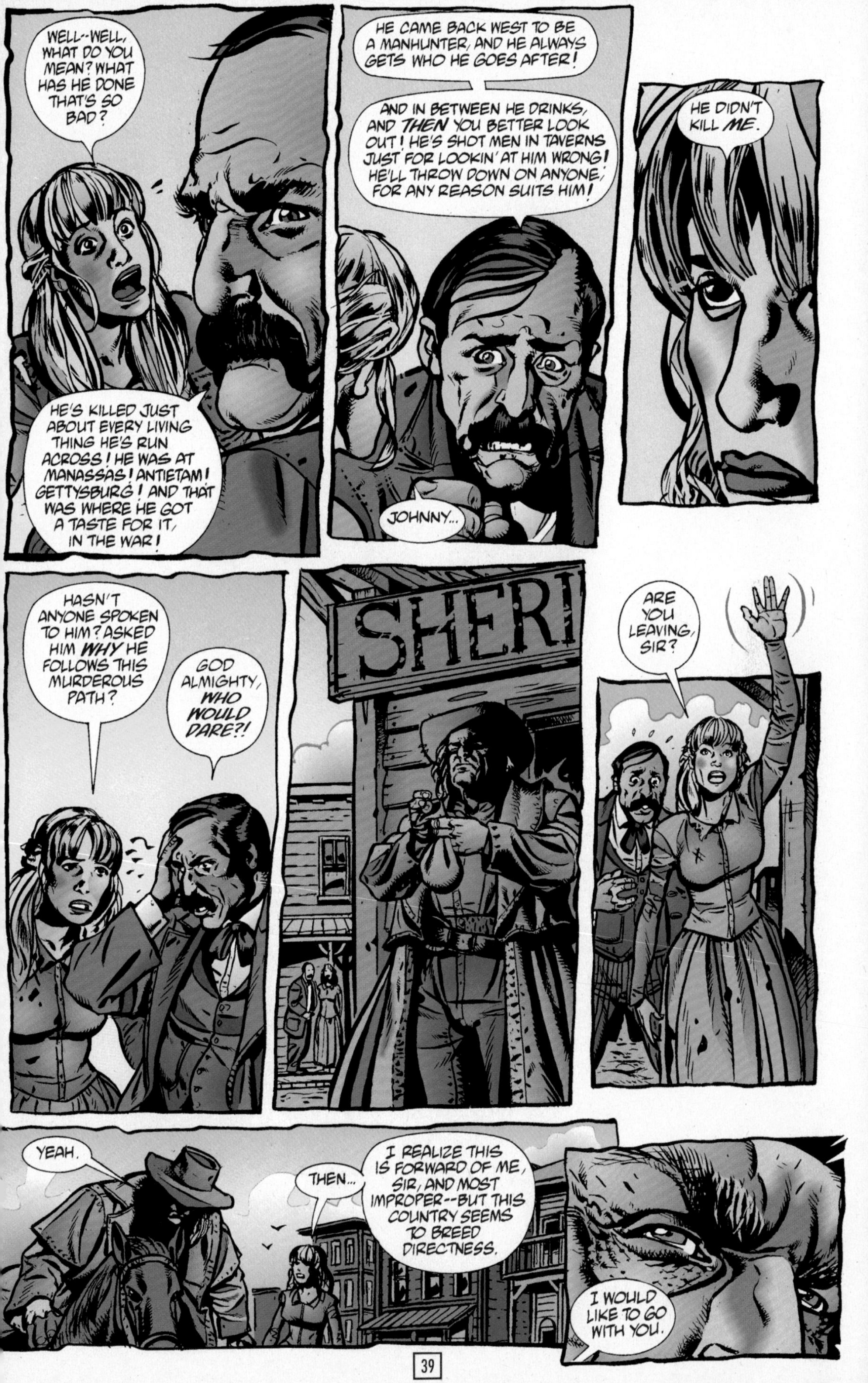
WELL--WELL, WHAT DO YOU MEAN? WHAT HAS HE DONE THAT'S SO BAD?
HE'S KILLED JUST ABOUT EVERY LIVING THING HE'S RUN ACROSS! HE WAS AT MANASSAS! ANTIETAM! GETTYSBURG! AND THAT WAS WHERE HE GOT A TASTE FOR IT, IN THE WAR!
HE CAME BACK WEST TO BE A MANHUNTER, AND HE ALWAYS GETS WHO HE GOES AFTER!
AND IN BETWEEN HE DRINKS, AND THEN YOU BETTER LOOK OUT! HE'S SHOT MEN IN TAVERNS JUST FOR LOOKIN' AT HIM WRONG! HE'LL THROW DOWN ON ANYONE, FOR ANY REASON SUITS HIM!
JOHNNY...
HE DIDN'T KILL ME.
HASN'T ANYONE SPOKEN TO HIM? ASKED HIM WHY HE FOLLOWS THIS MURDEROUS PATH?
GOD ALMIGHTY, WHO WOULD DARE?!
SHERI
ARE YOU LEAVING, SIR?
YEAH.
THEN...
I REALIZE THIS IS FORWARD OF ME, SIR, AND MOST IMPROPER--BUT THIS COUNTRY SEEMS TO BREED DIRECTNESS.
I WOULD LIKE TO GO WITH YOU.

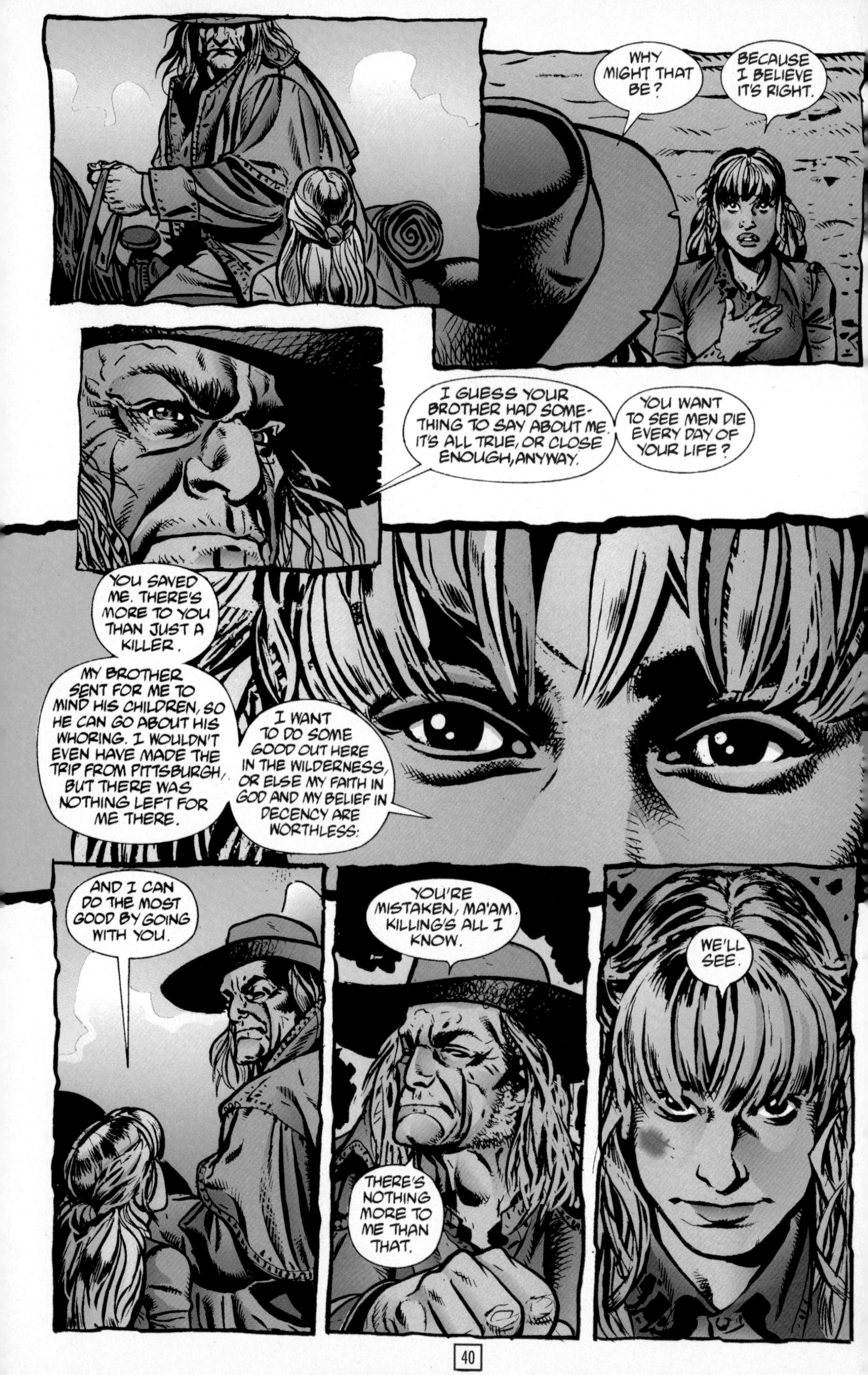
WHY MIGHT THAT BE?
BECAUSE I BELIEVE IT'S RIGHT.
I GUESS YOUR BROTHER HAD SOMETHING TO SAY ABOUT ME. IT'S ALL TRUE, OR CLOSE ENOUGH, ANYWAY.
YOU WANT TO SEE MEN DIE EVERY DAY OF YOUR LIFE?
YOU SAVED ME. THERE'S MORE TO YOU THAN JUST A KILLER.
MY BROTHER SENT FOR ME TO MIND HIS CHILDREN, SO HE CAN GO ABOUT HIS WHORING. I WOULDN'T EVEN HAVE MADE THE TRIP FROM PITTSBURGH, BUT THERE WAS NOTHING LEFT FOR ME THERE.
I WANT TO DO SOME GOOD OUT HERE IN THE WILDERNESS, OR ELSE MY FAITH IN GOD AND MY BELIEF IN DECENCY ARE WORTHLESS.
AND I CAN DO THE MOST GOOD BY GOING WITH YOU.
YOU'RE MISTAKEN, MA'AM. KILLING'S ALL I KNOW.
THERE'S NOTHING MORE TO ME THAN THAT.
WE'LL SEE.

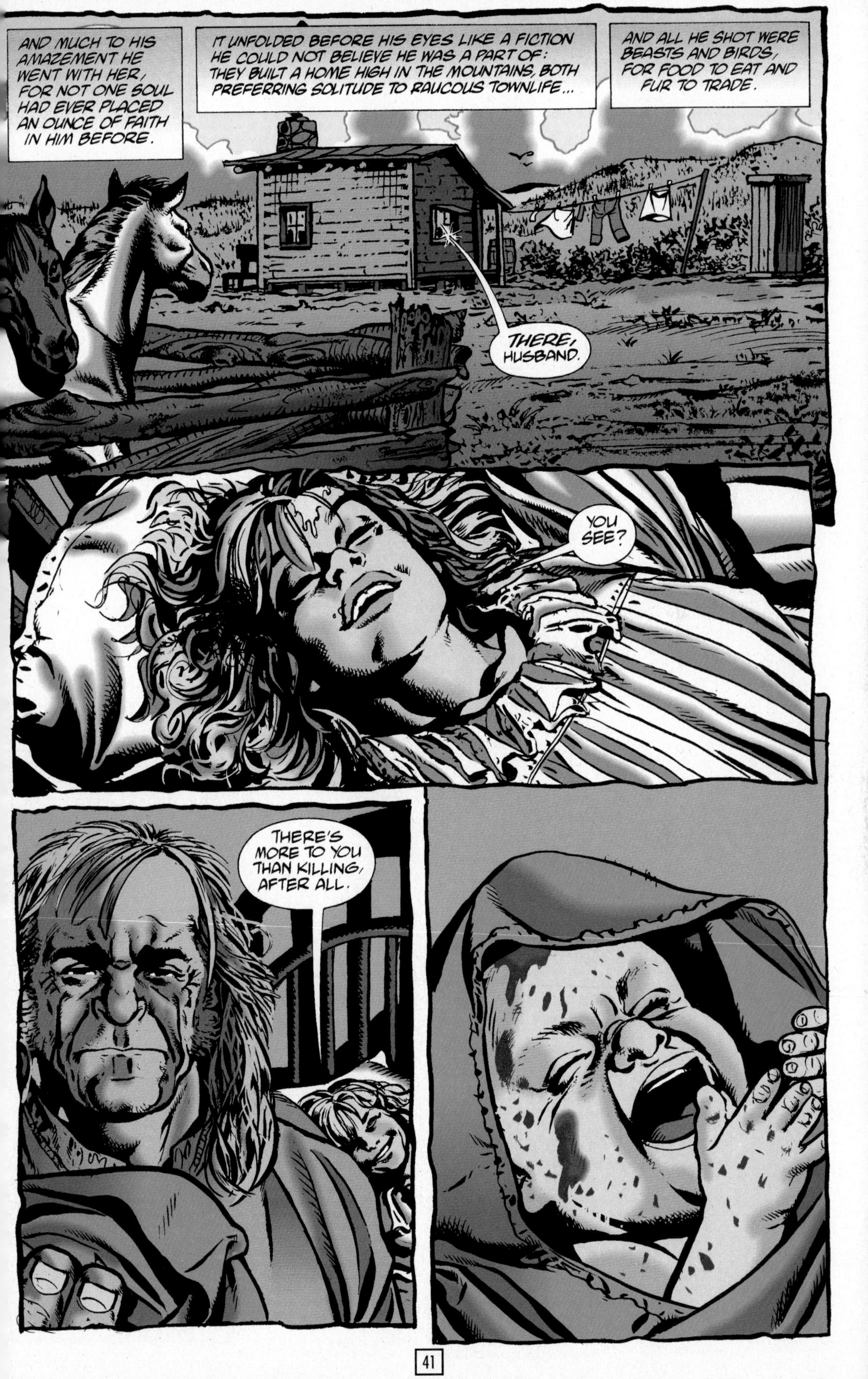
AND MUCH TO HIS AMAZEMENT HE WENT WITH HER, FOR NOT ONE SOUL HAD EVER PLACED AN OUNCE OF FAITH IN HIM BEFORE.
IT UNFOLDED BEFORE HIS EYES LIKE A FICTION HE COULD NOT BELIEVE HE WAS A PART OF: THEY BUILT A HOME HIGH IN THE MOUNTAINS, BOTH PREFERRING SOLITUDE TO RAUCOUS TOWNLIFE...
AND ALL HE SHOT WERE BEASTS AND BIRDS, FOR FOOD TO EAT AND FUR TO TRADE.
THERE, HUSBAND.
YOU SEE?
THERE'S MORE TO YOU THAN KILLING, AFTER ALL.

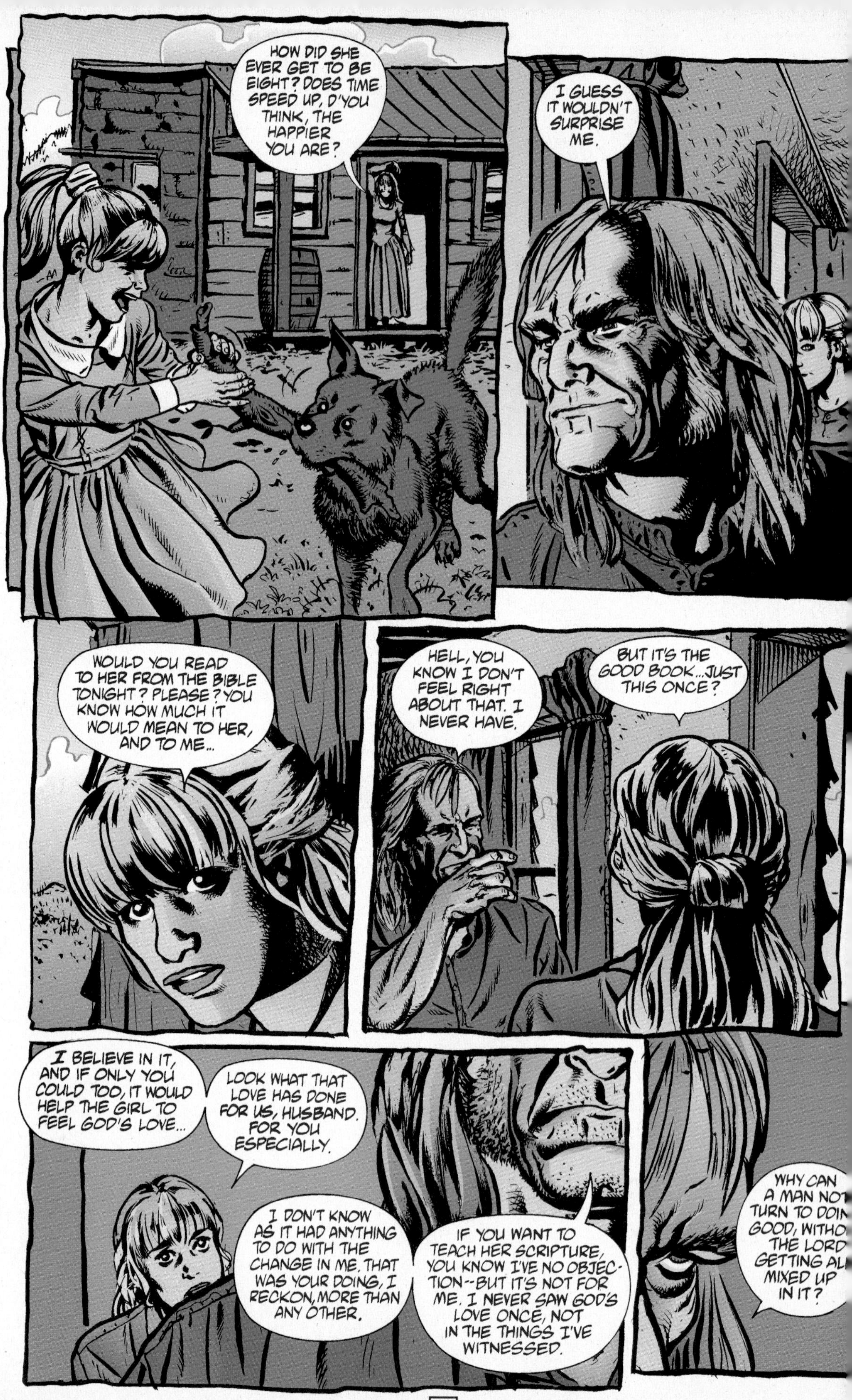
HOW DID SHE EVER GET TO BE EIGHT? DOES TIME SPEED UP, D'YOU THINK, THE HAPPIER YOU ARE?
I GUESS IT WOULDN'T SURPRISE ME.
WOULD YOU READ TO HER FROM THE BIBLE TONIGHT? PLEASE? YOU KNOW HOW MUCH IT WOULD MEAN TO HER, AND TO ME...
HELL, YOU KNOW I DON'T FEEL RIGHT ABOUT THAT. I NEVER HAVE.
BUT IT'S THE GOOD BOOK... JUST THIS ONCE?
I BELIEVE IN IT, AND IF ONLY YOU COULD TOO, IT WOULD HELP THE GIRL TO FEEL GOD'S LOVE...
LOOK WHAT THAT LOVE HAS DONE FOR US, HUSBAND. FOR YOU ESPECIALLY.
I DON'T KNOW AS IT HAD ANYTHING TO DO WITH THE CHANGE IN ME. THAT WAS YOUR DOING, I RECKON, MORE THAN ANY OTHER.
IF YOU WANT TO TEACH HER SCRIPTURE, YOU KNOW I'VE NO OBJEC-TION--BUT IT'S NOT FOR ME. I NEVER SAW GOD'S LOVE ONCE, NOT IN THE THINGS I'VE WITNESSED.
WHY CAN A MAN NOT TURN TO DOIN GOOD, WITHO THE LORD GETTING AL MIXED UP IN IT?

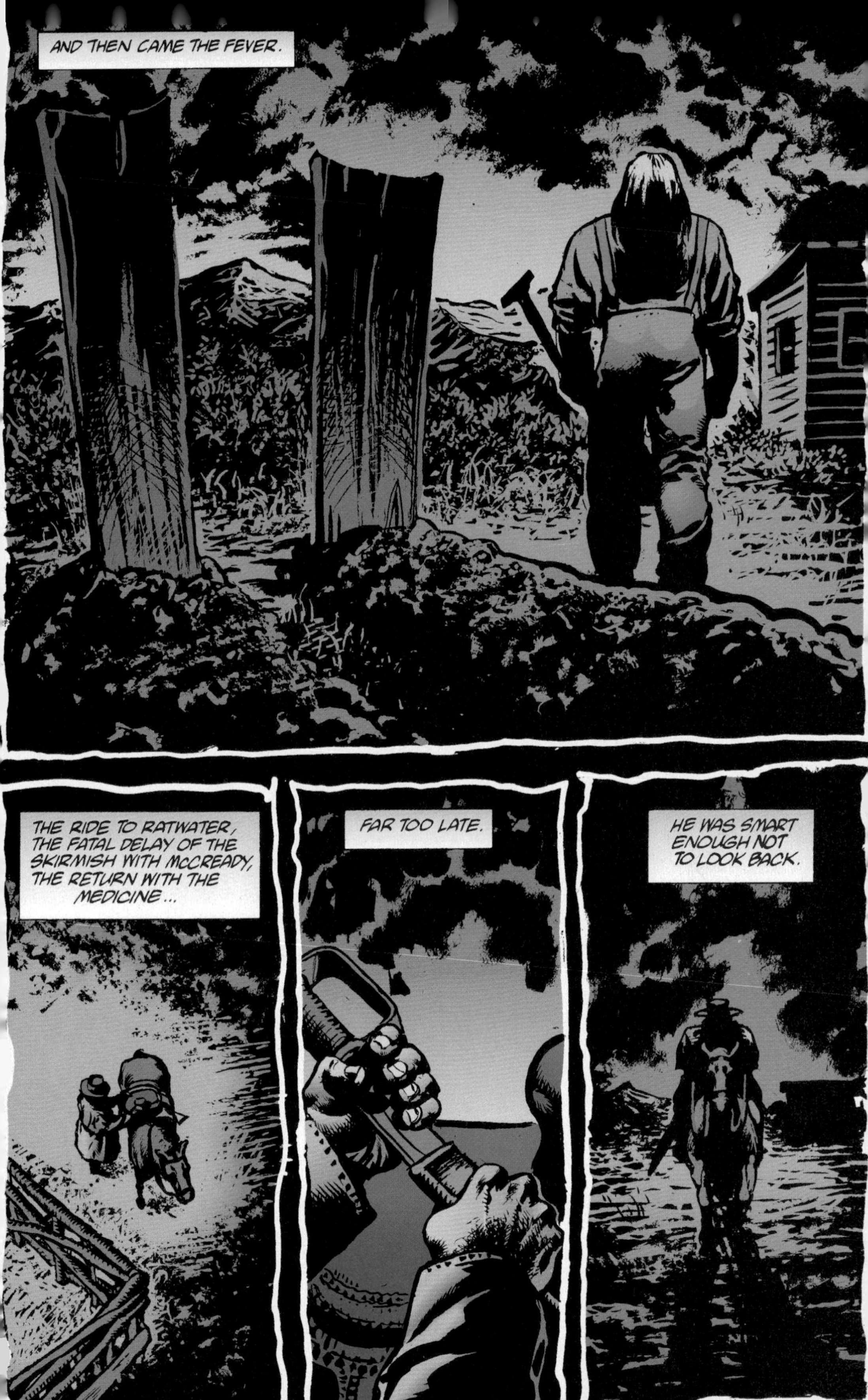
AND THEN CAME THE FEVER.
THE RIDE TO RATWATER, THE FATAL DELAY OF THE SKIRMISH WITH McCREADY, THE RETURN WITH THE MEDICINE...
FAR TOO LATE.
HE WAS SMART ENOUGH NOT TO LOOK BACK.

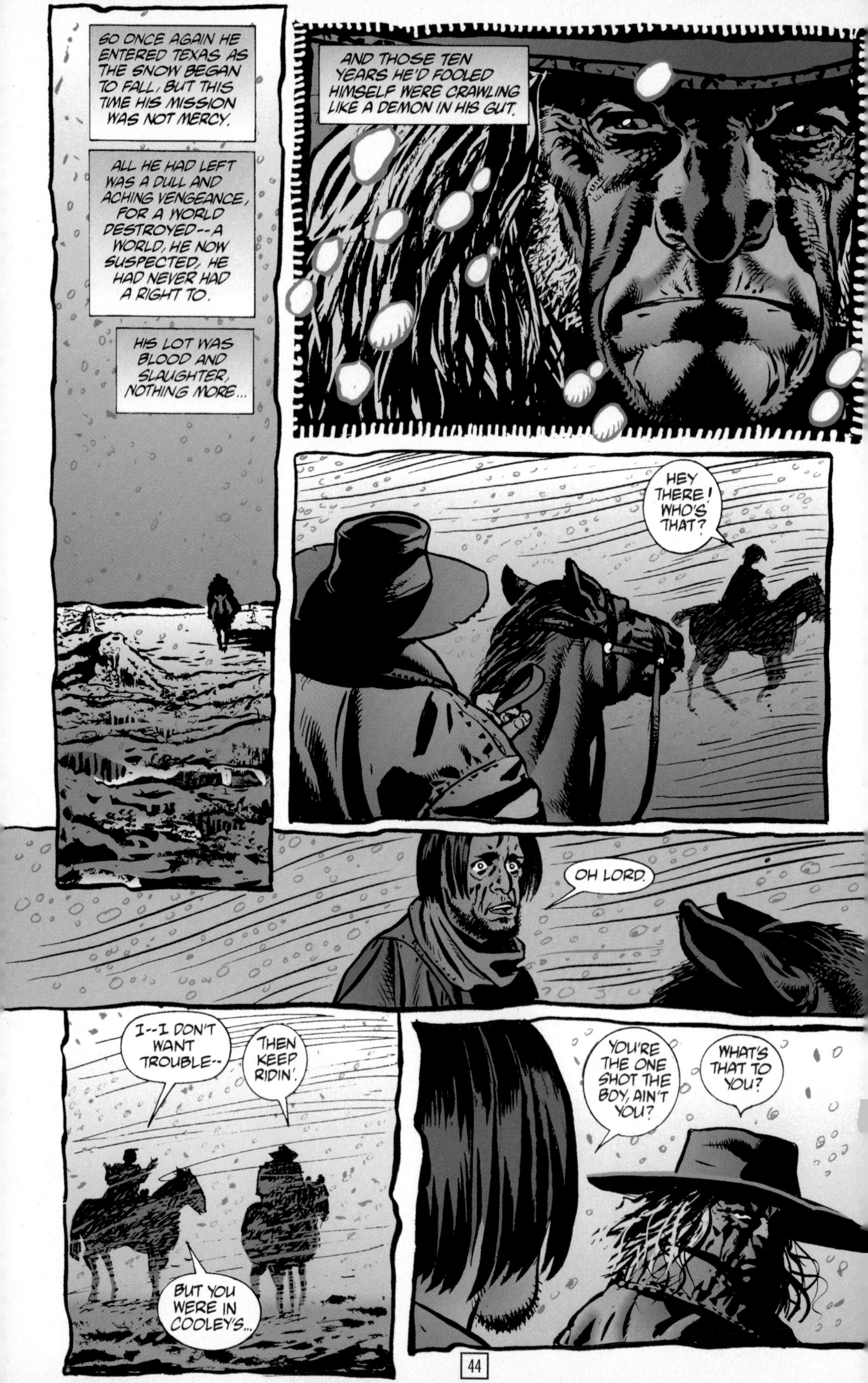
SO ONCE AGAIN HE ENTERED TEXAS AS THE SNOW BEGAN TO FALL, BUT THIS TIME HIS MISSION WAS NOT MERCY.
ALL HE HAD LEFT WAS A DULL AND ACHING VENGEANCE, FOR A WORLD DESTROYED--A WORLD, HE NOW SUSPECTED, HE HAD NEVER HAD A RIGHT TO.
HIS LOT WAS BLOOD AND SLAUGHTER, NOTHING MORE...
AND THOSE TEN YEARS HE'D FOOLED HIMSELF WERE CRAWLING LIKE A DEMON IN HIS GUT.
HEY THERE! WHO'S THAT?
OH LORD.
I--I DON'T WANT TROUBLE--
THEN KEEP RIDIN'.
BUT YOU WERE IN COOLEY'S...
YOU'RE THE ONE SHOT THE BOY, AIN'T YOU?
WHAT'S THAT TO YOU?

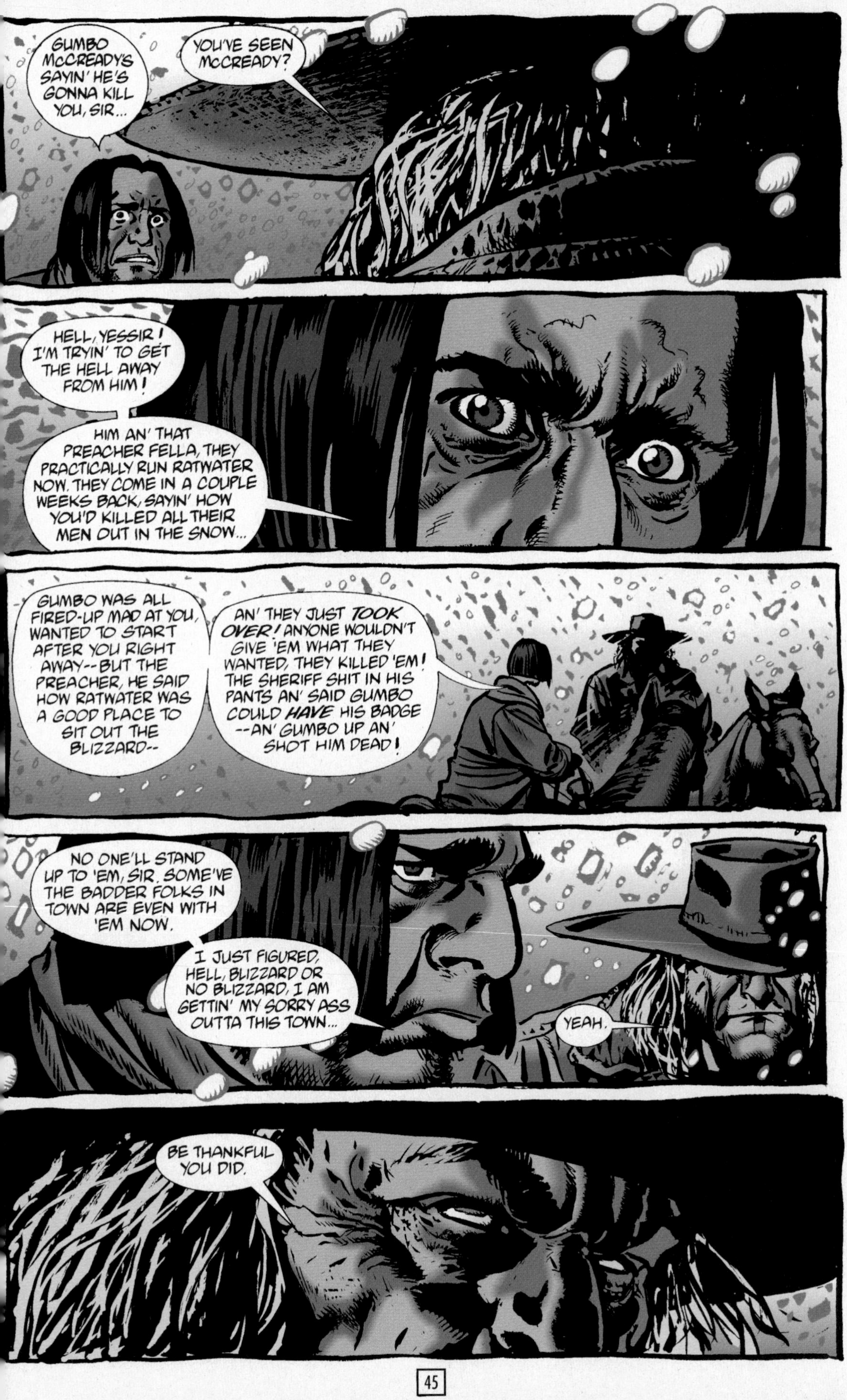
GUMBO McCREADY'S SAYIN' HE'S GONNA KILL YOU, SIR...
YOU'VE SEEN McCREADY?
HELL, YESSIR! I'M TRYIN' TO GET THE HELL AWAY FROM HIM!
HIM AN' THAT PREACHER FELLA, THEY PRACTICALLY RUN RATWATER NOW. THEY COME IN A COUPLE WEEKS BACK, SAYIN' HOW YOU'D KILLED ALL THEIR MEN OUT IN THE SNOW...
GUMBO WAS ALL FIRED-UP MAD AT YOU, WANTED TO START AFTER YOU RIGHT AWAY--BUT THE PREACHER, HE SAID HOW RATWATER WAS A GOOD PLACE TO SIT OUT THE BLIZZARD--
AN' THEY JUST *TOOK OVER!* ANYONE WOULDN'T GIVE 'EM WHAT THEY WANTED, THEY KILLED 'EM! THE SHERIFF SHIT IN HIS PANTS AN' SAID GUMBO COULD ***HAVE*** HIS BADGE --AN' GUMBO UP AN' SHOT HIM DEAD!
NO ONE'LL STAND UP TO 'EM, SIR. SOME'VE THE BADDER FOLKS IN TOWN ARE EVEN WITH 'EM NOW.
I JUST FIGURED, HELL, BLIZZARD OR NO BLIZZARD, I AM GETTIN' MY SORRY ASS OUTTA THIS TOWN...
YEAH.
BE THANKFUL YOU DID.

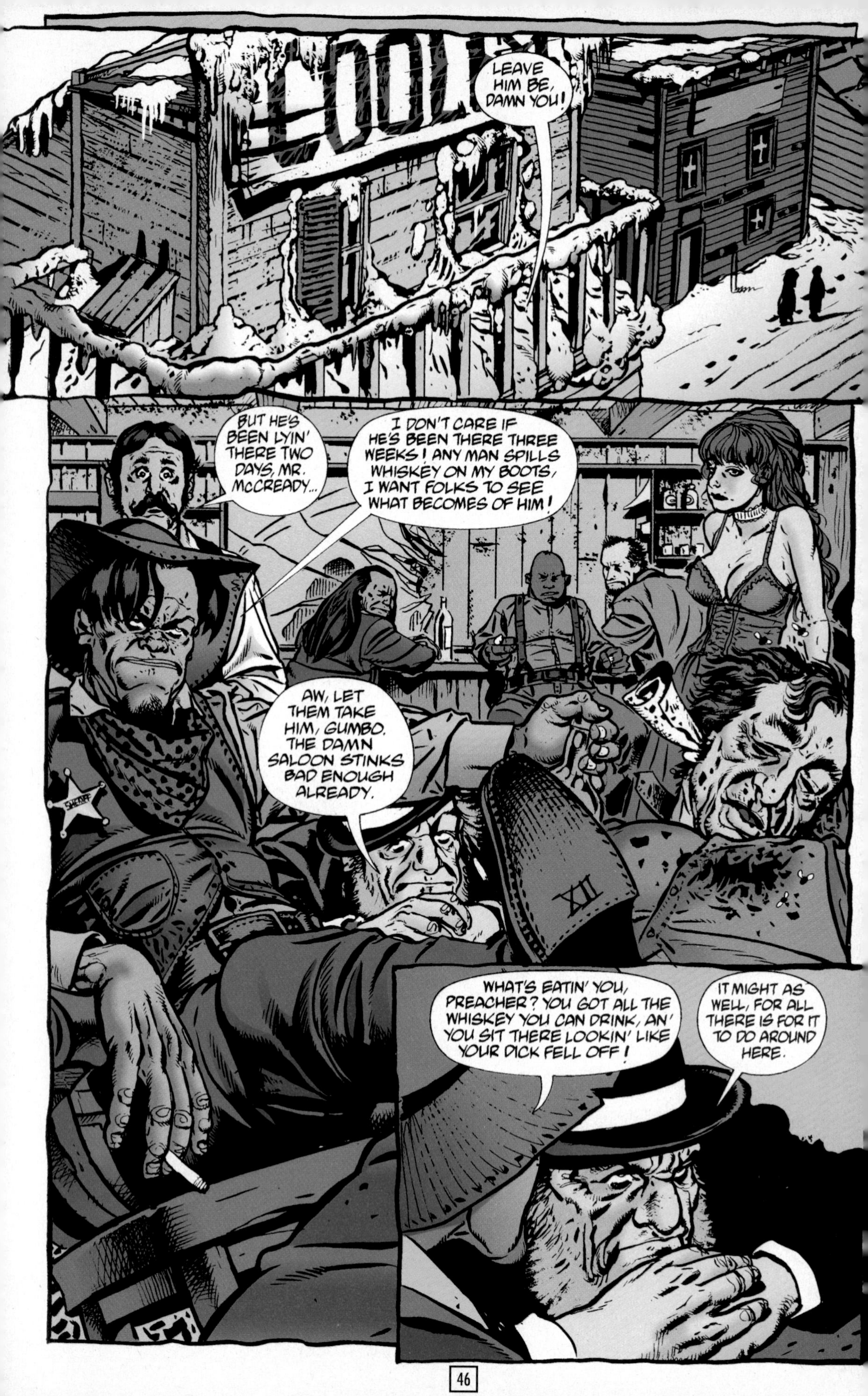
LEAVE HIM BE, DAMN YOU!
BUT HE'S BEEN LYIN' THERE TWO DAYS, MR. McCREADY...
I DON'T CARE IF HE'S BEEN THERE THREE WEEKS! ANY MAN SPILLS WHISKEY ON MY BOOTS, I WANT FOLKS TO SEE WHAT BECOMES OF HIM!
AW, LET THEM TAKE HIM, GUMBO. THE DAMN SALOON STINKS BAD ENOUGH ALREADY.
WHAT'S EATIN' YOU, PREACHER? YOU GOT ALL THE WHISKEY YOU CAN DRINK, AN' YOU SIT THERE LOOKIN' LIKE YOUR DICK FELL OFF!
IT MIGHT AS WELL, FOR ALL THERE IS FOR IT TO DO AROUND HERE.

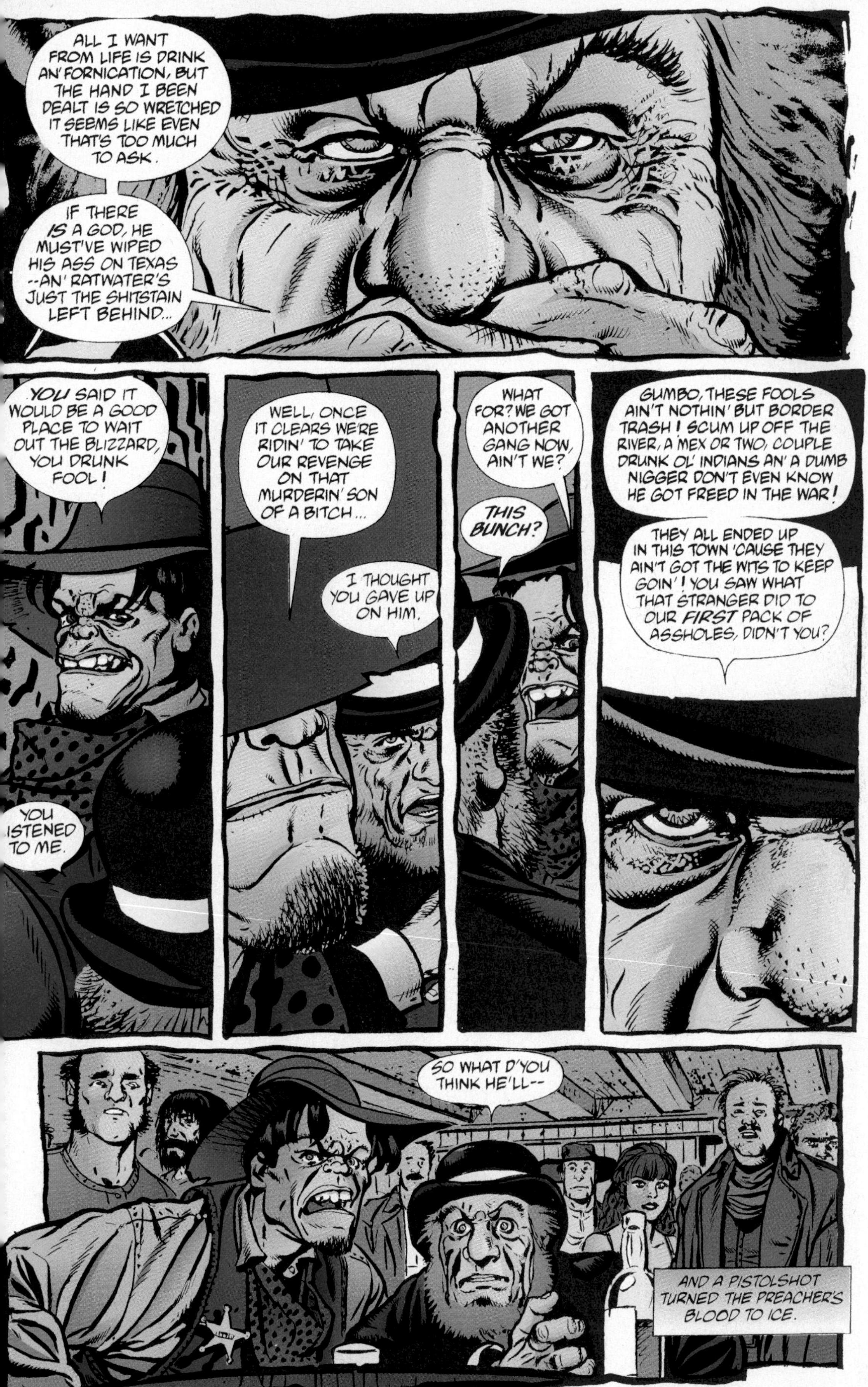

ALL I WANT FROM LIFE IS DRINK AN' FORNICATION, BUT THE HAND I BEEN DEALT IS SO WRETCHED IT SEEMS LIKE EVEN THAT'S TOO MUCH TO ASK.
IF THERE *IS* A GOD, HE MUST'VE WIPED HIS ASS ON TEXAS --AN' RATWATER'S JUST THE SHITSTAIN LEFT BEHIND...
YOU SAID IT WOULD BE A GOOD PLACE TO WAIT OUT THE BLIZZARD, YOU DRUNK FOOL!
YOU LISTENED TO ME.
WELL, ONCE IT CLEARS WE'RE RIDIN' TO TAKE OUR REVENGE ON THAT MURDERIN' SON OF A BITCH...
I THOUGHT YOU GAVE UP ON HIM.
WHAT FOR? WE GOT ANOTHER GANG NOW, AIN'T WE?
THIS BUNCH?
GUMBO, THESE FOOLS AIN'T NOTHIN' BUT BORDER TRASH! SCUM UP OFF THE RIVER, A MEX OR TWO, COUPLE DRUNK OL' INDIANS AN' A DUMB NIGGER DON'T EVEN KNOW HE GOT FREED IN THE WAR!
THEY ALL ENDED UP IN THIS TOWN 'CAUSE THEY AIN'T GOT THE WITS TO KEEP GOIN'! YOU SAW WHAT THAT STRANGER DID TO OUR *FIRST* PACK OF ASSHOLES, DIDN'T YOU?
SO WHAT D'YOU THINK HE'LL--
AND A PISTOLSHOT TURNED THE PREACHER'S BLOOD TO ICE.

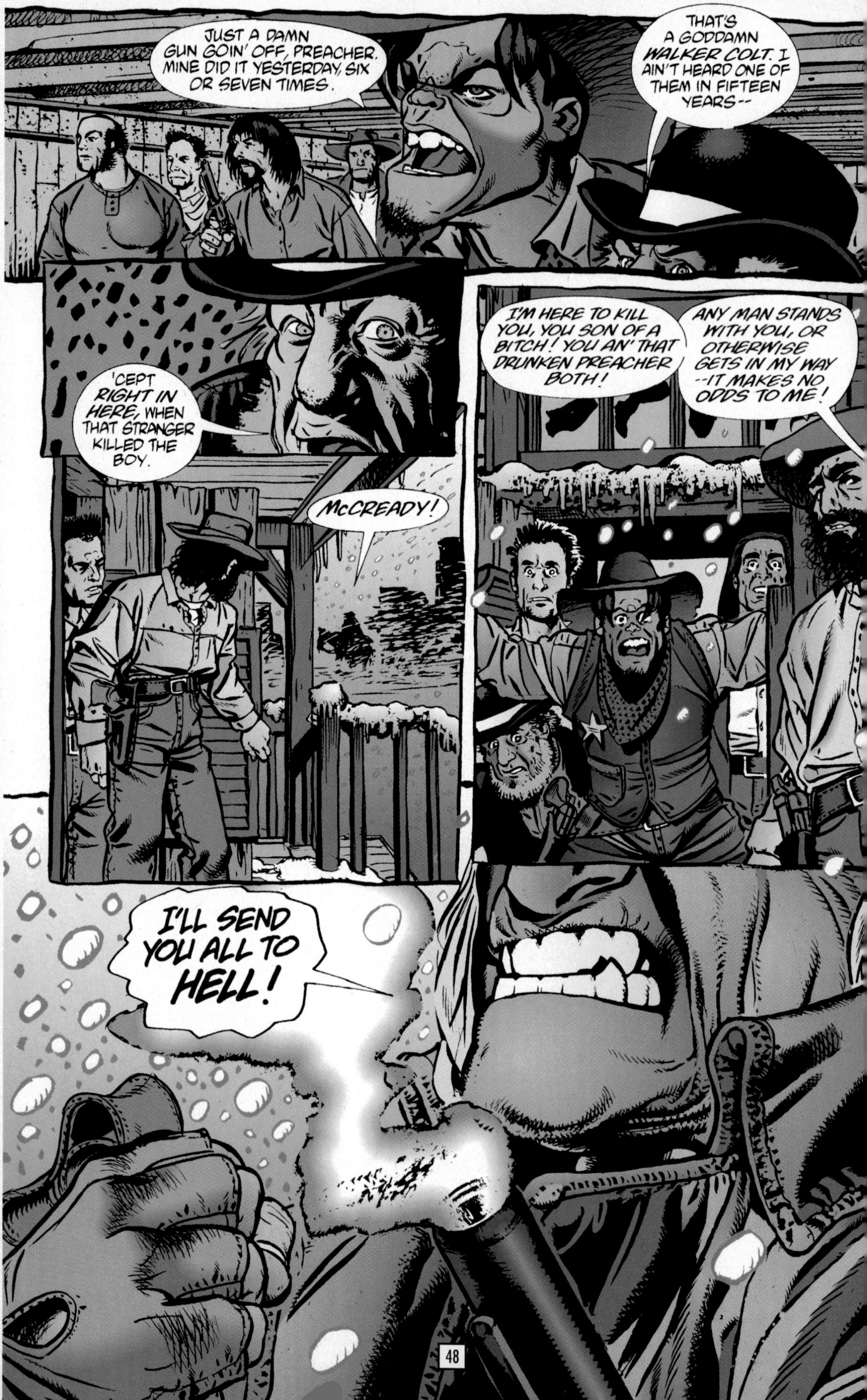

JUST A DAMN GUN GOIN' OFF, PREACHER. MINE DID IT YESTERDAY, SIX OR SEVEN TIMES.
THAT'S A GODDAMN WALKER COLT. I AIN'T HEARD ONE OF THEM IN FIFTEEN YEARS--
'CEPT RIGHT IN HERE, WHEN THAT STRANGER KILLED THE BOY.
McCREADY!
I'M HERE TO KILL YOU, YOU SON OF A BITCH! YOU AN' THAT DRUNKEN PREACHER BOTH!
ANY MAN STANDS WITH YOU, OR OTHERWISE GETS IN MY WAY --IT MAKES NO ODDS TO ME!
I'LL SEND YOU ALL TO HELL!

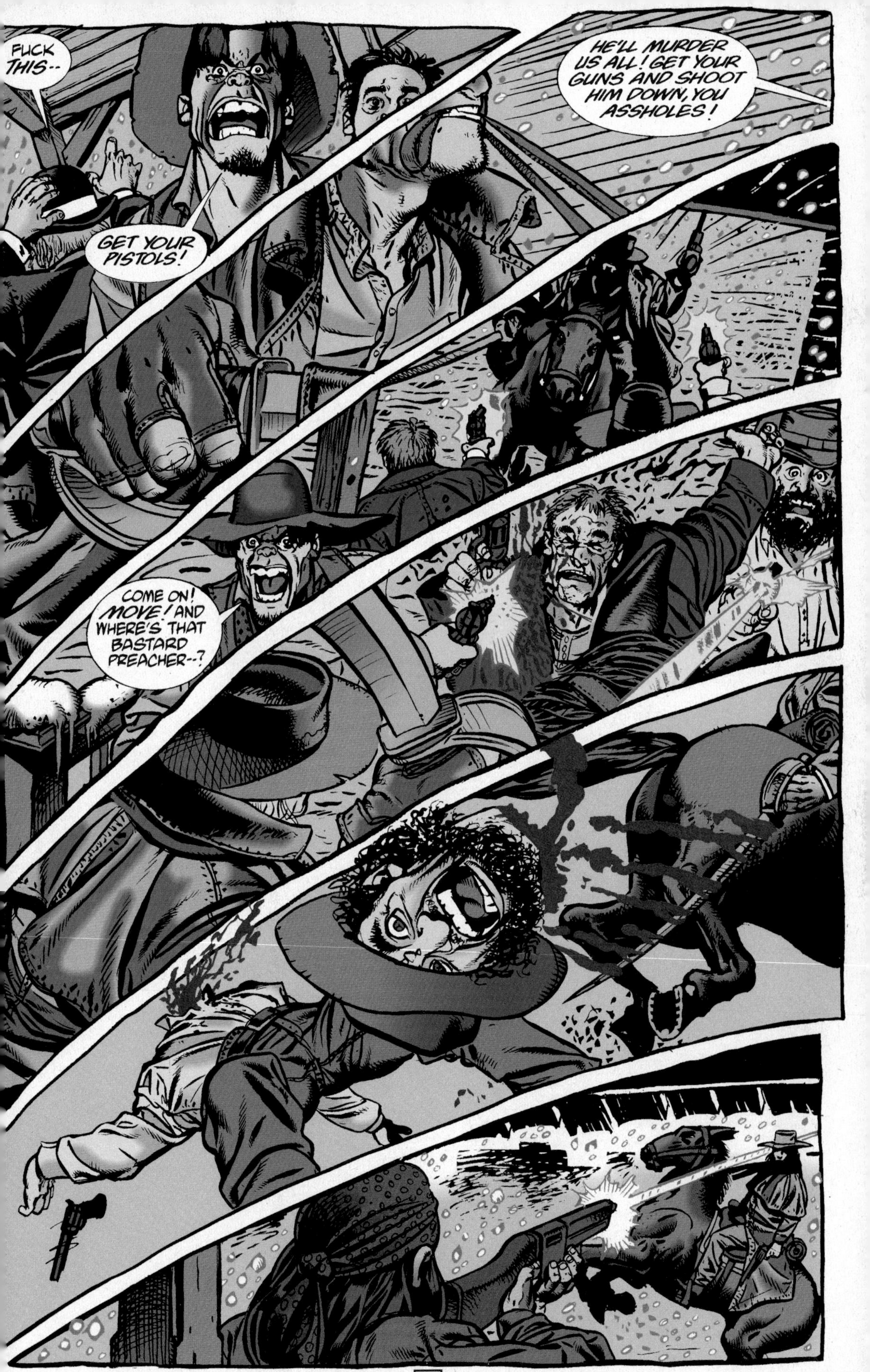
FUCK THIS--
HE'LL MURDER US ALL! GET YOUR GUNS AND SHOOT HIM DOWN, YOU ASSHOLES!
GET YOUR PISTOLS!
COME ON! MOVE! AND WHERE'S THAT BASTARD PREACHER--?

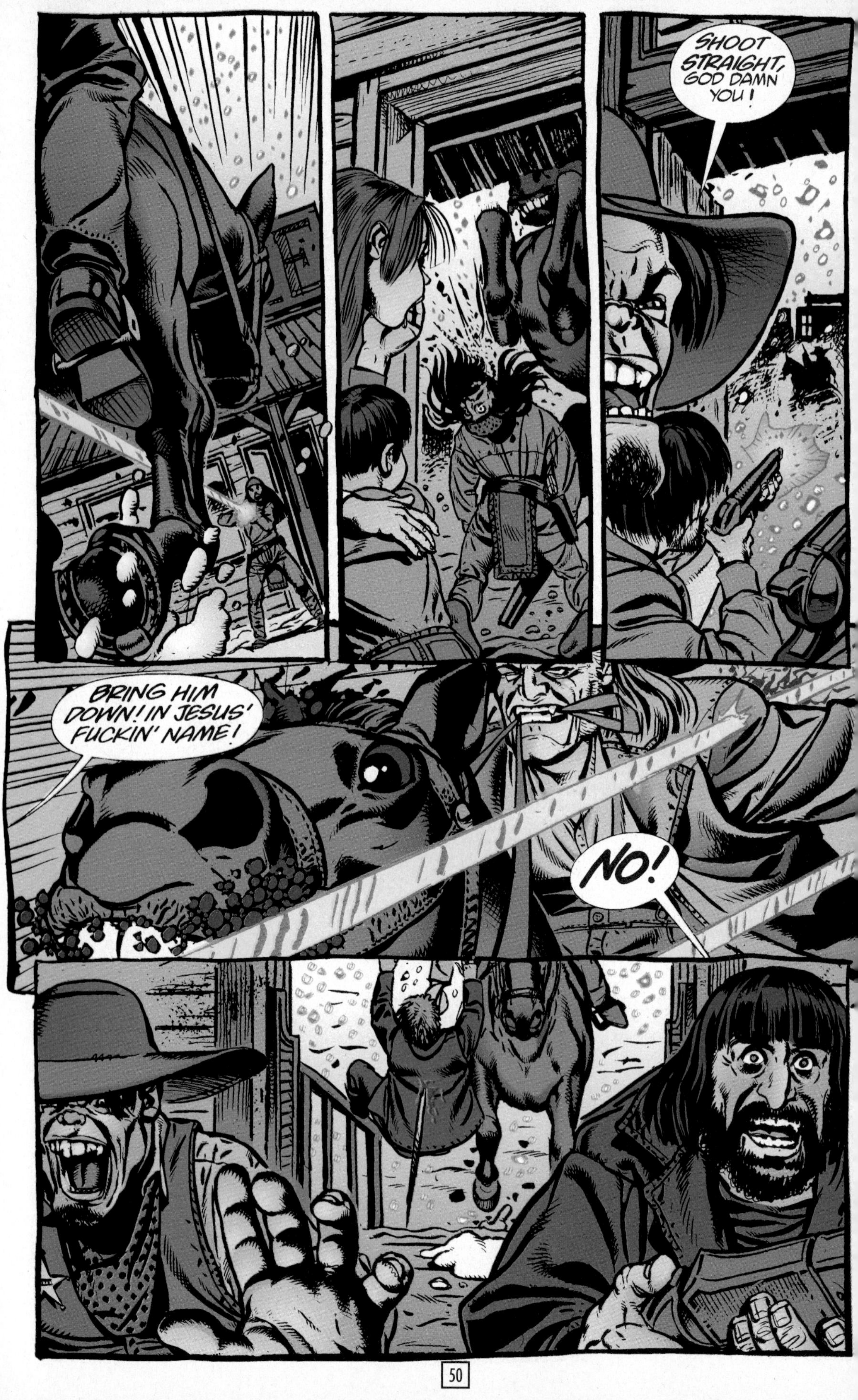
SHOOT STRAIGHT, GOD DAMN YOU!
BRING HIM DOWN! IN JESUS' FUCKIN' NAME!
NO!

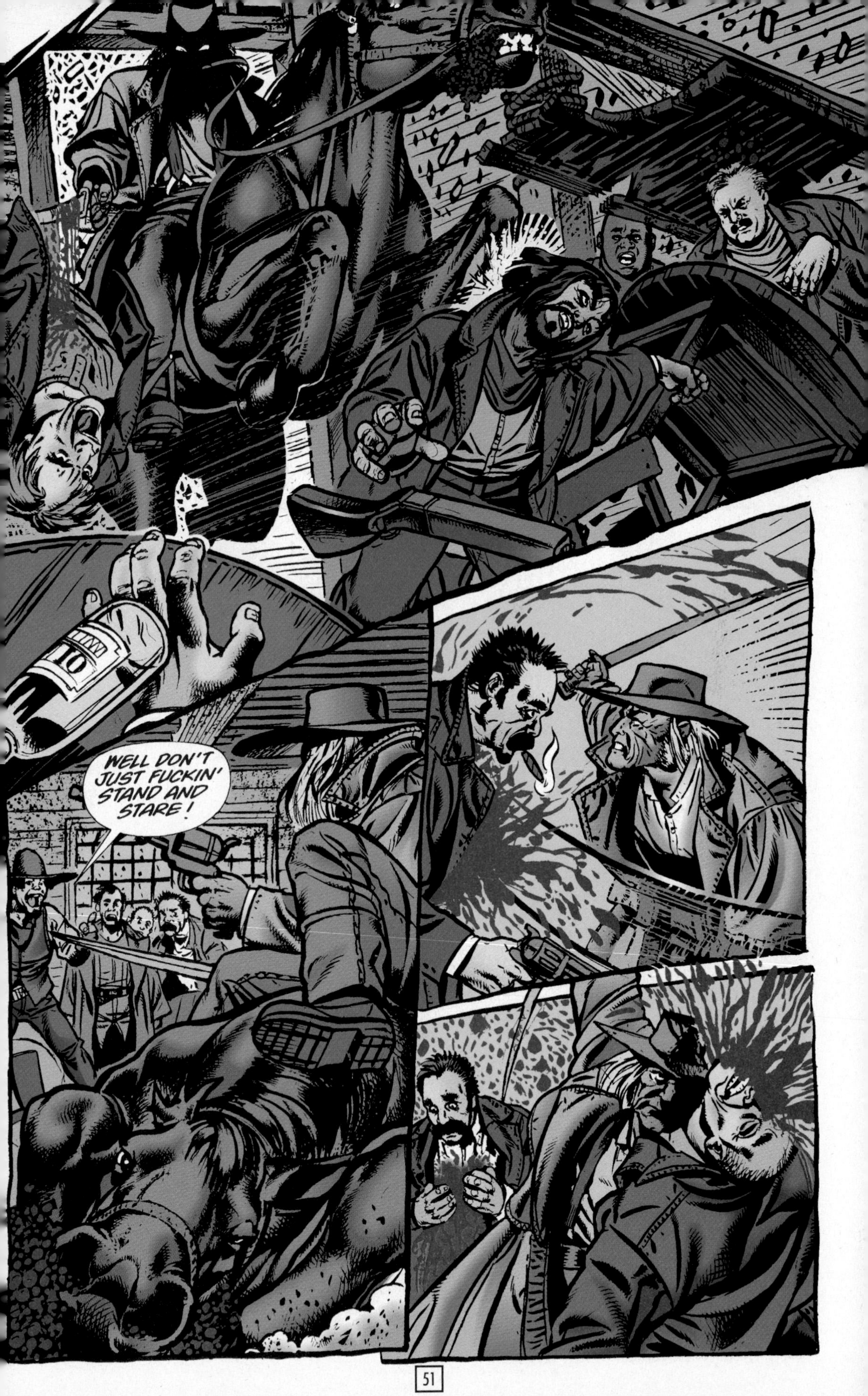
WELL DON'T JUST FUCKIN' STAND AND STARE!

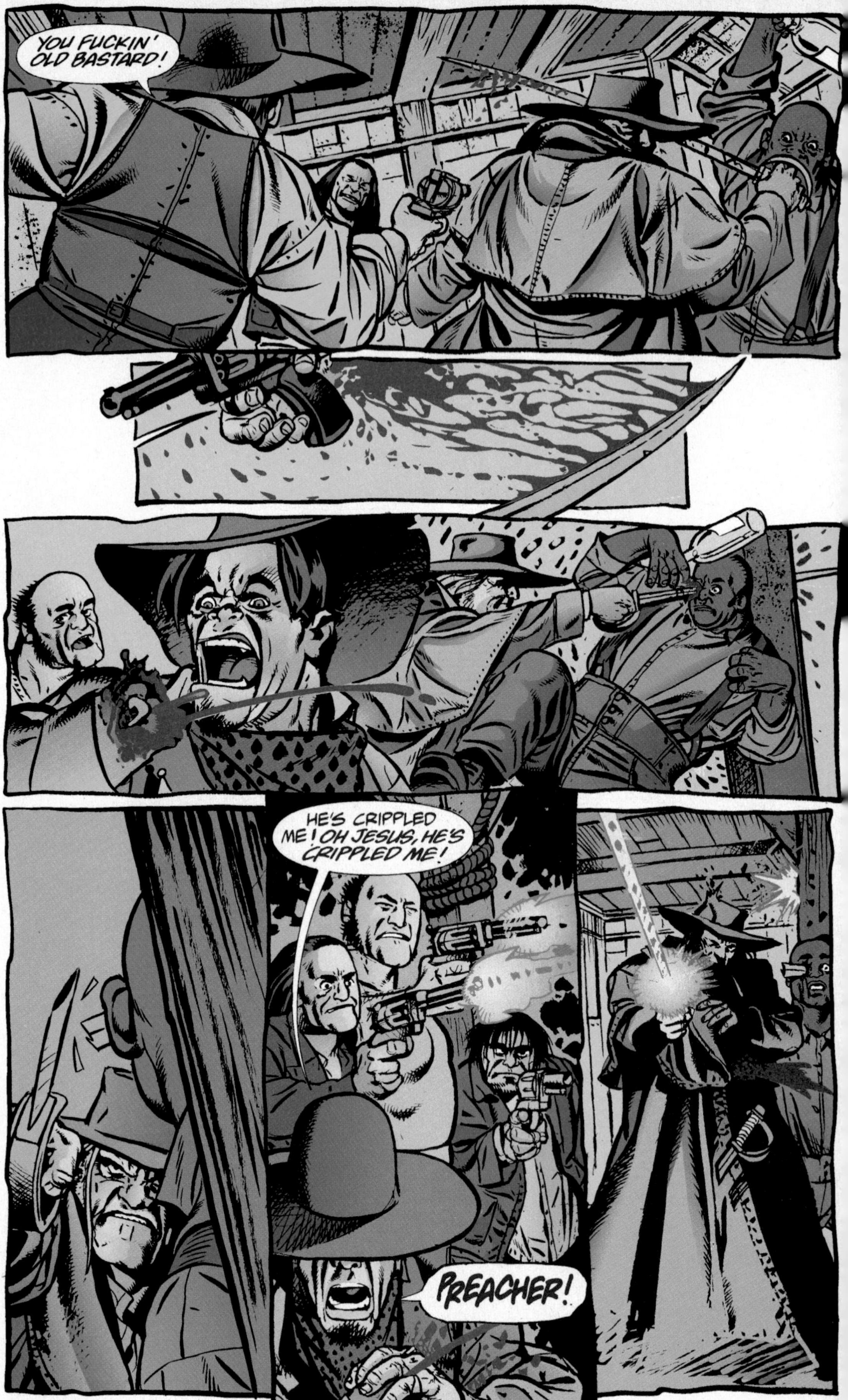
YOU FUCKIN' OLD BASTARD!
HE'S CRIPPLED ME! OH JESUS, HE'S CRIPPLED ME!
PREACHER!

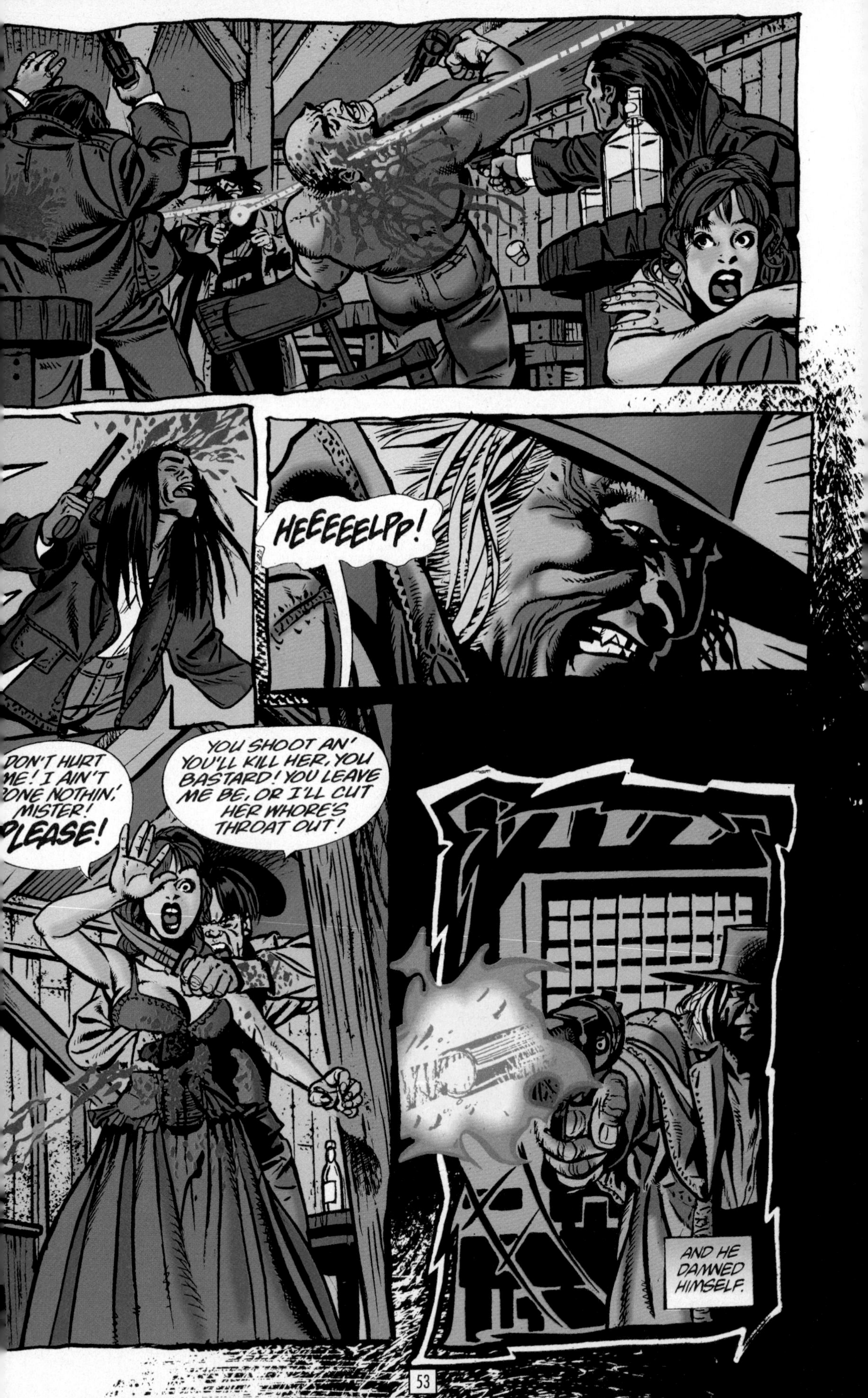
HEEEEELPP!
DON'T HURT ME! I AIN'T DONE NOTHIN,' MISTER! PLEASE!
YOU SHOOT AN' YOU'LL KILL HER, YOU BASTARD! YOU LEAVE ME BE, OR I'LL CUT HER WHORE'S THROAT OUT!
AND HE DAMNED HIMSELF.

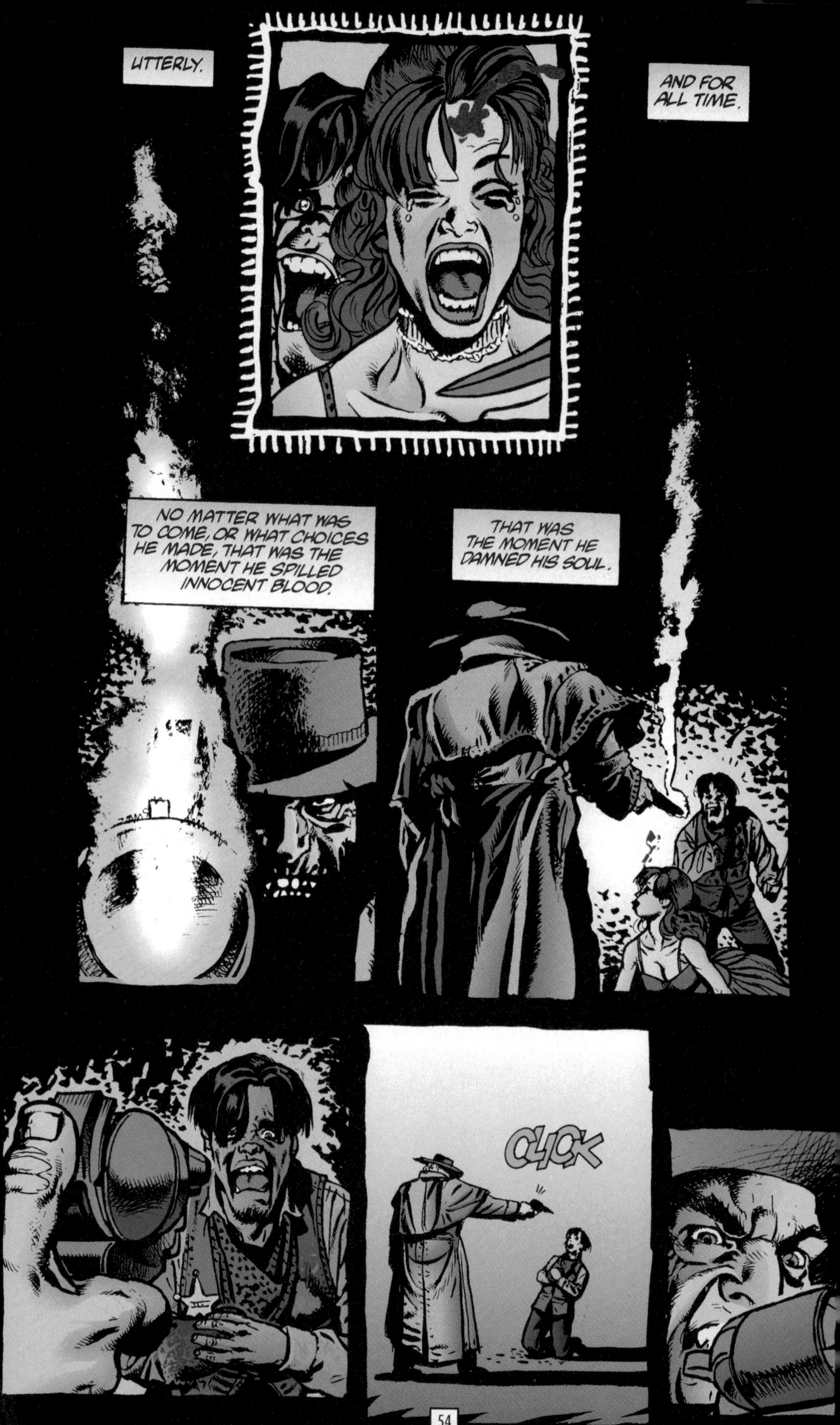
UTTERLY.
AND FOR ALL TIME.
NO MATTER WHAT WAS TO COME, OR WHAT CHOICES HE MADE, THAT WAS THE MOMENT HE SPILLED INNOCENT BLOOD.
THAT WAS THE MOMENT HE DAMNED HIS SOUL.
CLICK

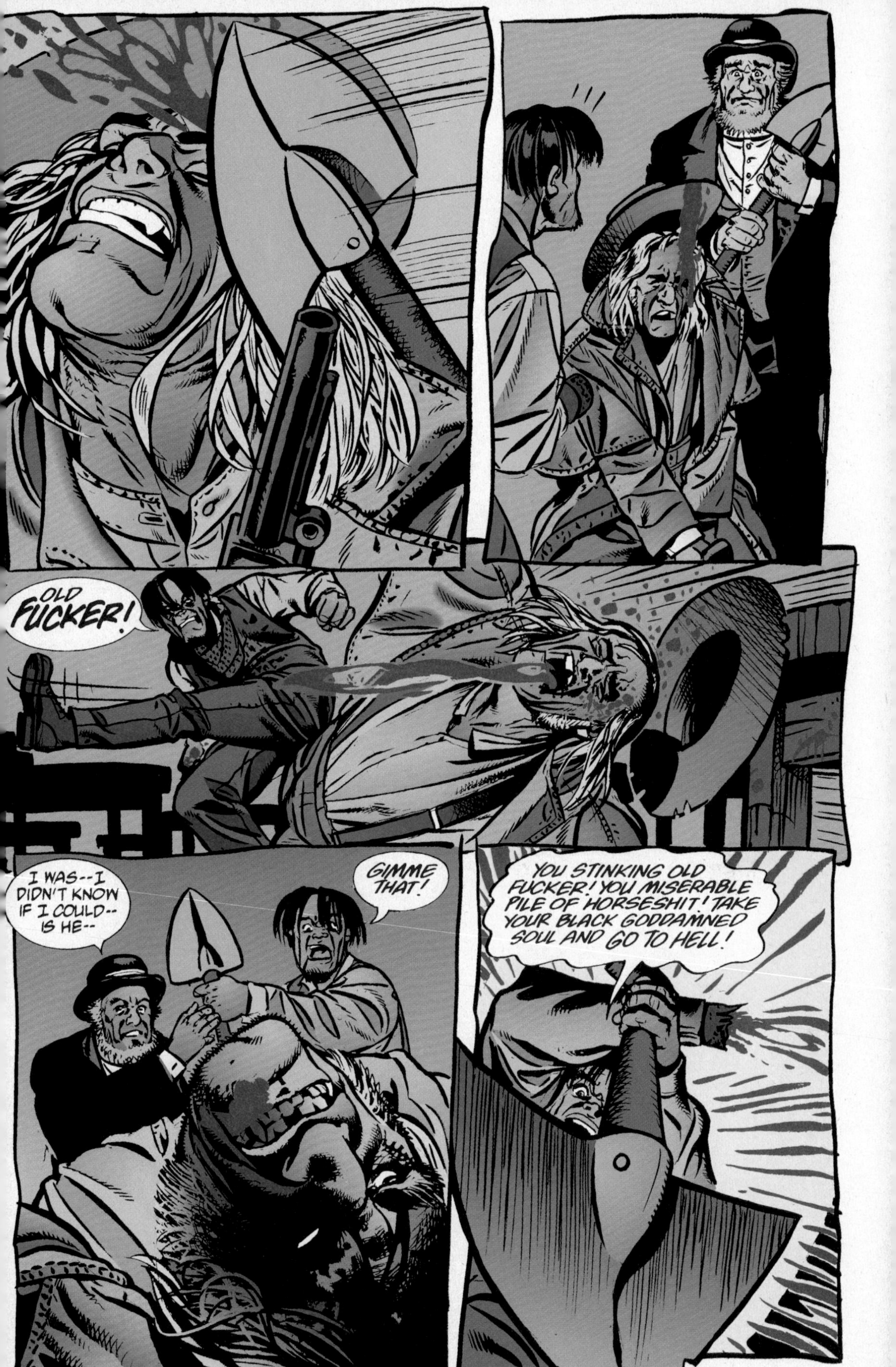
OLD FUCKER!
I WAS--I DIDN'T KNOW IF I COULD-- IS HE--
GIMME THAT!
YOU STINKING OLD FUCKER! YOU MISERABLE PILE OF HORSESHIT! TAKE YOUR BLACK GODDAMNED SOUL AND GO TO HELL!

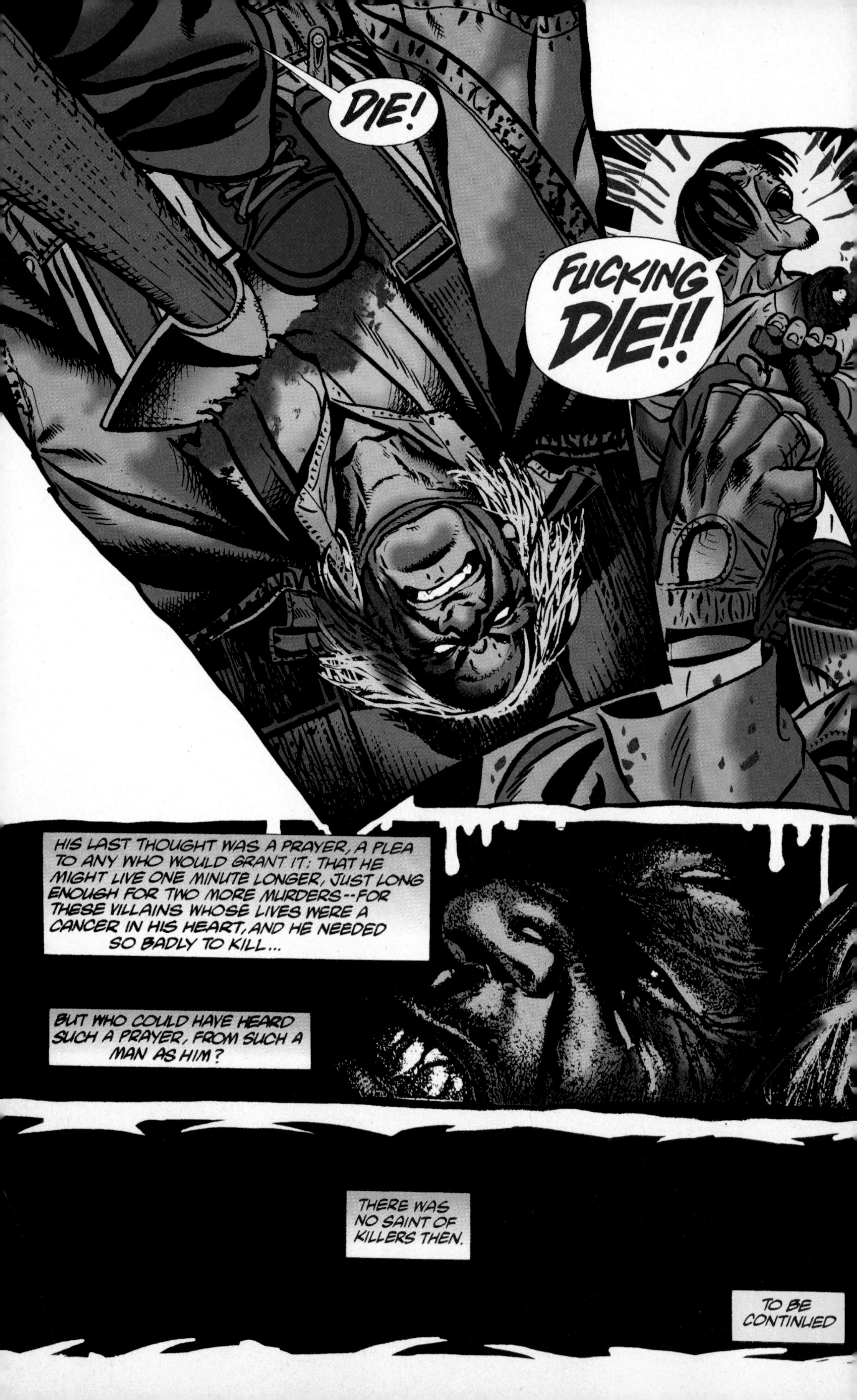
DIE!
FUCKING DIE!!
HIS LAST THOUGHT WAS A PRAYER, A PLEA TO ANY WHO WOULD GRANT IT: THAT HE MIGHT LIVE ONE MINUTE LONGER, JUST LONG ENOUGH FOR TWO MORE MURDERS--FOR THESE VILLAINS WHOSE LIVES WERE A CANCER IN HIS HEART, AND HE NEEDED SO BADLY TO KILL...
BUT WHO COULD HAVE HEARD SUCH A PRAYER, FROM SUCH A MAN AS HIM?
THERE WAS NO SAINT OF KILLERS THEN.
TO BE CONTINUED

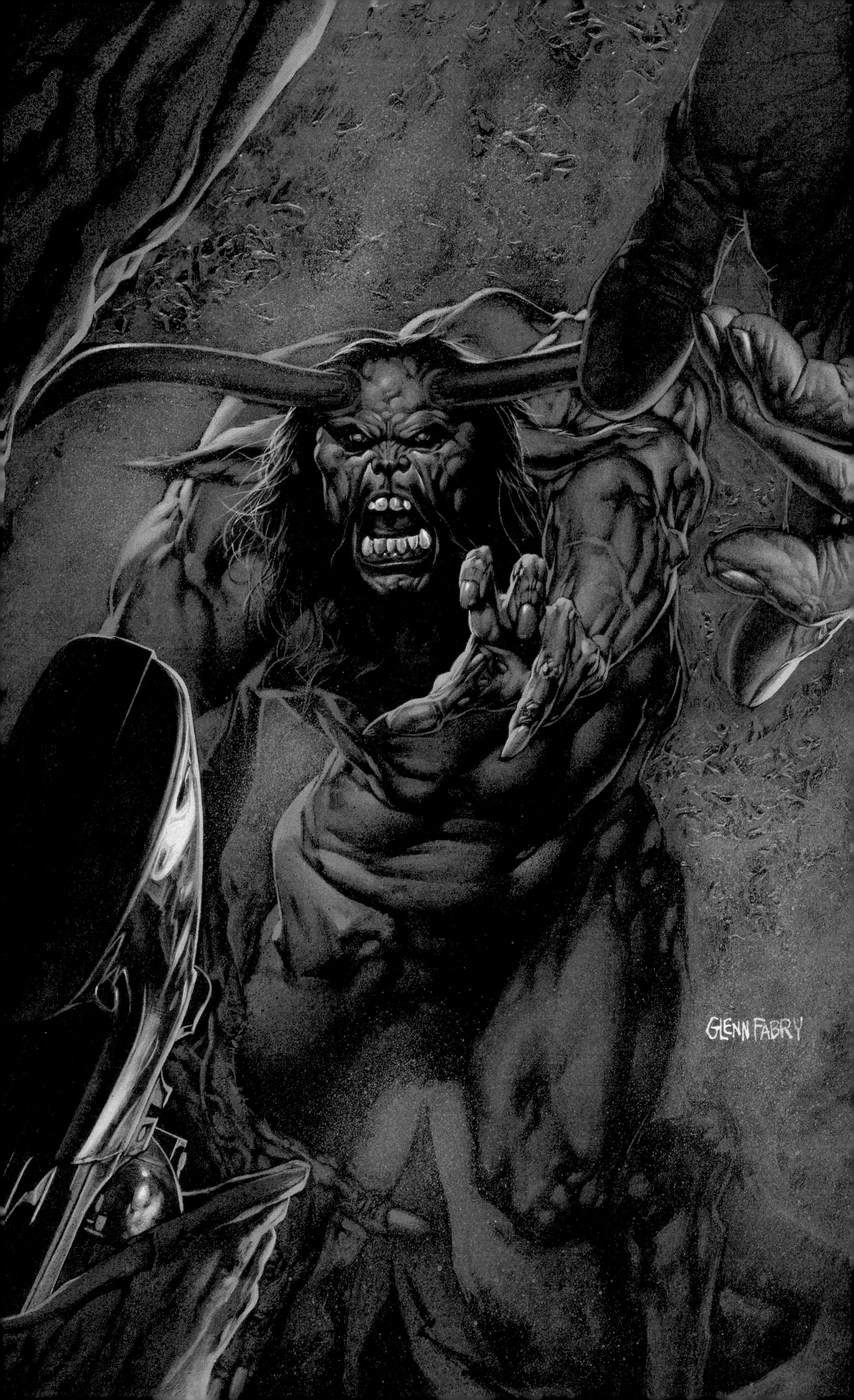
GLENN FABRY

HE AWOKE ON THE ROAD TO HELL, A BUTCHERED CORPSE SAT TALL IN THE SADDLE, LEADING THE SINNERS HE HAD SLAIN TO PERDITION.

THE HORSE THEY'D KILLED TWO WEEKS BEFORE HAD WAITED FOR ITS MASTER, GRAZING ON THE OTHER SIDE OF LIFE. IT WAS AS AIMLESS AND BLIND AS THE DEAD THAT FOLLOWED HIM, REQUIRING AS THEY DID SOME SMALL DIRECTION, SOME POINTING OF THE WAY--FOR ALL THEIR MINDS WERE GONE.

BUT HIS WAS NOT.

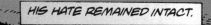

HIS HATE REMAINED INTACT.

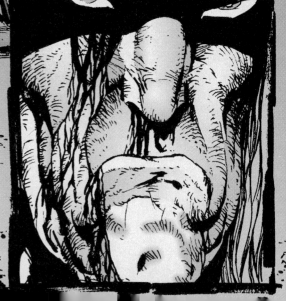

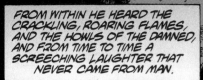

FROM WITHIN HE HEARD THE CRACKLING, ROARING FLAMES, AND THE HOWLS OF THE DAMNED, AND FROM TIME TO TIME A SCREECHING LAUGHTER THAT NEVER CAME FROM MAN.

HE DIDN'T CARE.

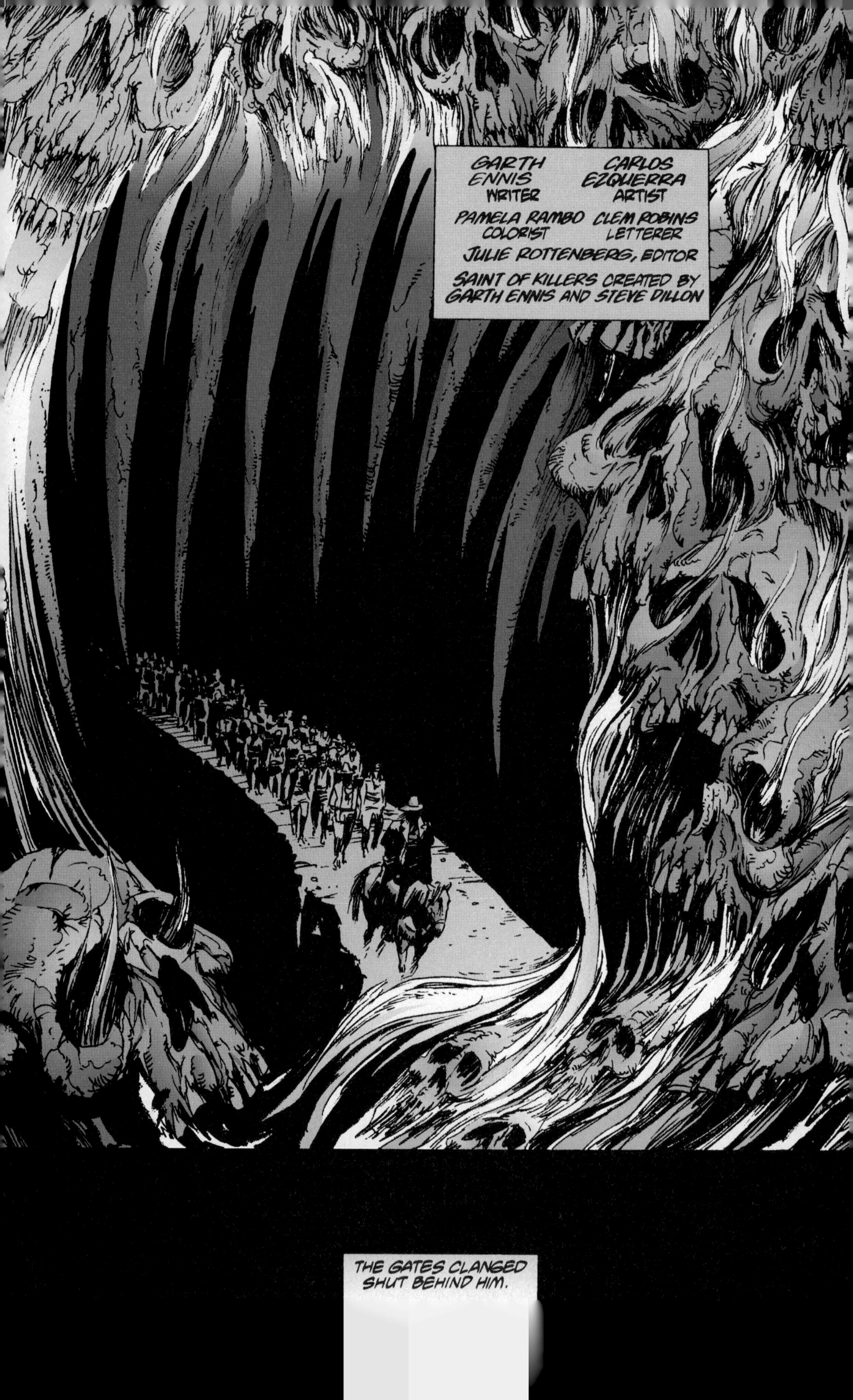
GARTH ENNIS WRITER
CARLOS EZQUERRA ARTIST
PAMELA RAMBO COLORIST
CLEM ROBINS LETTERER
JULIE ROTTENBERG, EDITOR
SAINT OF KILLERS CREATED BY GARTH ENNIS AND STEVE DILLON
THE GATES CLANGED SHUT BEHIND HIM.

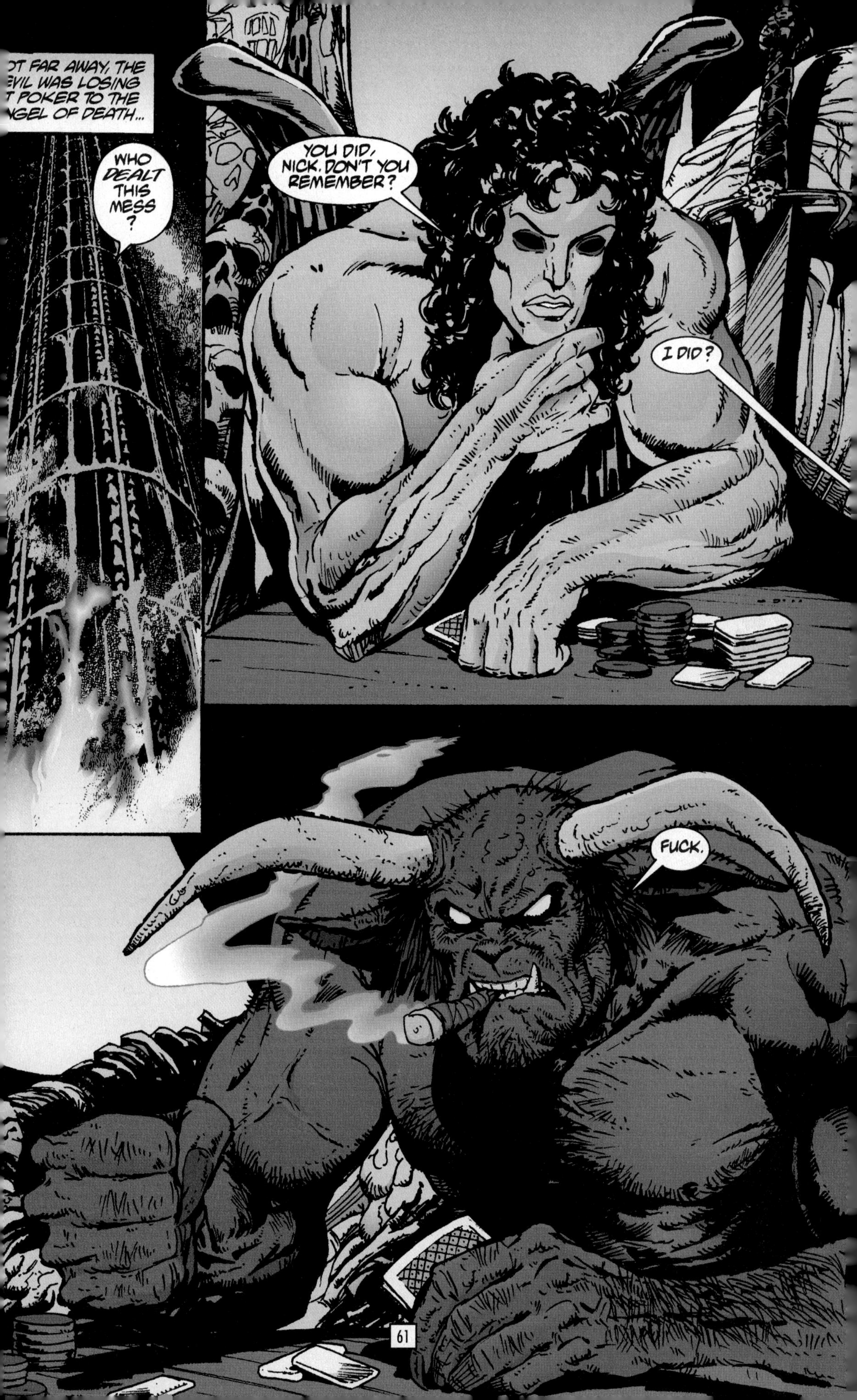
OT FAR AWAY, THE
EVIL WAS LOSING
T POKER TO THE
NGEL OF DEATH...
WHO DEALT THIS MESS?
YOU DID, NICK. DON'T YOU REMEMBER?
I DID?
FUCK.

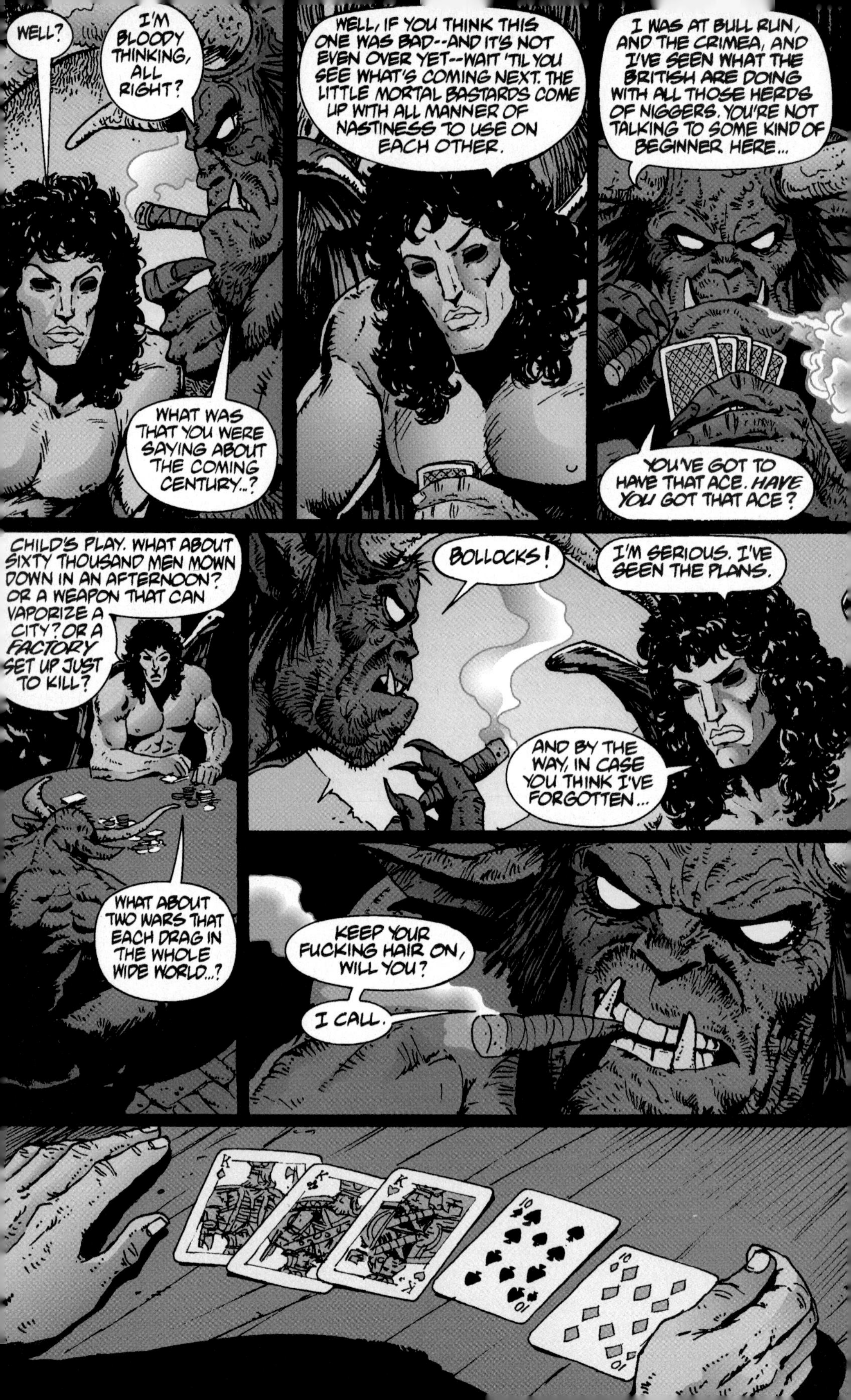
WELL?
I'M BLOODY THINKING, ALL RIGHT?
WHAT WAS THAT YOU WERE SAYING ABOUT THE COMING CENTURY..?
WELL, IF YOU THINK THIS ONE WAS BAD--AND IT'S NOT EVEN OVER YET--WAIT 'TIL YOU SEE WHAT'S COMING NEXT. THE LITTLE MORTAL BASTARDS COME UP WITH ALL MANNER OF NASTINESS TO USE ON EACH OTHER.
I WAS AT BULL RUN, AND THE CRIMEA, AND I'VE SEEN WHAT THE BRITISH ARE DOING WITH ALL THOSE HERDS OF NIGGERS. YOU'RE NOT TALKING TO SOME KIND OF BEGINNER HERE...
YOU'VE GOT TO HAVE THAT ACE. *HAVE YOU* GOT THAT ACE?
CHILD'S PLAY. WHAT ABOUT SIXTY THOUSAND MEN MOWN DOWN IN AN AFTERNOON? OR A WEAPON THAT CAN VAPORIZE A CITY? OR A *FACTORY* SET UP JUST TO KILL?
WHAT ABOUT TWO WARS THAT EACH DRAG IN THE WHOLE WIDE WORLD...?
BOLLOCKS!
I'M SERIOUS. I'VE SEEN THE PLANS.
AND BY THE WAY, IN CASE YOU THINK I'VE FORGOTTEN...
KEEP YOUR FUCKING HAIR ON, WILL YOU?
I CALL.

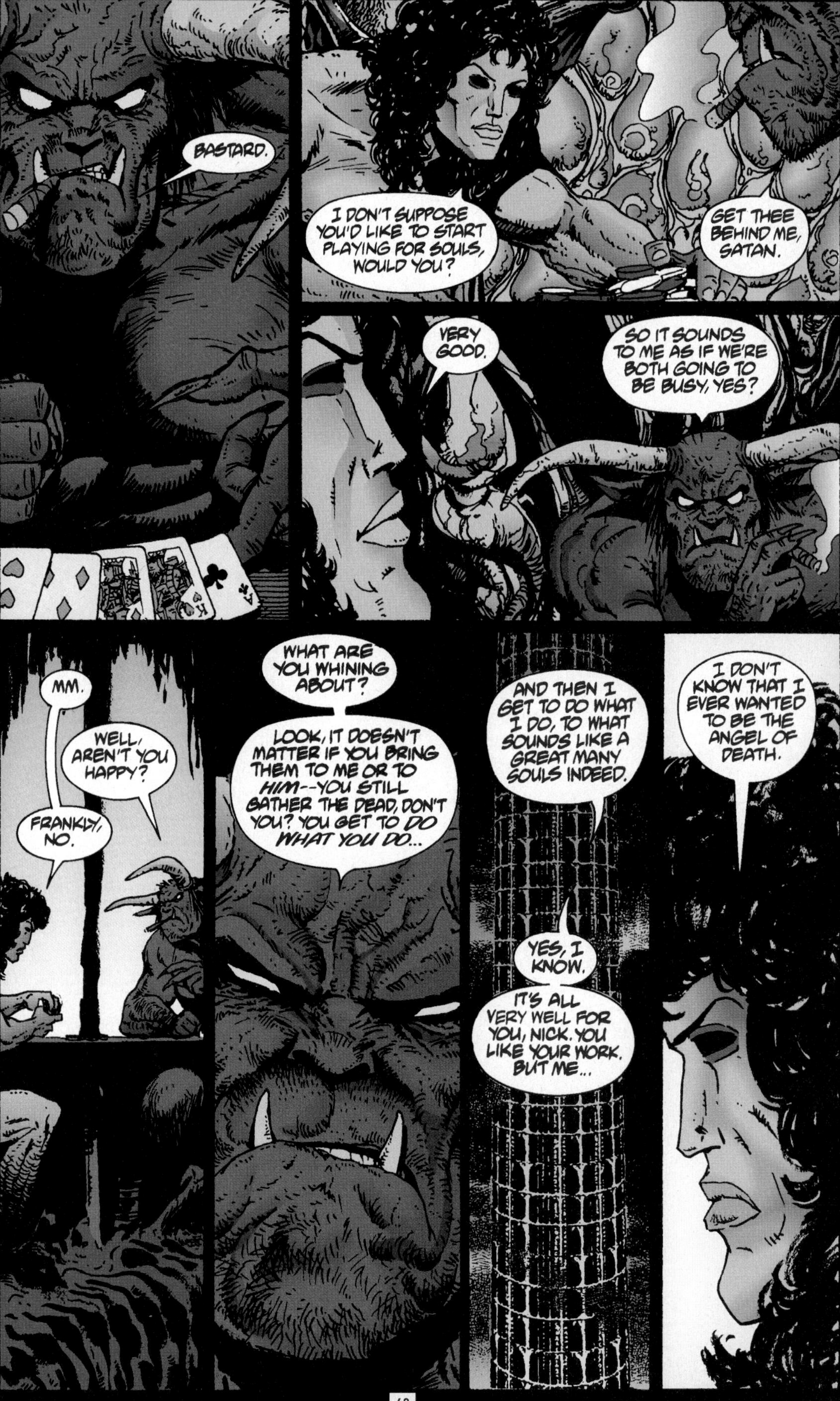
BASTARD.
I DON'T SUPPOSE YOU'D LIKE TO START PLAYING FOR SOULS, WOULD YOU?
GET THEE BEHIND ME, SATAN.
VERY GOOD.
SO IT SOUNDS TO ME AS IF WE'RE BOTH GOING TO BE BUSY, YES?
MM.
WELL, AREN'T YOU HAPPY?
FRANKLY, NO.
WHAT ARE YOU WHINING ABOUT?
LOOK, IT DOESN'T MATTER IF YOU BRING THEM TO ME OR TO *HIM*--YOU STILL GATHER THE DEAD, DON'T YOU? YOU GET TO *DO WHAT YOU DO*...
AND THEN I GET TO DO WHAT I DO, TO WHAT SOUNDS LIKE A GREAT MANY SOULS INDEED.
YES, I KNOW.
IT'S ALL VERY WELL FOR YOU, NICK. YOU LIKE YOUR WORK. BUT ME...
I DON'T KNOW THAT I EVER WANTED TO BE THE ANGEL OF DEATH.

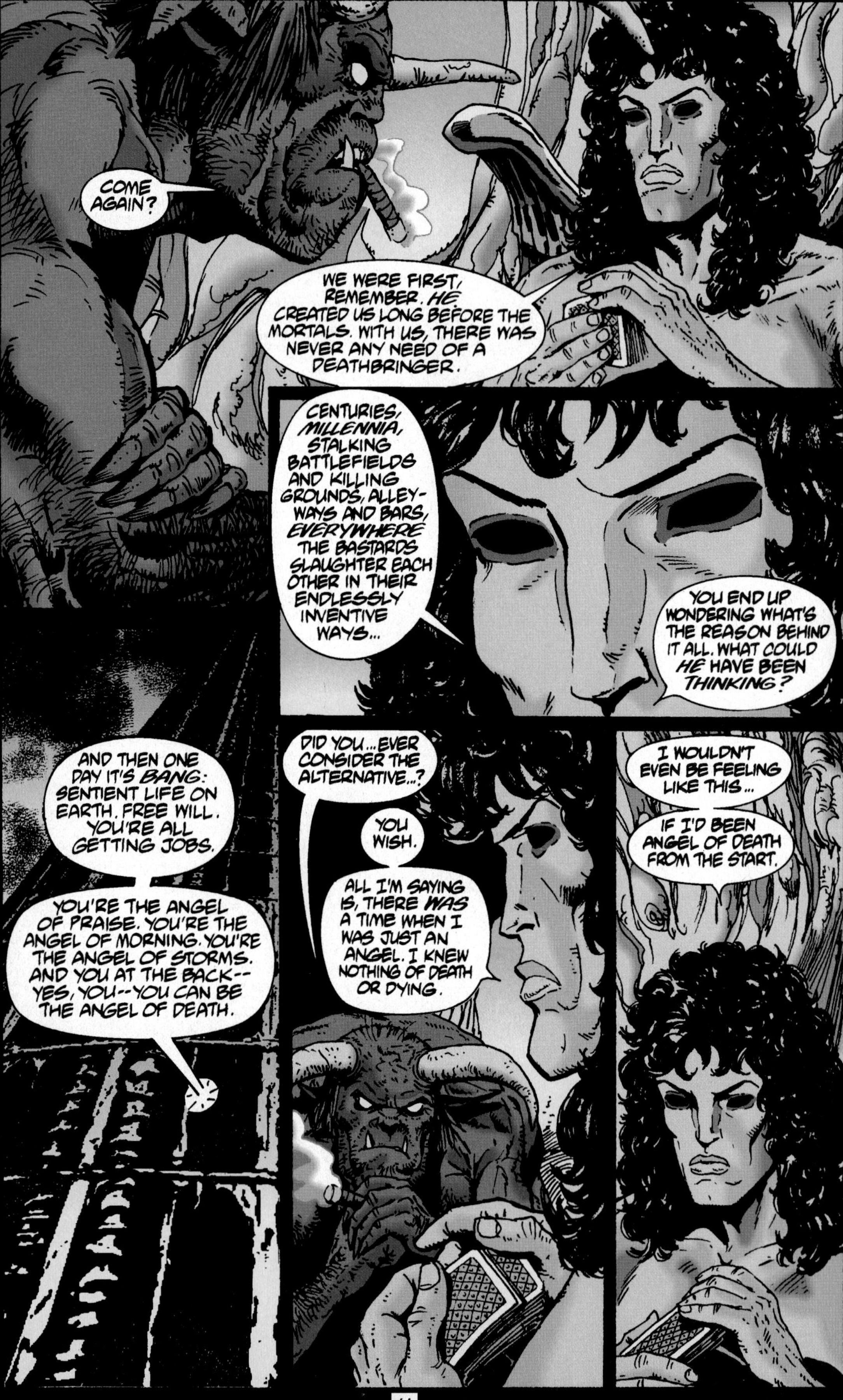
COME AGAIN?
WE WERE FIRST, REMEMBER. HE CREATED US LONG BEFORE THE MORTALS. WITH US, THERE WAS NEVER ANY NEED OF A DEATHBRINGER.
CENTURIES, MILLENNIA, STALKING BATTLEFIELDS AND KILLING GROUNDS, ALLEY-WAYS AND BARS, EVERYWHERE THE BASTARDS SLAUGHTER EACH OTHER IN THEIR ENDLESSLY INVENTIVE WAYS...
YOU END UP WONDERING WHAT'S THE REASON BEHIND IT ALL. WHAT COULD HE HAVE BEEN THINKING?
AND THEN ONE DAY IT'S BANG: SENTIENT LIFE ON EARTH. FREE WILL. YOU'RE ALL GETTING JOBS.
YOU'RE THE ANGEL OF PRAISE. YOU'RE THE ANGEL OF MORNING. YOU'RE THE ANGEL OF STORMS. AND YOU AT THE BACK-- YES, YOU--YOU CAN BE THE ANGEL OF DEATH.
DID YOU...EVER CONSIDER THE ALTERNATIVE...?
YOU WISH.
ALL I'M SAYING IS, THERE WAS A TIME WHEN I WAS JUST AN ANGEL. I KNEW NOTHING OF DEATH OR DYING.
I WOULDN'T EVEN BE FEELING LIKE THIS...
IF I'D BEEN ANGEL OF DEATH FROM THE START.

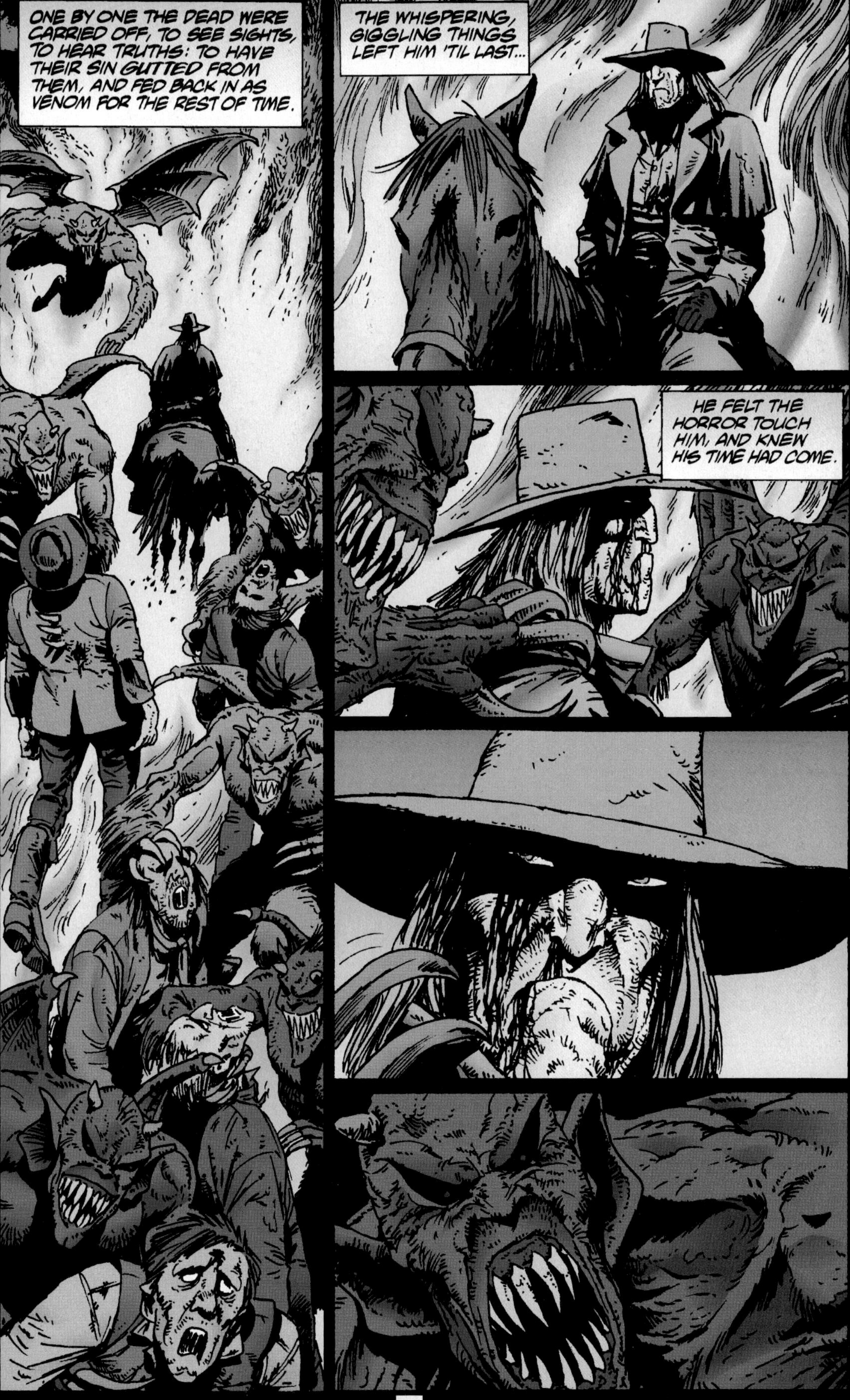
ONE BY ONE THE DEAD WERE CARRIED OFF, TO SEE SIGHTS, TO HEAR TRUTHS: TO HAVE THEIR SIN GUTTED FROM THEM, AND FED BACK IN AS VENOM FOR THE REST OF TIME.
THE WHISPERING, GIGGLING THINGS LEFT HIM 'TIL LAST...
HE FELT THE HORROR TOUCH HIM, AND KNEW HIS TIME HAD COME.

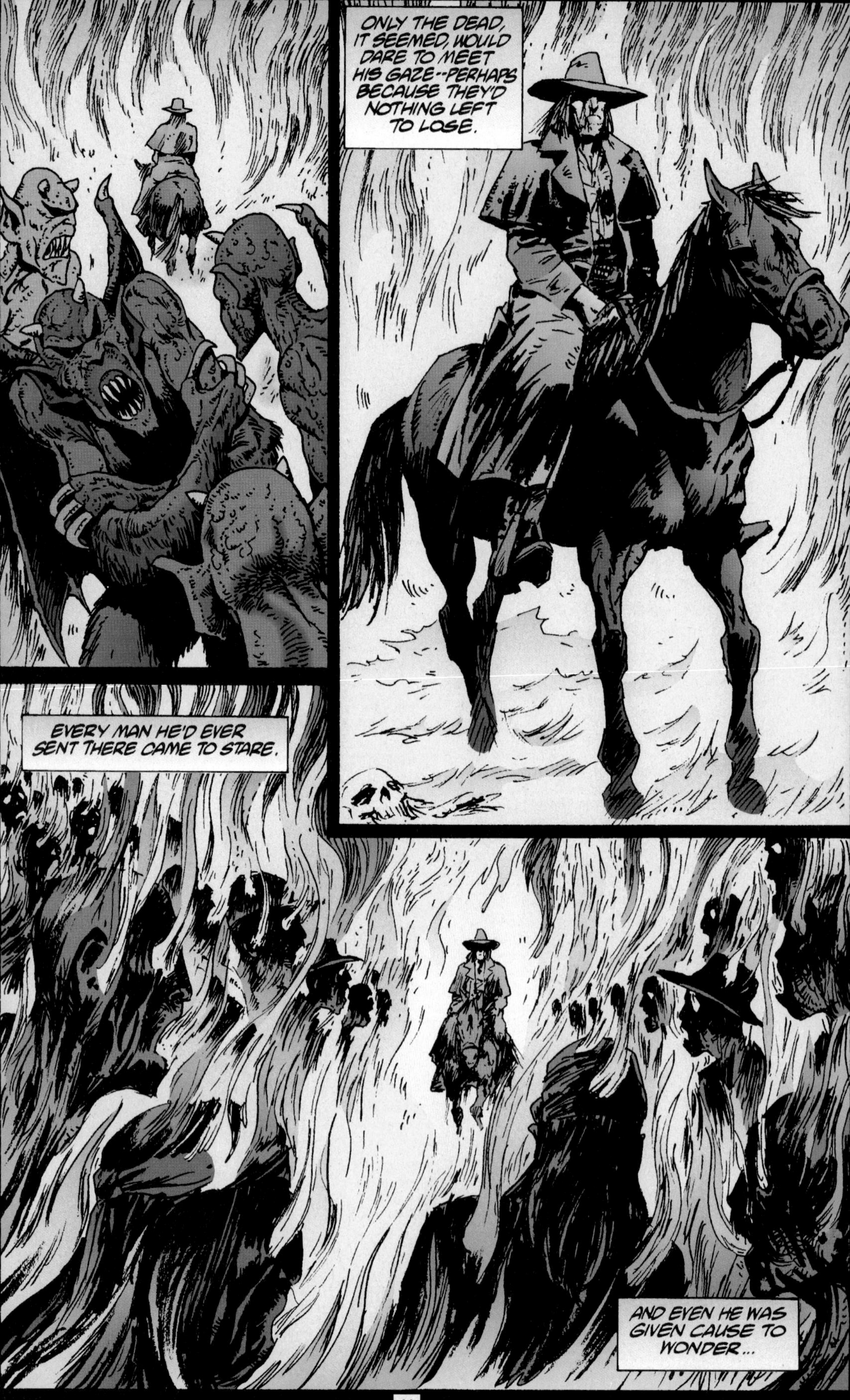
ONLY THE DEAD, IT SEEMED, WOULD DARE TO MEET HIS GAZE--PERHAPS BECAUSE THEY'D NOTHING LEFT TO LOSE.
EVERY MAN HE'D EVER SENT THERE CAME TO STARE.
AND EVEN HE WAS GIVEN CAUSE TO WONDER...

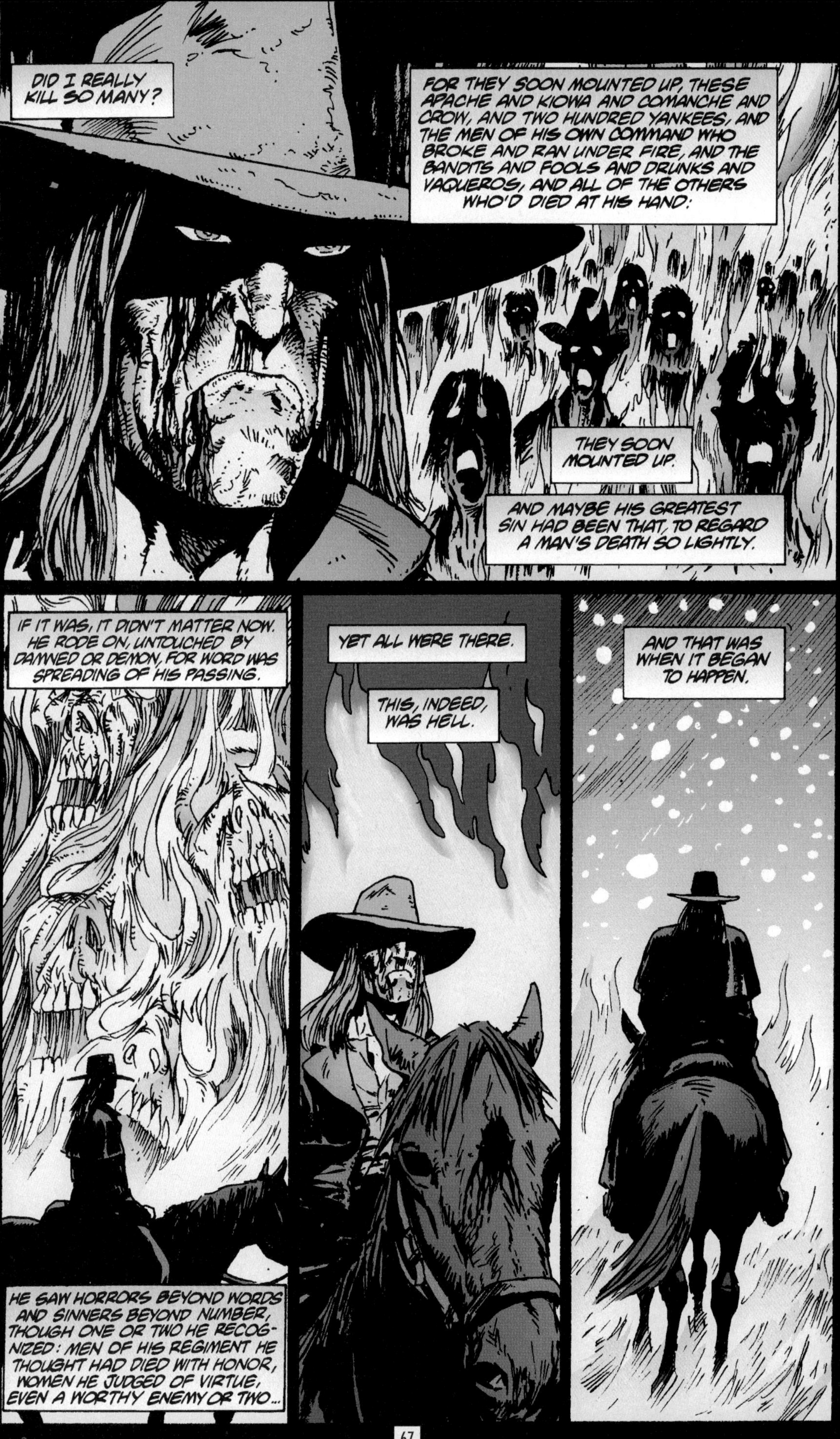
DID I REALLY KILL SO MANY?
FOR THEY SOON MOUNTED UP, THESE APACHE AND KIOWA AND COMANCHE AND CROW, AND TWO HUNDRED YANKEES, AND THE MEN OF HIS OWN COMMAND WHO BROKE AND RAN UNDER FIRE, AND THE BANDITS AND FOOLS AND DRUNKS AND VAQUEROS, AND ALL OF THE OTHERS WHO'D DIED AT HIS HAND:
THEY SOON MOUNTED UP.
AND MAYBE HIS GREATEST SIN HAD BEEN THAT, TO REGARD A MAN'S DEATH SO LIGHTLY.
IF IT WAS, IT DIDN'T MATTER NOW. HE RODE ON, UNTOUCHED BY DAMNED OR DEMON, FOR WORD WAS SPREADING OF HIS PASSING.
HE SAW HORRORS BEYOND WORDS AND SINNERS BEYOND NUMBER, THOUGH ONE OR TWO HE RECOG-NIZED: MEN OF HIS REGIMENT HE THOUGHT HAD DIED WITH HONOR, WOMEN HE JUDGED OF VIRTUE, EVEN A WORTHY ENEMY OR TWO...
YET ALL WERE THERE.
THIS, INDEED, WAS HELL.
AND THAT WAS WHEN IT BEGAN TO HAPPEN.

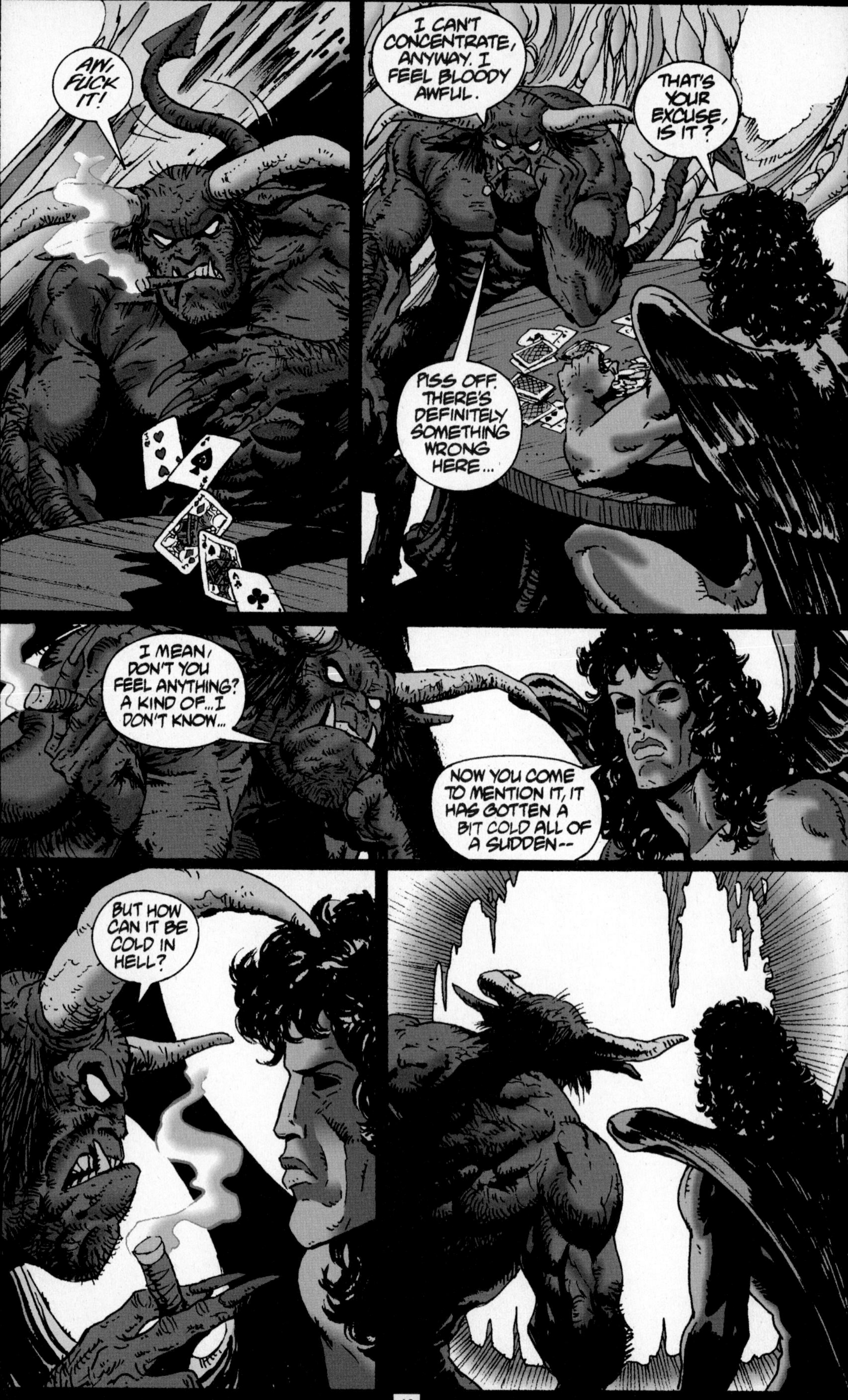

AW, FUCK IT!
I CAN'T CONCENTRATE, ANYWAY. I FEEL BLOODY AWFUL.
THAT'S YOUR EXCUSE, IS IT?
PISS OFF. THERE'S DEFINITELY SOMETHING WRONG HERE...
I MEAN, DON'T YOU FEEL ANYTHING? A KIND OF... I DON'T KNOW...
NOW YOU COME TO MENTION IT, IT HAS GOTTEN A BIT COLD ALL OF A SUDDEN--
BUT HOW CAN IT BE COLD IN HELL?

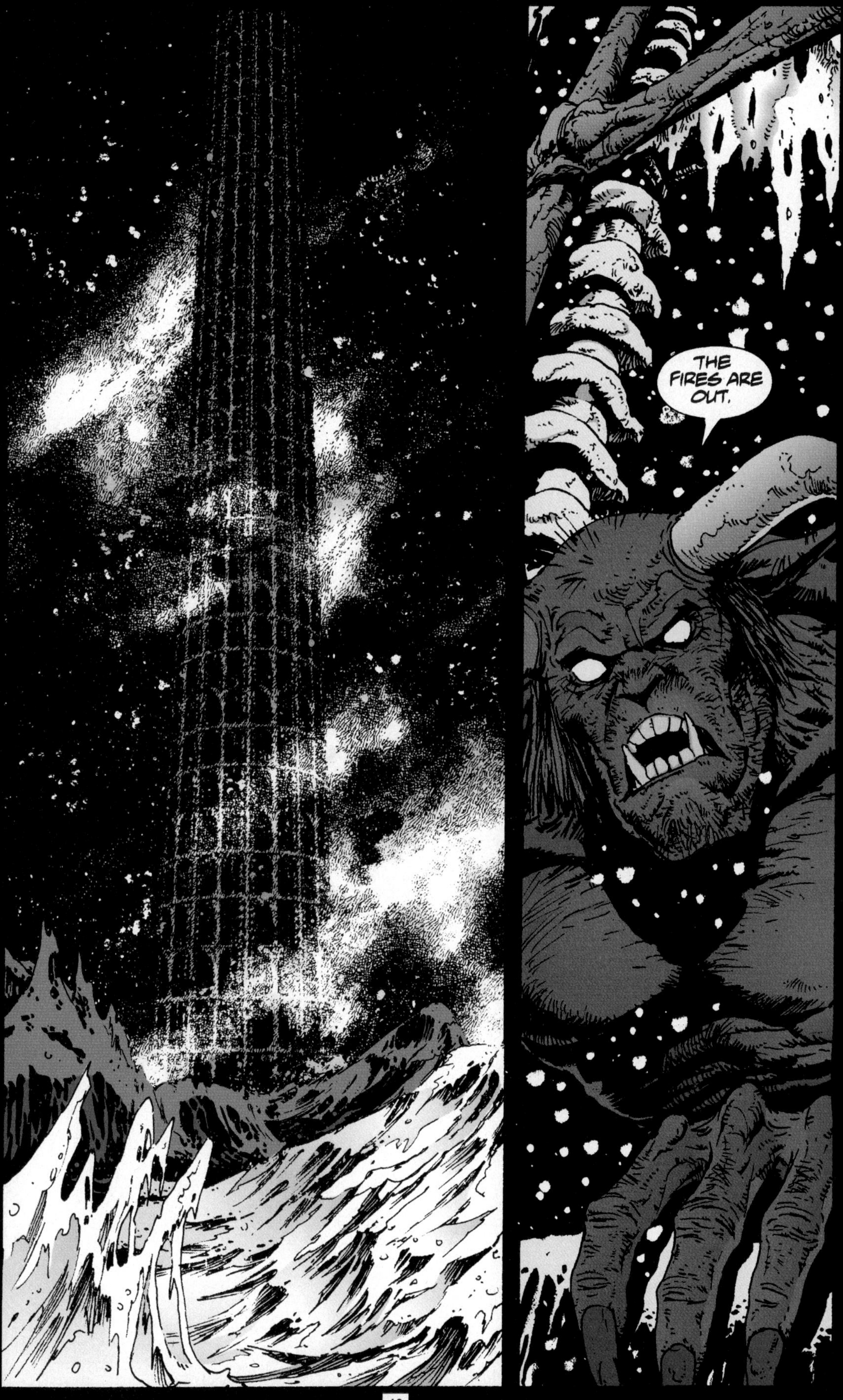
THE FIRES ARE OUT.

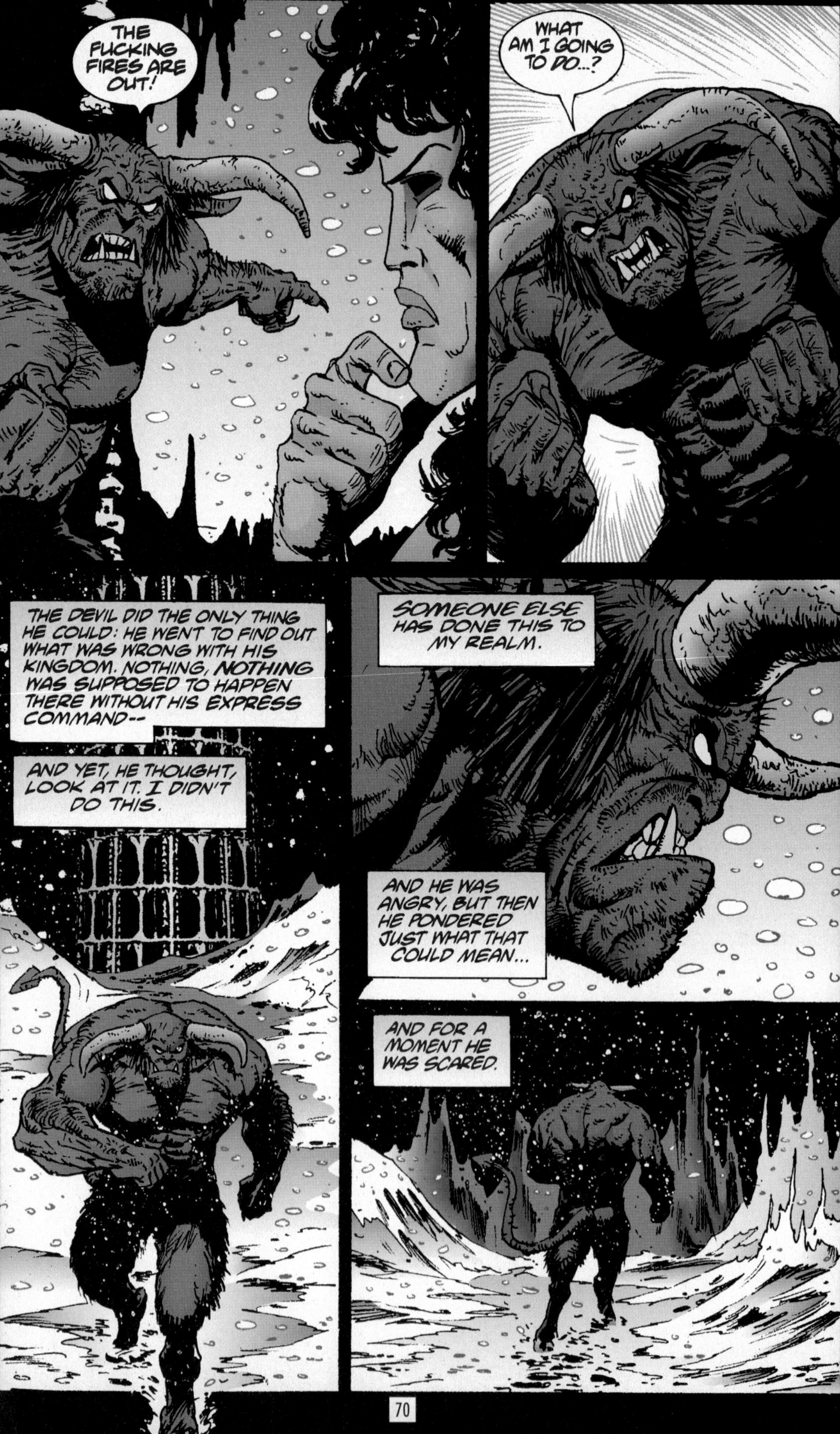

THE FUCKING FIRES ARE OUT!
WHAT AM I GOING TO DO...?
THE DEVIL DID THE ONLY THING HE COULD: HE WENT TO FIND OUT WHAT WAS WRONG WITH HIS KINGDOM. NOTHING, NOTHING WAS SUPPOSED TO HAPPEN THERE WITHOUT HIS EXPRESS COMMAND--
AND YET, HE THOUGHT, LOOK AT IT. I DIDN'T DO THIS.
SOMEONE ELSE HAS DONE THIS TO MY REALM.
AND HE WAS ANGRY, BUT THEN HE PONDERED JUST WHAT THAT COULD MEAN...
AND FOR A MOMENT HE WAS SCARED.

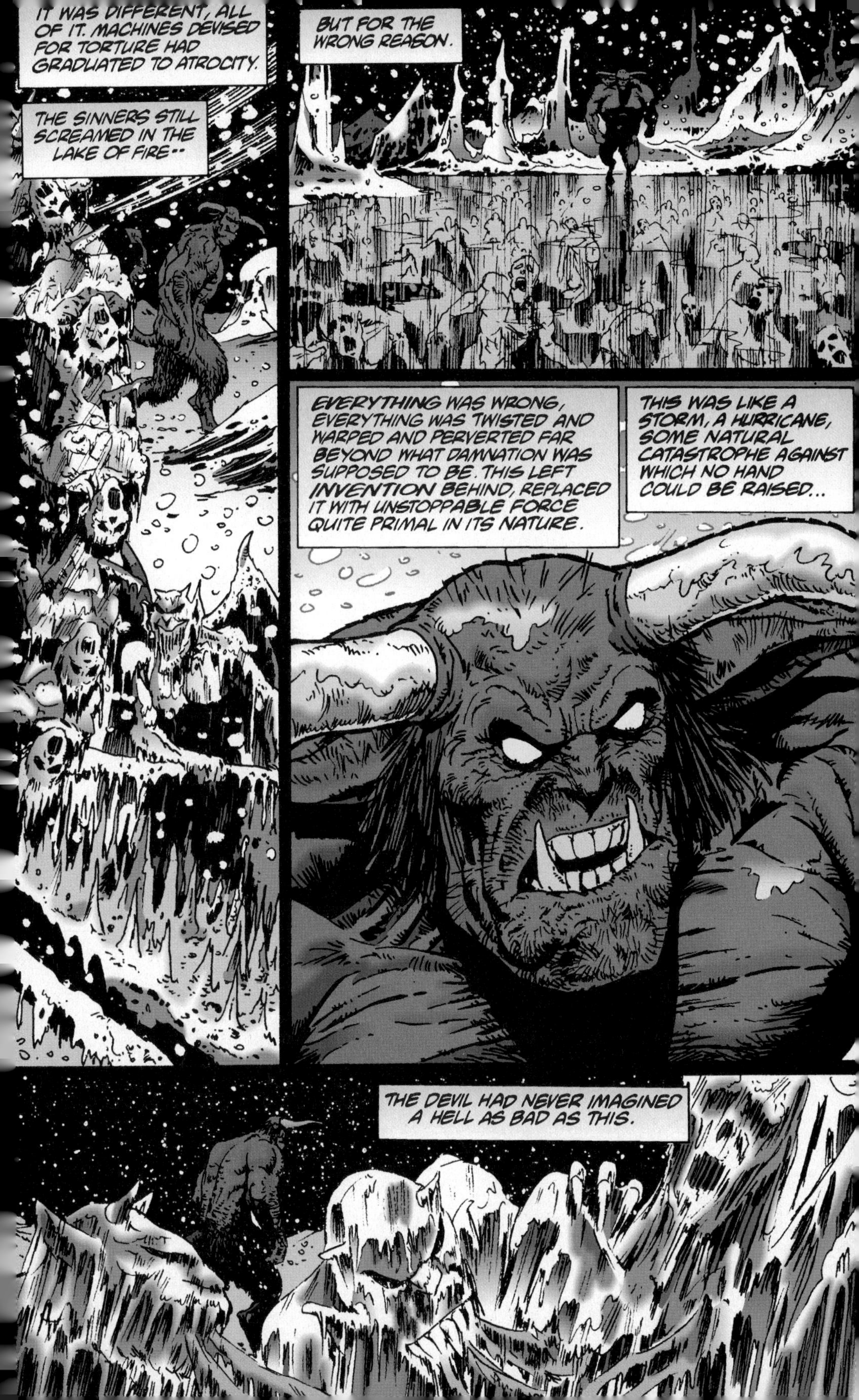
IT WAS DIFFERENT, ALL OF IT. MACHINES DEVISED FOR TORTURE HAD GRADUATED TO ATROCITY.
THE SINNERS STILL SCREAMED IN THE LAKE OF FIRE--
BUT FOR THE WRONG REASON.
EVERYTHING WAS WRONG, EVERYTHING WAS TWISTED AND WARPED AND PERVERTED FAR BEYOND WHAT DAMNATION WAS SUPPOSED TO BE. THIS LEFT INVENTION BEHIND, REPLACED IT WITH UNSTOPPABLE FORCE QUITE PRIMAL IN ITS NATURE.
THIS WAS LIKE A STORM, A HURRICANE, SOME NATURAL CATASTROPHE AGAINST WHICH NO HAND COULD BE RAISED...
THE DEVIL HAD NEVER IMAGINED A HELL AS BAD AS THIS.

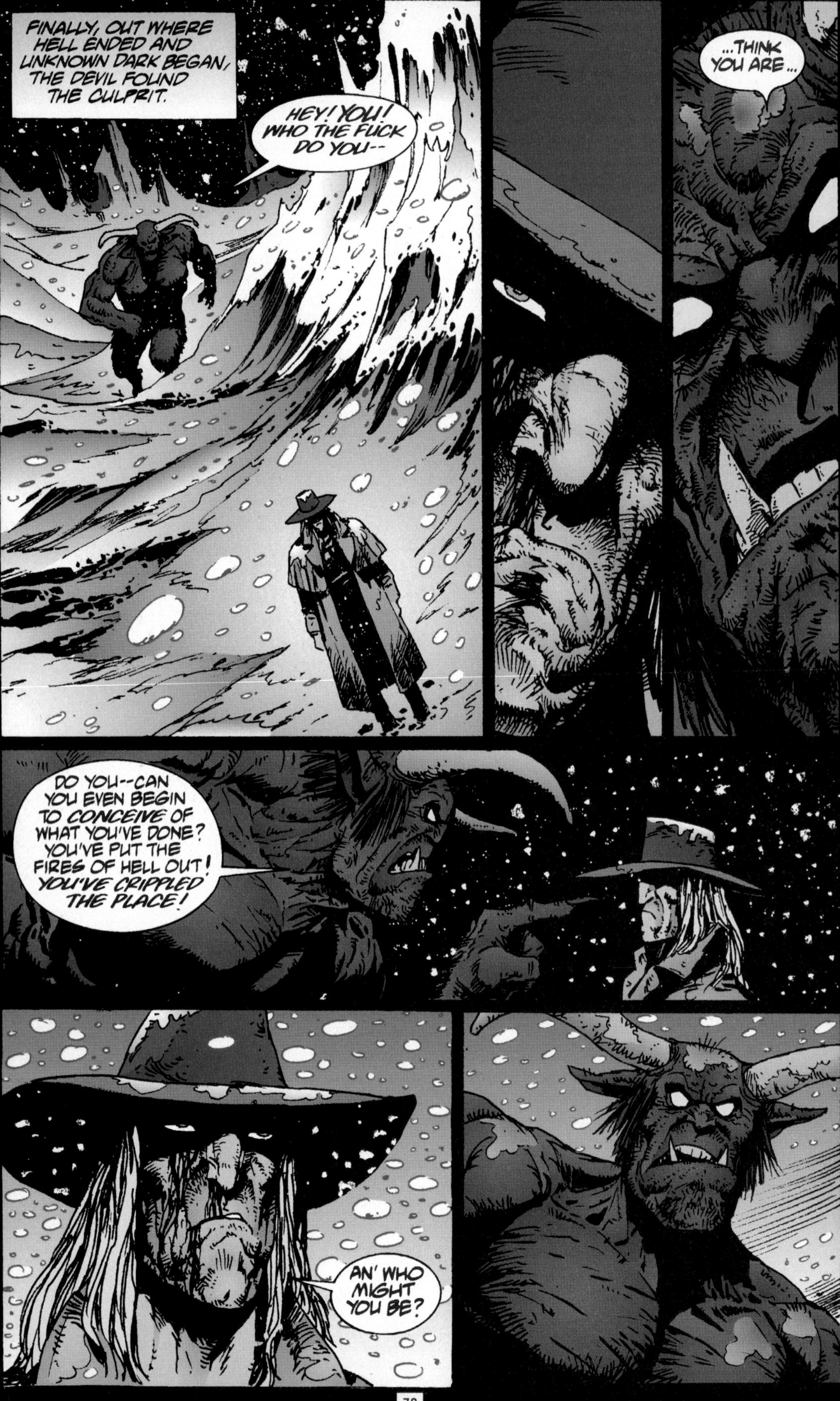
FINALLY, OUT WHERE HELL ENDED AND UNKNOWN DARK BEGAN, THE DEVIL FOUND THE CULPRIT.
HEY! YOU! WHO THE FUCK DO YOU--
...THINK YOU ARE...
DO YOU--CAN YOU EVEN BEGIN TO CONCEIVE OF WHAT YOU'VE DONE? YOU'VE PUT THE FIRES OF HELL OUT! YOU'VE CRIPPLED THE PLACE!
AN' WHO MIGHT YOU BE?

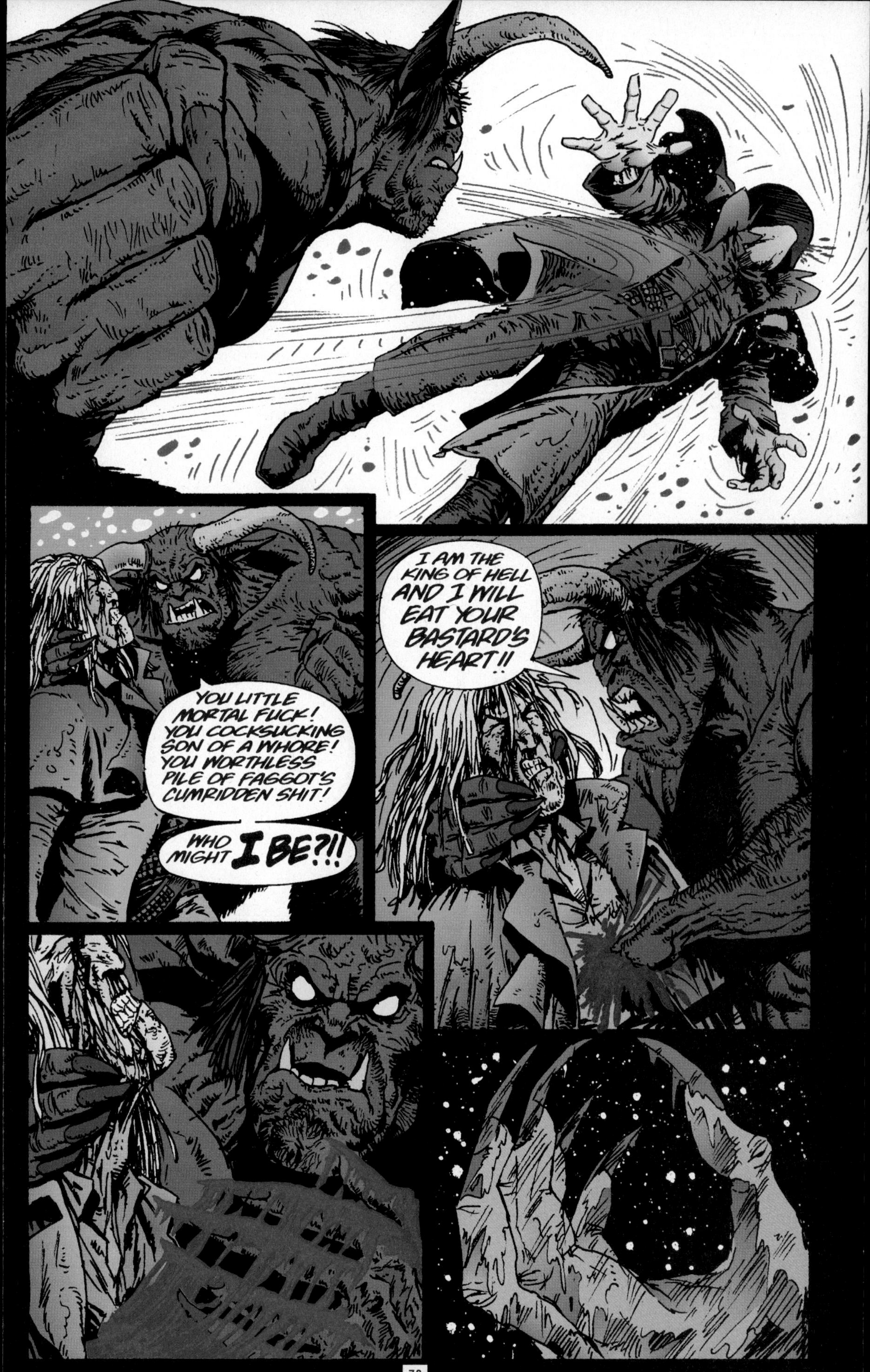
YOU LITTLE MORTAL FUCK! YOU COCKSUCKING SON OF A WHORE! YOU WORTHLESS PILE OF FAGGOT'S CUMRIDDEN SHIT!
WHO MIGHT I BE?!!
I AM THE KING OF HELL AND I WILL EAT YOUR BASTARD'S HEART!!

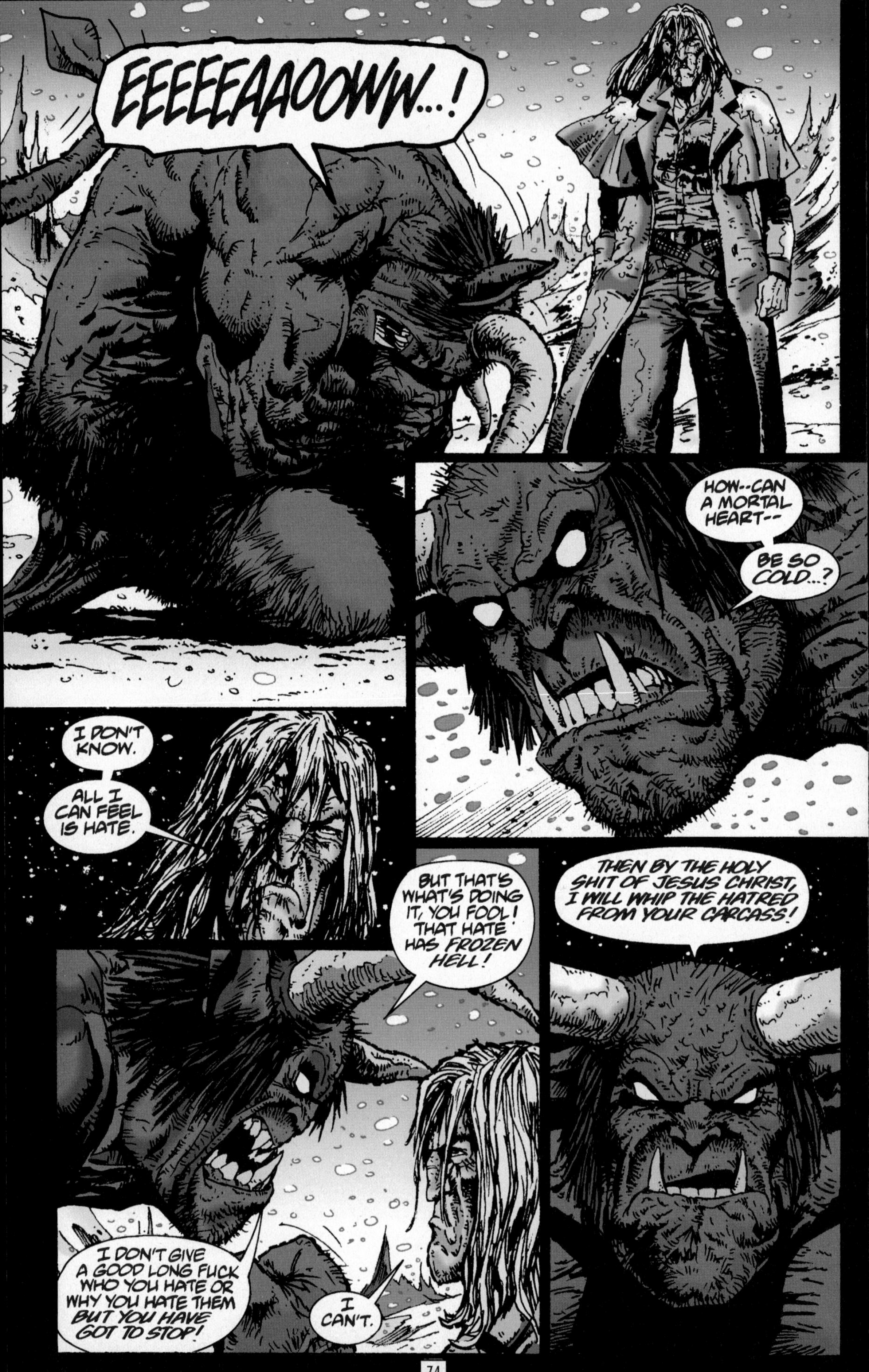
EEEEEAAOOWW...!
HOW--CAN A MORTAL HEART--
BE SO COLD...?
I DON'T KNOW.
ALL I CAN FEEL IS HATE.
BUT THAT'S WHAT'S DOING IT, YOU FOOL! THAT HATE HAS FROZEN HELL!
THEN BY THE HOLY SHIT OF JESUS CHRIST, I WILL WHIP THE HATRED FROM YOUR CARCASS!
I DON'T GIVE A GOOD LONG FUCK WHO YOU HATE OR WHY YOU HATE THEM BUT YOU HAVE GOT TO STOP!
I CAN'T.

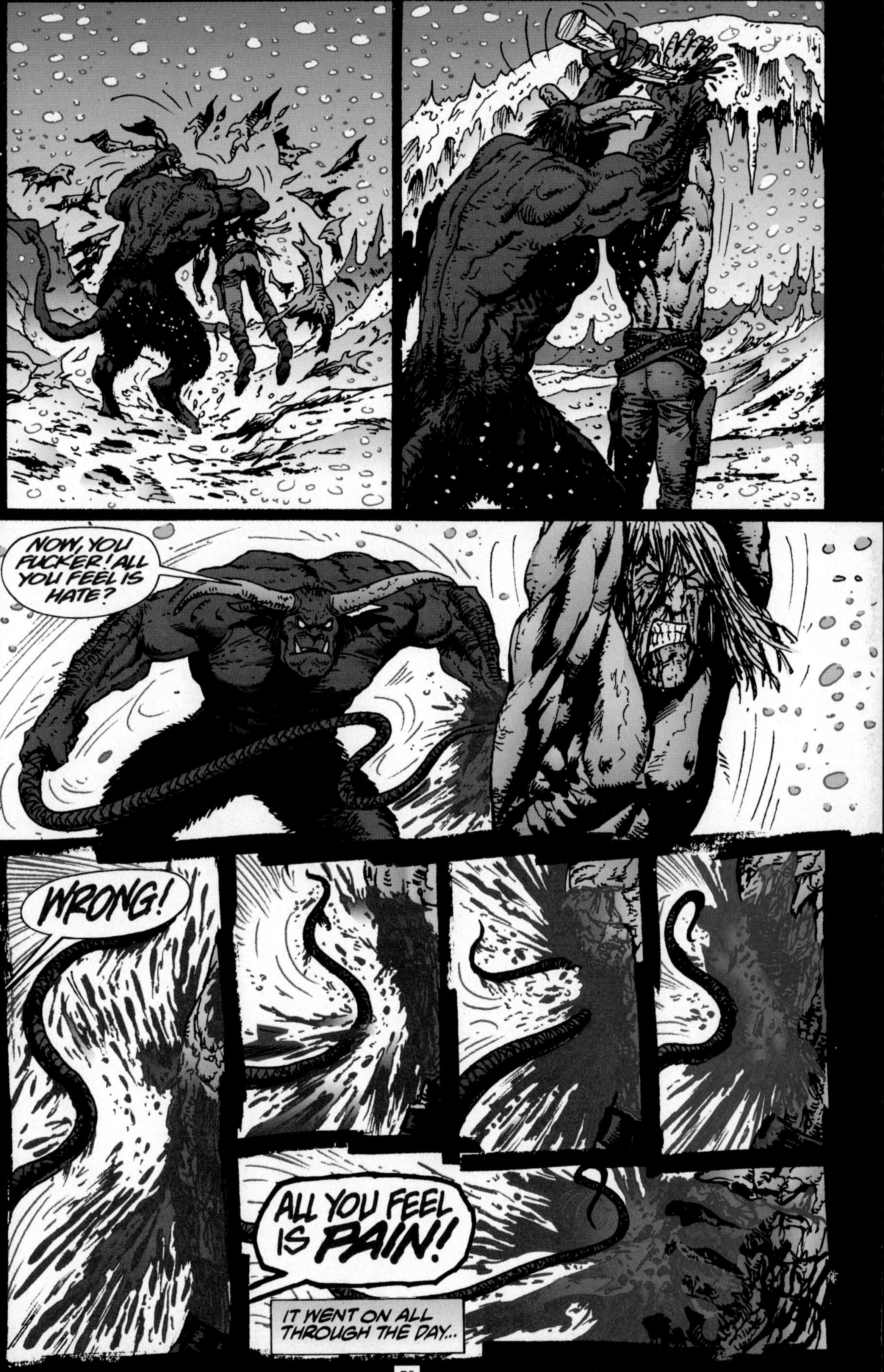
NOW, YOU FUCKER! ALL YOU FEEL IS HATE?
WRONG!
ALL YOU FEEL IS PAIN!
IT WENT ON ALL THROUGH THE DAY...

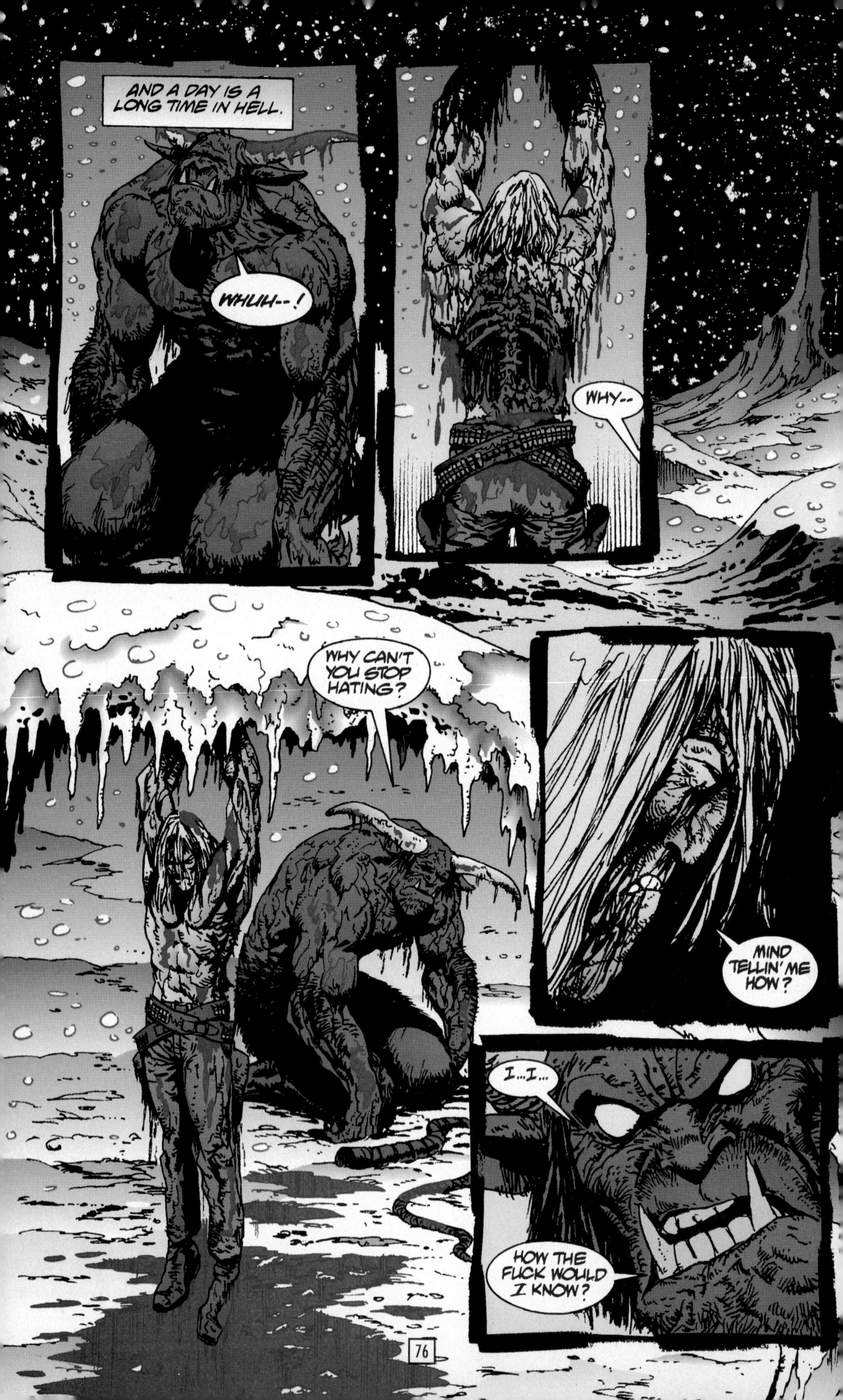
AND A DAY IS A LONG TIME IN HELL.
WHUH--!
WHY--
WHY CAN'T YOU STOP HATING?
MIND TELLIN' ME HOW?
I...I...
HOW THE FUCK WOULD I KNOW?

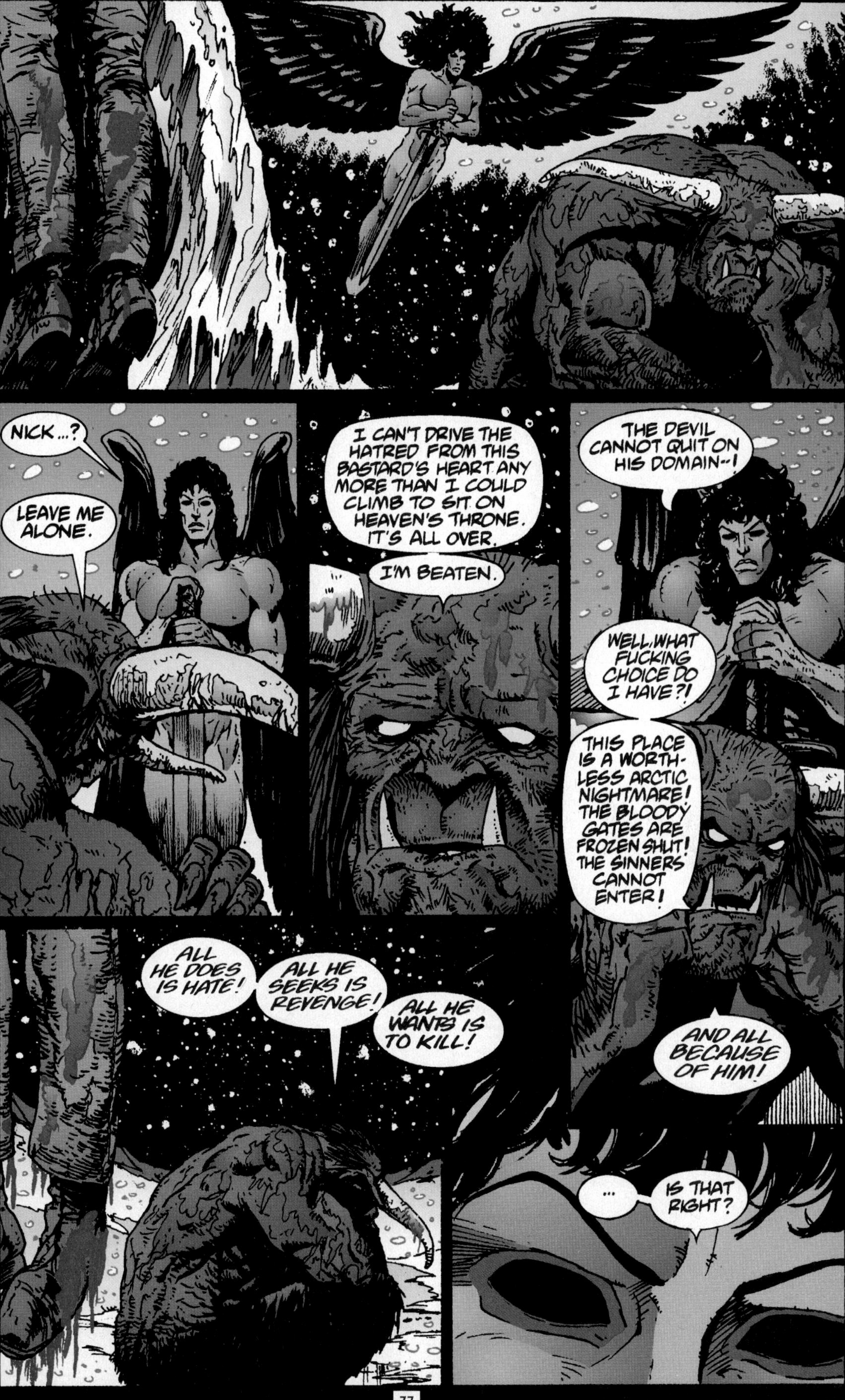
NICK...?
LEAVE ME ALONE.
I CAN'T DRIVE THE HATRED FROM THIS BASTARD'S HEART ANY MORE THAN I COULD CLIMB TO SIT ON HEAVEN'S THRONE. IT'S ALL OVER.
I'M BEATEN.
THE DEVIL CANNOT QUIT ON HIS DOMAIN--!
WELL, WHAT FUCKING CHOICE DO I HAVE?!
THIS PLACE IS A WORTHLESS ARCTIC NIGHTMARE! THE BLOODY GATES ARE FROZEN SHUT! THE SINNERS CANNOT ENTER!
ALL HE DOES IS HATE!
ALL HE SEEKS IS REVENGE!
ALL HE WANTS IS TO KILL!
AND ALL BECAUSE OF HIM!
...
IS THAT RIGHT?

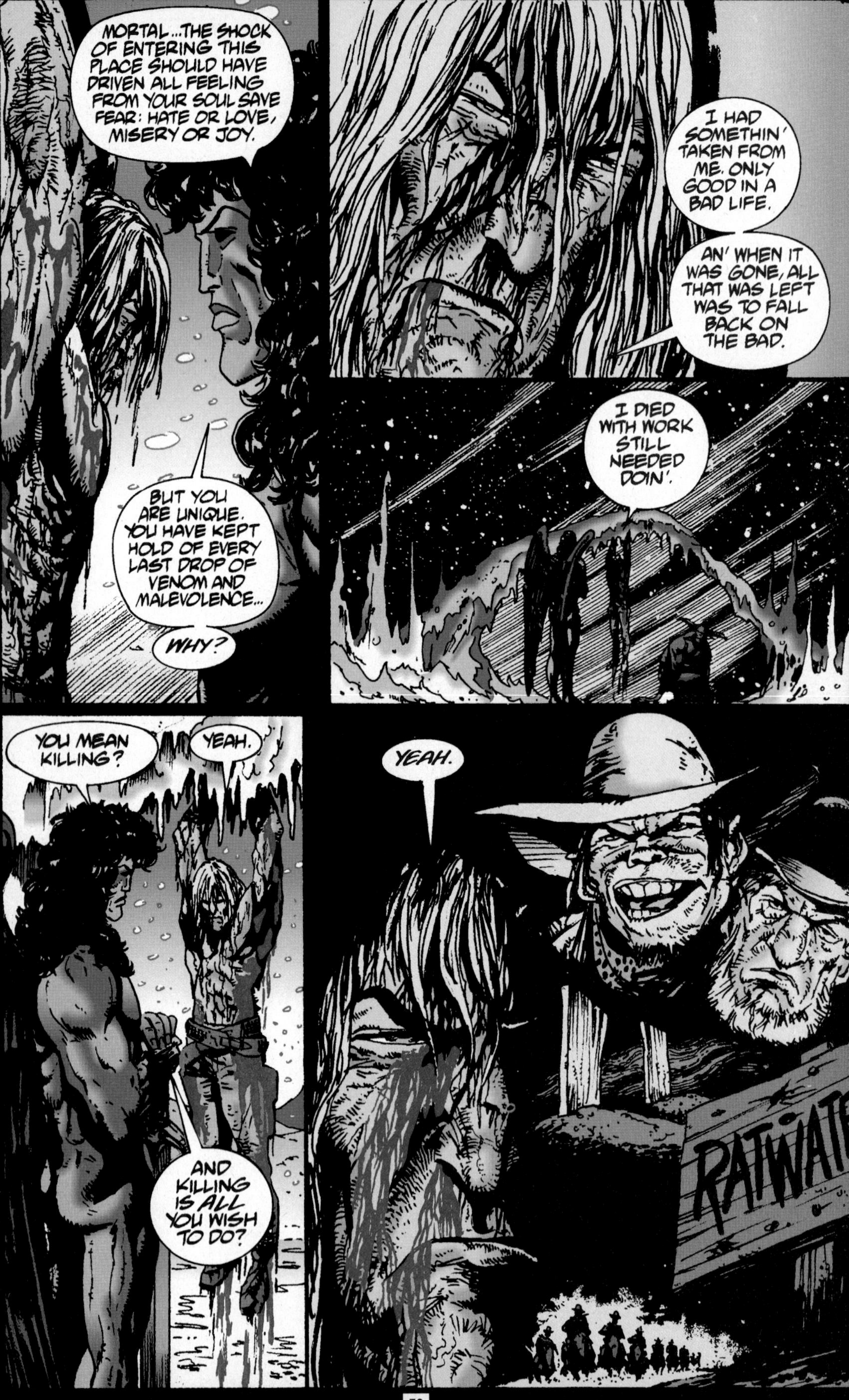
MORTAL...THE SHOCK OF ENTERING THIS PLACE SHOULD HAVE DRIVEN ALL FEELING FROM YOUR SOUL SAVE FEAR: HATE OR LOVE, MISERY OR JOY.
BUT YOU ARE UNIQUE. YOU HAVE KEPT HOLD OF EVERY LAST DROP OF VENOM AND MALEVOLENCE...
WHY?
I HAD SOMETHIN' TAKEN FROM ME. ONLY GOOD IN A BAD LIFE.
AN' WHEN IT WAS GONE, ALL THAT WAS LEFT WAS TO FALL BACK ON THE BAD.
I DIED WITH WORK STILL NEEDED DOIN'.
YOU MEAN KILLING?
YEAH.
AND KILLING IS ALL YOU WISH TO DO?
YEAH.
RATWAT

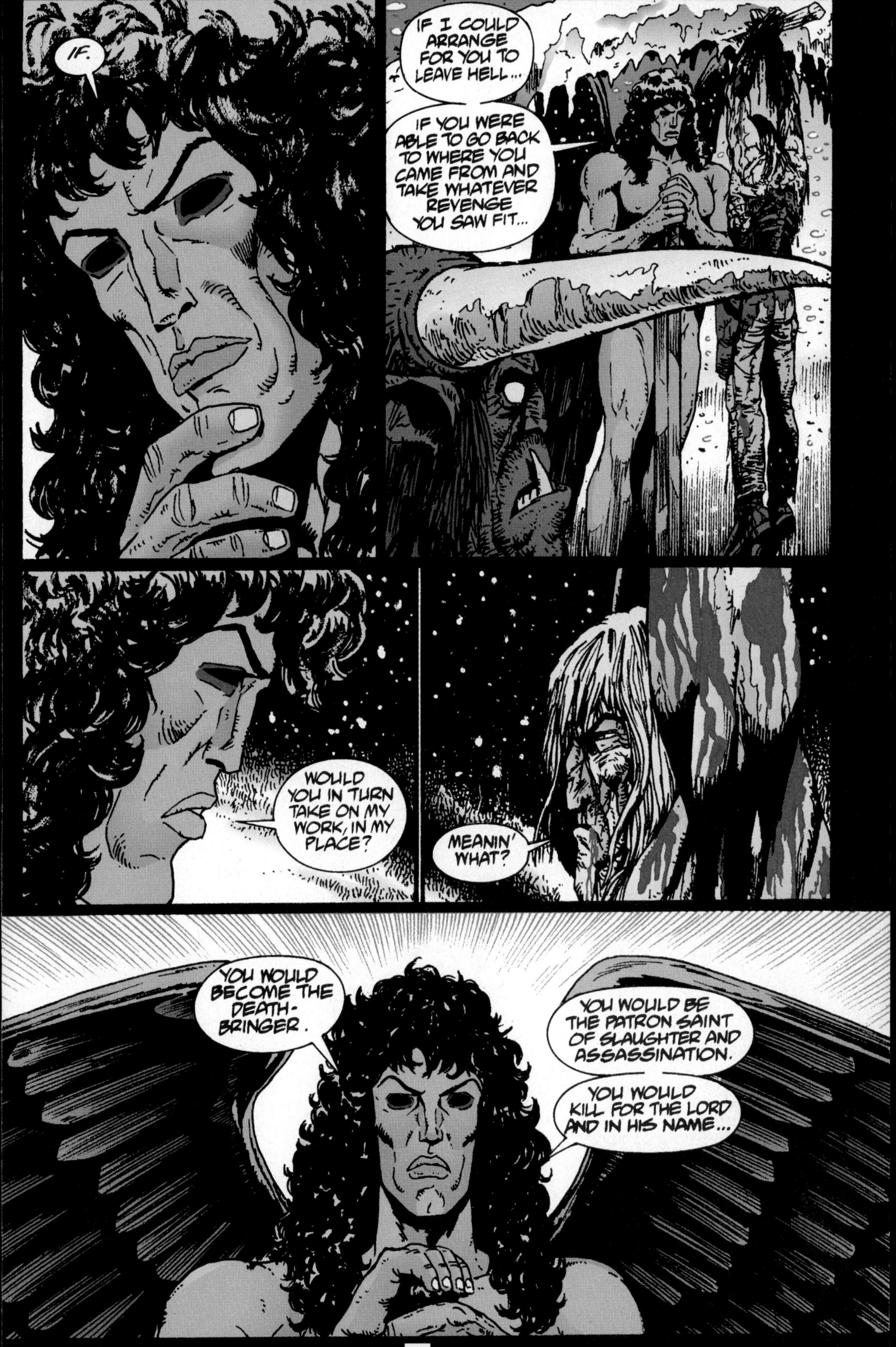
IF.
IF I COULD ARRANGE FOR YOU TO LEAVE HELL...
IF YOU WERE ABLE TO GO BACK TO WHERE YOU CAME FROM AND TAKE WHATEVER REVENGE YOU SAW FIT...
WOULD YOU IN TURN TAKE ON MY WORK, IN MY PLACE?
MEANIN' WHAT?
YOU WOULD BECOME THE DEATH-BRINGER.
YOU WOULD BE THE PATRON SAINT OF SLAUGHTER AND ASSASSINATION.
YOU WOULD KILL FOR THE LORD AND IN HIS NAME...

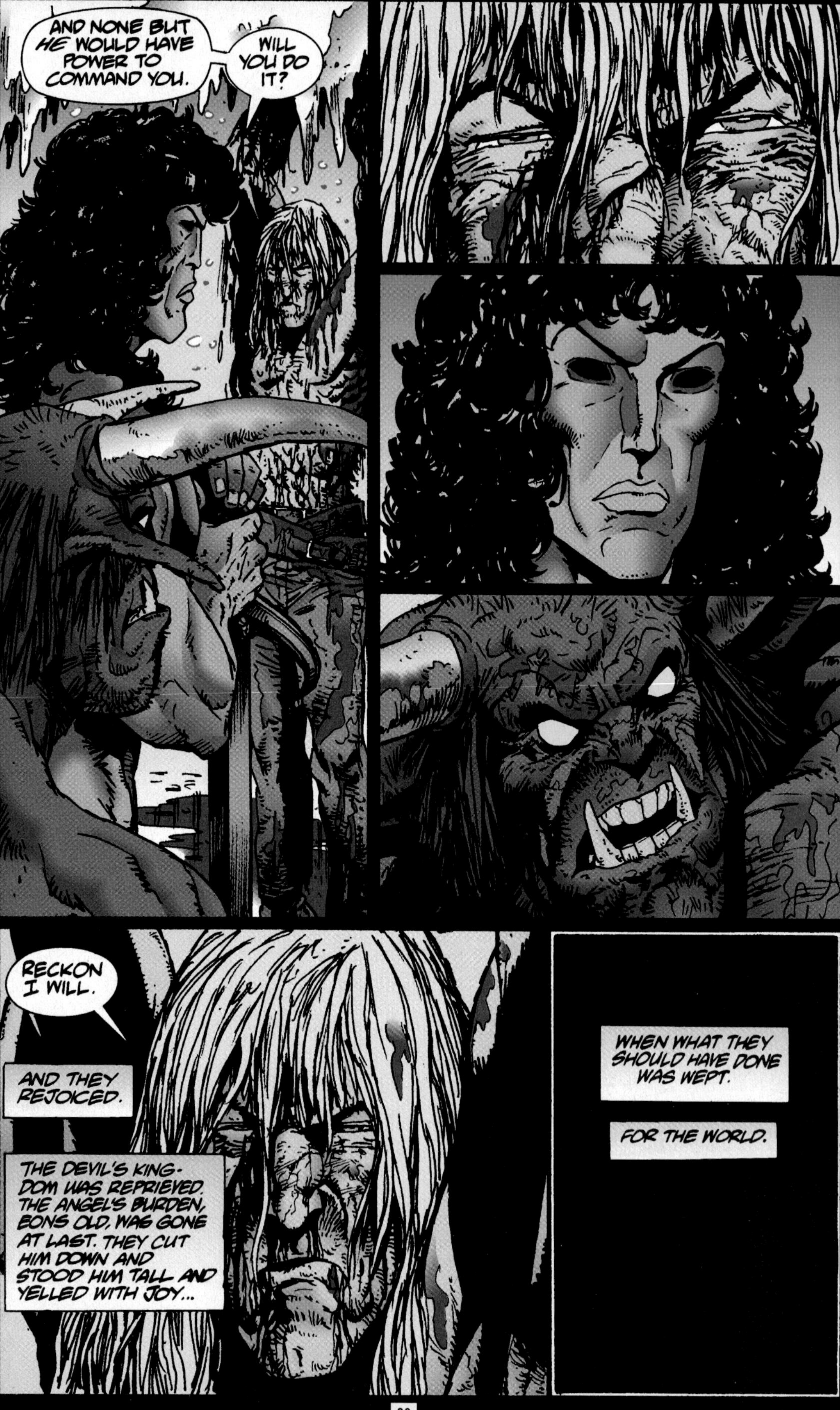
AND NONE BUT HE WOULD HAVE POWER TO COMMAND YOU.
WILL YOU DO IT?
RECKON I WILL.
AND THEY REJOICED.
THE DEVIL'S KING-DOM WAS REPRIEVED. THE ANGEL'S BURDEN, EONS OLD, WAS GONE AT LAST. THEY CUT HIM DOWN AND STOOD HIM TALL AND YELLED WITH JOY...
WHEN WHAT THEY SHOULD HAVE DONE WAS WEPT.
FOR THE WORLD.

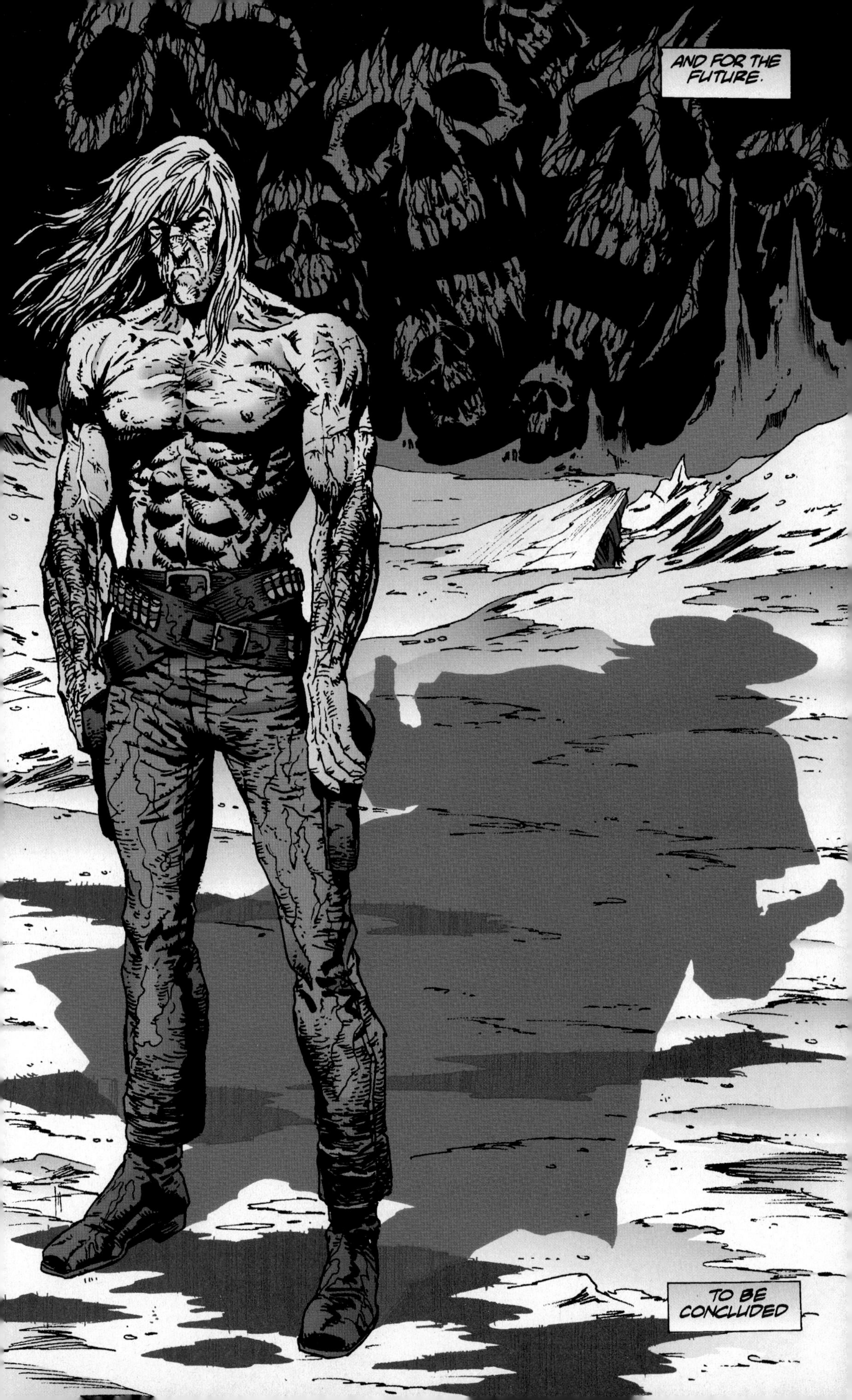
AND FOR THE FUTURE.
TO BE CONCLUDED

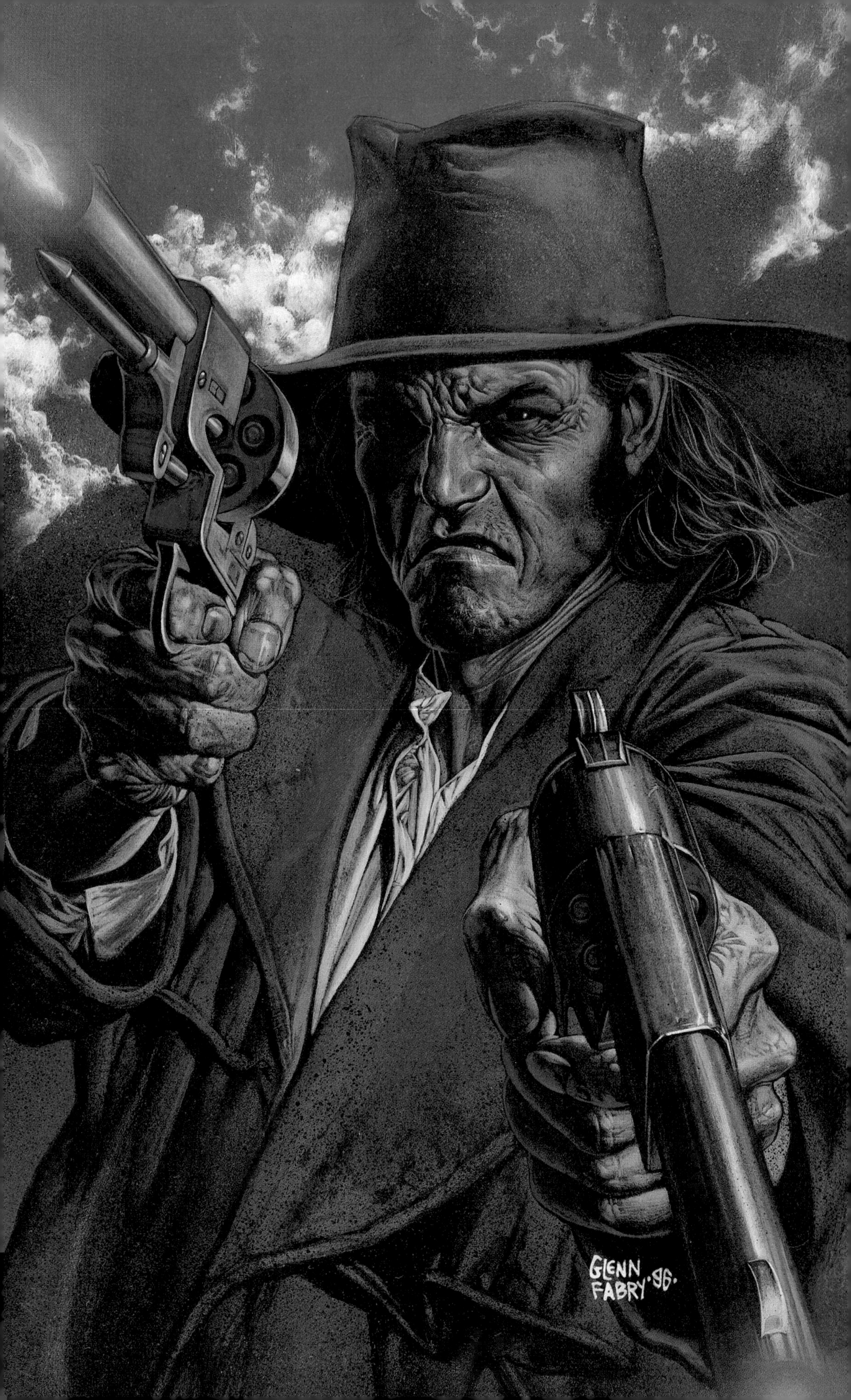
GLENN FABRY ·96·

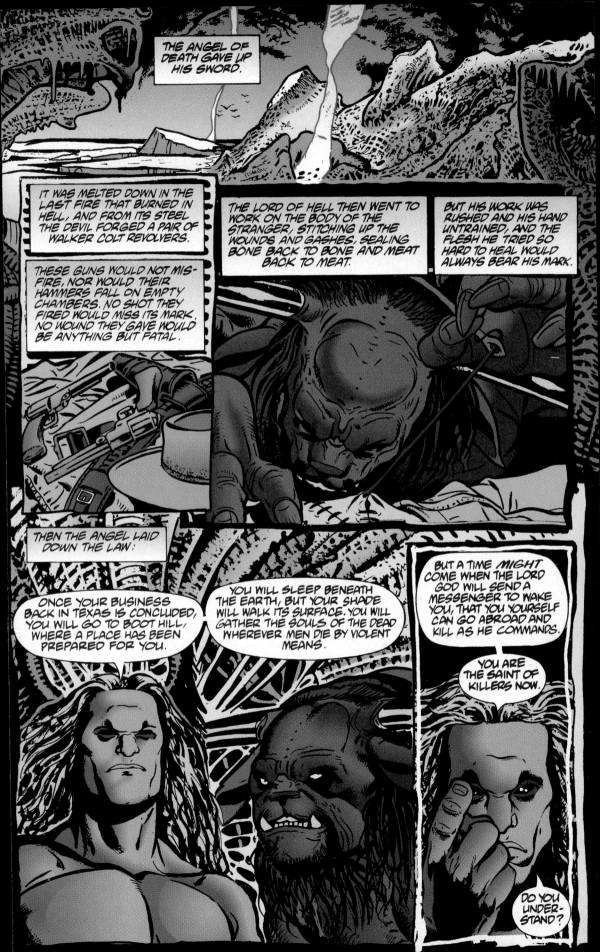

THE ANGEL OF DEATH GAVE UP HIS SWORD.

IT WAS MELTED DOWN IN THE LAST FIRE THAT BURNED IN HELL, AND FROM ITS STEEL THE DEVIL FORGED A PAIR OF WALKER COLT REVOLVERS.

THESE GUNS WOULD NOT MIS-FIRE, NOR WOULD THEIR HAMMERS FALL ON EMPTY CHAMBERS. NO SHOT THEY FIRED WOULD MISS ITS MARK. NO WOUND THEY GAVE WOULD BE ANYTHING BUT FATAL.

THE LORD OF HELL THEN WENT TO WORK ON THE BODY OF THE STRANGER, STITCHING UP THE WOUNDS AND GASHES, SEALING BONE BACK TO BONE AND MEAT BACK TO MEAT.

BUT HIS WORK WAS RUSHED AND HIS HAND UNTRAINED, AND THE FLESH HE TRIED SO HARD TO HEAL WOULD ALWAYS BEAR HIS MARK.

THEN THE ANGEL LAID DOWN THE LAW:

ONCE YOUR BUSINESS BACK IN TEXAS IS CONCLUDED, YOU WILL GO TO BOOT HILL, WHERE A PLACE HAS BEEN PREPARED FOR YOU.

YOU WILL SLEEP BENEATH THE EARTH, BUT YOUR SHADE WILL WALK ITS SURFACE. YOU WILL GATHER THE SOULS OF THE DEAD WHEREVER MEN DIE BY VIOLENT MEANS.

BUT A TIME MIGHT COME WHEN THE LORD GOD WILL SEND A MESSENGER TO WAKE YOU, THAT YOU YOURSELF CAN GO ABROAD AND KILL AS HE COMMANDS.

YOU ARE THE SAINT OF KILLERS NOW.

DO YOU UNDER-STAND?

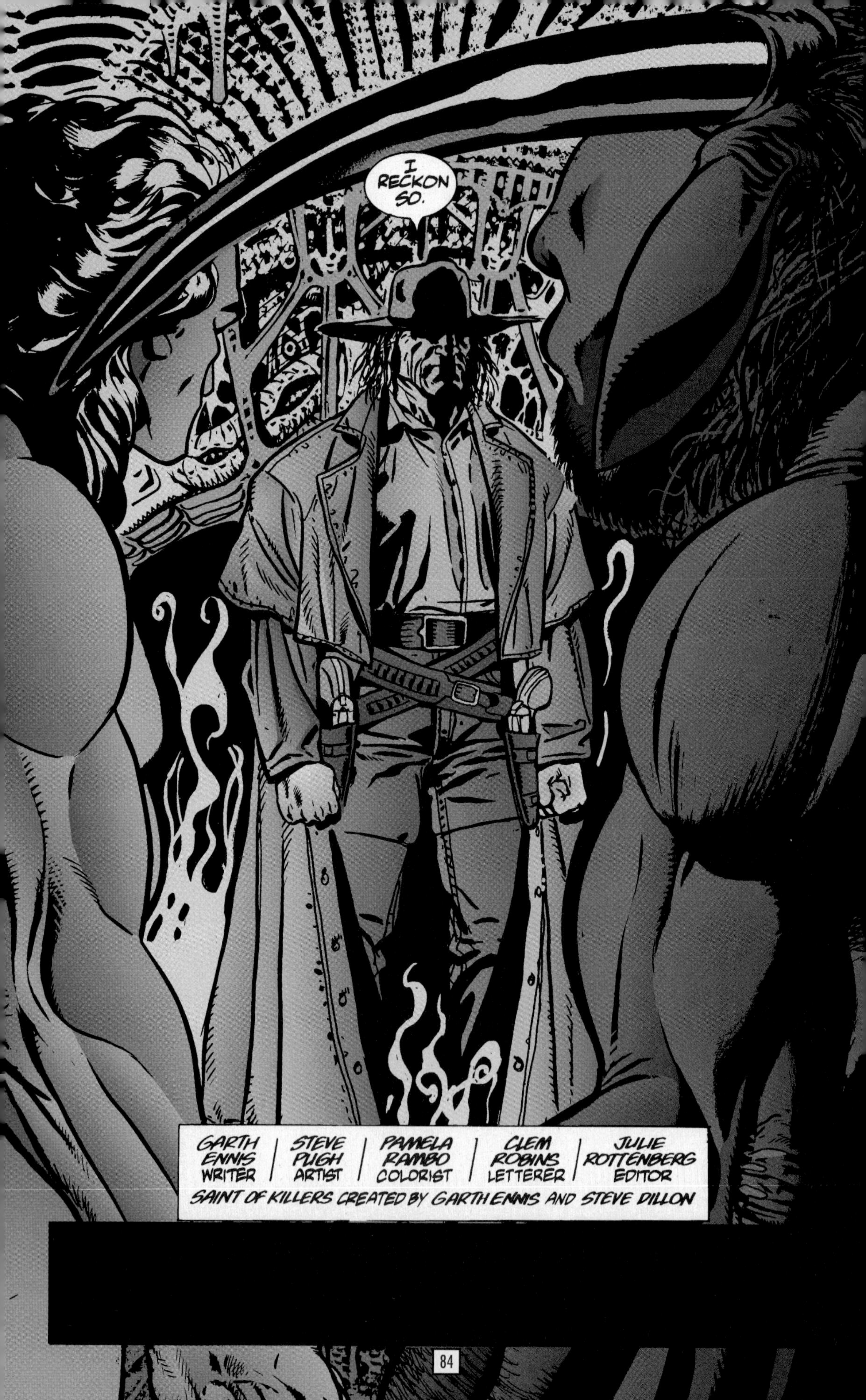
I RECKON SO.
GARTH ENNIS WRITER
STEVE PUGH ARTIST
PAMELA RAMBO COLORIST
CLEM ROBINS LETTERER
JULIE ROTTENBERG EDITOR
SAINT OF KILLERS CREATED BY GARTH ENNIS AND STEVE DILLON
[redacted]

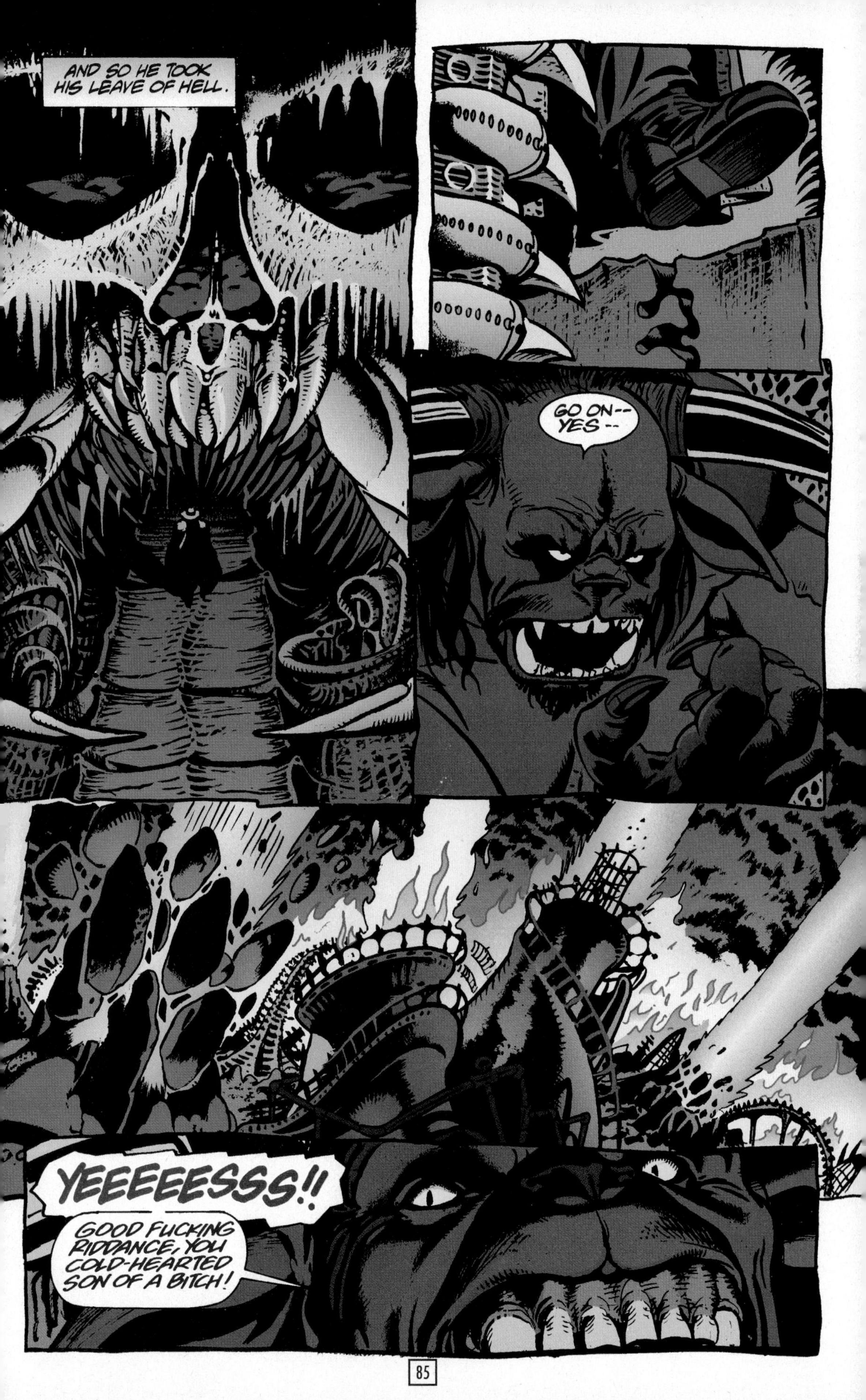
AND SO HE TOOK HIS LEAVE OF HELL.
GO ON-- YES --
YEEEEESSS!!
GOOD FUCKING RIDDANCE, YOU COLD-HEARTED SON OF A BITCH!

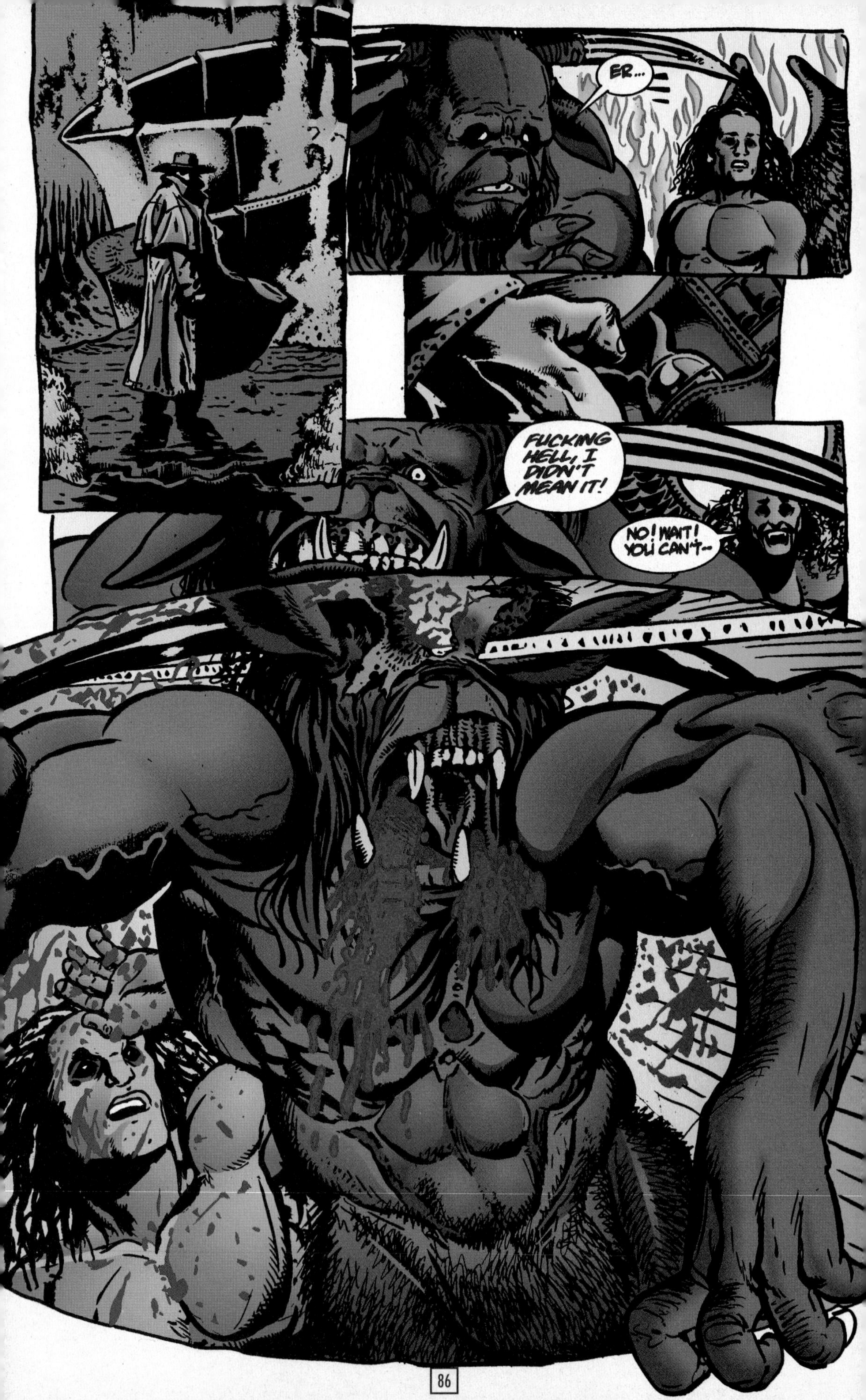
ER...
FUCKING HELL, I DIDN'T MEAN IT!
NO! WAIT! YOU CAN'T--

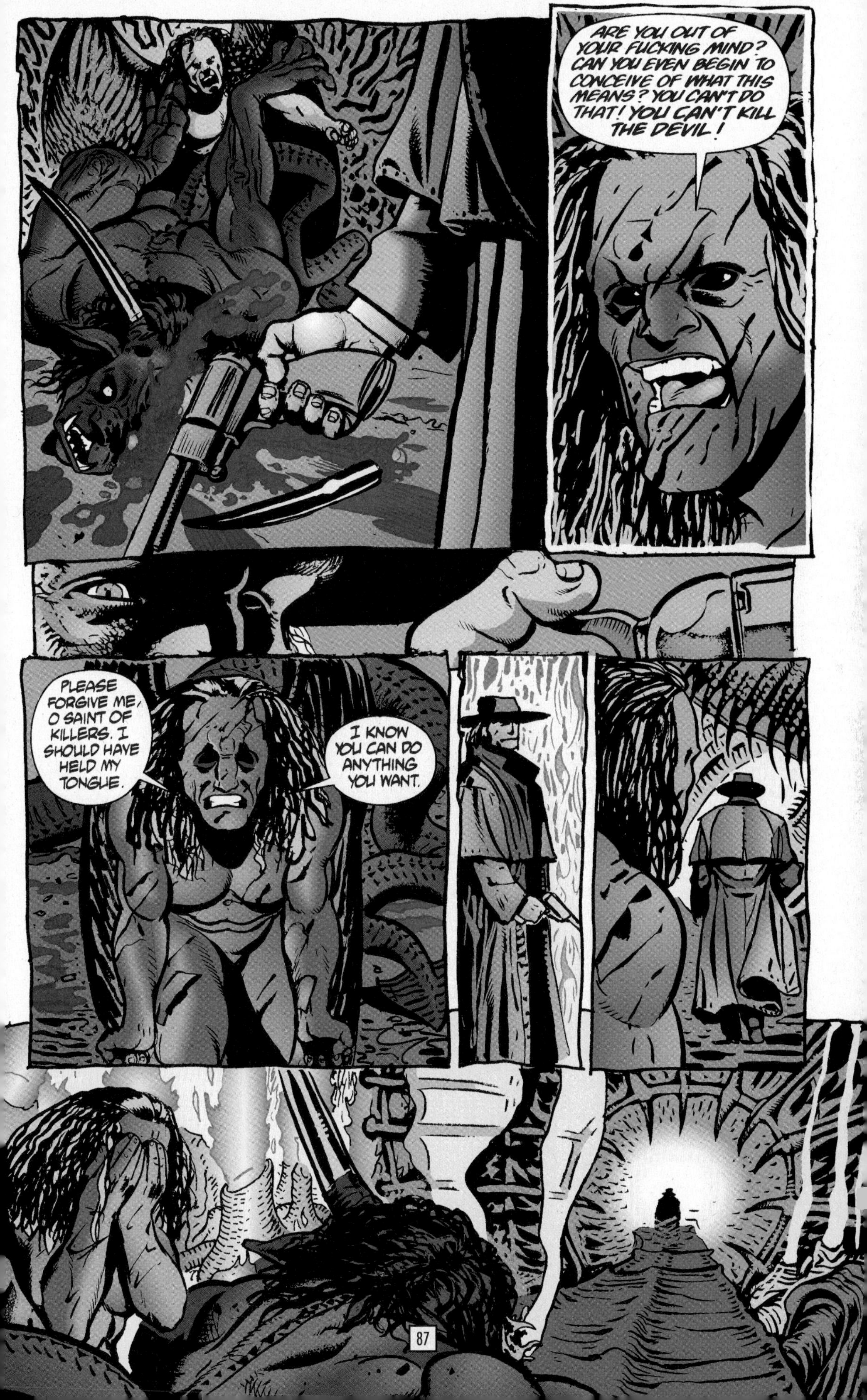
ARE YOU OUT OF YOUR FUCKING MIND? CAN YOU EVEN BEGIN TO CONCEIVE OF WHAT THIS MEANS? YOU CAN'T DO THAT! YOU CAN'T KILL THE DEVIL!
PLEASE FORGIVE ME, O SAINT OF KILLERS. I SHOULD HAVE HELD MY TONGUE.
I KNOW YOU CAN DO ANYTHING YOU WANT.

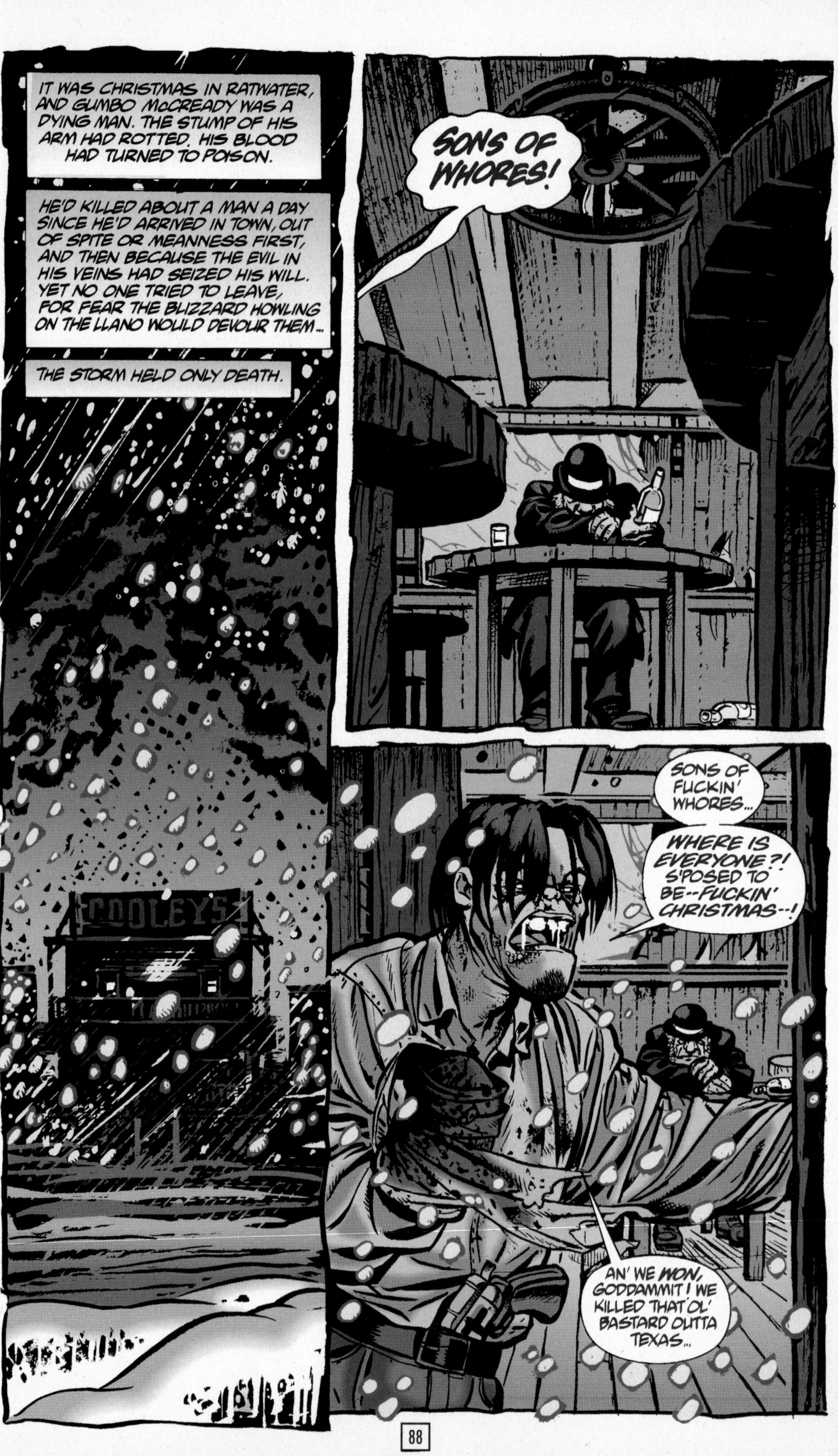
IT WAS CHRISTMAS IN RATWATER, AND GUMBO McCREADY WAS A DYING MAN. THE STUMP OF HIS ARM HAD ROTTED. HIS BLOOD HAD TURNED TO POISON.
HE'D KILLED ABOUT A MAN A DAY SINCE HE'D ARRIVED IN TOWN, OUT OF SPITE OR MEANNESS FIRST, AND THEN BECAUSE THE EVIL IN HIS VEINS HAD SEIZED HIS WILL. YET NO ONE TRIED TO LEAVE, FOR FEAR THE BLIZZARD HOWLING ON THE LLANO WOULD DEVOUR THEM...
THE STORM HELD ONLY DEATH.
SONS OF WHORES!
SONS OF FUCKIN' WHORES...
WHERE IS EVERYONE?! S'POSED TO BE--FUCKIN' CHRISTMAS--!
AN' WE WON, GODDAMMIT! WE KILLED THAT OL' BASTARD OUTTA TEXAS...

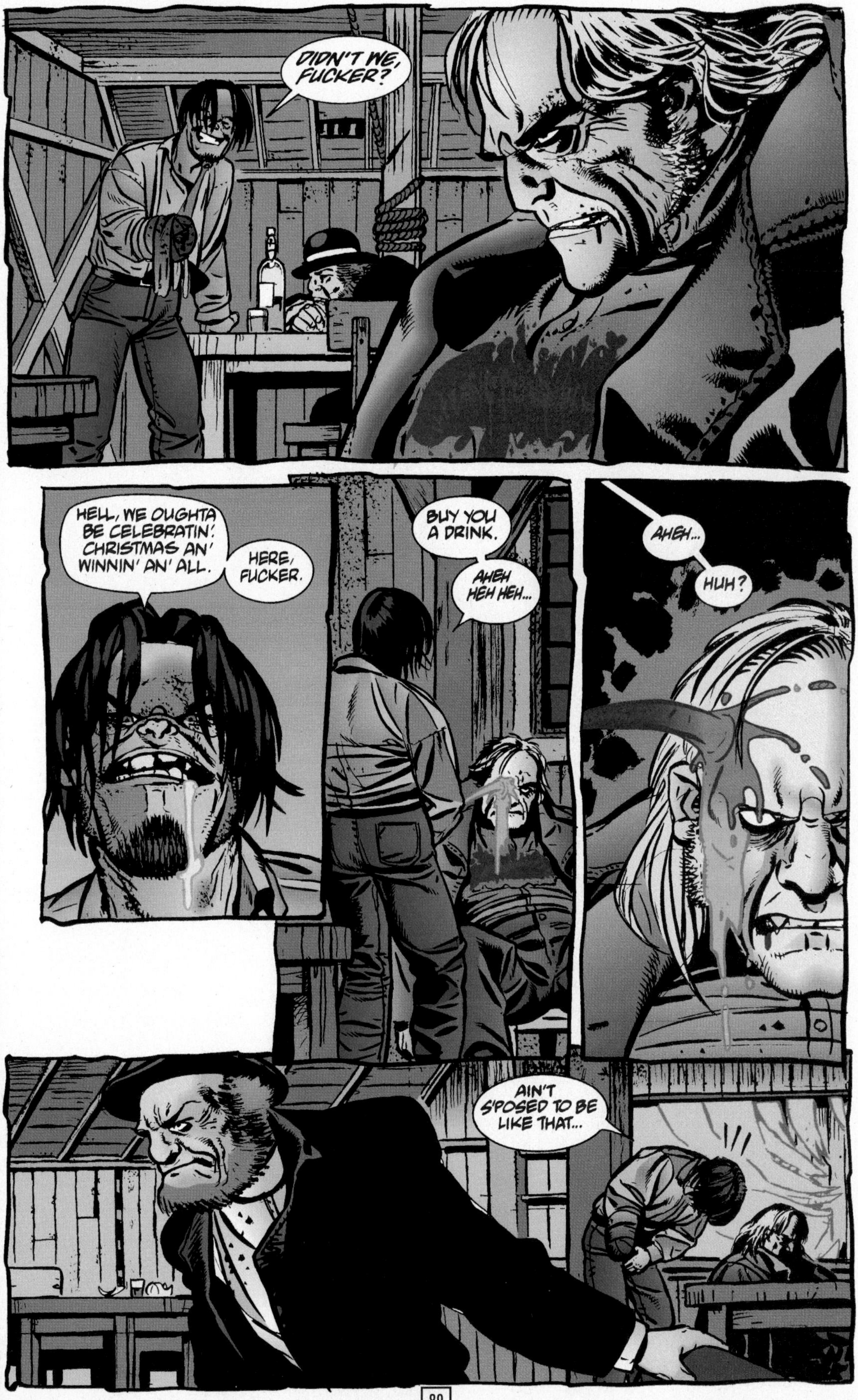
DIDN'T WE, FUCKER?
HELL, WE OUGHTA BE CELEBRATIN'. CHRISTMAS AN' WINNIN' AN' ALL.
HERE, FUCKER.
BUY YOU A DRINK.
AHEH HEH HEH...
AHEH...
HUH?
AIN'T S'POSED TO BE LIKE THAT...

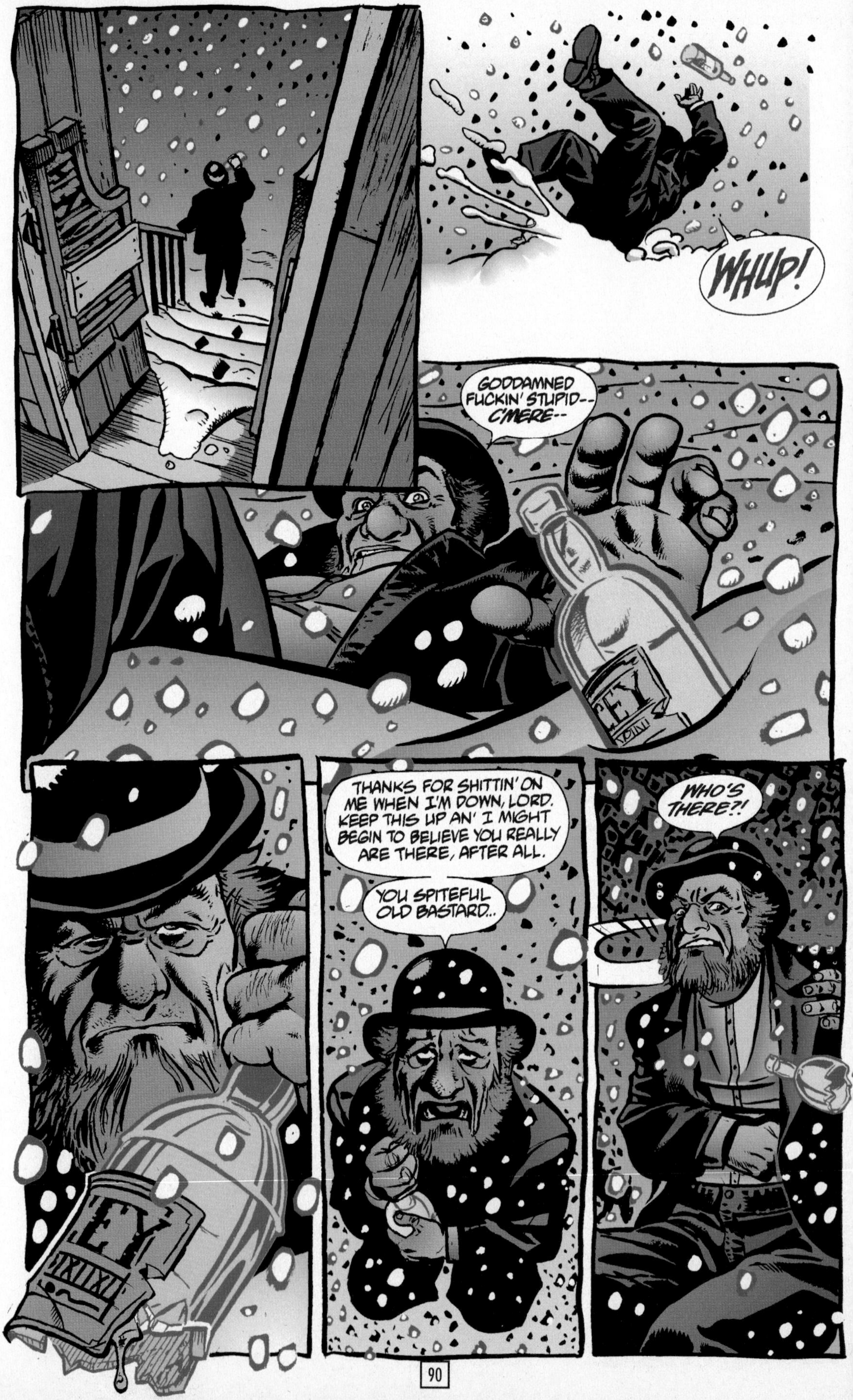
WHUP!
GODDAMNED FUCKIN' STUPID-- C'MERE--
THANKS FOR SHITTIN' ON ME WHEN I'M DOWN, LORD. KEEP THIS UP AN' I MIGHT BEGIN TO BELIEVE YOU REALLY ARE THERE, AFTER ALL.
YOU SPITEFUL OLD BASTARD...
WHO'S THERE?!

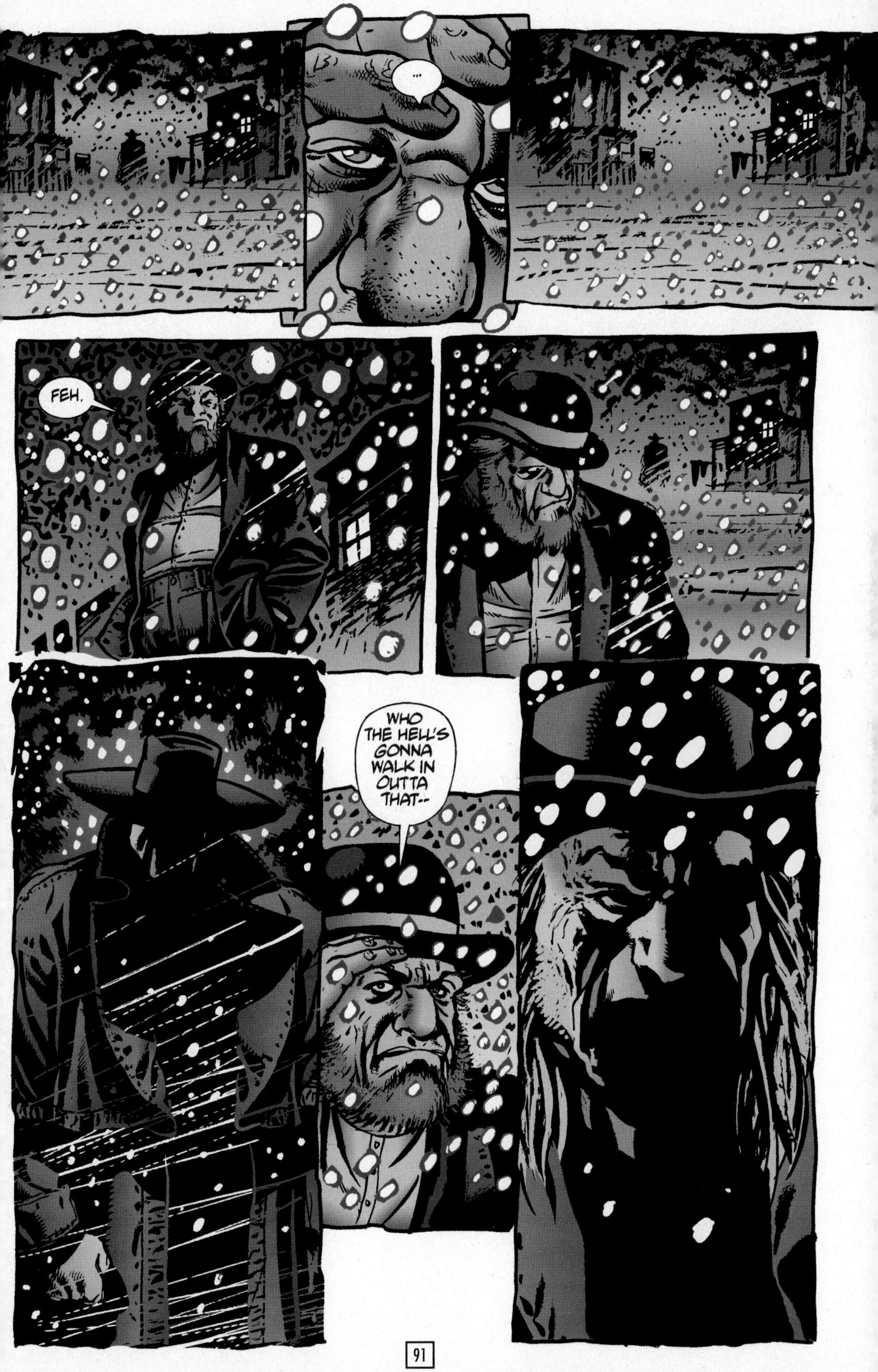
...
FEH.
WHO THE HELL'S GONNA WALK IN OUTTA THAT--

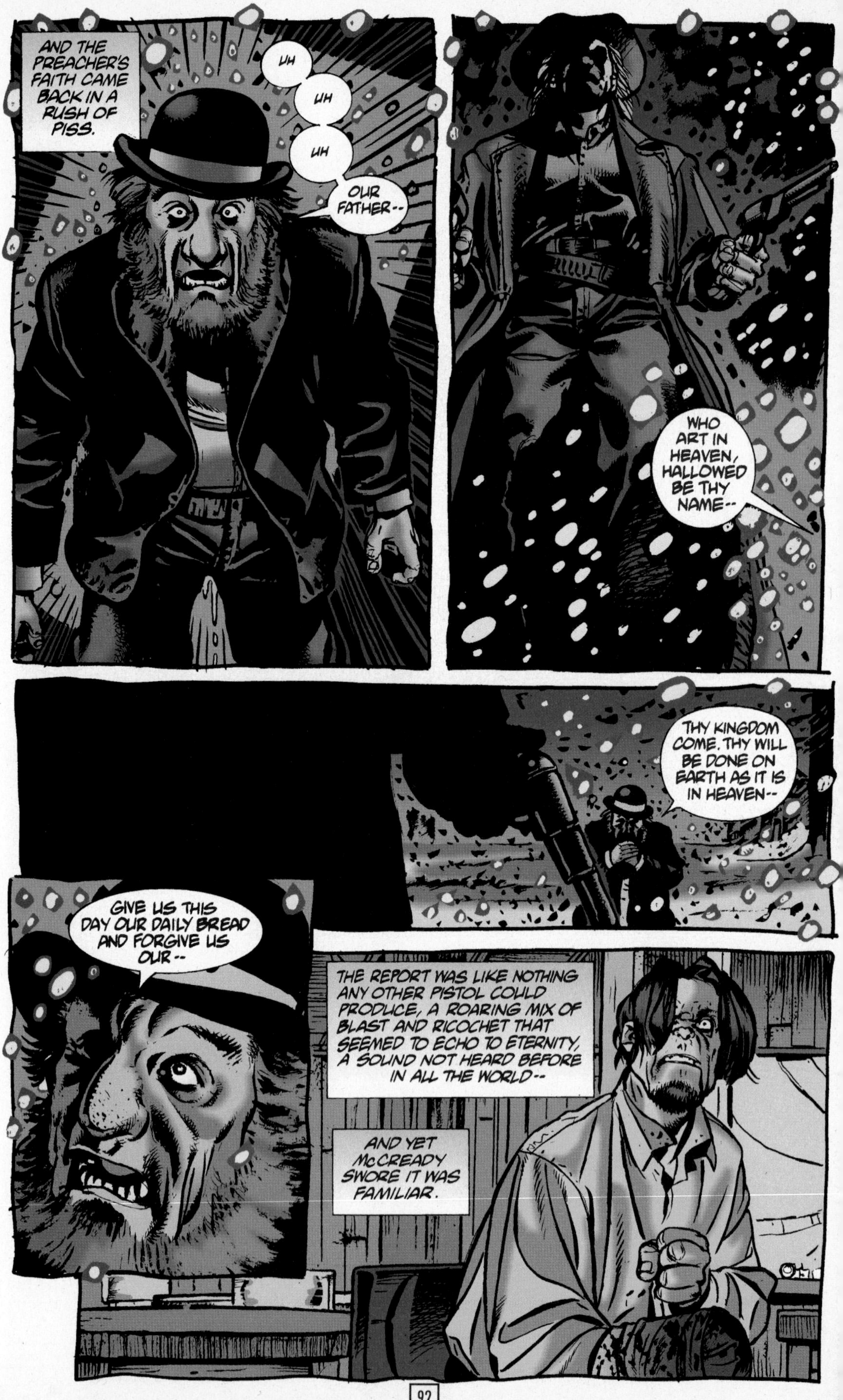

AND THE PREACHER'S FAITH CAME BACK IN A RUSH OF PISS.
UH
UH
UH
OUR FATHER--
WHO ART IN HEAVEN, HALLOWED BE THY NAME--
THY KINGDOM COME. THY WILL BE DONE ON EARTH AS IT IS IN HEAVEN--
GIVE US THIS DAY OUR DAILY BREAD AND FORGIVE US OUR--
THE REPORT WAS LIKE NOTHING ANY OTHER PISTOL COULD PRODUCE, A ROARING MIX OF BLAST AND RICOCHET THAT SEEMED TO ECHO TO ETERNITY, A SOUND NOT HEARD BEFORE IN ALL THE WORLD--
AND YET McCREADY SWORE IT WAS FAMILIAR.

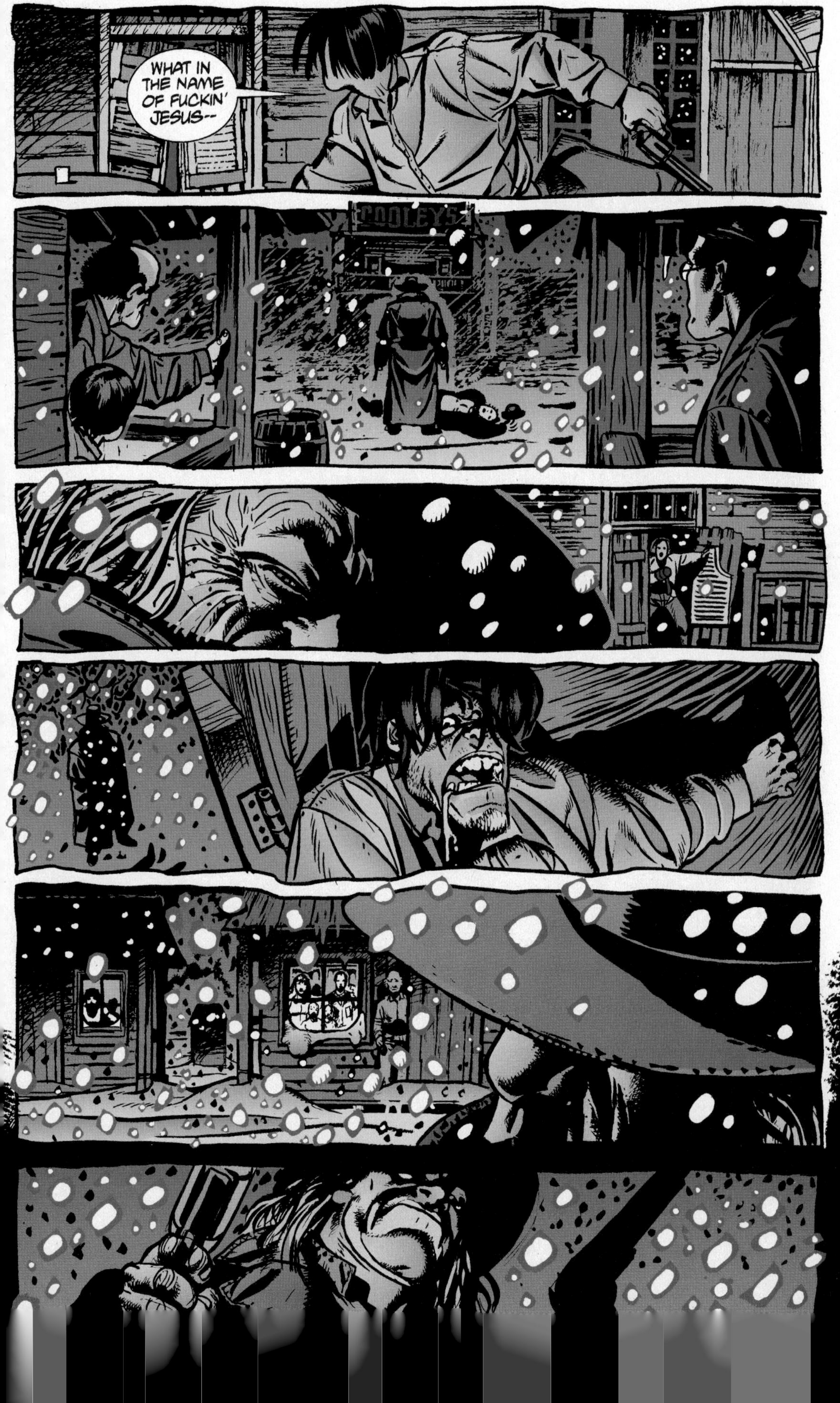
WHAT IN THE NAME OF FUCKIN' JESUS--
DOOLEY'S

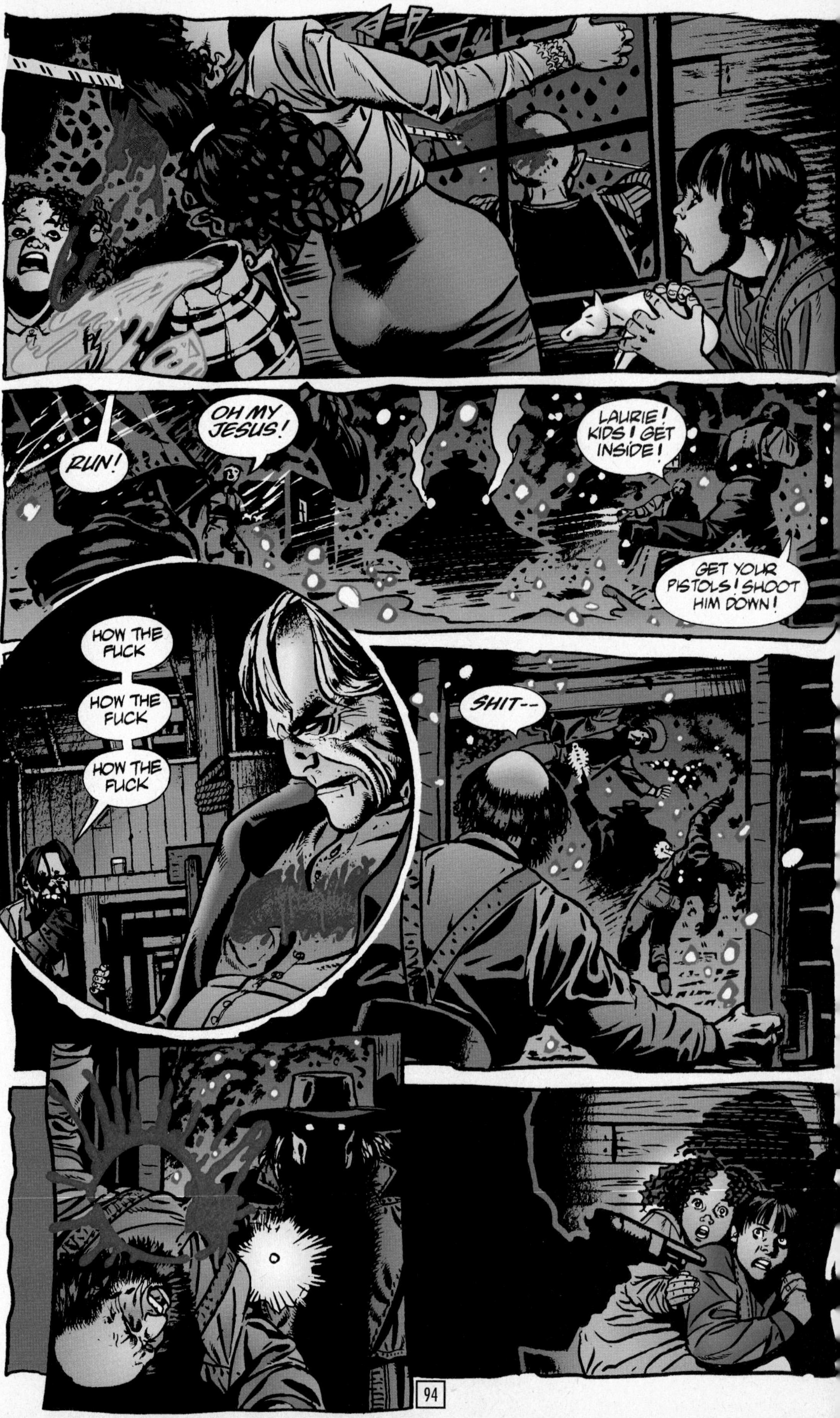
RUN!
OH MY JESUS!
LAURIE! KIDS! GET INSIDE!
GET YOUR PISTOLS! SHOOT HIM DOWN!
HOW THE FUCK
HOW THE FUCK
HOW THE FUCK
SHIT--

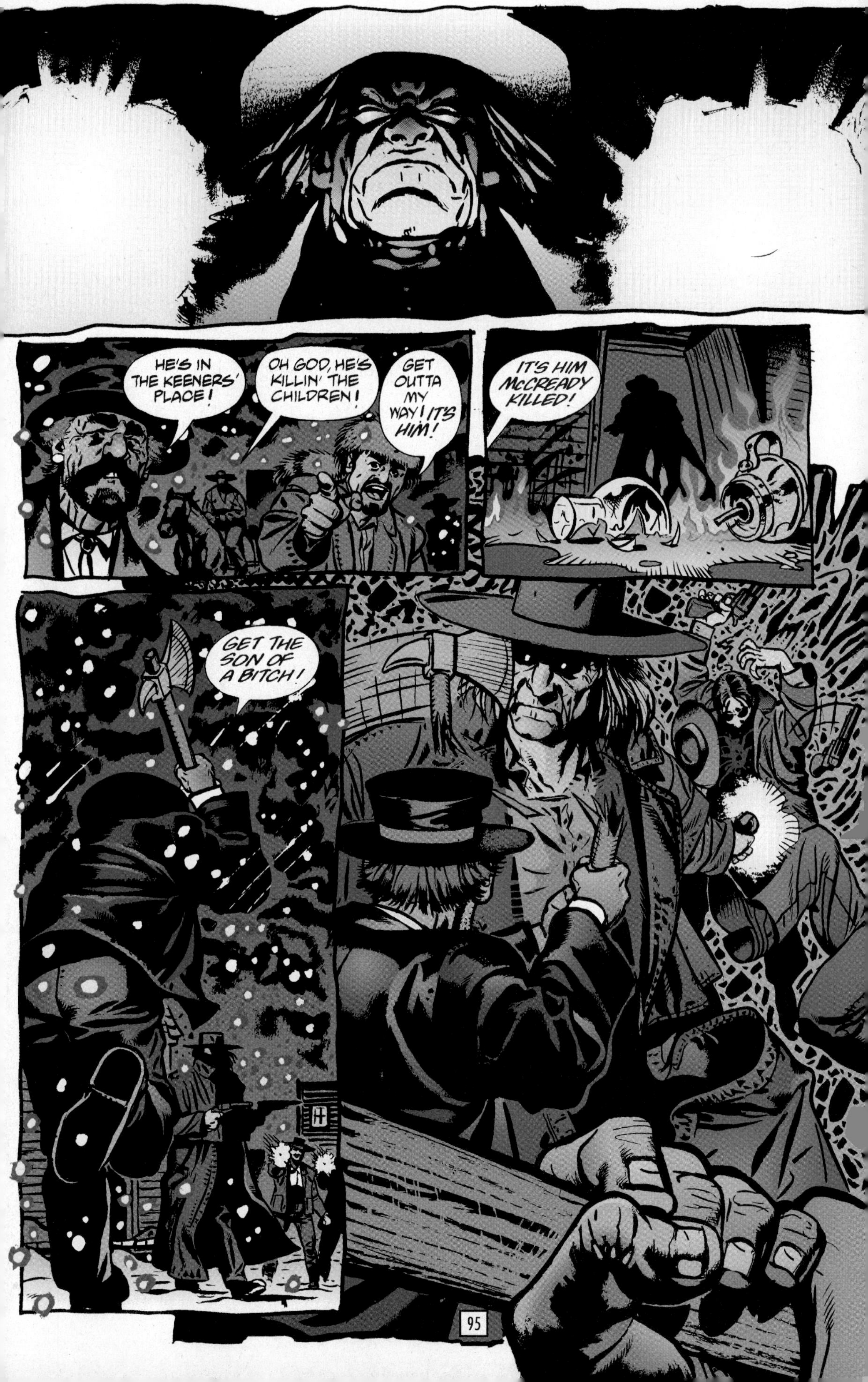
HE'S IN THE KEENERS' PLACE!
OH GOD, HE'S KILLIN' THE CHILDREN!
GET OUTTA MY WAY! IT'S HIM!
IT'S HIM McCREADY KILLED!
GET THE SON OF A BITCH!

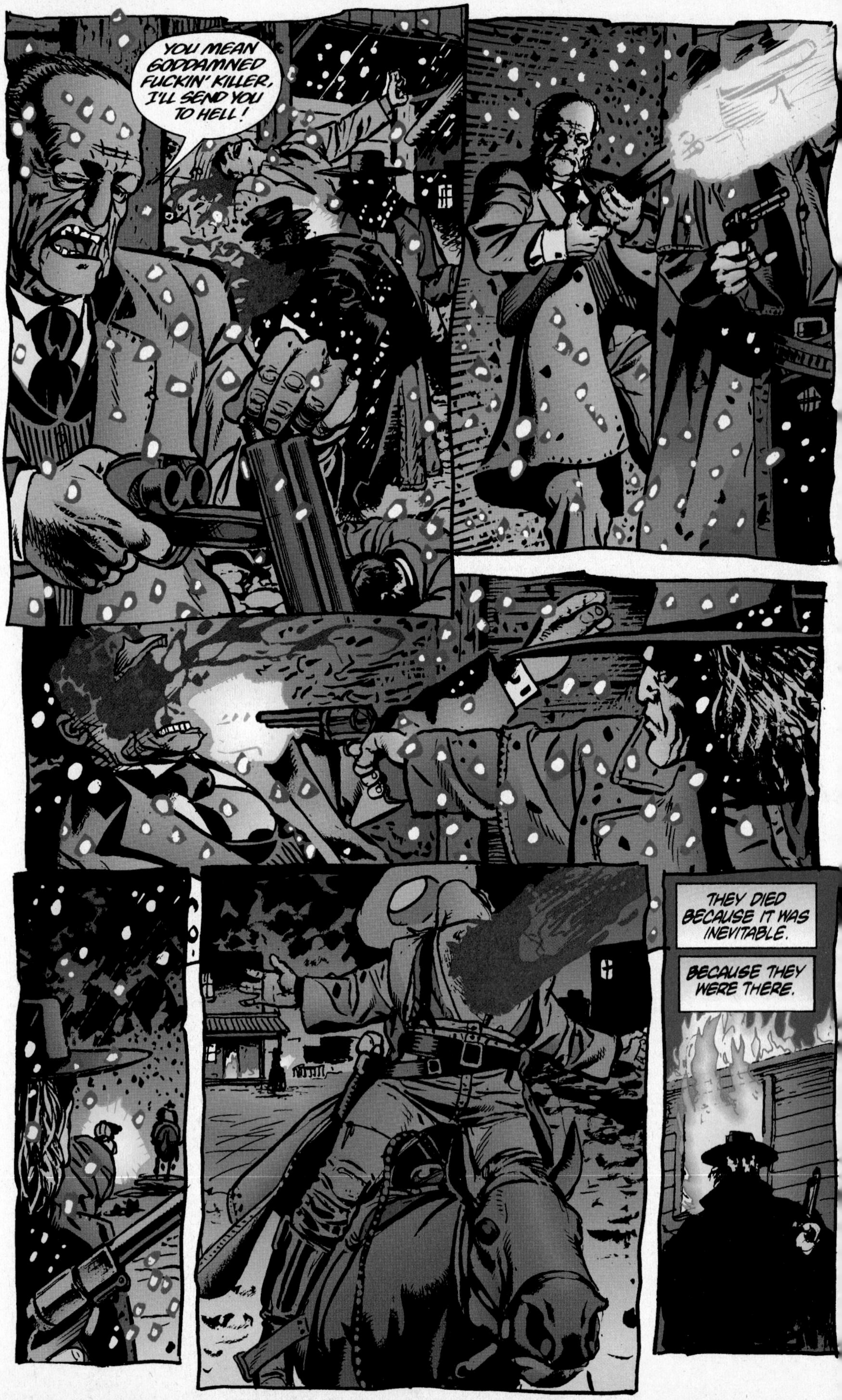
YOU MEAN GODDAMNED FUCKIN' KILLER, I'LL SEND YOU TO HELL!
THEY DIED BECAUSE IT WAS INEVITABLE.
BECAUSE THEY WERE THERE.

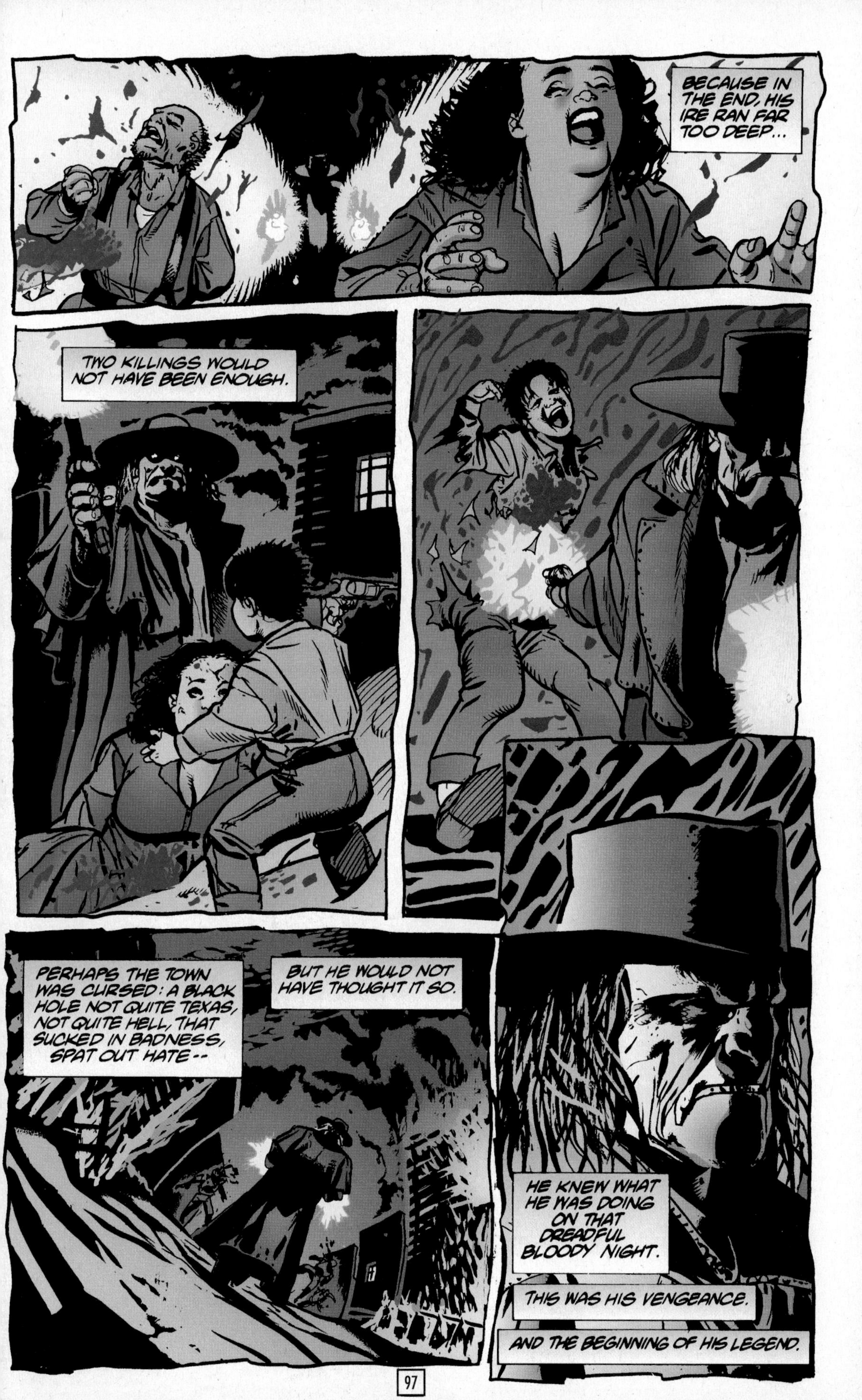

BECAUSE IN THE END, HIS IRE RAN FAR TOO DEEP...
TWO KILLINGS WOULD NOT HAVE BEEN ENOUGH.
PERHAPS THE TOWN WAS CURSED: A BLACK HOLE NOT QUITE TEXAS, NOT QUITE HELL, THAT SUCKED IN BADNESS, SPAT OUT HATE--
BUT HE WOULD NOT HAVE THOUGHT IT SO.
HE KNEW WHAT HE WAS DOING ON THAT DREADFUL BLOODY NIGHT.
THIS WAS HIS VENGEANCE.
AND THE BEGINNING OF HIS LEGEND.

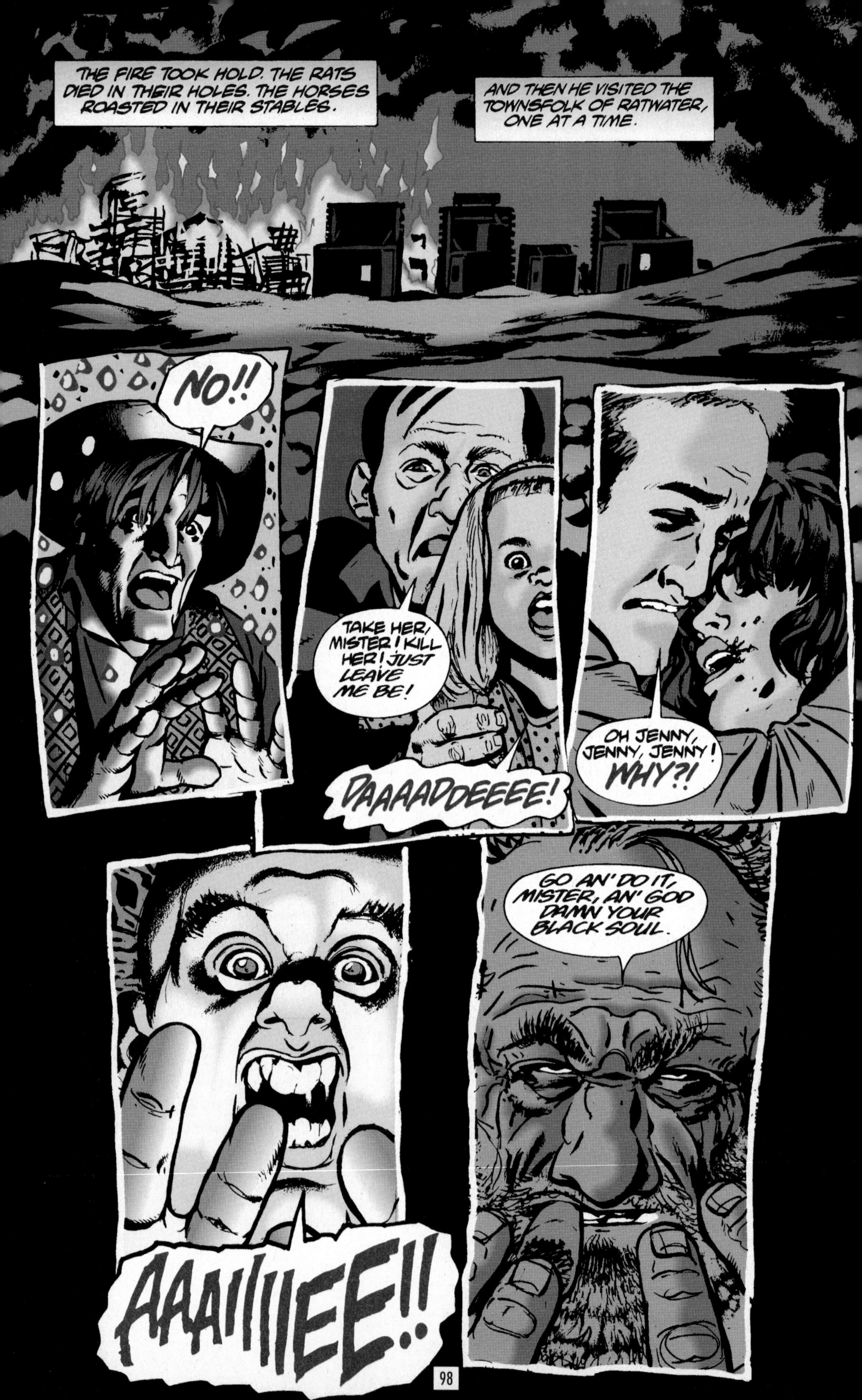

THE FIRE TOOK HOLD. THE RATS DIED IN THEIR HOLES. THE HORSES ROASTED IN THEIR STABLES.
AND THEN HE VISITED THE TOWNSFOLK OF RATWATER, ONE AT A TIME.
NO!!
TAKE HER, MISTER! KILL HER! JUST LEAVE ME BE!
DAAAADDEEEE!
OH JENNY, JENNY, JENNY! WHY?!
AAAIIIIEE!!
GO AN' DO IT, MISTER, AN' GOD DAMN YOUR BLACK SOUL.

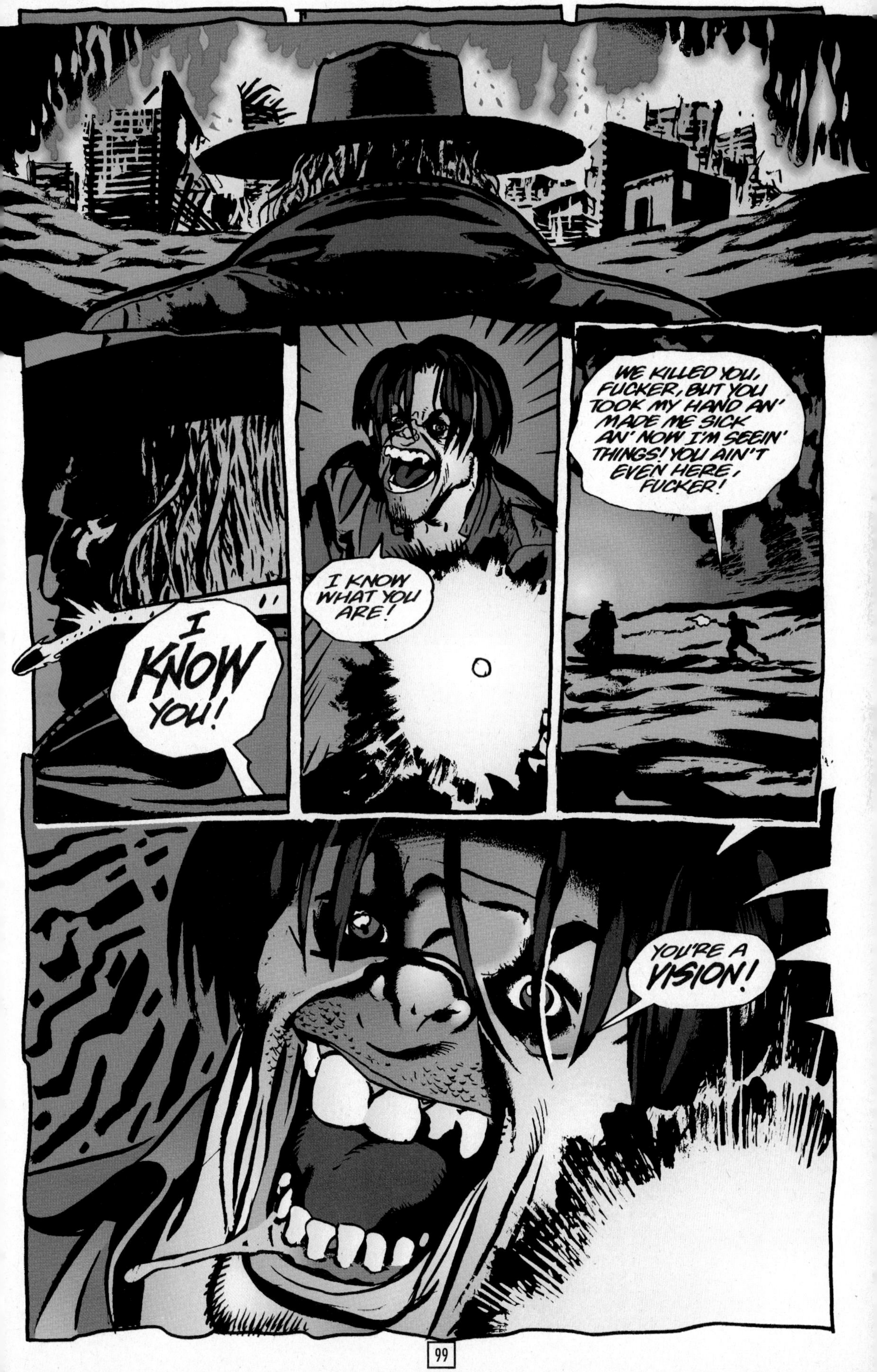
I KNOW YOU!
I KNOW WHAT YOU ARE!
WE KILLED YOU, FUCKER, BUT YOU TOOK MY HAND AN' MADE ME SICK AN' NOW I'M SEEIN' THINGS! YOU AIN'T EVEN HERE, FUCKER!
YOU'RE A VISION!

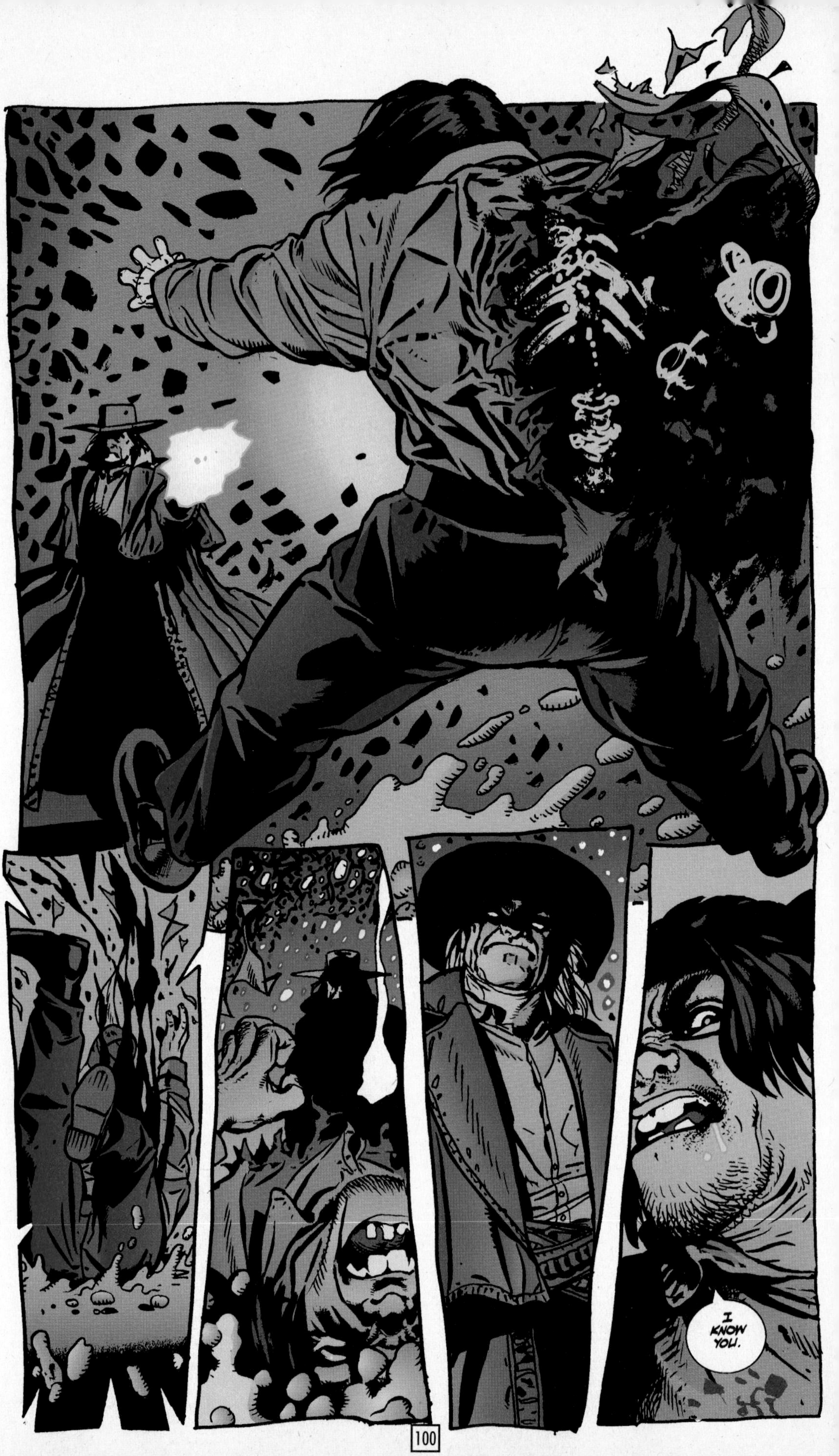
I KNOW YOU.

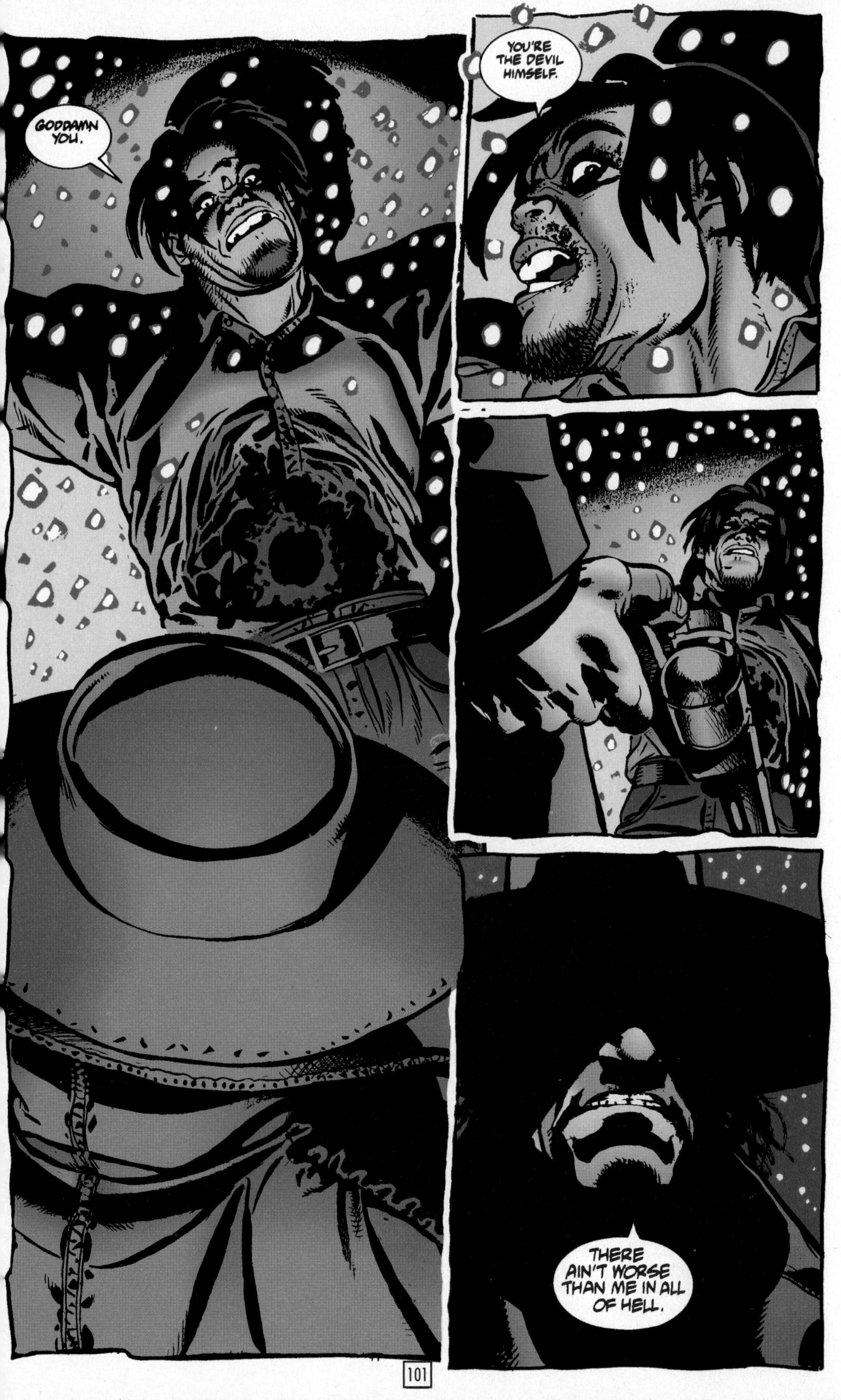
GODDAMN YOU.
YOU'RE THE DEVIL HIMSELF.
THERE AIN'T WORSE THAN ME IN ALL OF HELL.

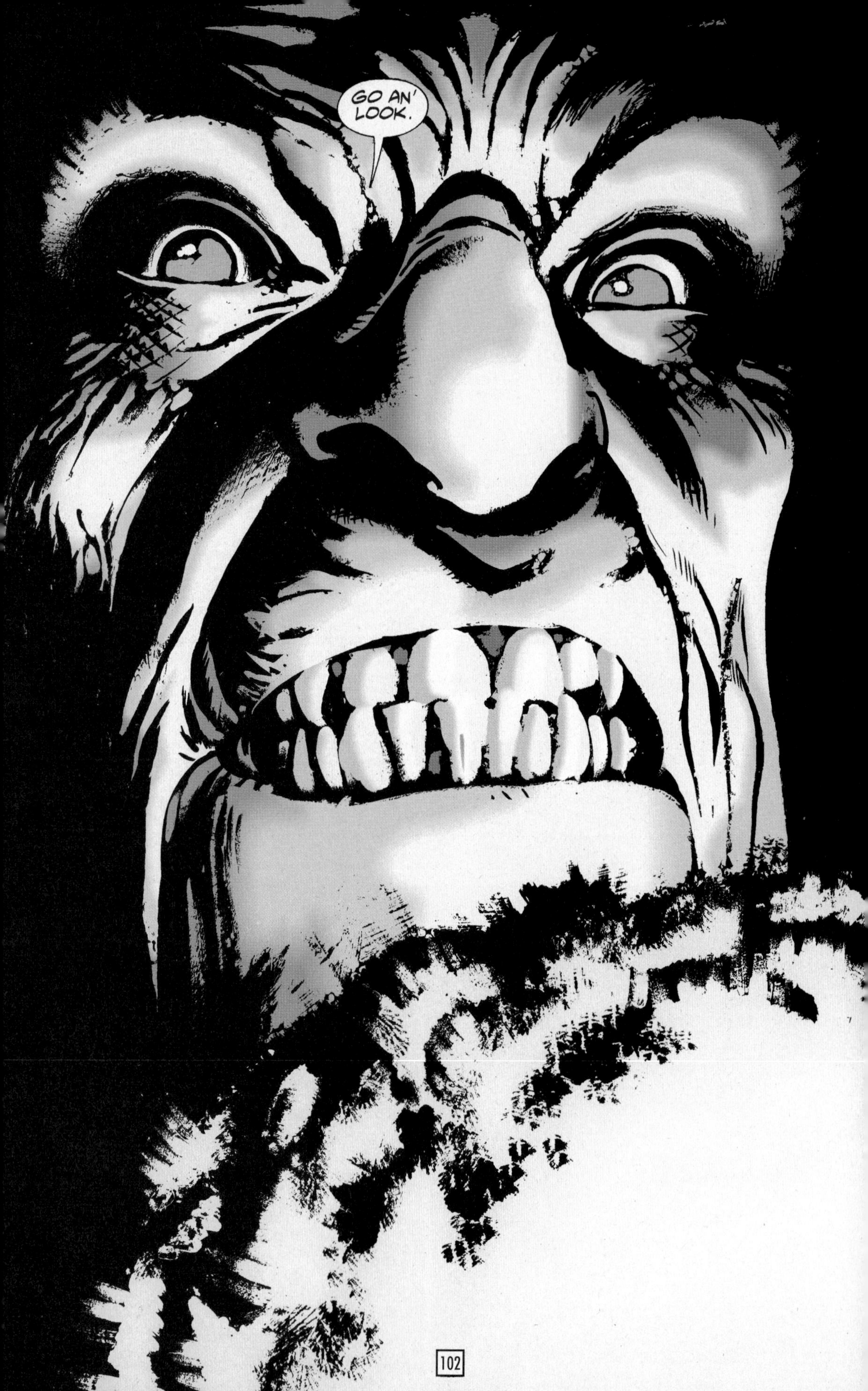
GO AN' LOOK.

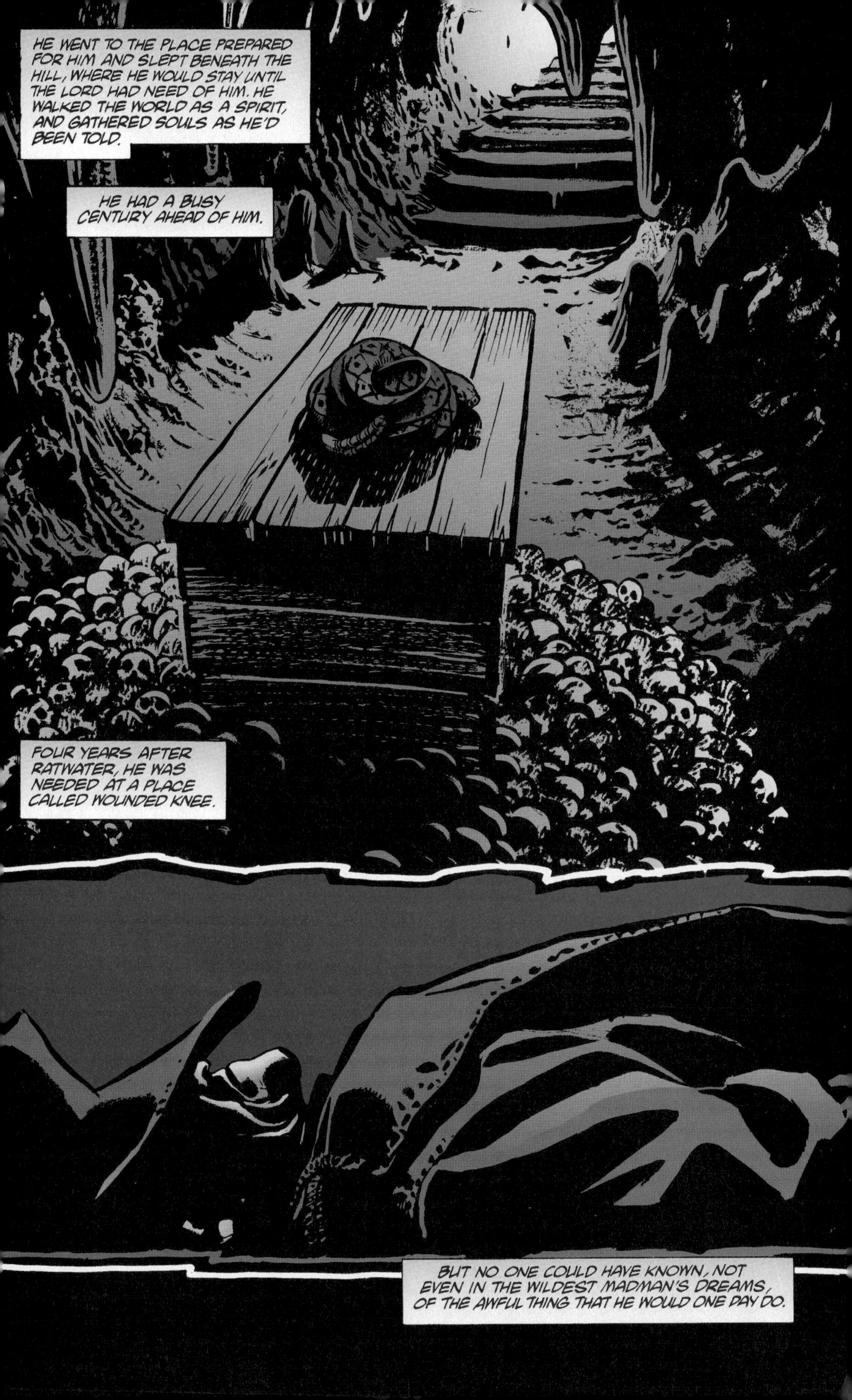
HE WENT TO THE PLACE PREPARED FOR HIM AND SLEPT BENEATH THE HILL, WHERE HE WOULD STAY UNTIL THE LORD HAD NEED OF HIM. HE WALKED THE WORLD AS A SPIRIT, AND GATHERED SOULS AS HE'D BEEN TOLD.
HE HAD A BUSY CENTURY AHEAD OF HIM.
FOUR YEARS AFTER RATWATER, HE WAS NEEDED AT A PLACE CALLED WOUNDED KNEE.
BUT NO ONE COULD HAVE KNOWN, NOT EVEN IN THE WILDEST MADMAN'S DREAMS, OF THE AWFUL THING THAT HE WOULD ONE DAY DO.

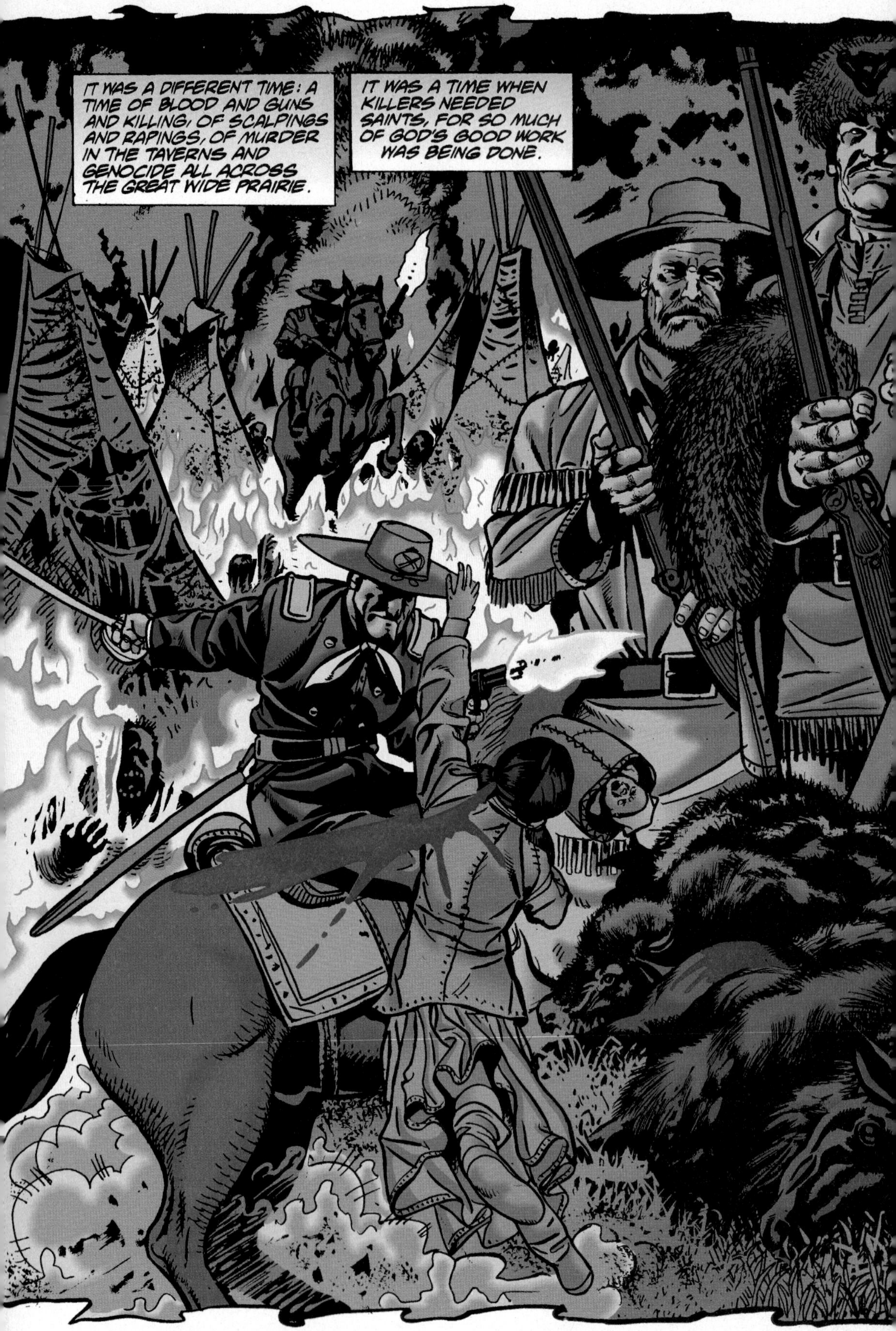
IT WAS A DIFFERENT TIME: A TIME OF BLOOD AND GUNS AND KILLING, OF SCALPINGS AND RAPINGS, OF MURDER IN THE TAVERNS AND GENOCIDE ALL ACROSS THE GREAT WIDE PRAIRIE.
IT WAS A TIME WHEN KILLERS NEEDED SAINTS, FOR SO MUCH OF GOD'S GOOD WORK WAS BEING DONE.

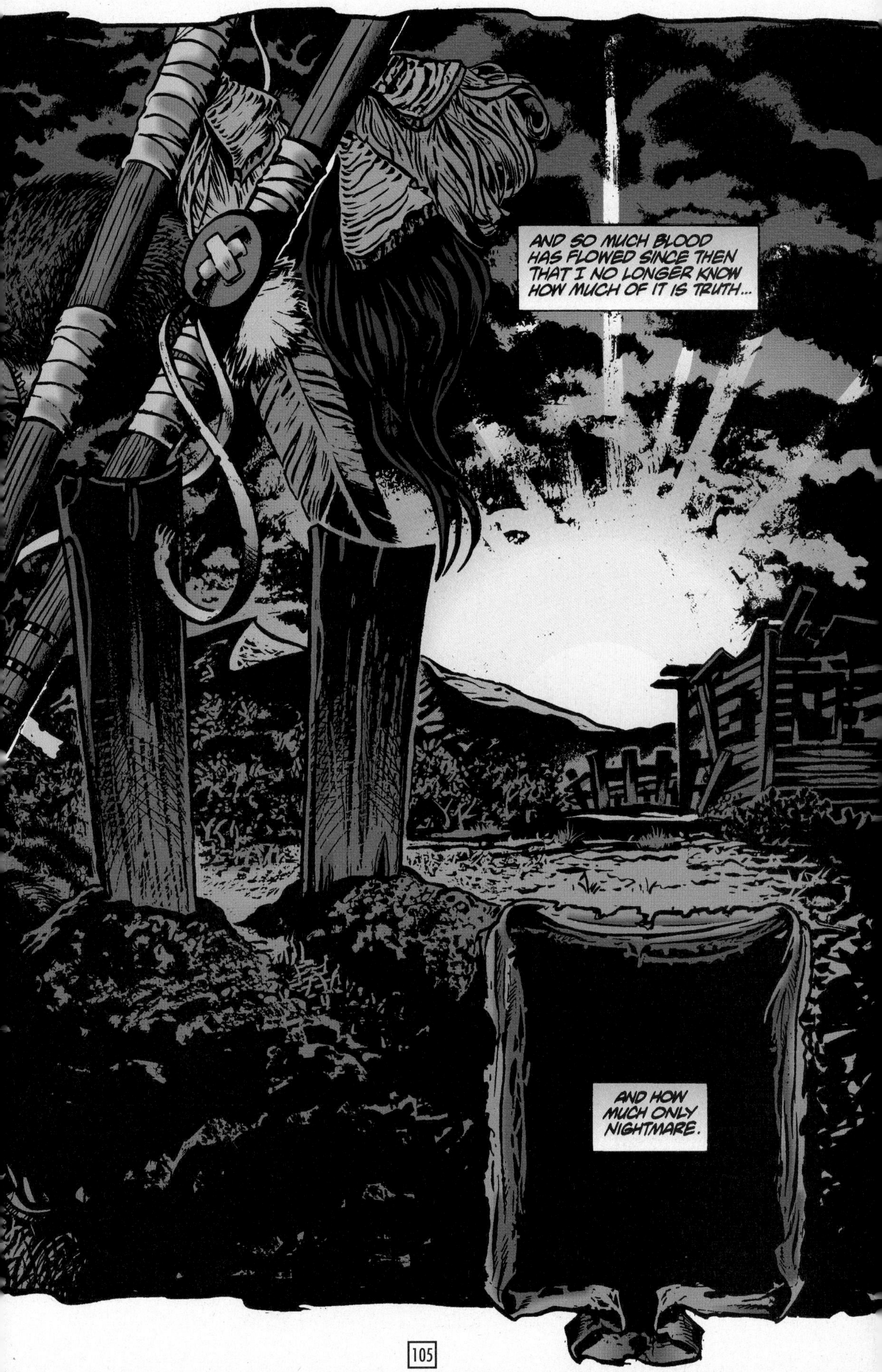
AND SO MUCH BLOOD HAS FLOWED SINCE THEN THAT I NO LONGER KNOW HOW MUCH OF IT IS TRUTH...
AND HOW MUCH ONLY NIGHTMARE.

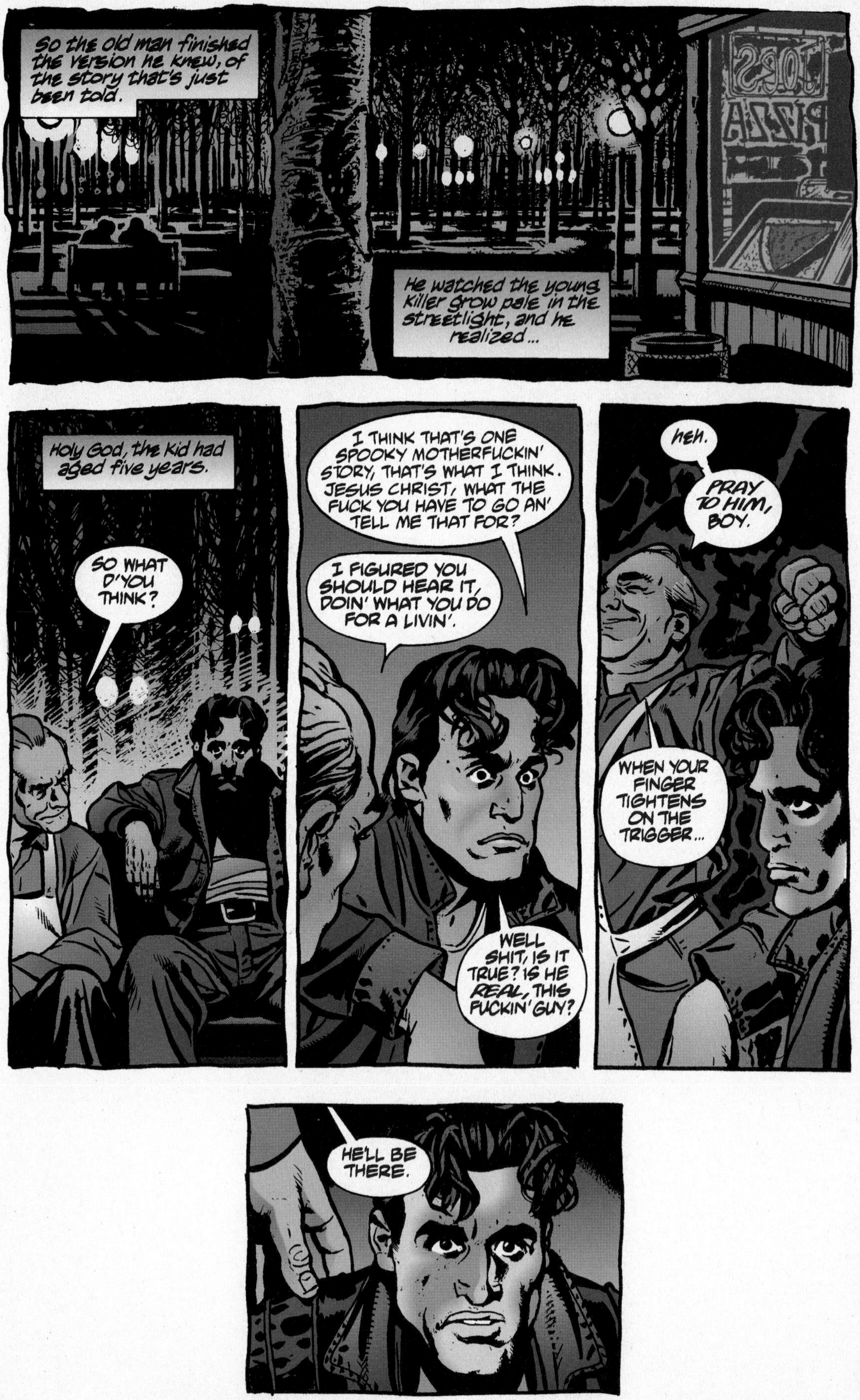
So the old man finished the version he knew, of the story that's just been told.
He watched the young killer grow pale in the streetlight, and he realized...
Holy God, the kid had aged five years.
SO WHAT D'YOU THINK?
I THINK THAT'S ONE SPOOKY MOTHERFUCKIN' STORY, THAT'S WHAT I THINK. JESUS CHRIST, WHAT THE FUCK YOU HAVE TO GO AN' TELL ME THAT FOR?
I FIGURED YOU SHOULD HEAR IT, DOIN' WHAT YOU DO FOR A LIVIN'.
WELL SHIT, IS IT TRUE? IS HE REAL, THIS FUCKIN' GUY?
heh.
PRAY TO HIM, BOY.
WHEN YOUR FINGER TIGHTENS ON THE TRIGGER...
HE'LL BE THERE.

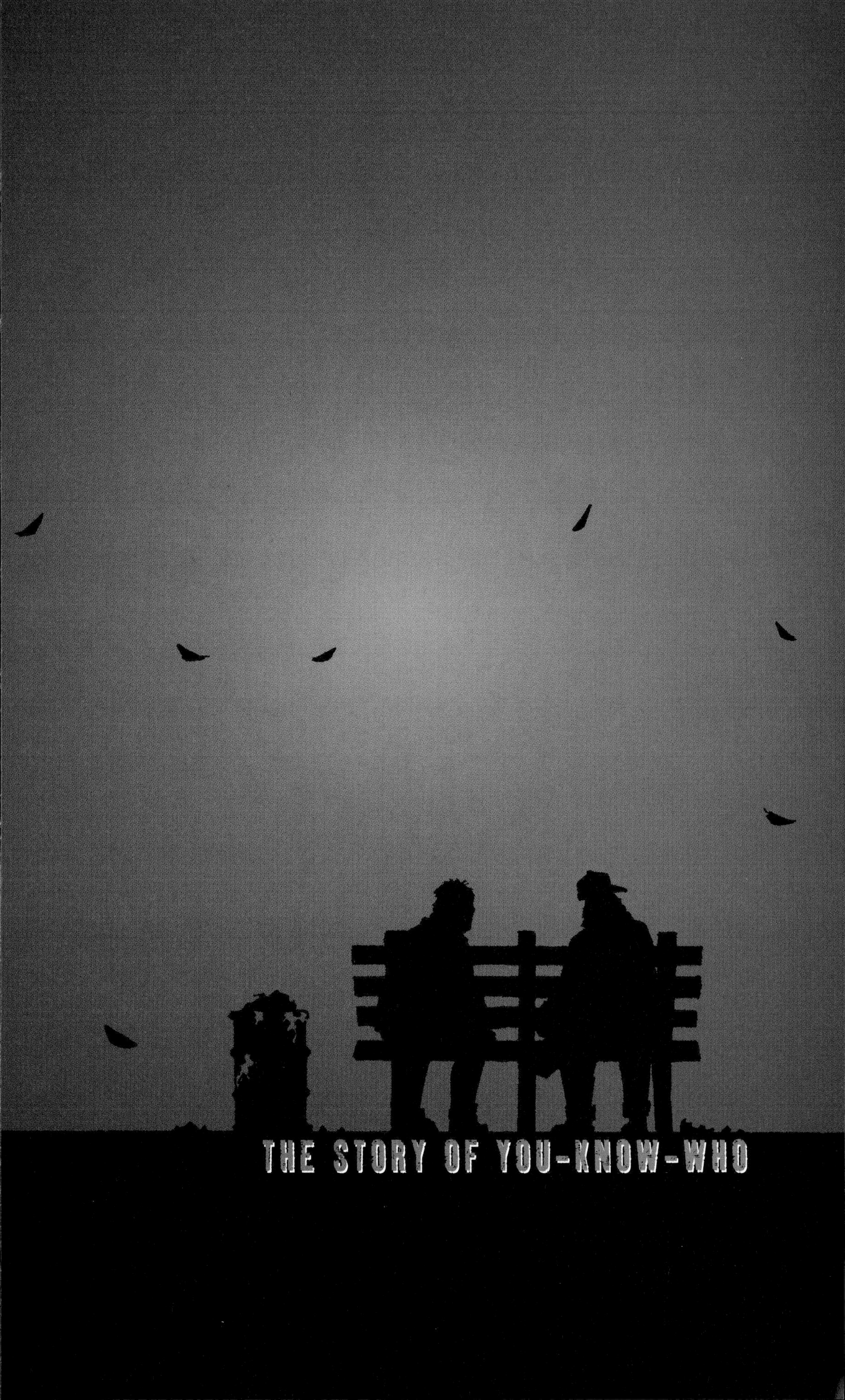

THE STORY OF YOU-KNOW-WHO

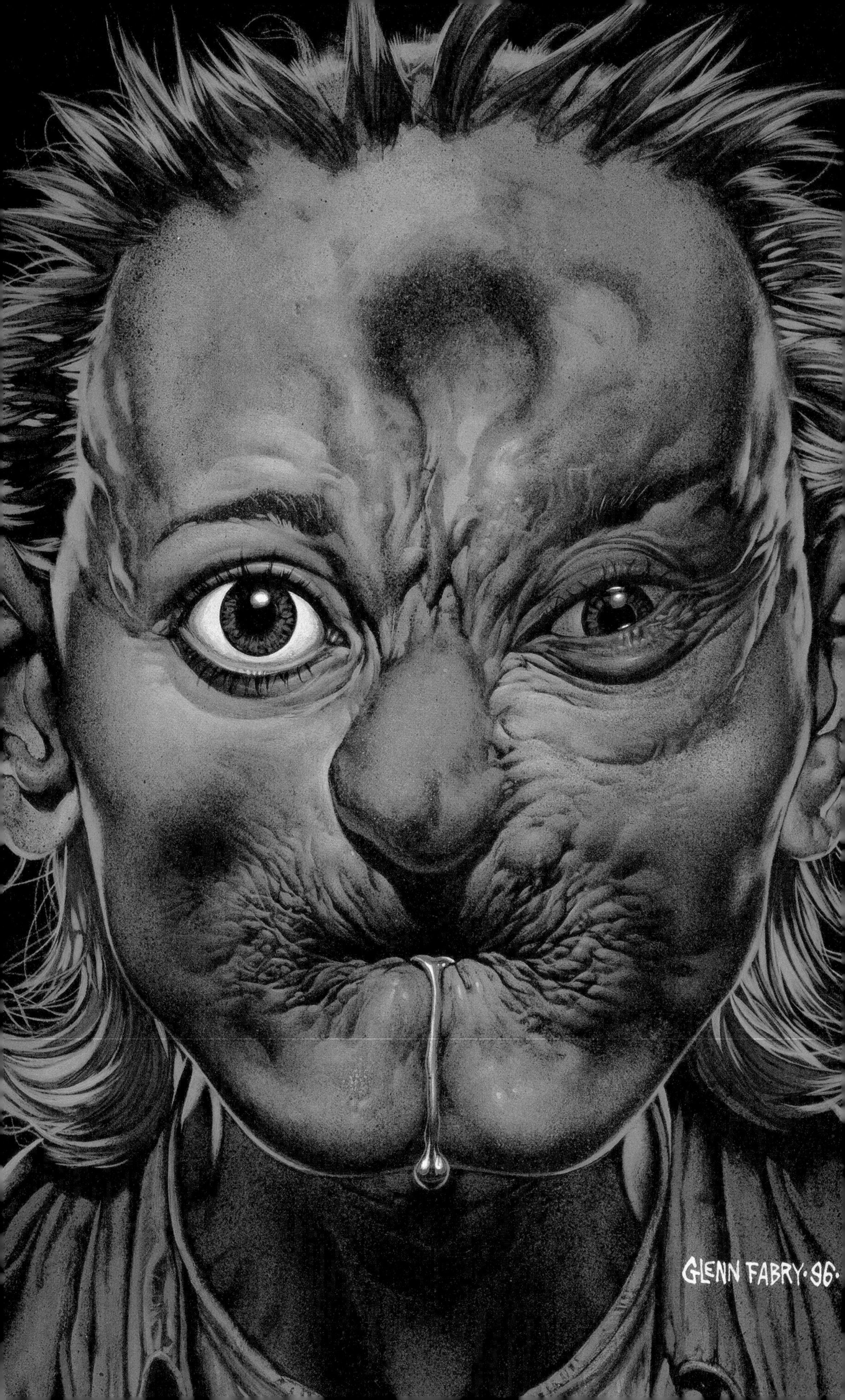
GLENN FABRY·96·

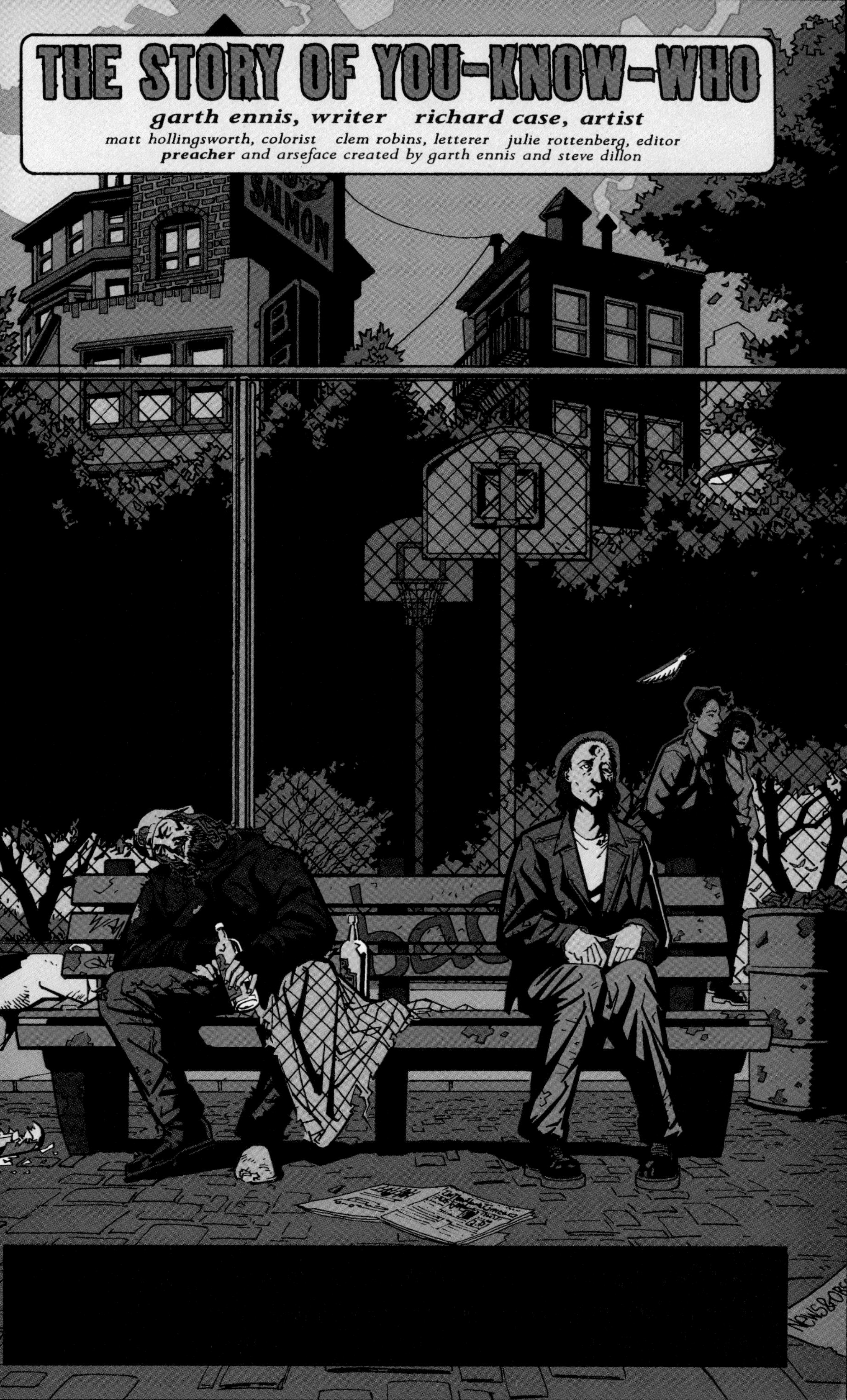
THE STORY OF YOU-KNOW-WHO
garth ennis, writer richard case, artist
matt hollingsworth, colorist clem robins, letterer julie rottenberg, editor
preacher and arseface created by garth ennis and steve dillon
SALMON
[redacted]

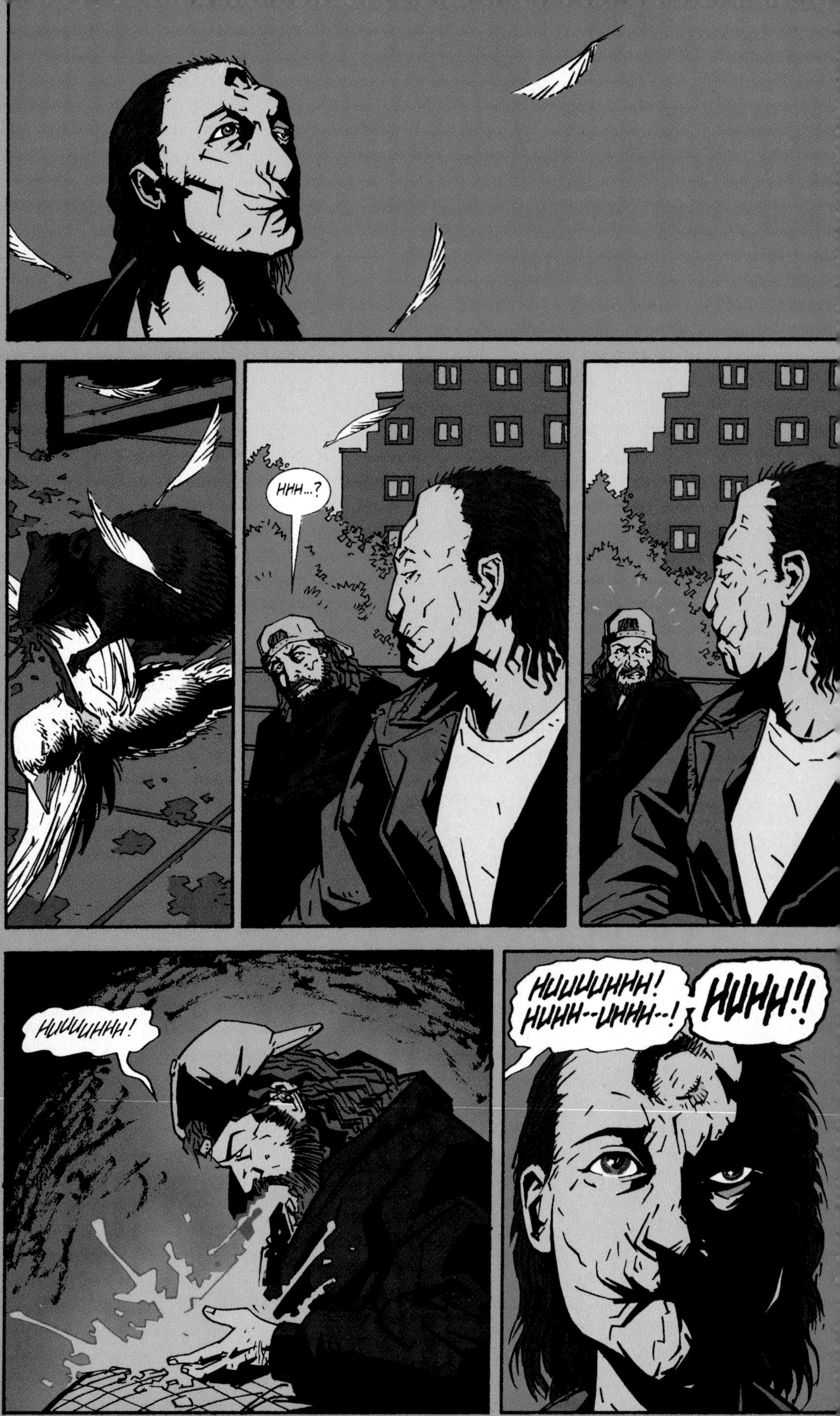
HHH...?
HUUUHHH!
HUUUHHH!
HHHH--UHHH--!
HUHH!!

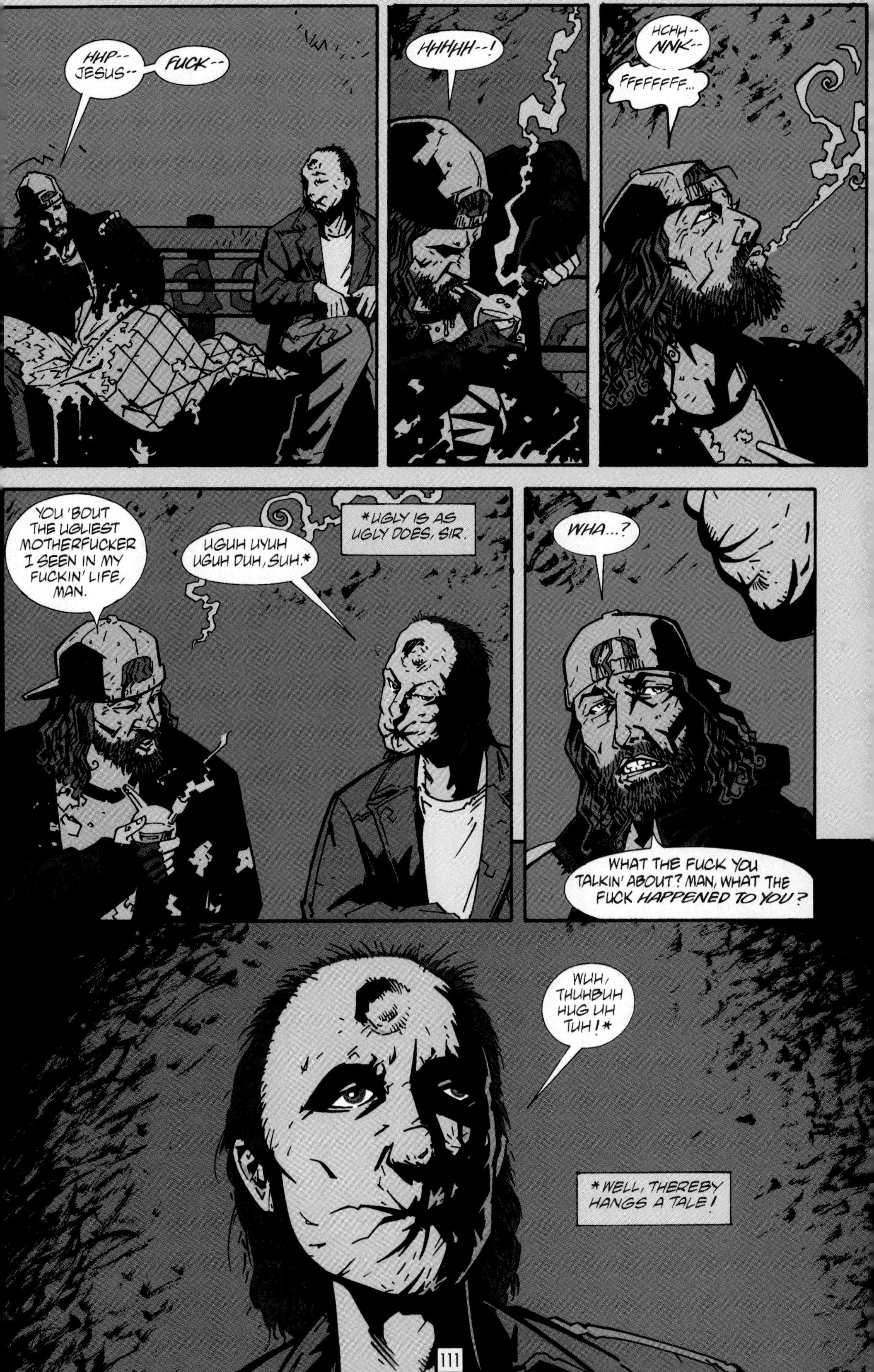
HHP-- JESUS--
FUCK--
HHHHH--!
HCHH-- NNK--
FFFFFFFF...
YOU 'BOUT THE UGLIEST MOTHERFUCKER I SEEN IN MY FUCKIN' LIFE, MAN.
UGUH UYUH UGUH DUH, SUH.*
*UGLY IS AS UGLY DOES, SIR.
WHA...?
WHAT THE FUCK YOU TALKIN' ABOUT? MAN, WHAT THE FUCK HAPPENED TO YOU?
WUH, THUHBUH HUG UH TUH!*
*WELL, THEREBY HANGS A TALE!

1. A Day in the Life

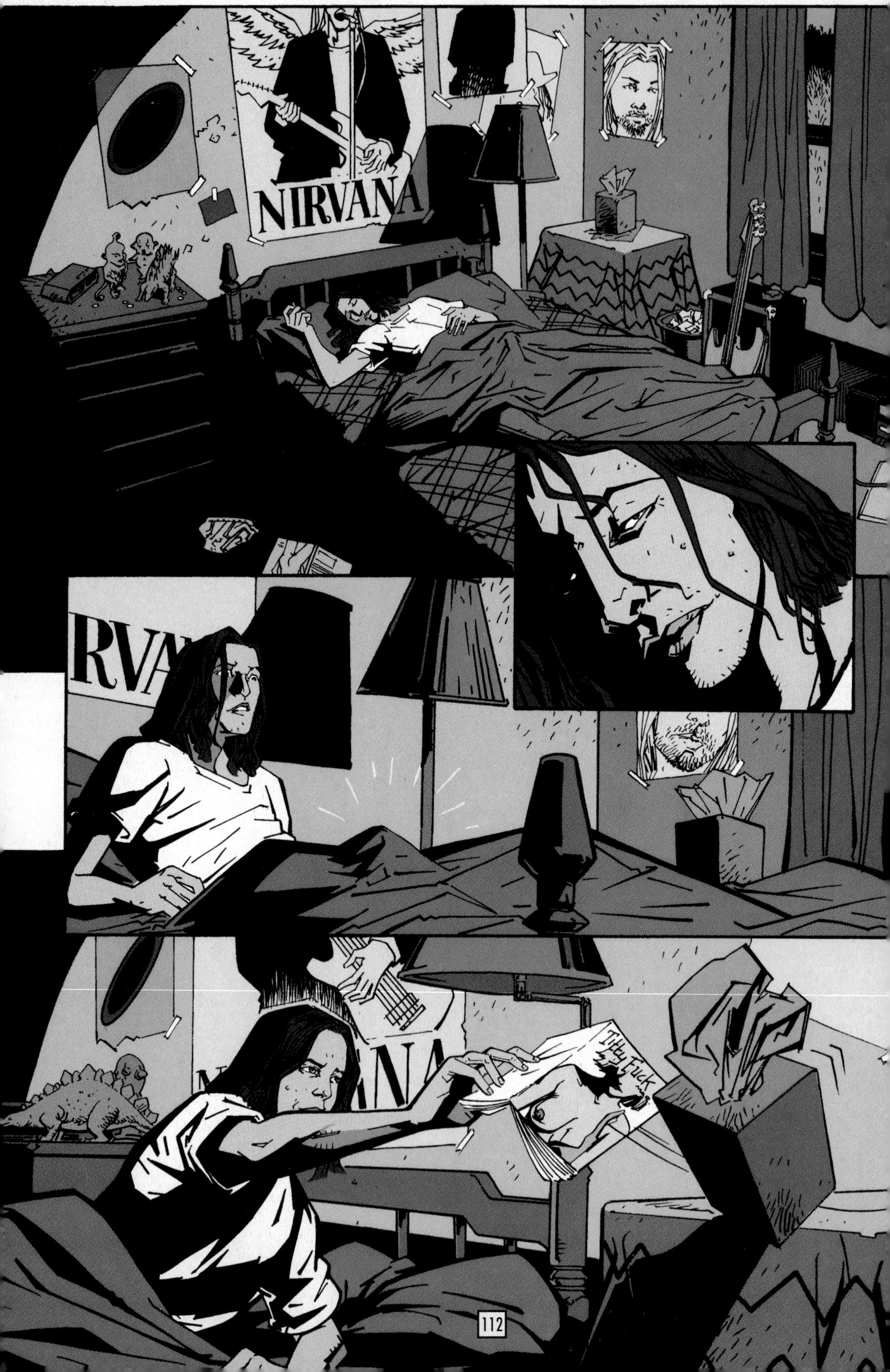

NIRVANA
RVA
Titty Fuck

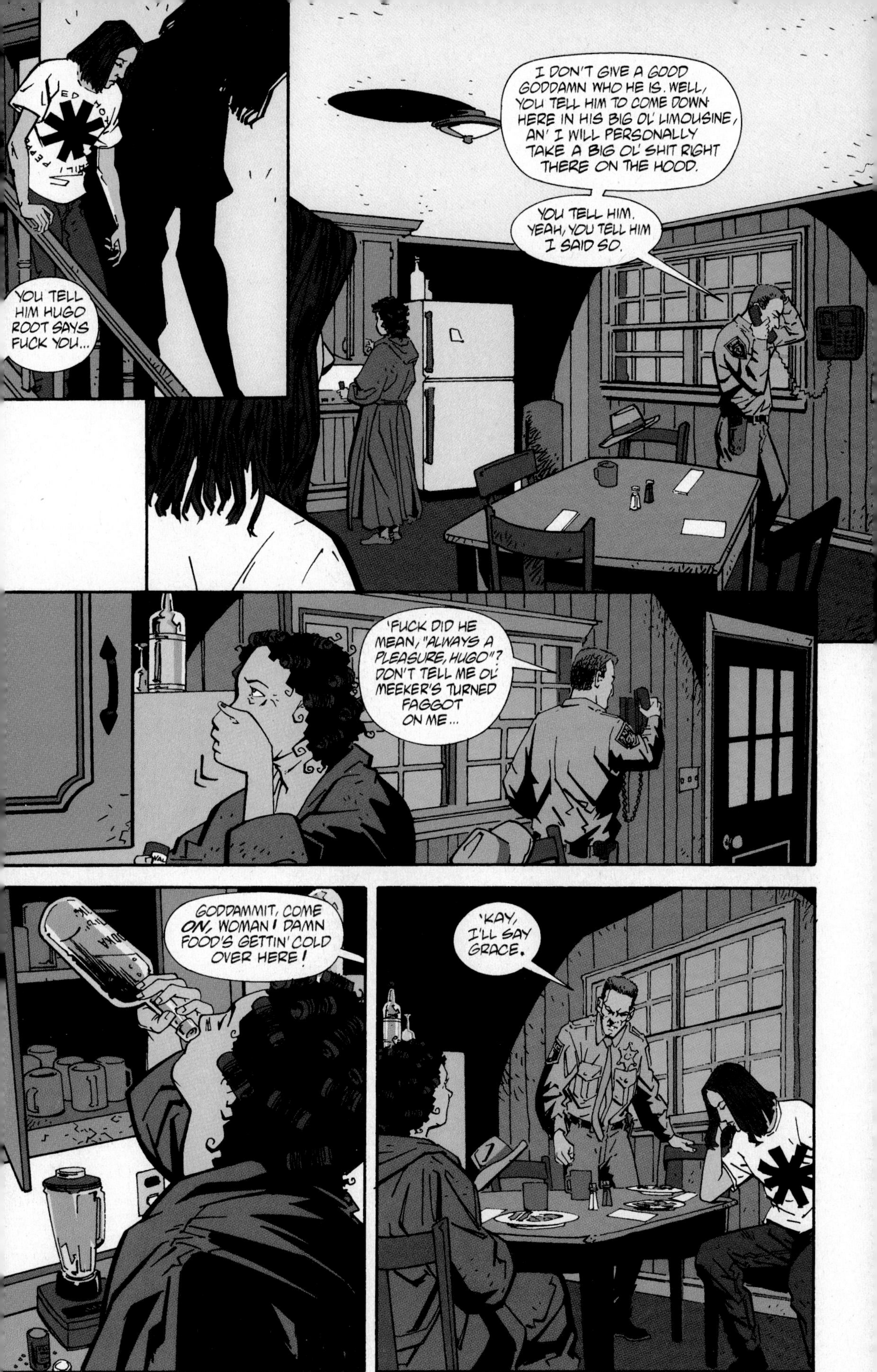
I DON'T GIVE A GOOD GODDAMN WHO HE IS. WELL, YOU TELL HIM TO COME DOWN HERE IN HIS BIG OL' LIMOUSINE, AN' I WILL PERSONALLY TAKE A BIG OL' SHIT RIGHT THERE ON THE HOOD.
YOU TELL HIM. YEAH, YOU TELL HIM I SAID SO.
YOU TELL HIM HUGO ROOT SAYS FUCK YOU...
'FUCK DID HE MEAN, "ALWAYS A PLEASURE, HUGO"? DON'T TELL ME OL' MEEKER'S TURNED FAGGOT ON ME...
GODDAMMIT, COME ON, WOMAN! DAMN FOOD'S GETTIN' COLD OVER HERE!
'KAY, I'LL SAY GRACE.

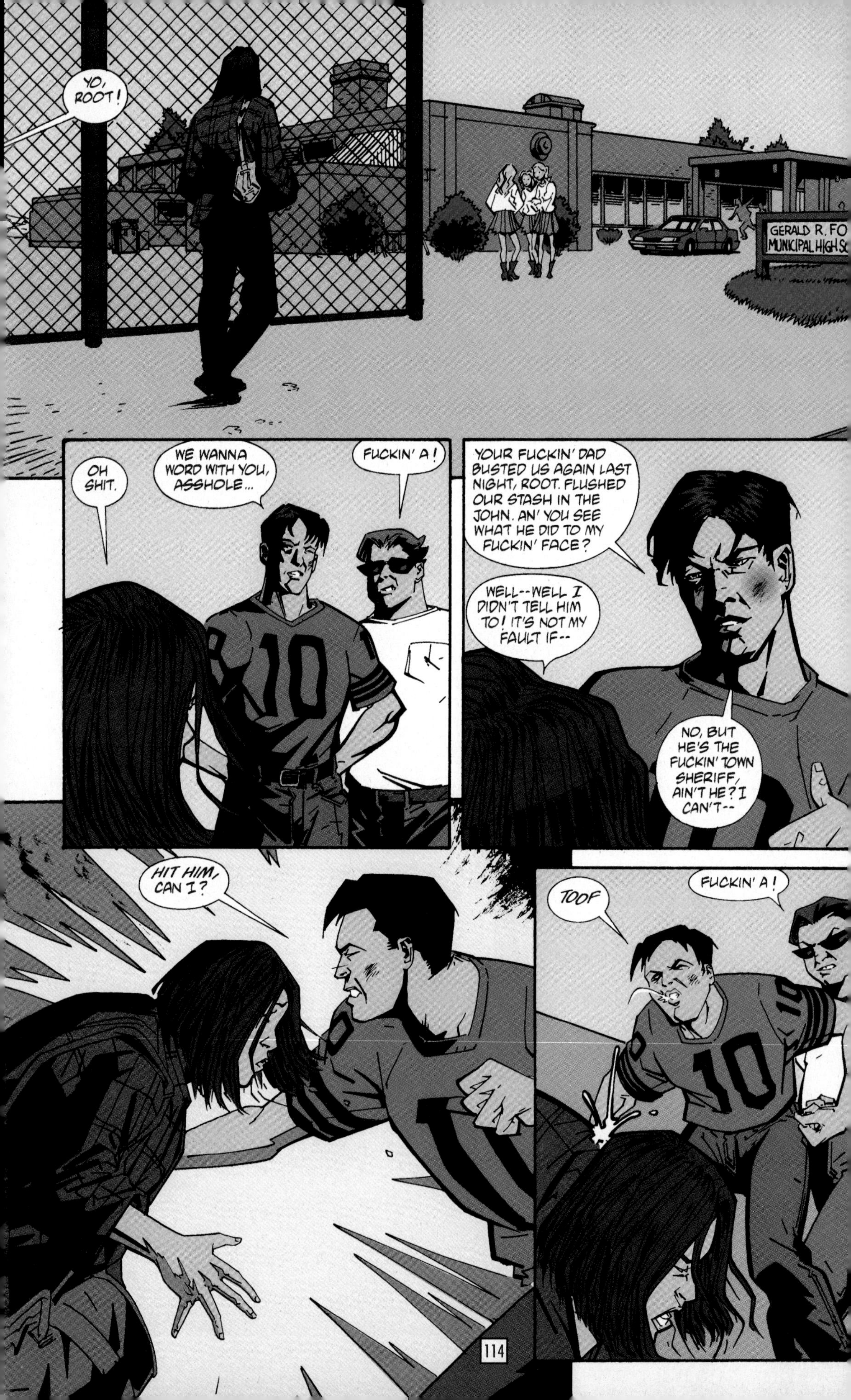
YO, ROOT!
GERALD R. FO
MUNICIPAL HIGH SC
OH SHIT.
WE WANNA WORD WITH YOU, ASSHOLE...
FUCKIN' A!
YOUR FUCKIN' DAD BUSTED US AGAIN LAST NIGHT, ROOT. FLUSHED OUR STASH IN THE JOHN. AN' YOU SEE WHAT HE DID TO MY FUCKIN' FACE?
WELL--WELL I DIDN'T TELL HIM TO! IT'S NOT MY FAULT IF--
NO, BUT HE'S THE FUCKIN' TOWN SHERIFF, AIN'T HE? I CAN'T--
HIT HIM, CAN I?
TOOF
FUCKIN' A!

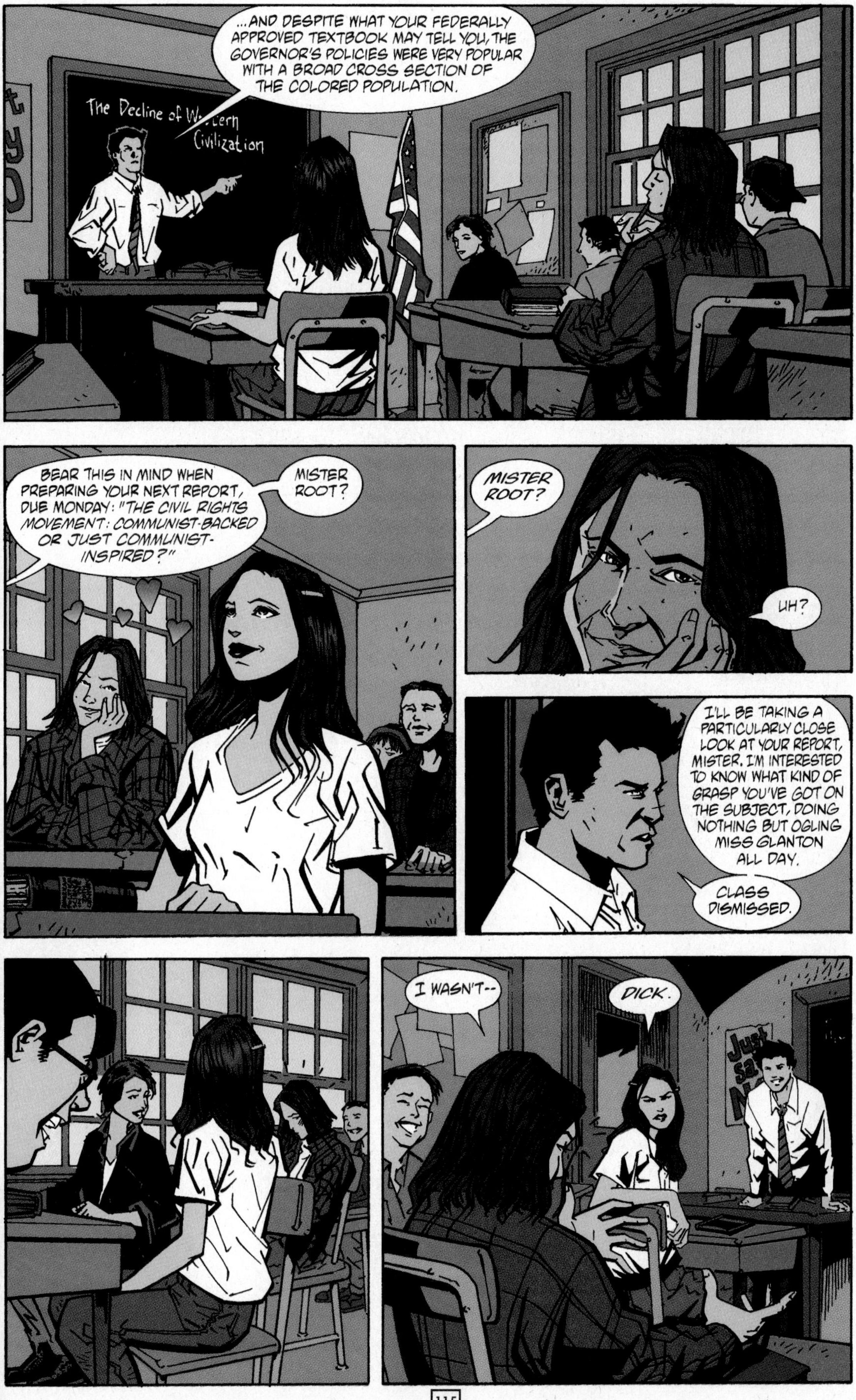
...AND DESPITE WHAT YOUR FEDERALLY APPROVED TEXTBOOK MAY TELL YOU, THE GOVERNOR'S POLICIES WERE VERY POPULAR WITH A BROAD CROSS SECTION OF THE COLORED POPULATION.
Civilization
BEAR THIS IN MIND WHEN PREPARING YOUR NEXT REPORT, DUE MONDAY: "THE CIVIL RIGHTS MOVEMENT: COMMUNIST-BACKED OR JUST COMMUNIST-INSPIRED?"
MISTER ROOT?
MISTER ROOT?
UH?
I'LL BE TAKING A PARTICULARLY CLOSE LOOK AT YOUR REPORT, MISTER. I'M INTERESTED TO KNOW WHAT KIND OF GRASP YOU'VE GOT ON THE SUBJECT, DOING NOTHING BUT OGLING MISS GLANTON ALL DAY.
CLASS DISMISSED.
I WASN'T--
DICK.

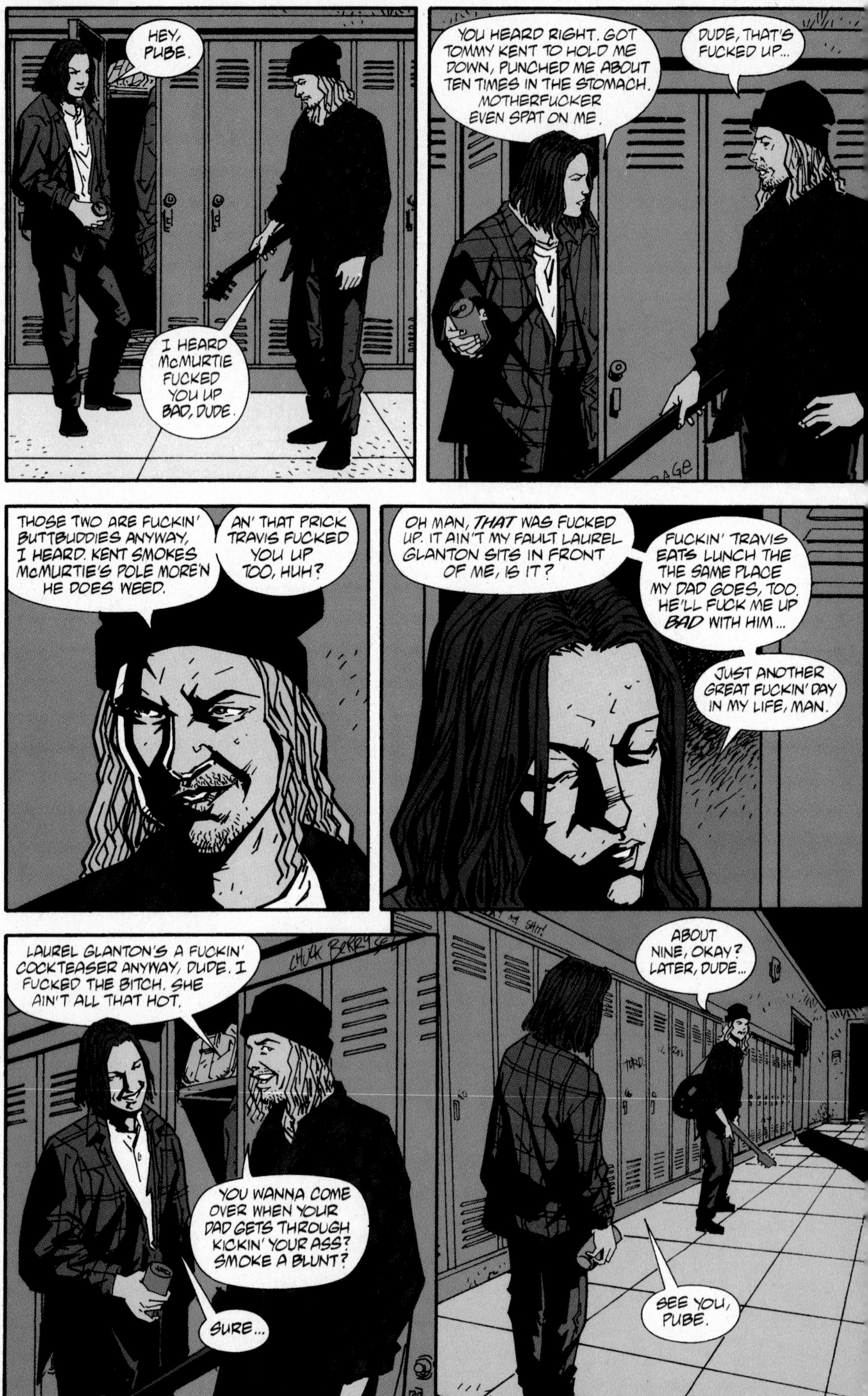
HEY, PUBE.
I HEARD McMURTIE FUCKED YOU UP BAD, DUDE.
YOU HEARD RIGHT. GOT TOMMY KENT TO HOLD ME DOWN, PUNCHED ME ABOUT TEN TIMES IN THE STOMACH. MOTHERFUCKER EVEN SPAT ON ME.
DUDE, THAT'S FUCKED UP...
THOSE TWO ARE FUCKIN' BUTTBUDDIES ANYWAY, I HEARD. KENT SMOKES McMURTIE'S POLE MORE'N HE DOES WEED.
AN' THAT PRICK TRAVIS FUCKED YOU UP TOO, HUH?
OH MAN, THAT WAS FUCKED UP. IT AIN'T MY FAULT LAUREL GLANTON SITS IN FRONT OF ME, IS IT?
FUCKIN' TRAVIS EATS LUNCH THE THE SAME PLACE MY DAD GOES, TOO. HE'LL FUCK ME UP BAD WITH HIM...
JUST ANOTHER GREAT FUCKIN' DAY IN MY LIFE, MAN.
LAUREL GLANTON'S A FUCKIN' COCKTEASER ANYWAY, DUDE. I FUCKED THE BITCH. SHE AIN'T ALL THAT HOT.
YOU WANNA COME OVER WHEN YOUR DAD GETS THROUGH KICKIN' YOUR ASS? SMOKE A BLUNT?
SURE...
ABOUT NINE, OKAY? LATER, DUDE...
SEE YOU, PUBE.

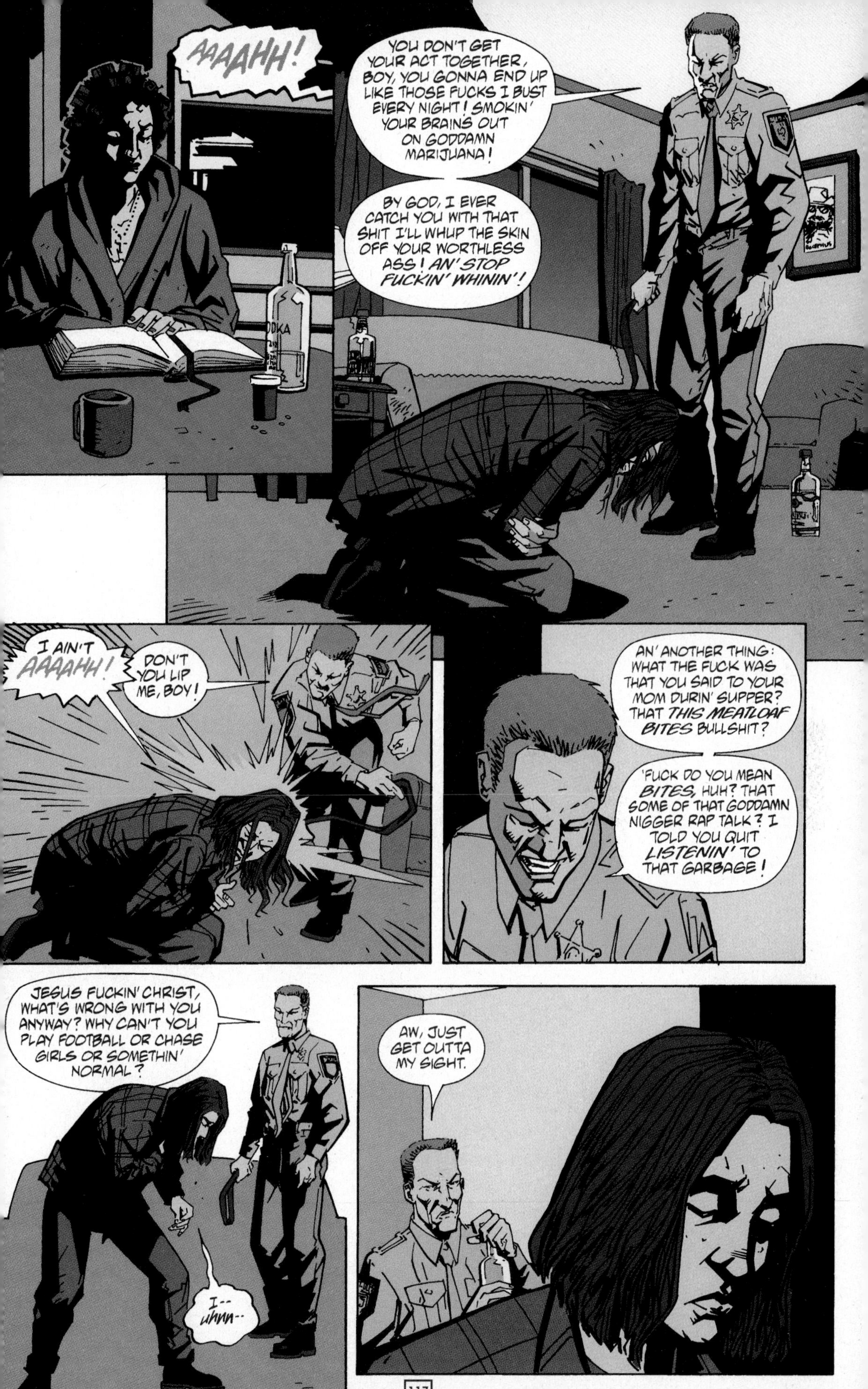
AAAAHH!
YOU DON'T GET YOUR ACT TOGETHER, BOY, YOU GONNA END UP LIKE THOSE FUCKS I BUST EVERY NIGHT! SMOKIN' YOUR BRAINS OUT ON GODDAMN MARIJUANA!
BY GOD, I EVER CATCH YOU WITH THAT SHIT I'LL WHUP THE SKIN OFF YOUR WORTHLESS ASS! AN' STOP FUCKIN' WHININ'!
I AIN'T AAAAHH!
DON'T YOU LIP ME, BOY!
AN' ANOTHER THING: WHAT THE FUCK WAS THAT YOU SAID TO YOUR MOM DURIN' SUPPER? THAT THIS MEATLOAF BITES BULLSHIT?
'FUCK DO YOU MEAN BITES, HUH? THAT SOME OF THAT GODDAMN NIGGER RAP TALK? I TOLD YOU QUIT LISTENIN' TO THAT GARBAGE!
JESUS FUCKIN' CHRIST, WHAT'S WRONG WITH YOU ANYWAY? WHY CAN'T YOU PLAY FOOTBALL OR CHASE GIRLS OR SOMETHIN' NORMAL?
I-- uhnn--
AW, JUST GET OUTTA MY SIGHT.

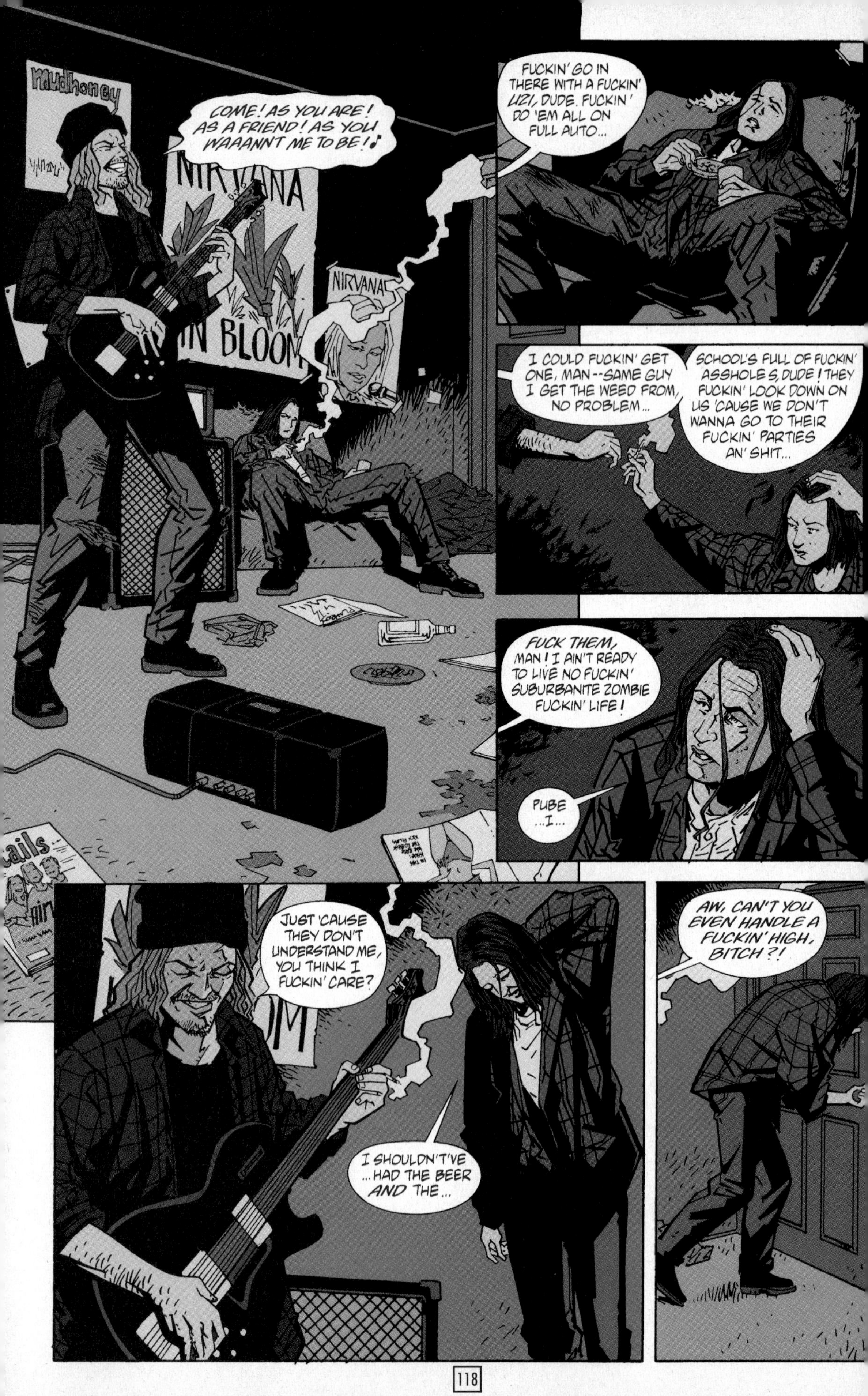
mudhoney
NIRVANA
IN BLOOM
NIRVANA
COME! AS YOU ARE! AS A FRIEND! AS YOU WAAANNT ME TO BE! ♪
FUCKIN' GO IN THERE WITH A FUCKIN' UZI, DUDE. FUCKIN' DO 'EM ALL ON FULL AUTO...
I COULD FUCKIN' GET ONE, MAN--SAME GUY I GET THE WEED FROM, NO PROBLEM...
SCHOOL'S FULL OF FUCKIN' ASSHOLES, DUDE! THEY FUCKIN' LOOK DOWN ON US 'CAUSE WE DON'T WANNA GO TO THEIR FUCKIN' PARTIES AN' SHIT...
FUCK THEM, MAN! I AIN'T READY TO LIVE NO FUCKIN' SUBURBANITE ZOMBIE FUCKIN' LIFE!
PUBE ...I...
JUST 'CAUSE THEY DON'T UNDERSTAND ME, YOU THINK I FUCKIN' CARE?
I SHOULDN'T'VE ...HAD THE BEER AND THE...
AW, CAN'T YOU EVEN HANDLE A FUCKIN' HIGH, BITCH?!

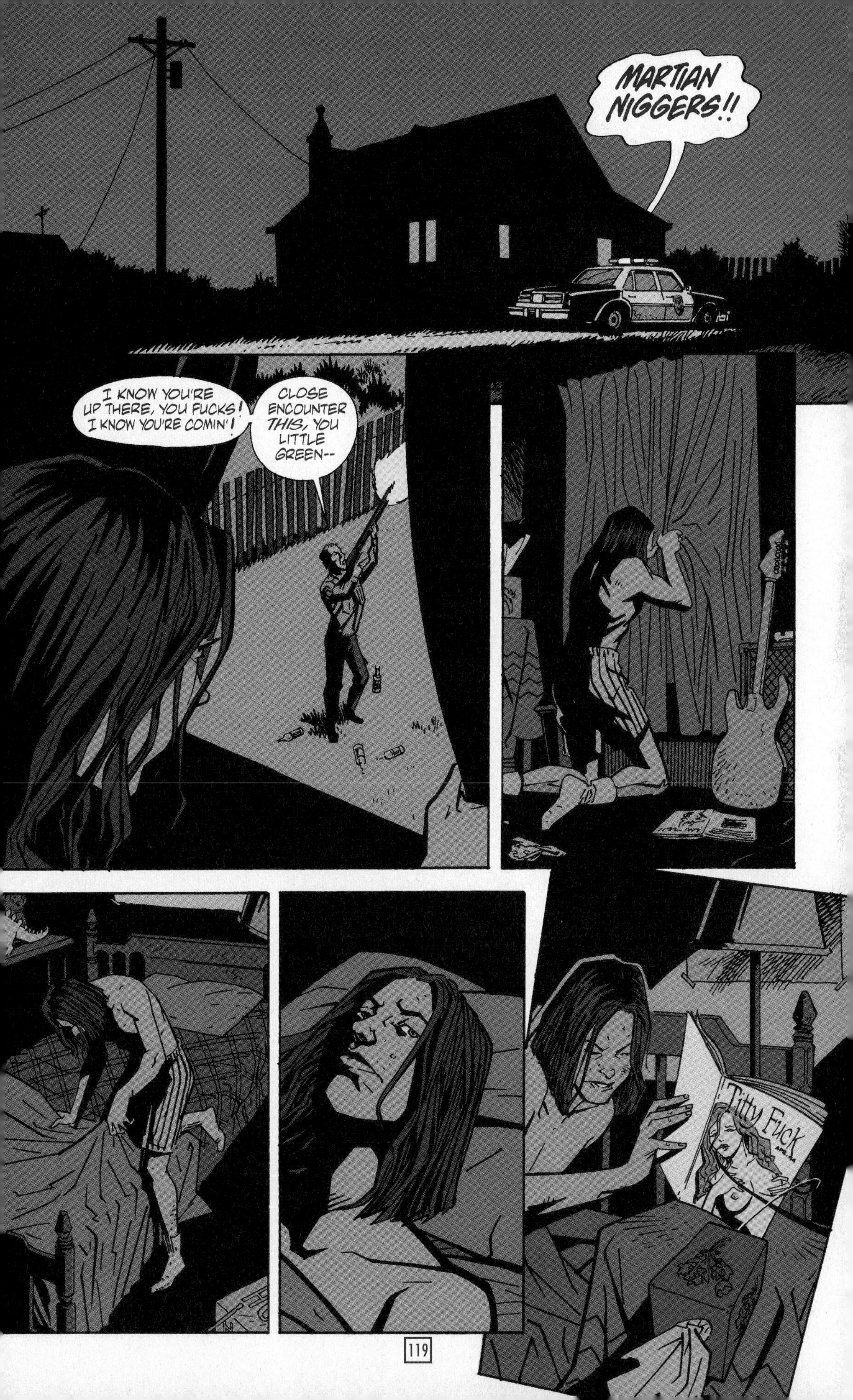
MARTIAN NIGGERS!!
I KNOW YOU'RE UP THERE, YOU FUCKS! I KNOW YOU'RE COMIN'!
CLOSE ENCOUNTER THIS, YOU LITTLE GREEN--
Titty Fuck

2. Rebel Rebel

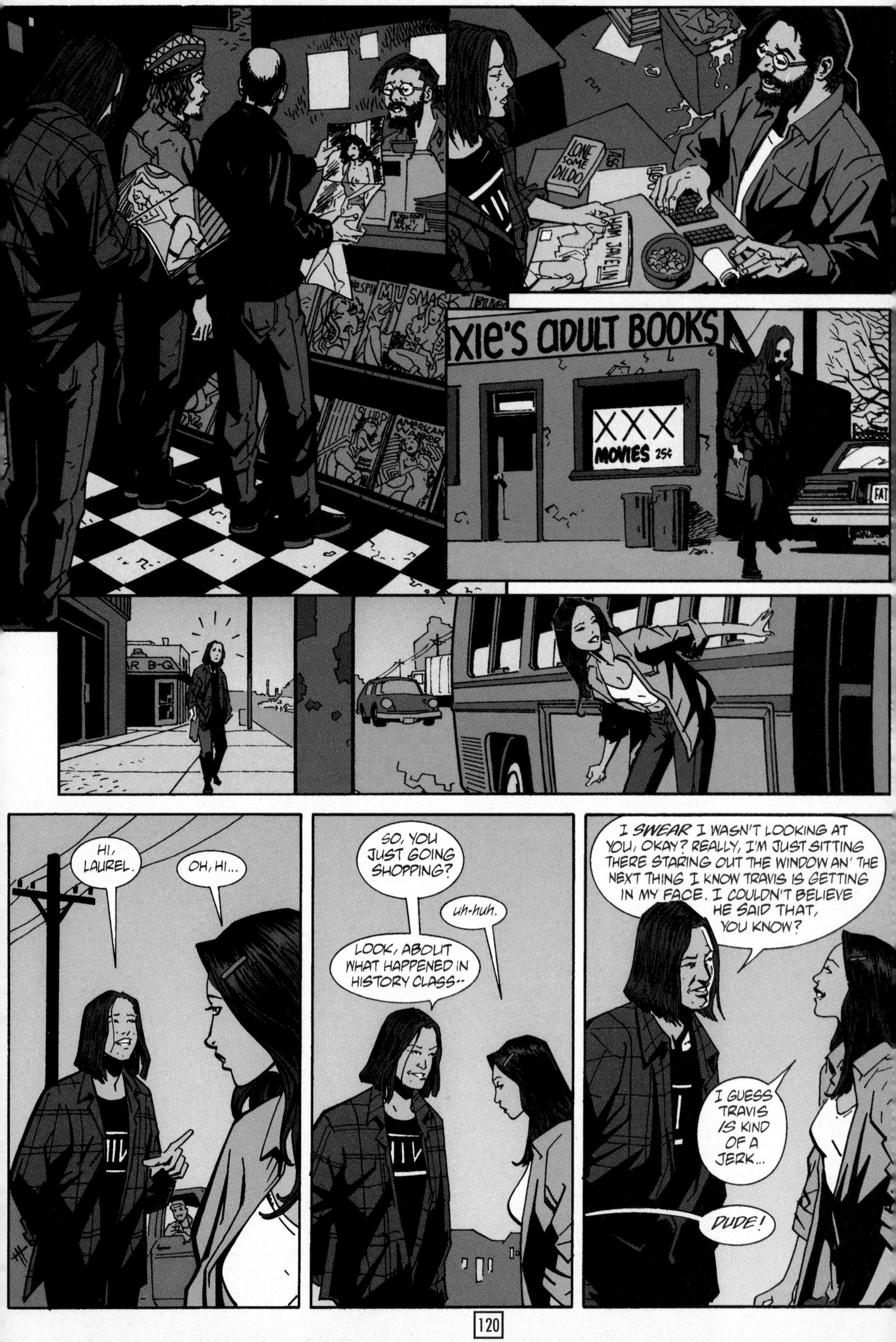

LONE SOME DILDO
HAM JAVELIN
XIE'S ADULT BOOKS
XXX
MOVIES 25¢
FAT
HI, LAUREL.
OH, HI...
SO, YOU JUST GOING SHOPPING?
uh-huh.
LOOK, ABOUT WHAT HAPPENED IN HISTORY CLASS--
I SWEAR I WASN'T LOOKING AT YOU, OKAY? REALLY, I'M JUST SITTING THERE STARING OUT THE WINDOW AN' THE NEXT THING I KNOW TRAVIS IS GETTING IN MY FACE. I COULDN'T BELIEVE HE SAID THAT, YOU KNOW?
I GUESS TRAVIS IS KIND OF A JERK...
DUDE!

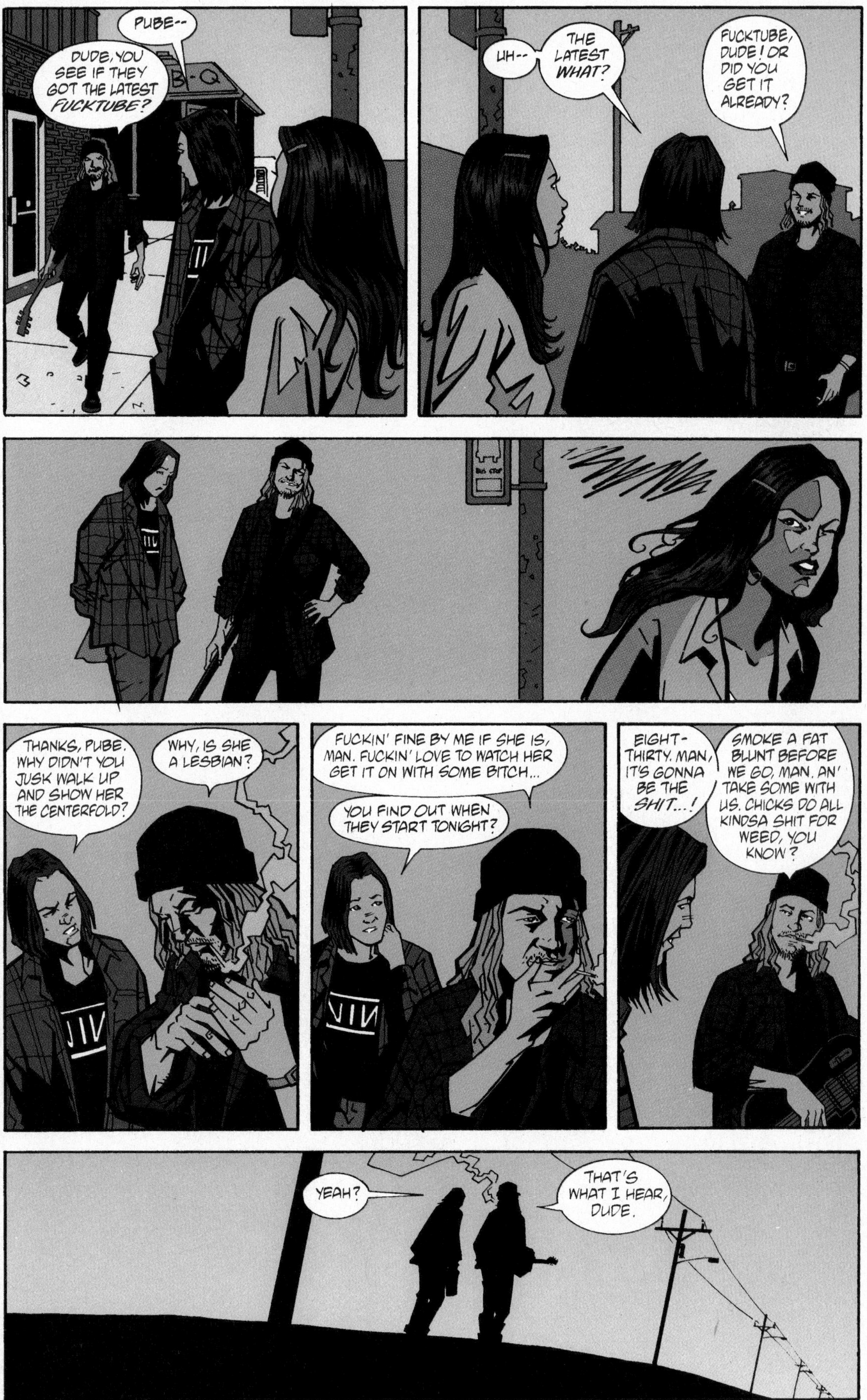
PUBE--
DUDE, YOU SEE IF THEY GOT THE LATEST FUCKTUBE?
UH--
THE LATEST WHAT?
FUCKTUBE, DUDE! OR DID YOU GET IT ALREADY?
BUS STOP
THANKS, PUBE. WHY DIDN'T YOU JUSK WALK UP AND SHOW HER THE CENTERFOLD?
WHY, IS SHE A LESBIAN?
FUCKIN' FINE BY ME IF SHE IS, MAN. FUCKIN' LOVE TO WATCH HER GET IT ON WITH SOME BITCH...
YOU FIND OUT WHEN THEY START TONIGHT?
EIGHT-THIRTY. MAN, IT'S GONNA BE THE SHIT...!
SMOKE A FAT BLUNT BEFORE WE GO, MAN. AN' TAKE SOME WITH US. CHICKS DO ALL KINDSA SHIT FOR WEED, YOU KNOW?
YEAH?
THAT'S WHAT I HEAR, DUDE.

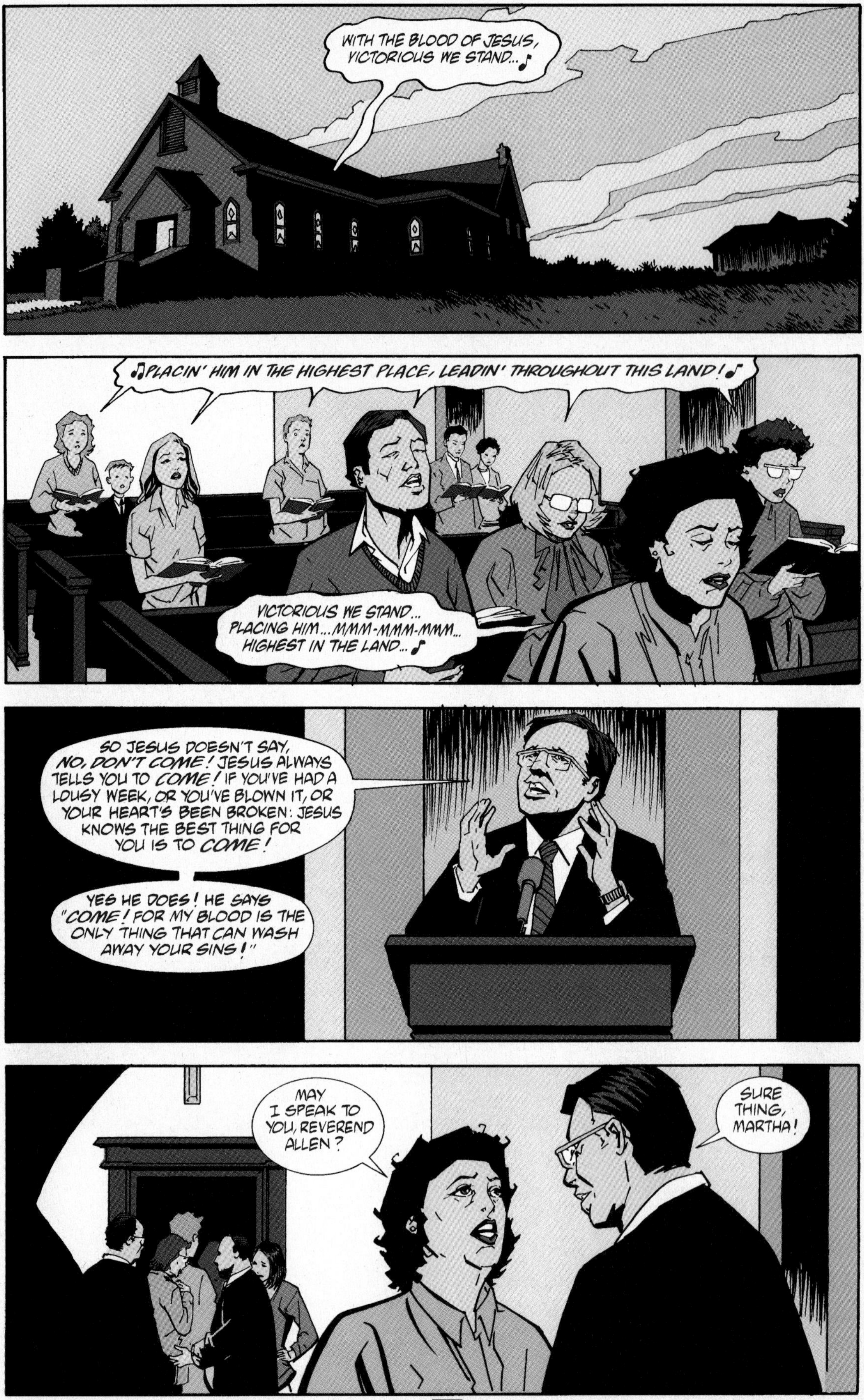
WITH THE BLOOD OF JESUS, VICTORIOUS WE STAND...♪
♫PLACIN' HIM IN THE HIGHEST PLACE, LEADIN' THROUGHOUT THIS LAND!♪
VICTORIOUS WE STAND... PLACING HIM...MMM-MMM-MMM... HIGHEST IN THE LAND...♪
SO JESUS DOESN'T SAY, *NO, DON'T COME!* JESUS ALWAYS TELLS YOU TO *COME!* IF YOU'VE HAD A LOUSY WEEK, OR YOU'VE BLOWN IT, OR YOUR HEART'S BEEN BROKEN: JESUS KNOWS THE BEST THING FOR YOU IS TO *COME!*
YES HE DOES! HE SAYS "*COME!* FOR MY BLOOD IS THE ONLY THING THAT CAN WASH AWAY YOUR SINS!"
MAY I SPEAK TO YOU, REVEREND ALLEN?
SURE THING, MARTHA!

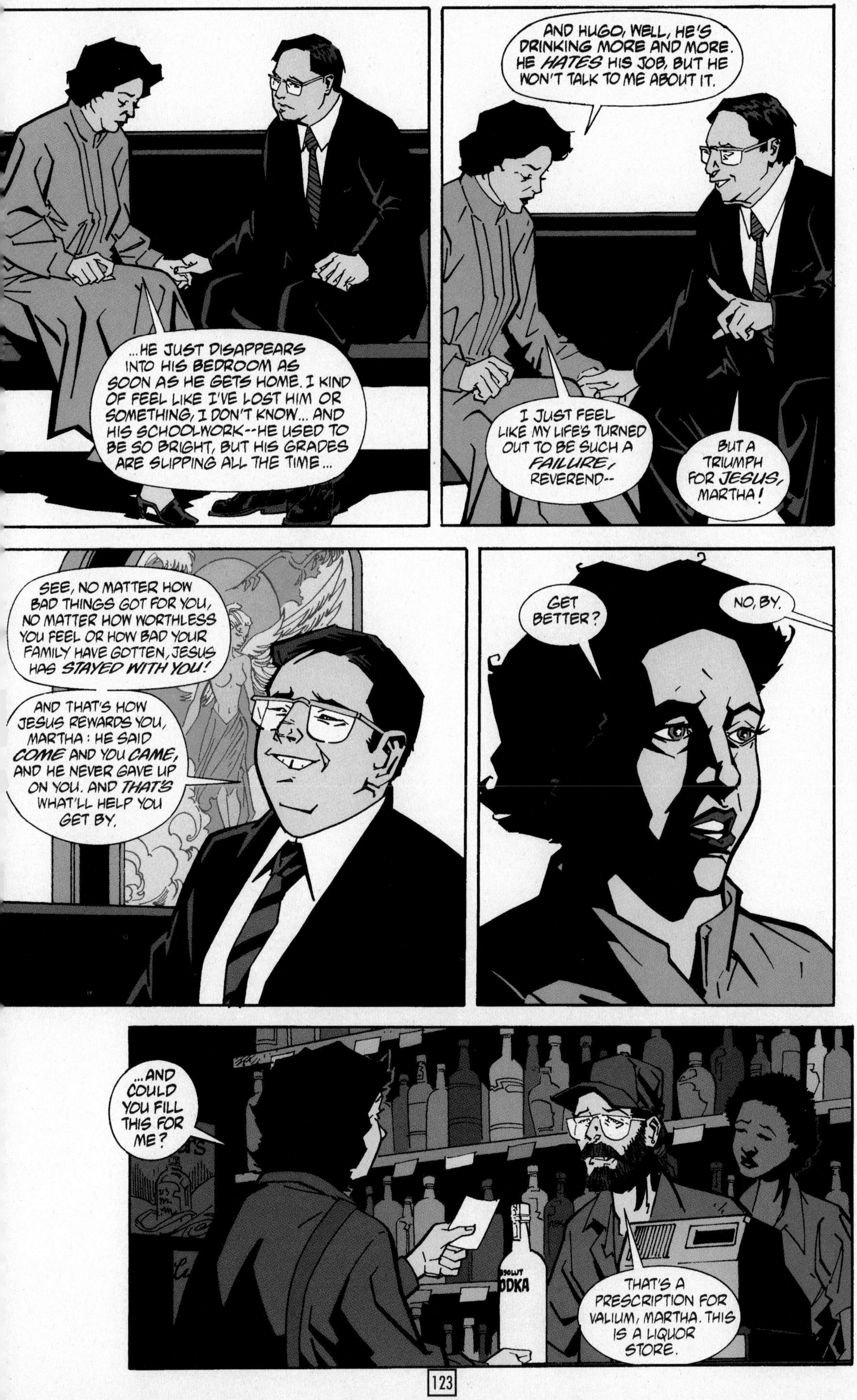
...HE JUST DISAPPEARS INTO HIS BEDROOM AS SOON AS HE GETS HOME. I KIND OF FEEL LIKE I'VE LOST HIM OR SOMETHING, I DON'T KNOW... AND HIS SCHOOLWORK--HE USED TO BE SO BRIGHT, BUT HIS GRADES ARE SLIPPING ALL THE TIME...
AND HUGO, WELL, HE'S DRINKING MORE AND MORE. HE HATES HIS JOB, BUT HE WON'T TALK TO ME ABOUT IT.
I JUST FEEL LIKE MY LIFE'S TURNED OUT TO BE SUCH A FAILURE, REVEREND--
BUT A TRIUMPH FOR JESUS, MARTHA!
SEE, NO MATTER HOW BAD THINGS GOT FOR YOU, NO MATTER HOW WORTHLESS YOU FEEL OR HOW BAD YOUR FAMILY HAVE GOTTEN, JESUS HAS STAYED WITH YOU!
AND THAT'S HOW JESUS REWARDS YOU, MARTHA: HE SAID COME AND YOU CAME, AND HE NEVER GAVE UP ON YOU. AND THAT'S WHAT'LL HELP YOU GET BY.
GET BETTER?
NO, BY.
...AND COULD YOU FILL THIS FOR ME?
ODKA
THAT'S A PRESCRIPTION FOR VALIUM, MARTHA. THIS IS A LIQUOR STORE.

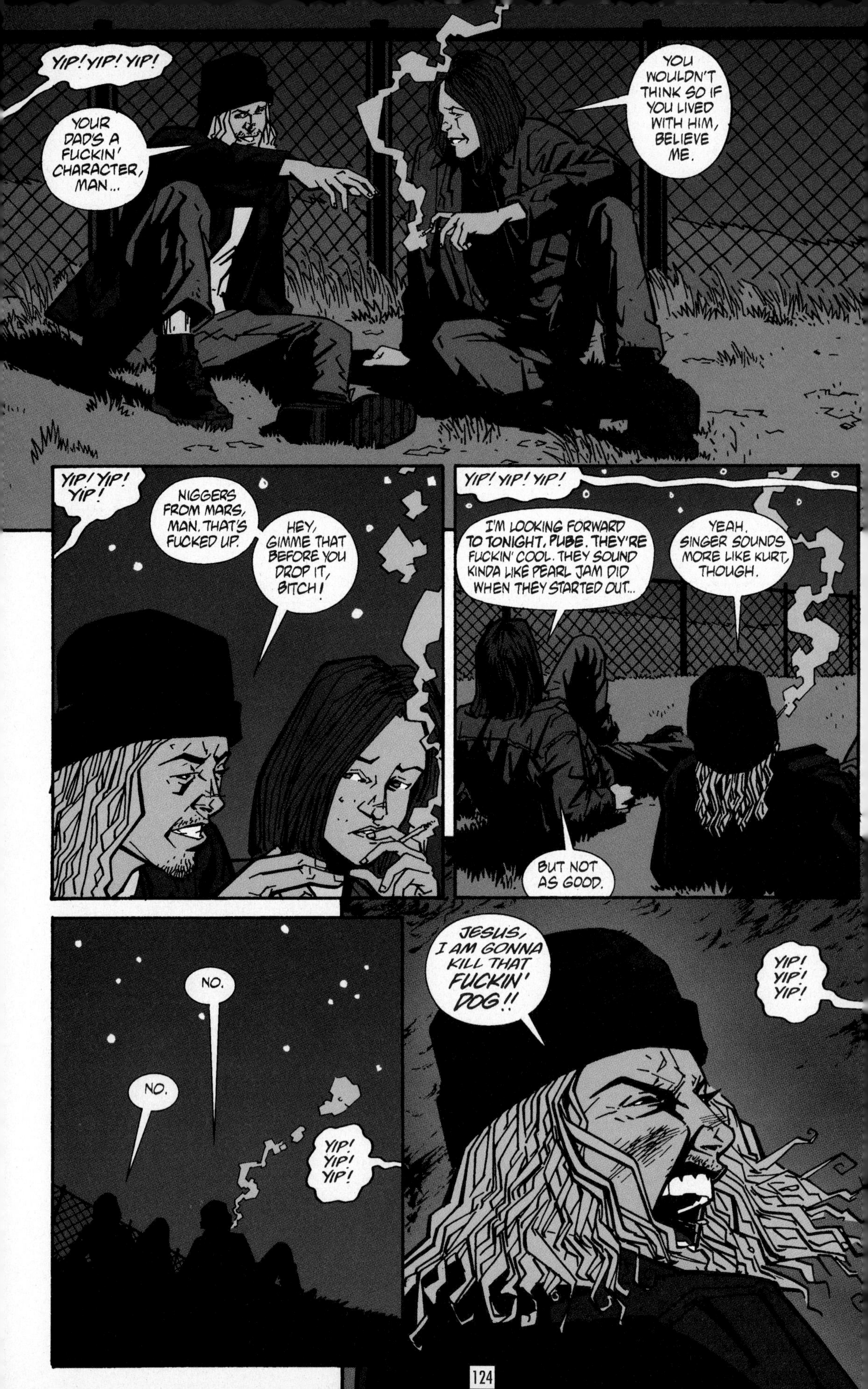
YIP! YIP! YIP!
YOUR DAD'S A FUCKIN' CHARACTER, MAN...
YOU WOULDN'T THINK SO IF YOU LIVED WITH HIM, BELIEVE ME.
YIP! YIP! YIP!
NIGGERS FROM MARS, MAN. THAT'S FUCKED UP.
HEY, GIMME THAT BEFORE YOU DROP IT, BITCH!
YIP! YIP! YIP!
I'M LOOKING FORWARD TO TONIGHT, PUBE. THEY'RE FUCKIN' COOL. THEY SOUND KINDA LIKE PEARL JAM DID WHEN THEY STARTED OUT...
YEAH. SINGER SOUNDS MORE LIKE KURT, THOUGH.
BUT NOT AS GOOD.
NO.
NO.
YIP! YIP! YIP!
JESUS, I AM GONNA KILL THAT FUCKIN' DOG!!
YIP! YIP! YIP!

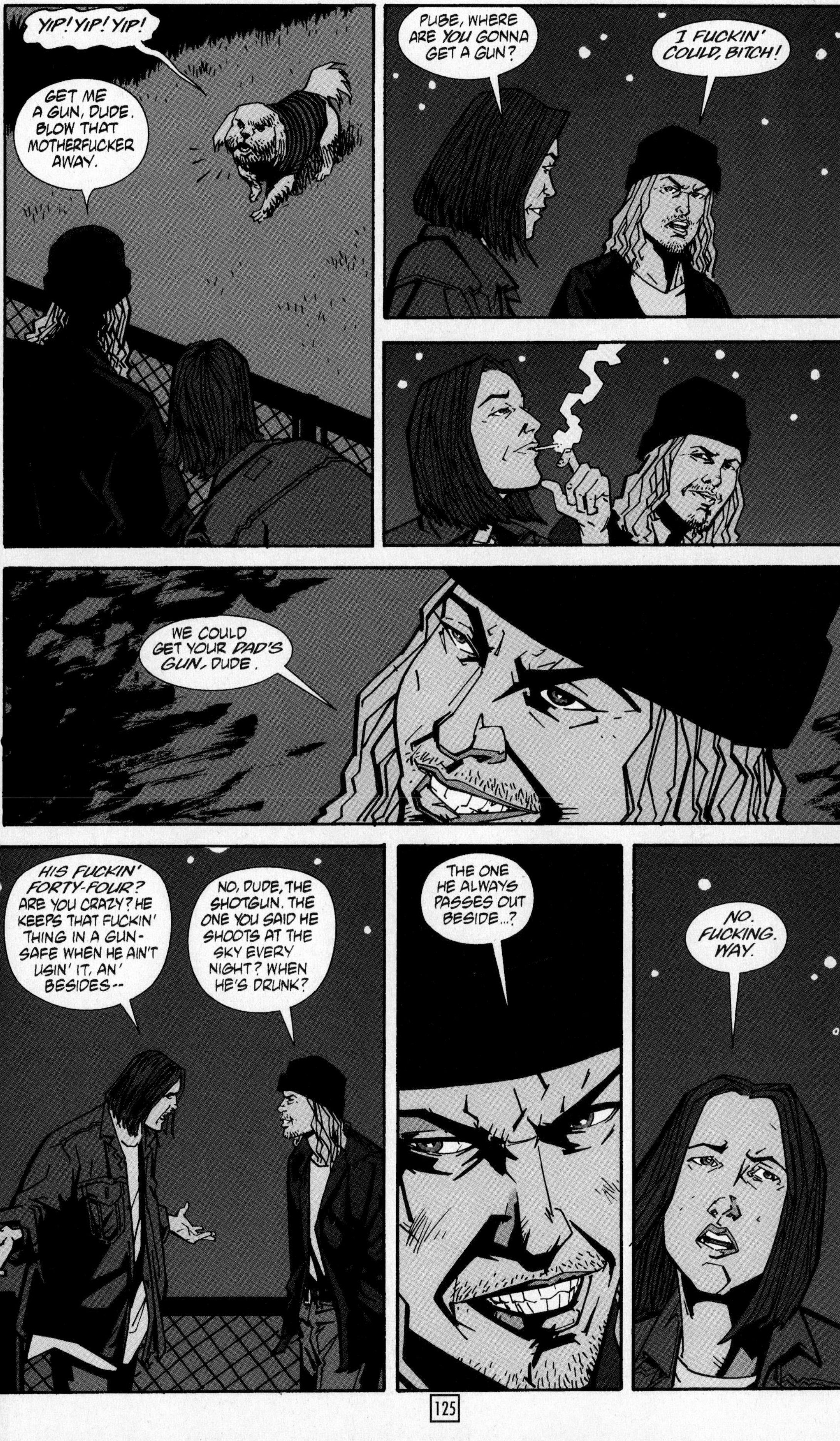
YIP! YIP! YIP!
GET ME A GUN, DUDE. BLOW THAT MOTHERFUCKER AWAY.
PUBE, WHERE ARE YOU GONNA GET A GUN?
I FUCKIN' COULD, BITCH!
WE COULD GET YOUR DAD'S GUN, DUDE.
HIS FUCKIN' FORTY-FOUR? ARE YOU CRAZY? HE KEEPS THAT FUCKIN' THING IN A GUN-SAFE WHEN HE AIN'T USIN' IT, AN' BESIDES--
NO, DUDE, THE SHOTGUN. THE ONE YOU SAID HE SHOOTS AT THE SKY EVERY NIGHT? WHEN HE'S DRUNK?
THE ONE HE ALWAYS PASSES OUT BESIDE...?
NO. FUCKING. WAY.

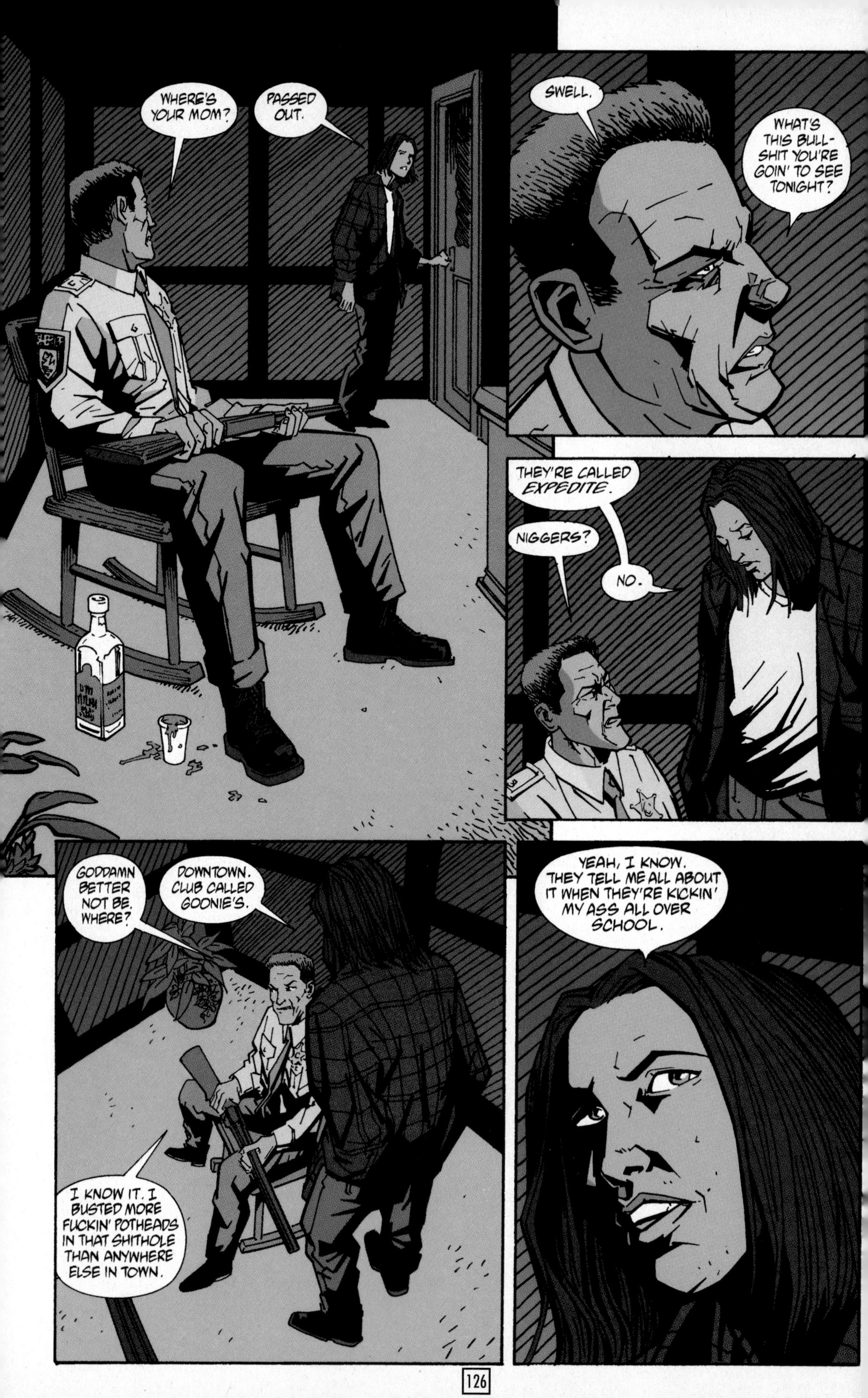
WHERE'S YOUR MOM?
PASSED OUT.
SWELL.
WHAT'S THIS BULL-SHIT YOU'RE GOIN' TO SEE TONIGHT?
THEY'RE CALLED *EXPEDITE*.
NIGGERS?
NO.
GODDAMN BETTER NOT BE. WHERE?
DOWNTOWN. CLUB CALLED GOONIE'S.
I KNOW IT. I BUSTED MORE FUCKIN' POTHEADS IN THAT SHITHOLE THAN ANYWHERE ELSE IN TOWN.
YEAH, I KNOW. THEY TELL ME ALL ABOUT IT WHEN THEY'RE KICKIN' MY ASS ALL OVER SCHOOL.

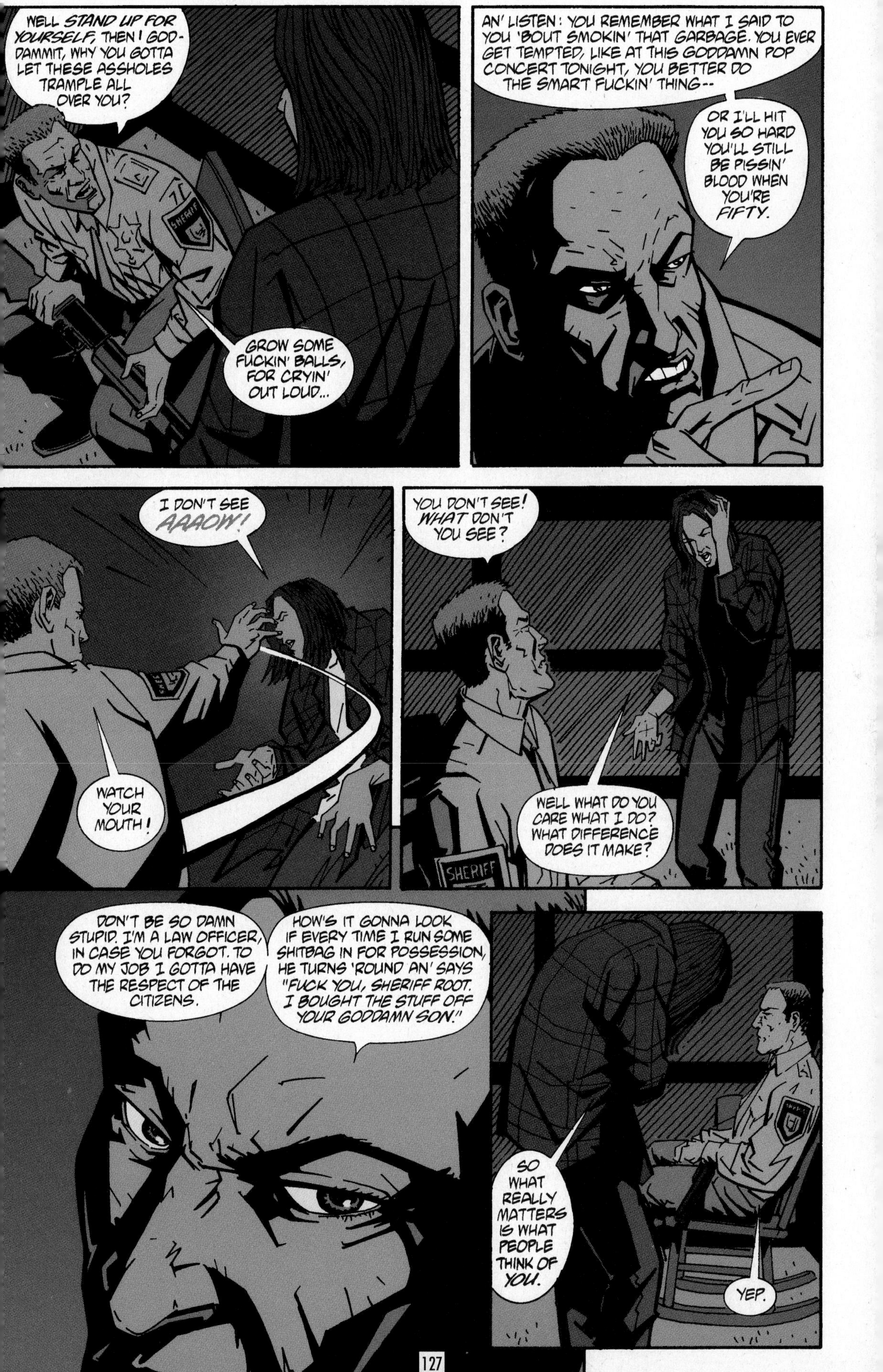
WELL STAND UP FOR YOURSELF, THEN! GOD-DAMMIT, WHY YOU GOTTA LET THESE ASSHOLES TRAMPLE ALL OVER YOU?
GROW SOME FUCKIN' BALLS, FOR CRYIN' OUT LOUD...
AN' LISTEN: YOU REMEMBER WHAT I SAID TO YOU 'BOUT SMOKIN' THAT GARBAGE. YOU EVER GET TEMPTED, LIKE AT THIS GODDAMN POP CONCERT TONIGHT, YOU BETTER DO THE SMART FUCKIN' THING--
OR I'LL HIT YOU SO HARD YOU'LL STILL BE PISSIN' BLOOD WHEN YOU'RE FIFTY.
I DON'T SEE AAAOW!
WATCH YOUR MOUTH!
YOU DON'T SEE! WHAT DON'T YOU SEE?
WELL WHAT DO YOU CARE WHAT I DO? WHAT DIFFERENCE DOES IT MAKE?
SHERIFF
DON'T BE SO DAMN STUPID. I'M A LAW OFFICER, IN CASE YOU FORGOT. TO DO MY JOB I GOTTA HAVE THE RESPECT OF THE CITIZENS.
HOW'S IT GONNA LOOK IF EVERY TIME I RUN SOME SHITBAG IN FOR POSSESSION, HE TURNS 'ROUND AN' SAYS "FUCK YOU, SHERIFF ROOT. I BOUGHT THE STUFF OFF YOUR GODDAMN SON."
SO WHAT REALLY MATTERS IS WHAT PEOPLE THINK OF YOU.
YEP.

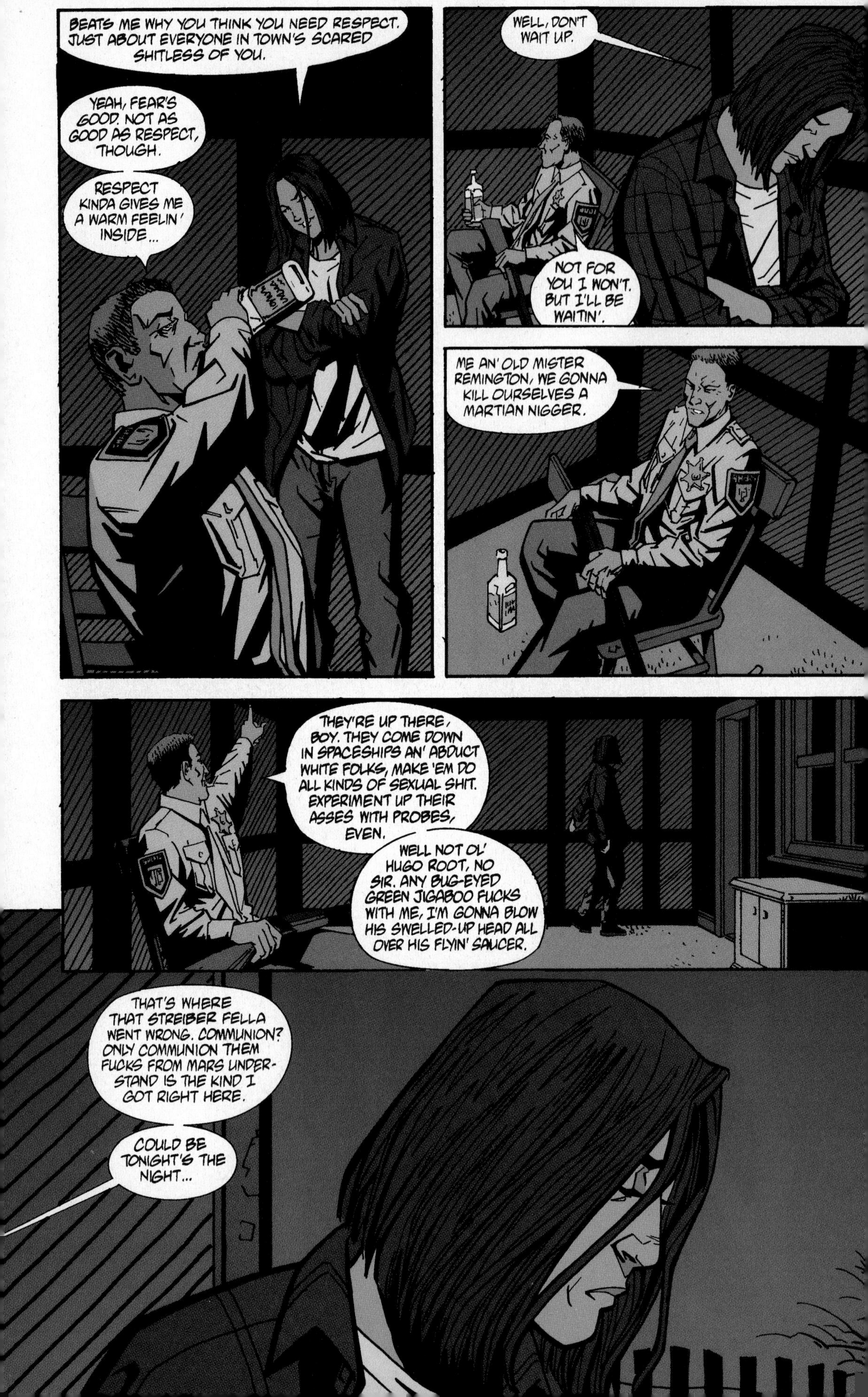
BEATS ME WHY YOU THINK YOU NEED RESPECT. JUST ABOUT EVERYONE IN TOWN'S SCARED SHITLESS OF YOU.
YEAH, FEAR'S GOOD. NOT AS GOOD AS RESPECT, THOUGH.
RESPECT KINDA GIVES ME A WARM FEELIN' INSIDE...
WELL, DON'T WAIT UP.
NOT FOR YOU I WON'T. BUT I'LL BE WAITIN'.
ME AN' OLD MISTER REMINGTON, WE GONNA KILL OURSELVES A MARTIAN NIGGER.
THEY'RE UP THERE, BOY. THEY COME DOWN IN SPACESHIPS AN' ABDUCT WHITE FOLKS, MAKE 'EM DO ALL KINDS OF SEXUAL SHIT. EXPERIMENT UP THEIR ASSES WITH PROBES, EVEN.
WELL NOT OL' HUGO ROOT, NO SIR. ANY BUG-EYED GREEN JIGABOO FUCKS WITH ME, I'M GONNA BLOW HIS SWELLED-UP HEAD ALL OVER HIS FLYIN' SAUCER.
THAT'S WHERE THAT STREIBER FELLA WENT WRONG. COMMUNION? ONLY COMMUNION THEM FUCKS FROM MARS UNDER-STAND IS THE KIND I GOT RIGHT HERE.
COULD BE TONIGHT'S THE NIGHT...

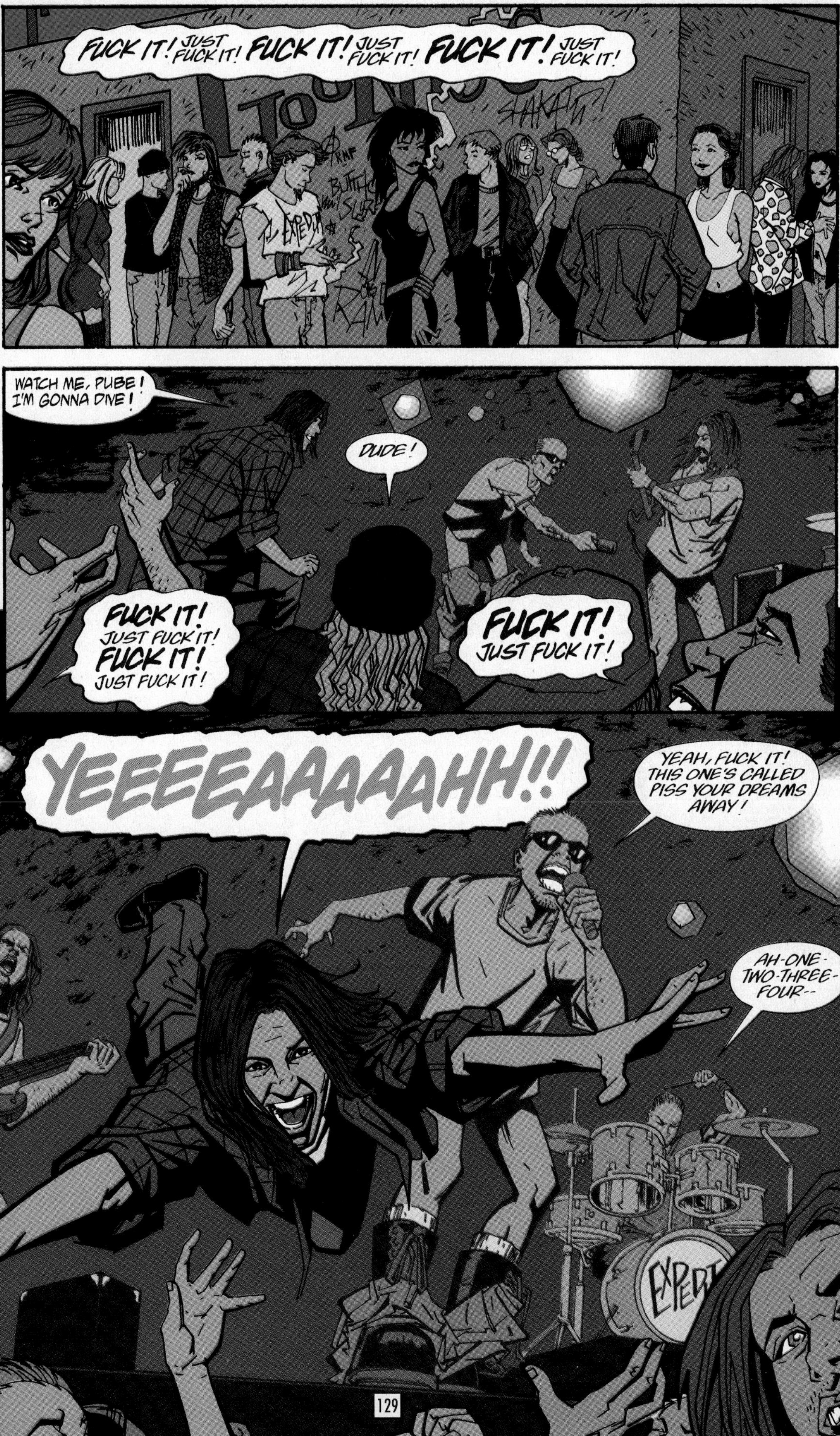
FUCK IT! JUST FUCK IT! FUCK IT! JUST FUCK IT! FUCK IT! JUST FUCK IT!
WATCH ME, PUBE! I'M GONNA DIVE!
DUDE!
FUCK IT! JUST FUCK IT! FUCK IT! JUST FUCK IT!
FUCK IT! JUST FUCK IT!
YEEEEAAAAAHH!!
YEAH, FUCK IT! THIS ONE'S CALLED PISS YOUR DREAMS AWAY!
AH-ONE-TWO-THREE-FOUR--

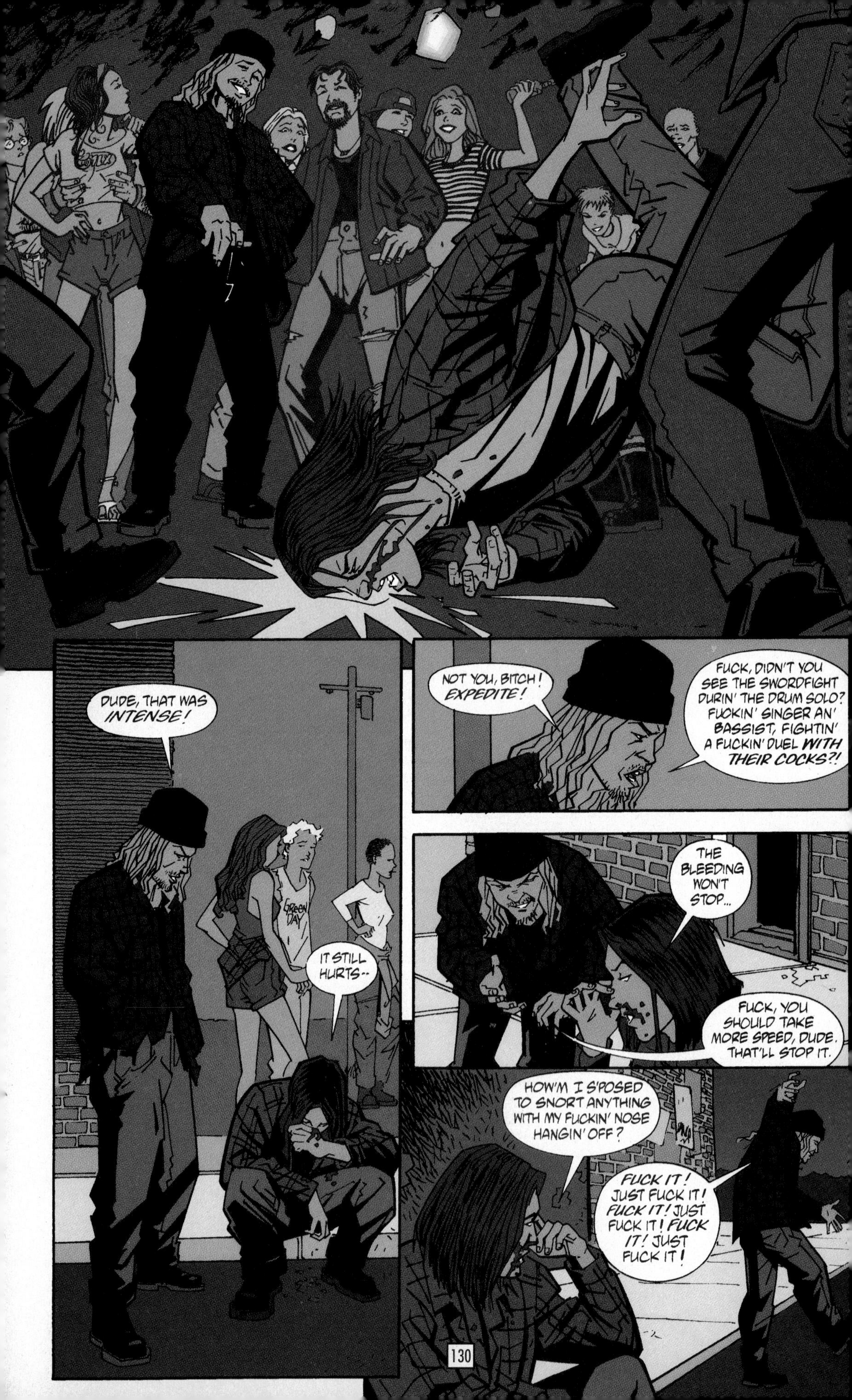
DUDE, THAT WAS INTENSE!
IT STILL HURTS--
NOT YOU, BITCH! EXPEDITE!
FUCK, DIDN'T YOU SEE THE SWORDFIGHT DURIN' THE DRUM SOLO? FUCKIN' SINGER AN' BASSIST, FIGHTIN' A FUCKIN' DUEL WITH THEIR COCKS?!
THE BLEEDING WON'T STOP...
FUCK, YOU SHOULD TAKE MORE SPEED, DUDE. THAT'LL STOP IT.
HOW'M I S'POSED TO SNORT ANYTHING WITH MY FUCKIN' NOSE HANGIN' OFF?
FUCK IT! JUST FUCK IT! FUCK IT! JUST FUCK IT! FUCK IT! JUST FUCK IT!

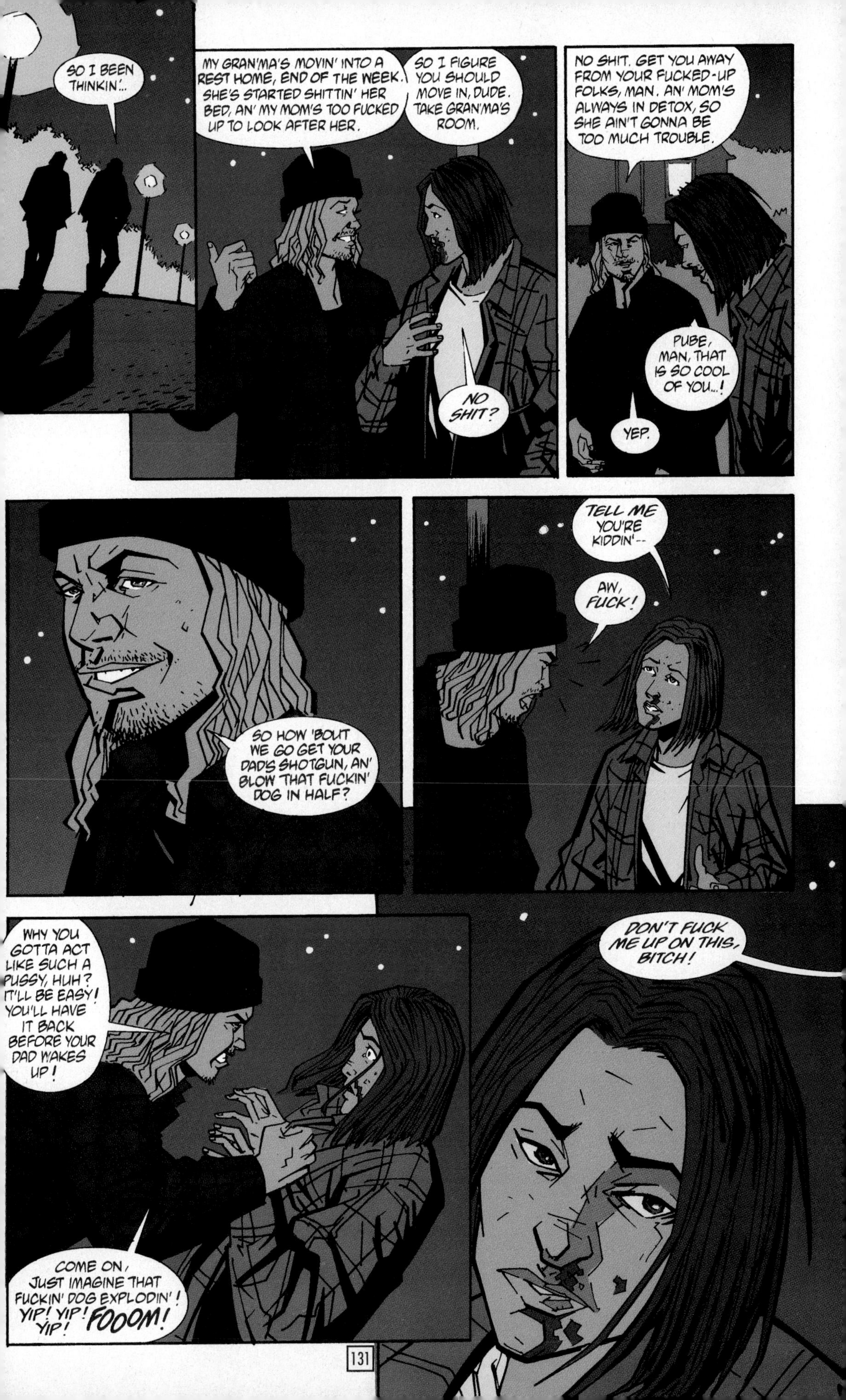
SO I BEEN THINKIN'...
MY GRAN'MA'S MOVIN' INTO A REST HOME, END OF THE WEEK. SHE'S STARTED SHITTIN' HER BED, AN' MY MOM'S TOO FUCKED UP TO LOOK AFTER HER.
SO I FIGURE YOU SHOULD MOVE IN, DUDE. TAKE GRAN'MA'S ROOM.
NO SHIT?
NO SHIT. GET YOU AWAY FROM YOUR FUCKED-UP FOLKS, MAN. AN' MOM'S ALWAYS IN DETOX, SO SHE AIN'T GONNA BE TOO MUCH TROUBLE.
PUBE, MAN, THAT IS SO COOL OF YOU...!
YEP.
SO HOW 'BOUT WE GO GET YOUR DAD'S SHOTGUN, AN' BLOW THAT FUCKIN' DOG IN HALF?
TELL ME YOU'RE KIDDIN'--
AW, FUCK!
WHY YOU GOTTA ACT LIKE SUCH A PUSSY, HUH? IT'LL BE EASY! YOU'LL HAVE IT BACK BEFORE YOUR DAD WAKES UP!
COME ON, JUST IMAGINE THAT FUCKIN' DOG EXPLODIN'! YIP! YIP! YIP! FOOOM!
DON'T FUCK ME UP ON THIS, BITCH!

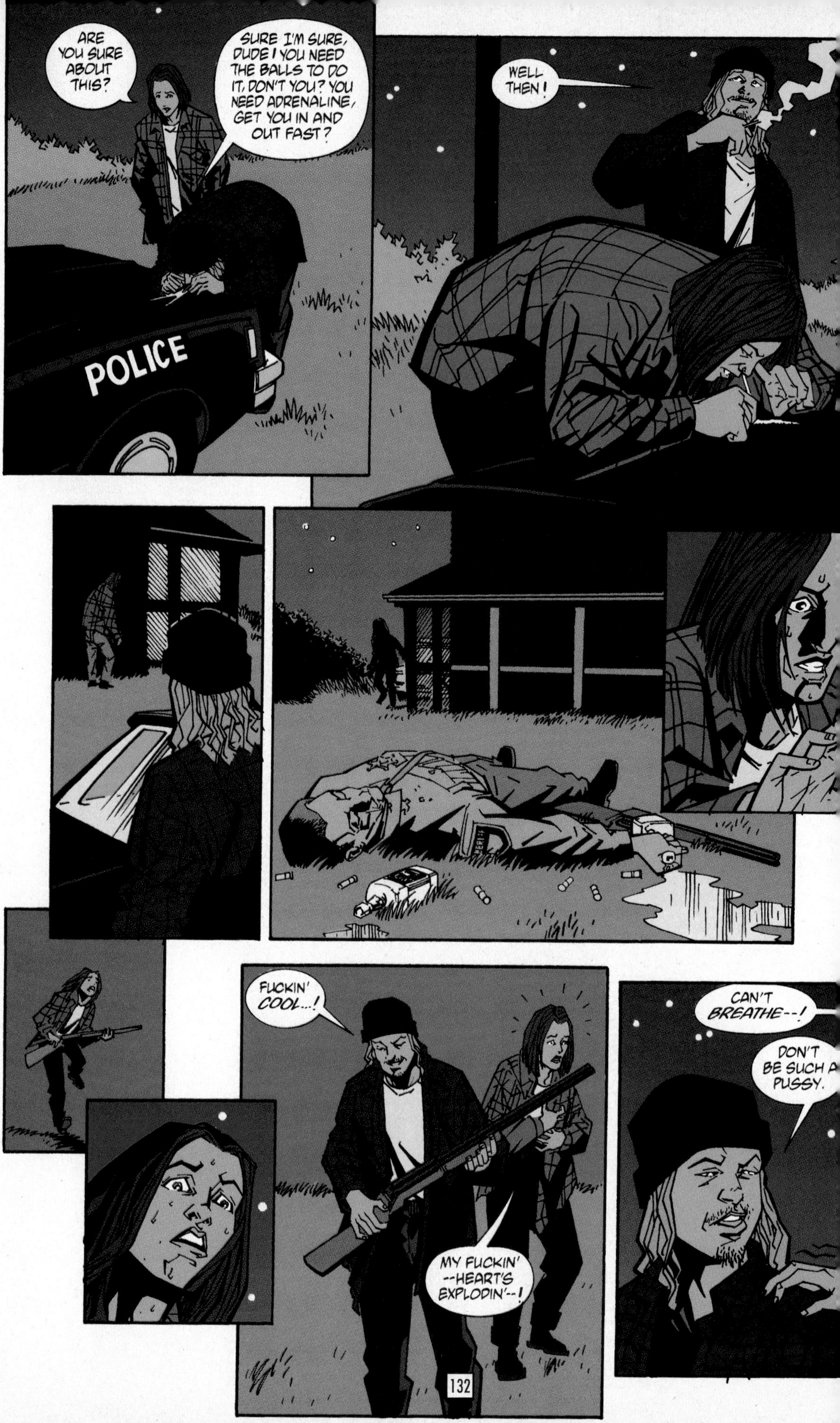
ARE YOU SURE ABOUT THIS?
SURE I'M SURE, DUDE! YOU NEED THE BALLS TO DO IT, DON'T YOU? YOU NEED ADRENALINE, GET YOU IN AND OUT FAST?
POLICE
WELL THEN!
FUCKIN' COOL...!
MY FUCKIN' --HEART'S EXPLODIN'--!
CAN'T BREATHE--!
DON'T BE SUCH A PUSSY.

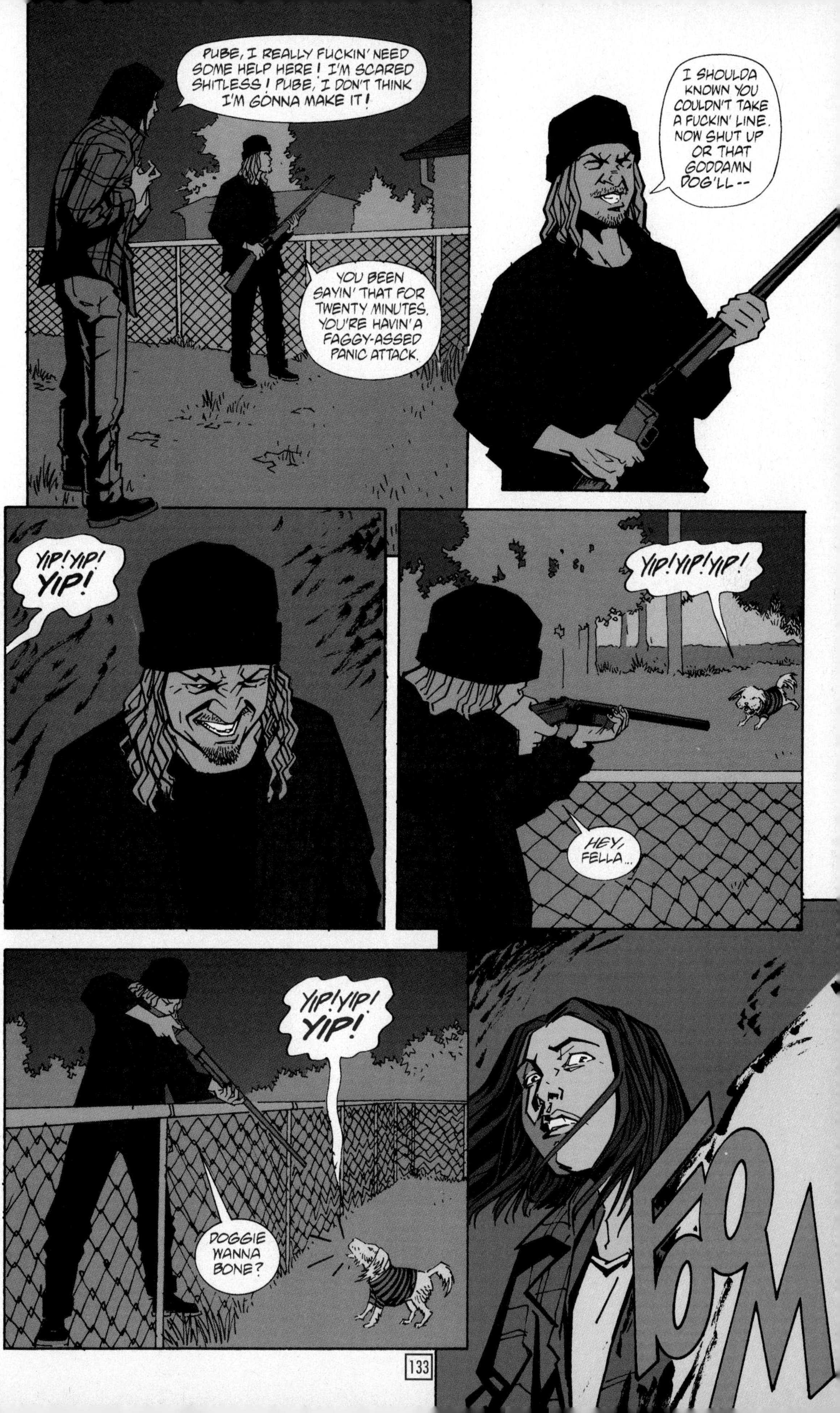
PUBE, I REALLY FUCKIN' NEED SOME HELP HERE! I'M SCARED SHITLESS! PUBE, I DON'T THINK I'M GONNA MAKE IT!
YOU BEEN SAYIN' THAT FOR TWENTY MINUTES. YOU'RE HAVIN' A FAGGY-ASSED PANIC ATTACK.
I SHOULDA KNOWN YOU COULDN'T TAKE A FUCKIN' LINE. NOW SHUT UP OR THAT GODDAMN DOG'LL --
YIP! YIP! YIP!
YIP! YIP! YIP!
HEY, FELLA...
YIP! YIP! YIP!
DOGGIE WANNA BONE?
TOOM

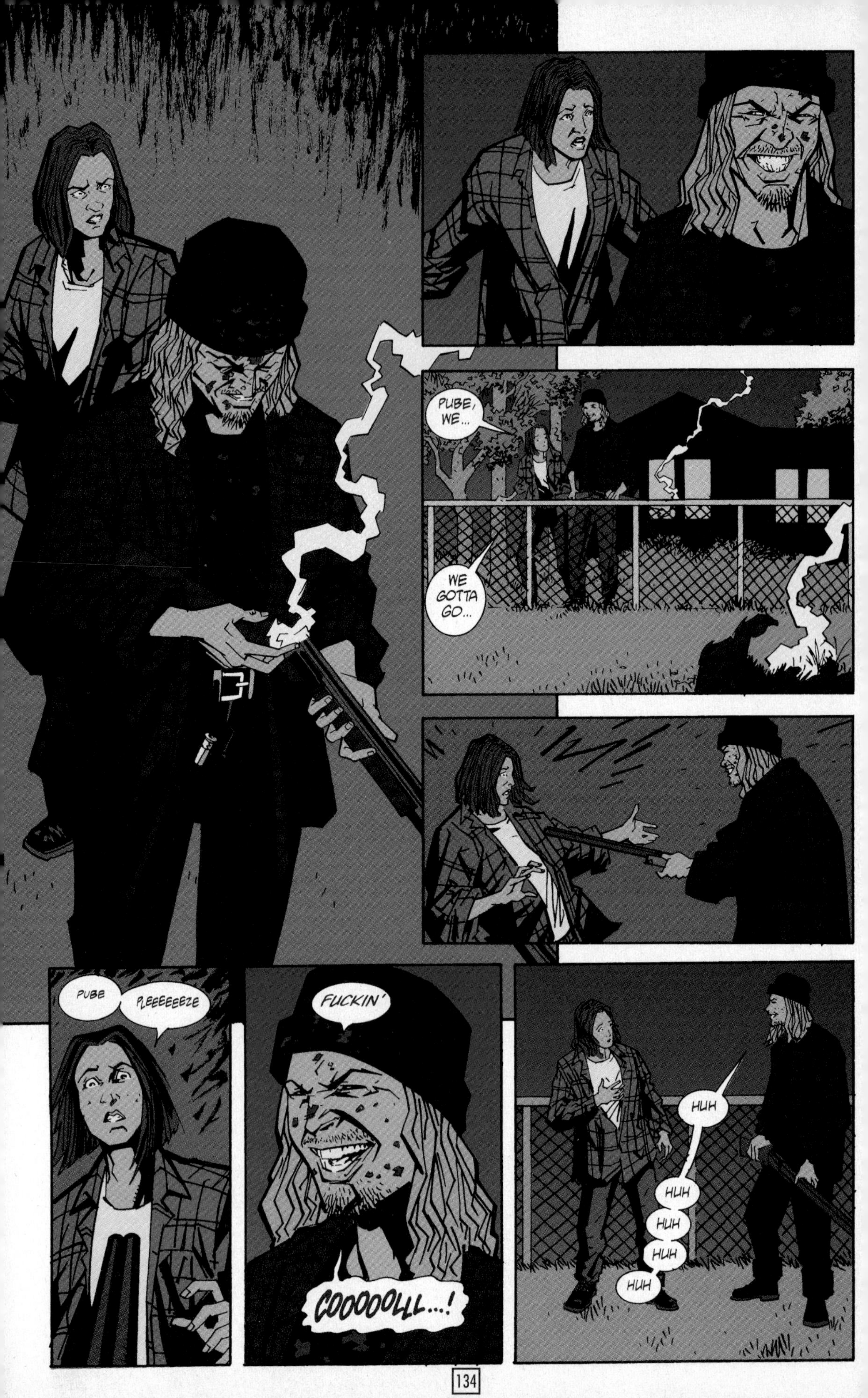
PUBE, WE...
WE GOTTA GO...
PUBE
PLEEEEEEZE
FUCKIN'
COOOOOLLL...!
HUH
HUH
HUH
HUH
HUH

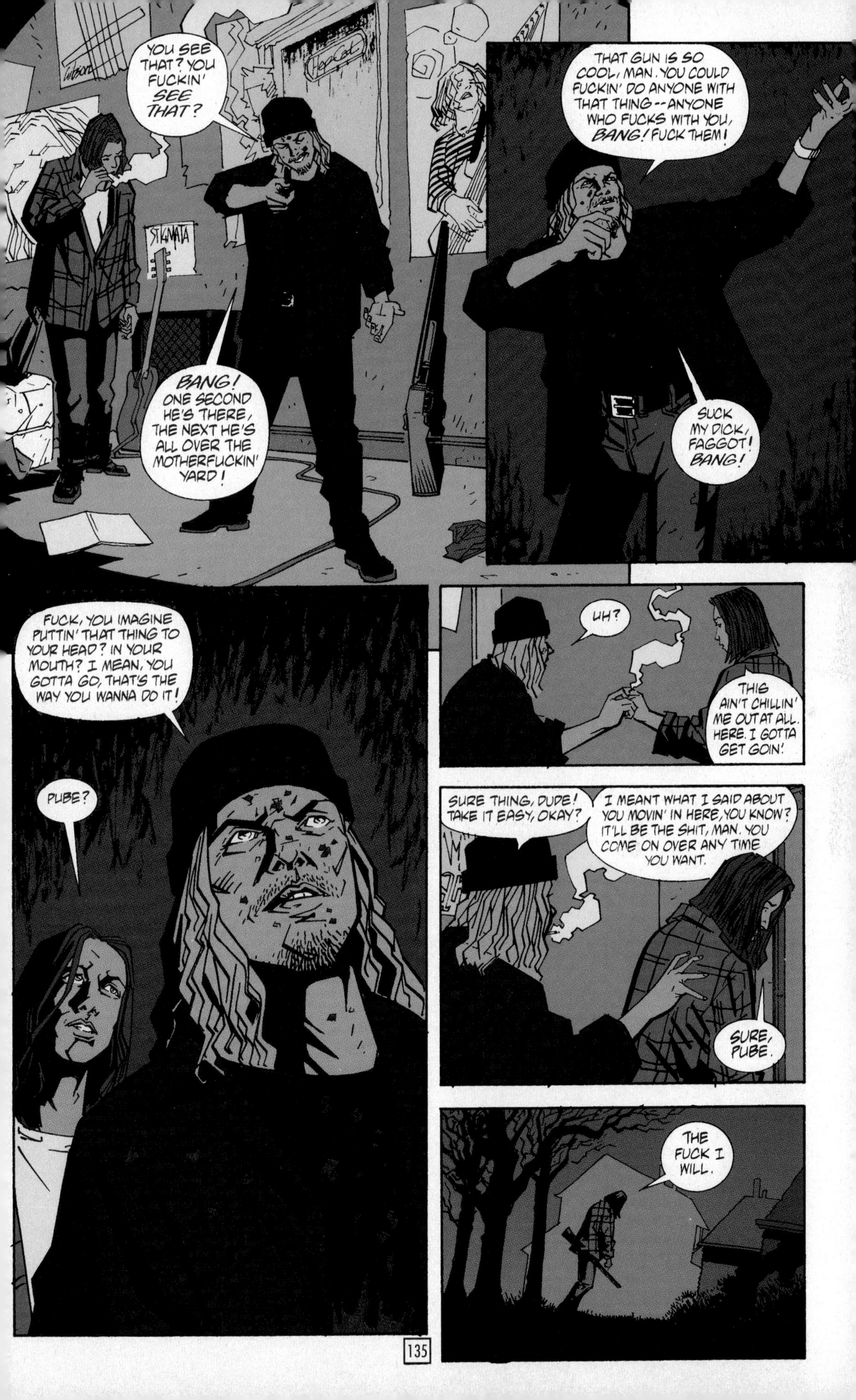

GIBSON
YOU SEE THAT? YOU FUCKIN' SEE THAT?
HEP CAT
STIGMATA
BANG! ONE SECOND HE'S THERE, THE NEXT HE'S ALL OVER THE MOTHERFUCKIN' YARD!
THAT GUN IS SO COOL, MAN. YOU COULD FUCKIN' DO ANYONE WITH THAT THING--ANYONE WHO FUCKS WITH YOU, BANG! FUCK THEM!
SUCK MY DICK, FAGGOT! BANG!
FUCK, YOU IMAGINE PUTTIN' THAT THING TO YOUR HEAD? IN YOUR MOUTH? I MEAN, YOU GOTTA GO, THAT'S THE WAY YOU WANNA DO IT!
PUBE?
UH?
THIS AIN'T CHILLIN' ME OUT AT ALL. HERE. I GOTTA GET GOIN'.
SURE THING, DUDE! TAKE IT EASY, OKAY?
I MEANT WHAT I SAID ABOUT YOU MOVIN' IN HERE, YOU KNOW? IT'LL BE THE SHIT, MAN. YOU COME ON OVER ANY TIME YOU WANT.
SURE, PUBE.
THE FUCK I WILL.

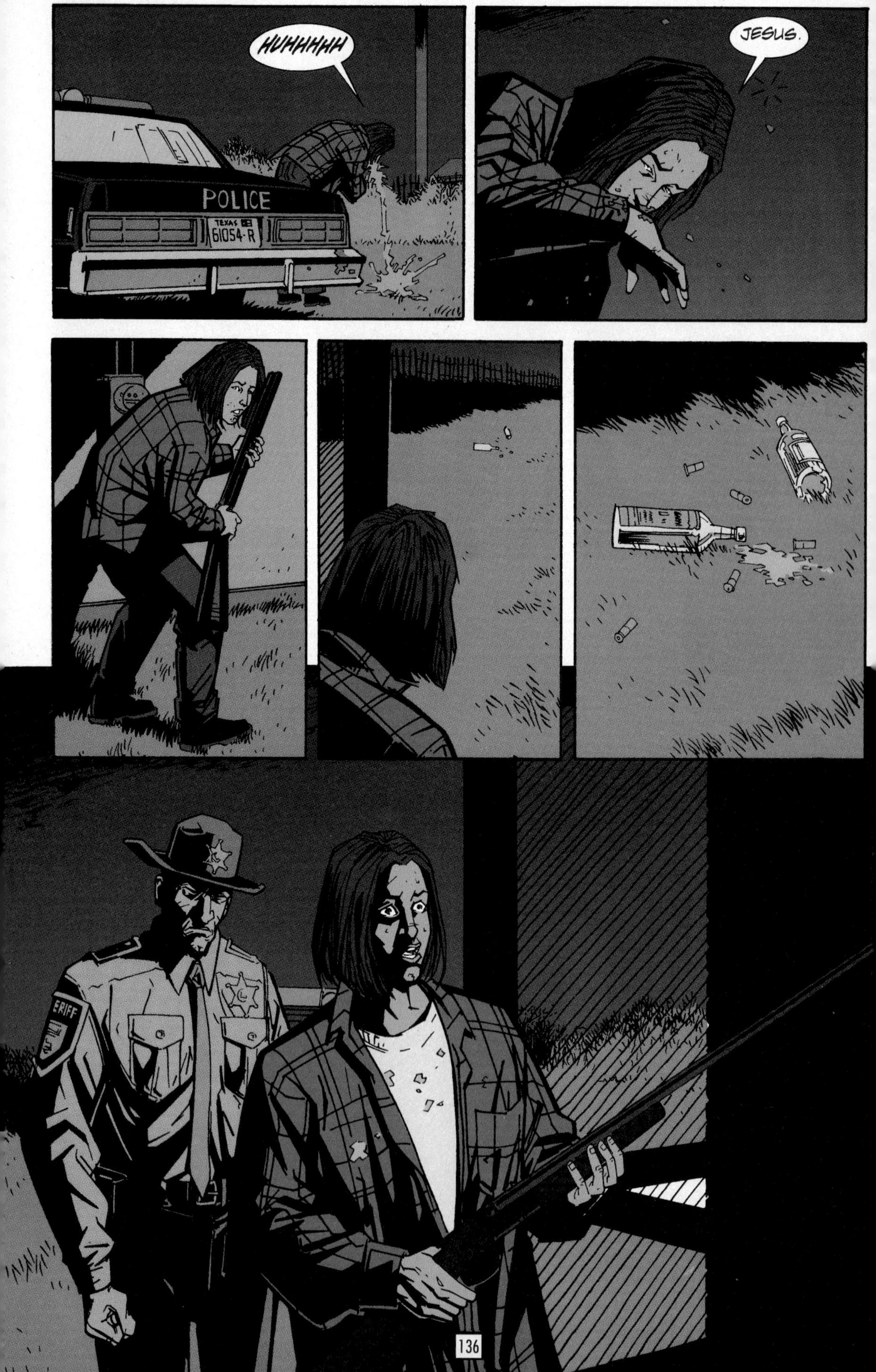
HUHHHHH
POLICE
TEXAS
61054-R
JESUS.
ERIFF

3. New Horizons

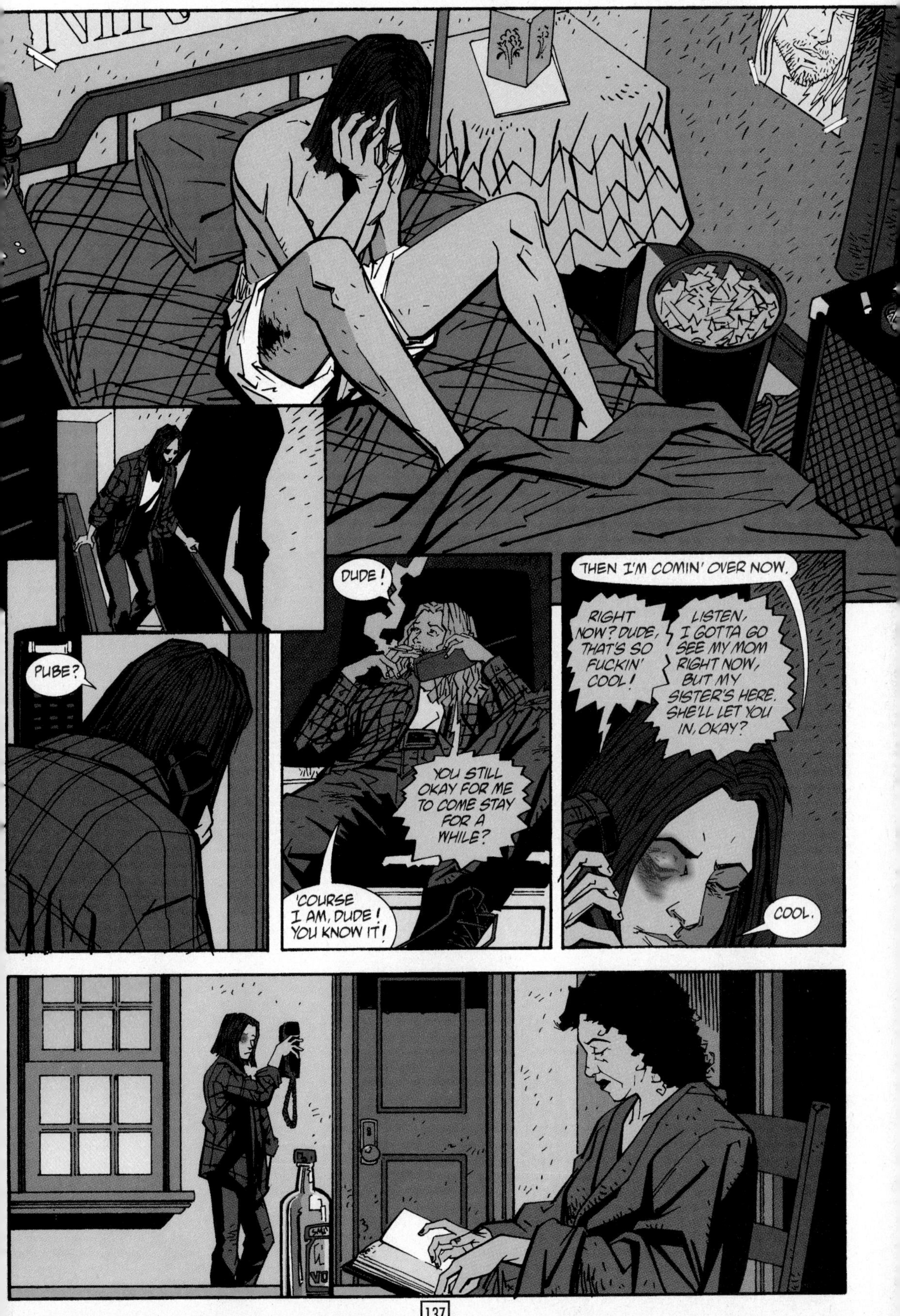
PUBE?
DUDE!
YOU STILL OKAY FOR ME TO COME STAY FOR A WHILE?
'COURSE I AM, DUDE! YOU KNOW IT!
THEN I'M COMIN' OVER NOW.
RIGHT NOW? DUDE, THAT'S SO FUCKIN' COOL!
LISTEN, I GOTTA GO SEE MY MOM RIGHT NOW, BUT MY SISTER'S HERE. SHE'LL LET YOU IN, OKAY?
COOL.

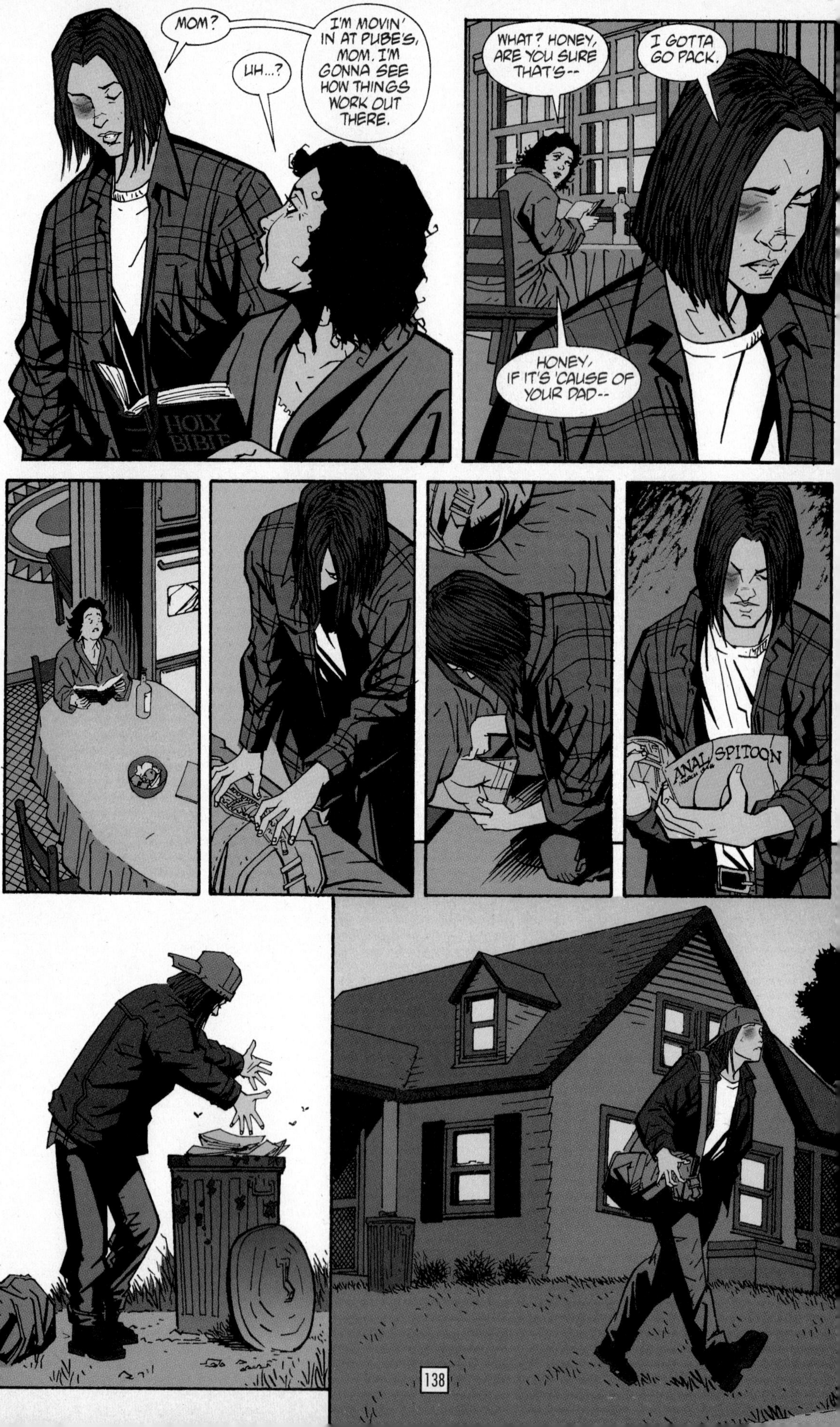

MOM?
UH...?
I'M MOVIN' IN AT PUBE'S, MOM. I'M GONNA SEE HOW THINGS WORK OUT THERE.
HOLY BIBLE
WHAT? HONEY, ARE YOU SURE THAT'S--
I GOTTA GO PACK.
HONEY, IF IT'S 'CAUSE OF YOUR DAD--
ANAL SPITOON

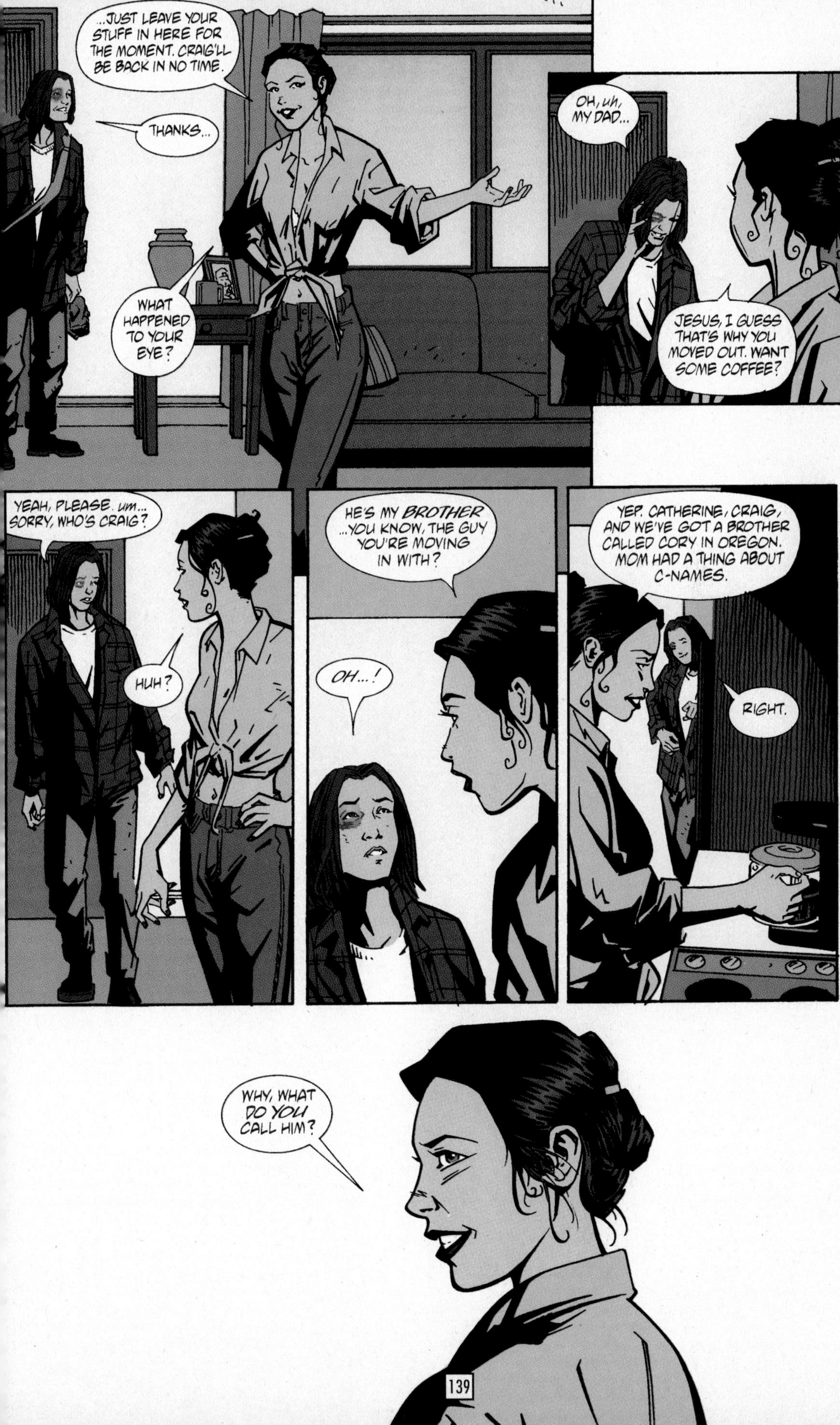
...JUST LEAVE YOUR STUFF IN HERE FOR THE MOMENT. CRAIG'LL BE BACK IN NO TIME.
THANKS...
WHAT HAPPENED TO YOUR EYE?
OH, uh, MY DAD...
JESUS, I GUESS THAT'S WHY YOU MOVED OUT. WANT SOME COFFEE?
YEAH, PLEASE. um... SORRY, WHO'S CRAIG?
HUH?
HE'S MY BROTHER ...YOU KNOW, THE GUY YOU'RE MOVING IN WITH?
OH...!
YEP. CATHERINE, CRAIG, AND WE'VE GOT A BROTHER CALLED CORY IN OREGON. MOM HAD A THING ABOUT C-NAMES.
RIGHT.
WHY, WHAT DO YOU CALL HIM?

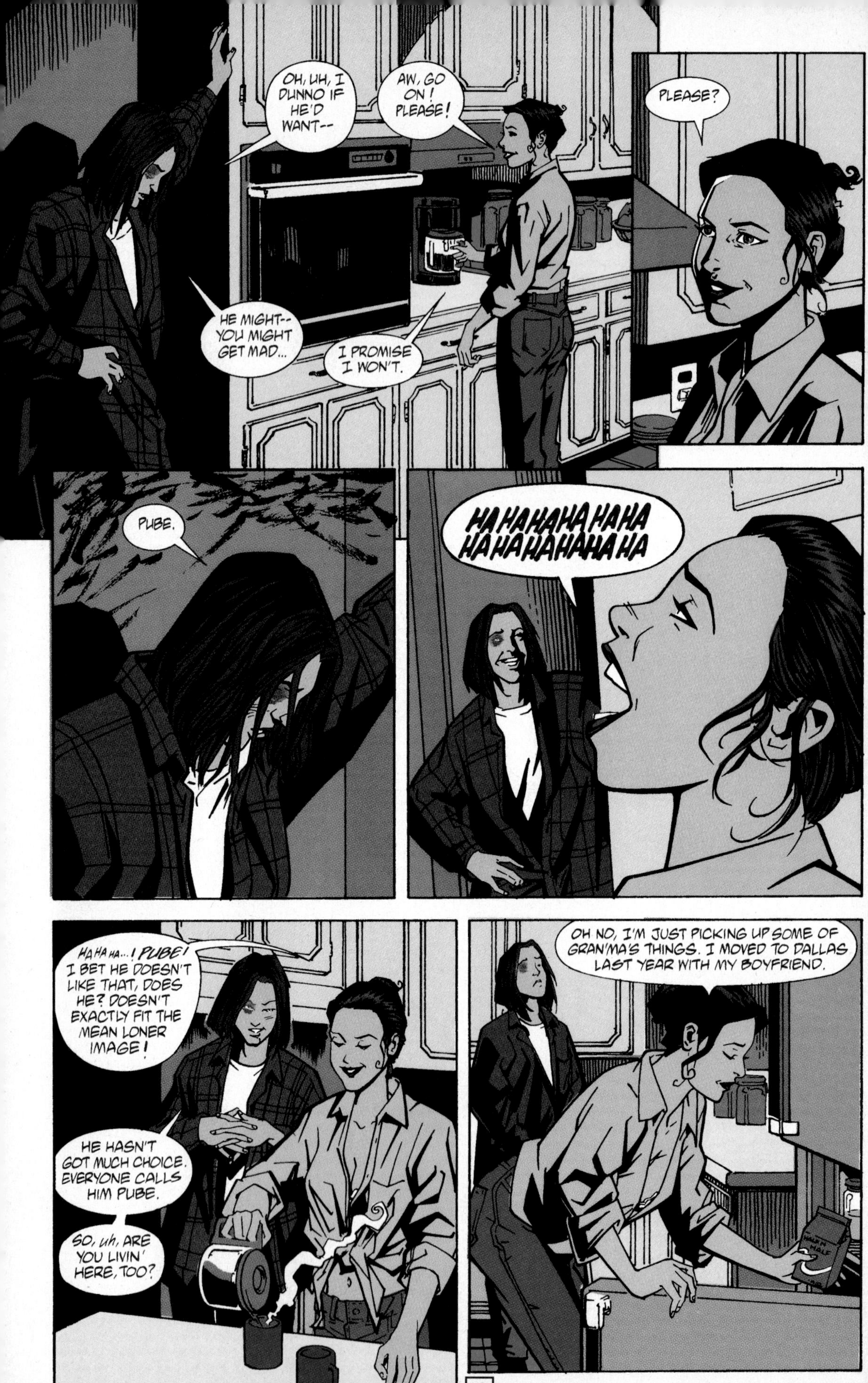
OH, UH, I DUNNO IF HE'D WANT--
AW, GO ON! PLEASE!
HE MIGHT-- YOU MIGHT GET MAD...
I PROMISE I WON'T.
PLEASE?
PUBE.
HA HA HA HA HA HA HA HA HA HA HA HA HA HA HA
HA HA HA...! PUBE! I BET HE DOESN'T LIKE THAT, DOES HE? DOESN'T EXACTLY FIT THE MEAN LONER IMAGE!
HE HASN'T GOT MUCH CHOICE. EVERYONE CALLS HIM PUBE.
SO, uh, ARE YOU LIVIN' HERE, TOO?
OH NO, I'M JUST PICKING UP SOME OF GRAN'MA'S THINGS. I MOVED TO DALLAS LAST YEAR WITH MY BOYFRIEND.

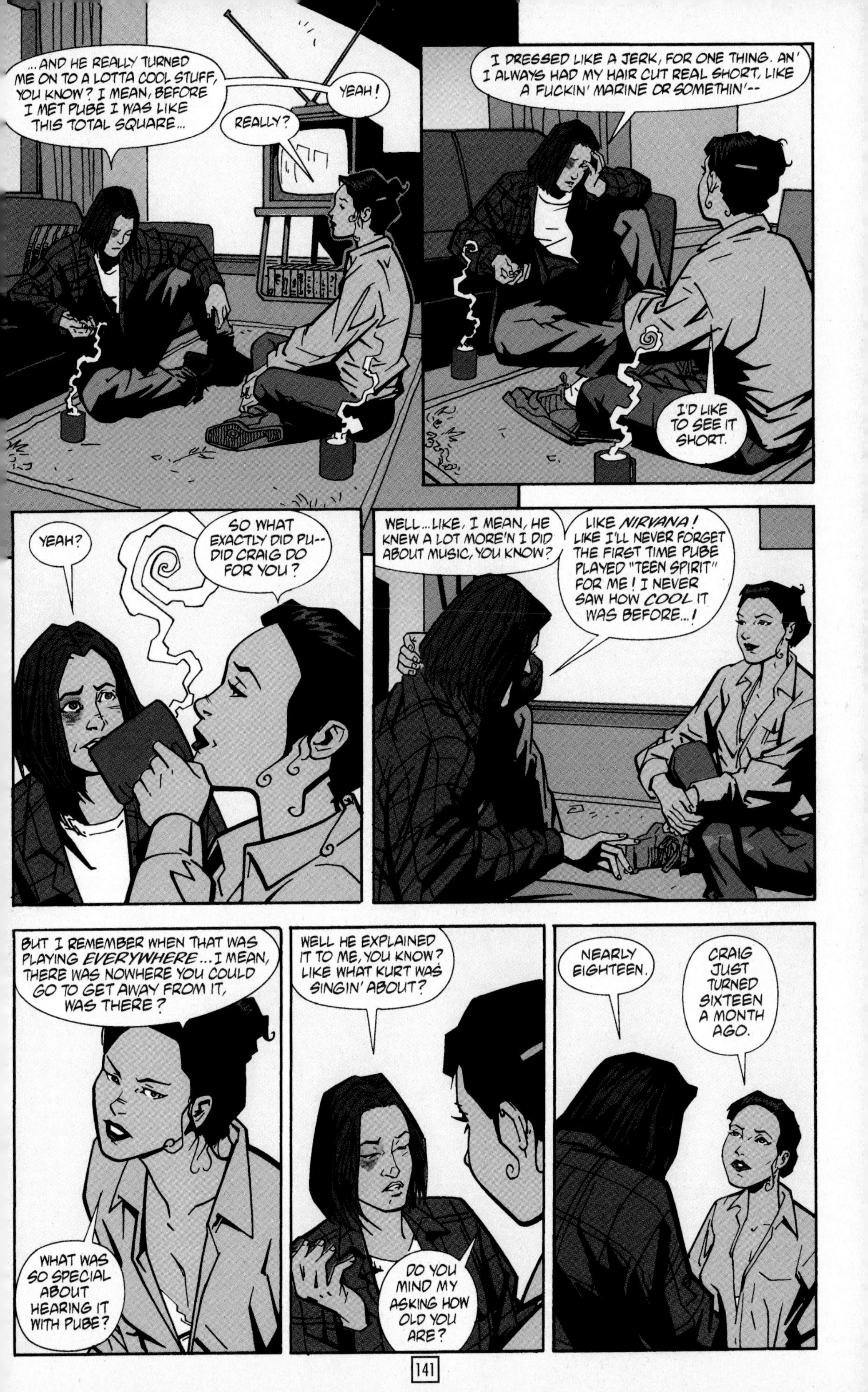
...AND HE REALLY TURNED ME ON TO A LOTTA COOL STUFF, YOU KNOW? I MEAN, BEFORE I MET PUBE I WAS LIKE THIS TOTAL SQUARE...
REALLY?
YEAH!
I DRESSED LIKE A JERK, FOR ONE THING. AN' I ALWAYS HAD MY HAIR CUT REAL SHORT, LIKE A FUCKIN' MARINE OR SOMETHIN'--
I'D LIKE TO SEE IT SHORT.
YEAH?
SO WHAT EXACTLY DID PU-- DID CRAIG DO FOR YOU?
WELL... LIKE, I MEAN, HE KNEW A LOT MORE'N I DID ABOUT MUSIC, YOU KNOW?
LIKE *NIRVANA*! LIKE I'LL NEVER FORGET THE FIRST TIME PUBE PLAYED "TEEN SPIRIT" FOR ME! I NEVER SAW HOW *COOL* IT WAS BEFORE...!
BUT I REMEMBER WHEN THAT WAS PLAYING *EVERYWHERE*... I MEAN, THERE WAS NOWHERE YOU COULD GO TO GET AWAY FROM IT, WAS THERE?
WHAT WAS SO SPECIAL ABOUT HEARING IT WITH PUBE?
WELL HE EXPLAINED IT TO ME, YOU KNOW? LIKE WHAT KURT WAS SINGIN' ABOUT?
DO YOU MIND MY ASKING HOW OLD YOU ARE?
NEARLY EIGHTEEN.
CRAIG JUST TURNED SIXTEEN A MONTH AGO.

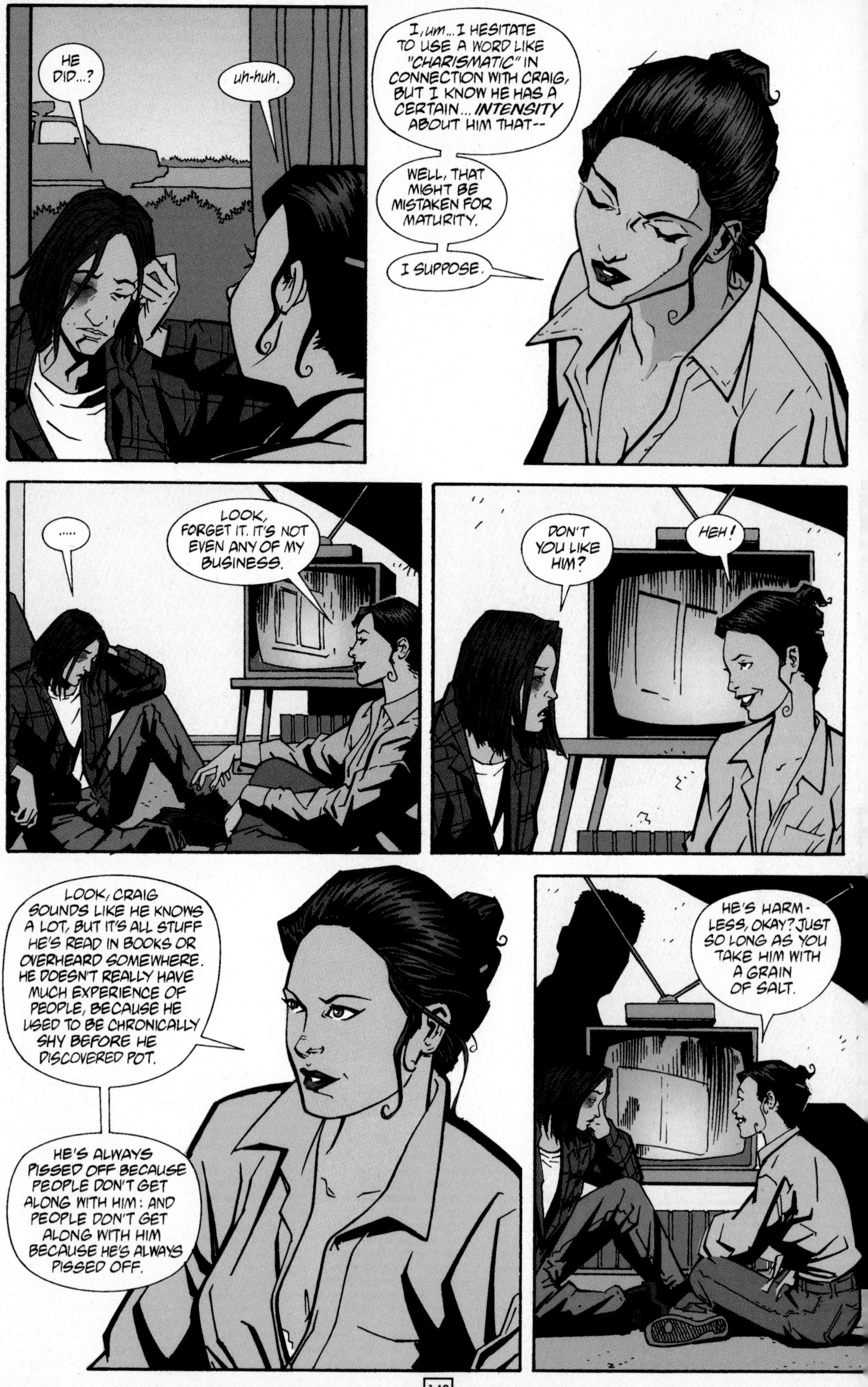
HE DID...?
uh-huh.
I, um... I HESITATE TO USE A WORD LIKE "CHARISMATIC" IN CONNECTION WITH CRAIG, BUT I KNOW HE HAS A CERTAIN... INTENSITY ABOUT HIM THAT--
WELL, THAT MIGHT BE MISTAKEN FOR MATURITY.
I SUPPOSE.
.....
LOOK, FORGET IT. IT'S NOT EVEN ANY OF MY BUSINESS.
DON'T YOU LIKE HIM?
HEH!
LOOK, CRAIG SOUNDS LIKE HE KNOWS A LOT, BUT IT'S ALL STUFF HE'S READ IN BOOKS OR OVERHEARD SOMEWHERE. HE DOESN'T REALLY HAVE MUCH EXPERIENCE OF PEOPLE, BECAUSE HE USED TO BE CHRONICALLY SHY BEFORE HE DISCOVERED POT.
HE'S ALWAYS PISSED OFF BECAUSE PEOPLE DON'T GET ALONG WITH HIM: AND PEOPLE DON'T GET ALONG WITH HIM BECAUSE HE'S ALWAYS PISSED OFF.
HE'S HARM-LESS, OKAY? JUST SO LONG AS YOU TAKE HIM WITH A GRAIN OF SALT.

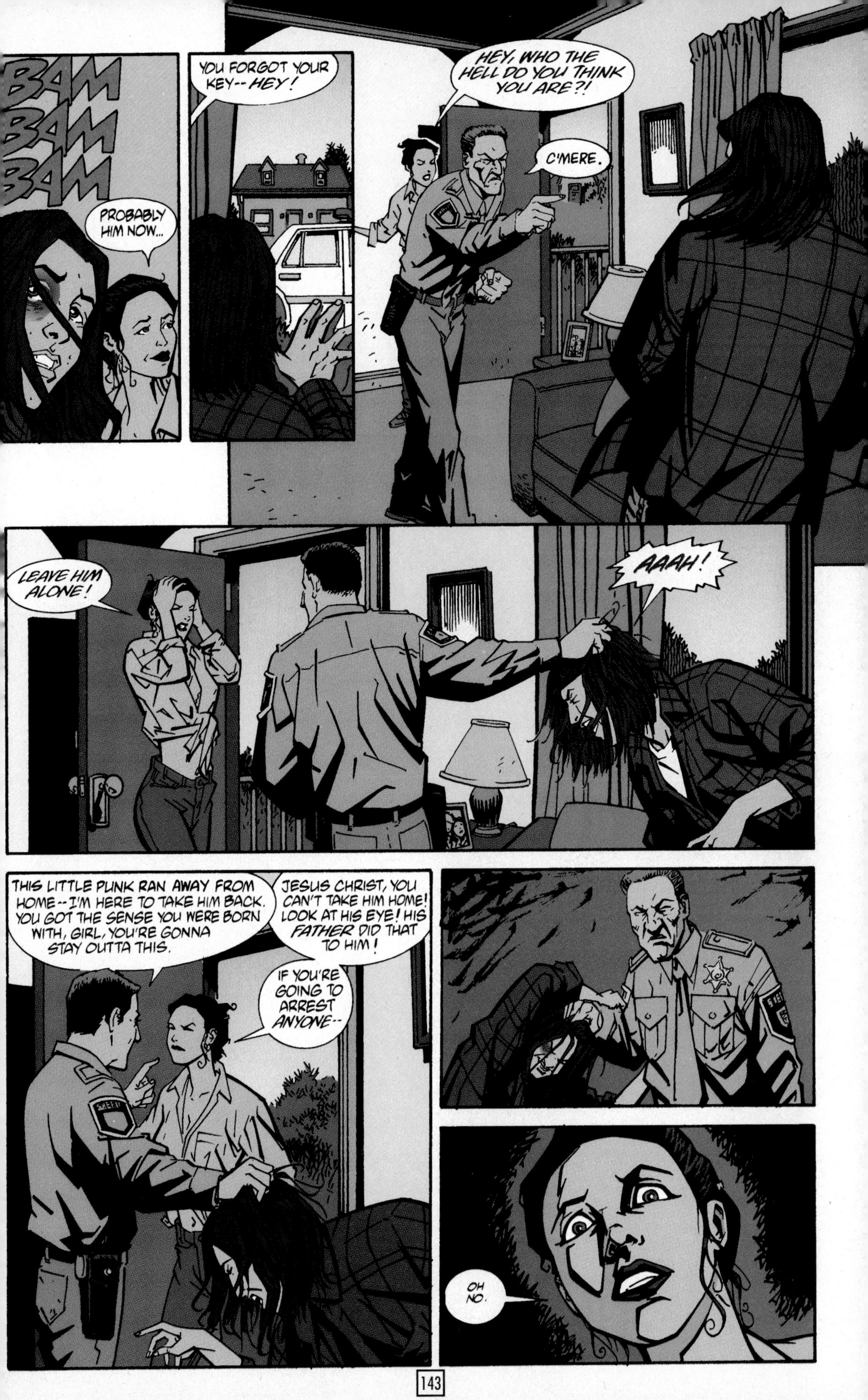
BAM
BAM
BAM
PROBABLY HIM NOW...
YOU FORGOT YOUR KEY-- HEY!
HEY, WHO THE HELL DO YOU THINK YOU ARE?!
C'MERE.
LEAVE HIM ALONE!
AAAH!
THIS LITTLE PUNK RAN AWAY FROM HOME-- I'M HERE TO TAKE HIM BACK. YOU GOT THE SENSE YOU WERE BORN WITH, GIRL, YOU'RE GONNA STAY OUTTA THIS.
JESUS CHRIST, YOU CAN'T TAKE HIM HOME! LOOK AT HIS EYE! HIS FATHER DID THAT TO HIM!
IF YOU'RE GOING TO ARREST ANYONE--
OH NO.

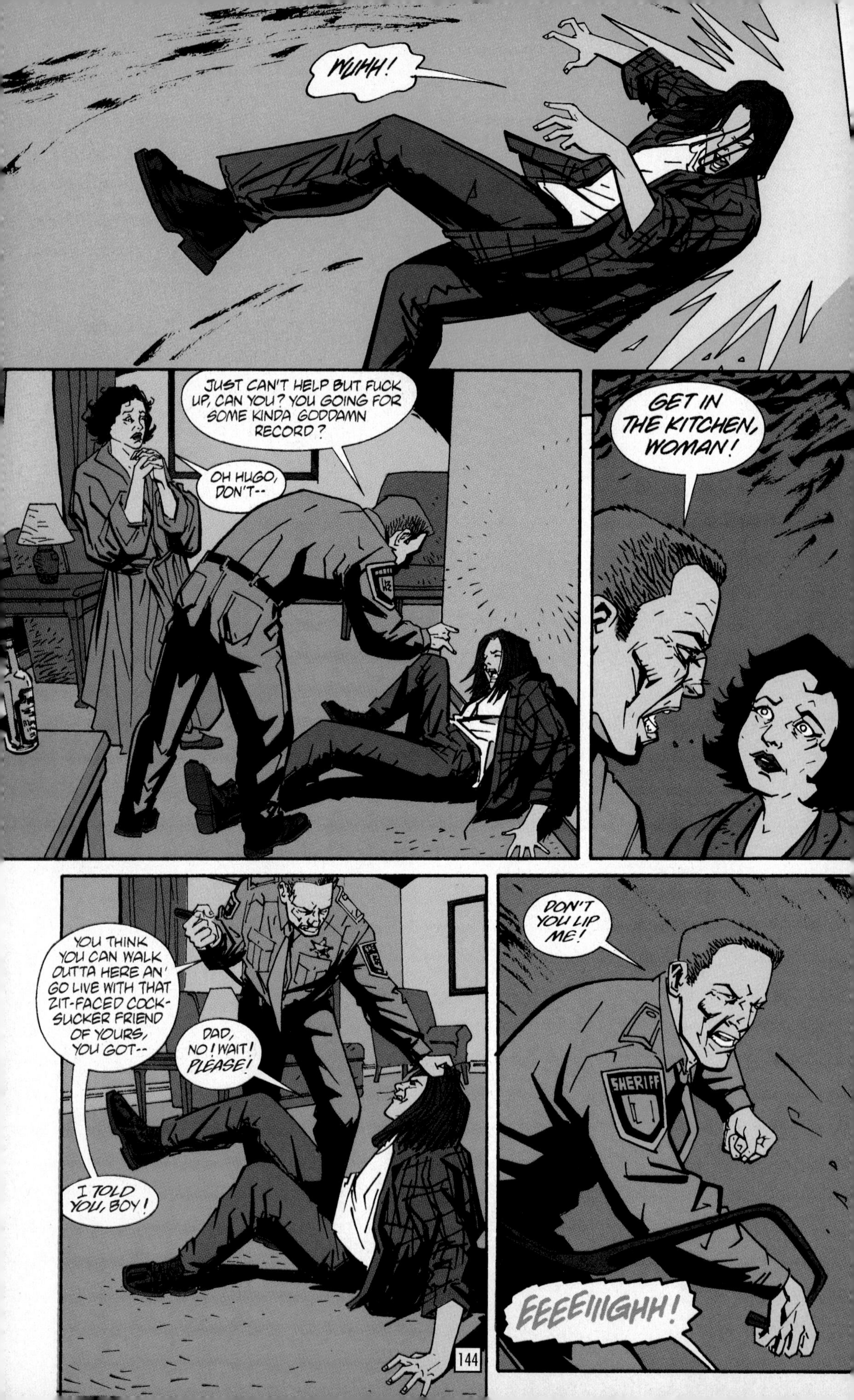

WUHH!
JUST CAN'T HELP BUT FUCK UP, CAN YOU? YOU GOING FOR SOME KINDA GODDAMN RECORD?
OH HUGO, DON'T--
GET IN THE KITCHEN, WOMAN!
YOU THINK YOU CAN WALK OUTTA HERE AN' GO LIVE WITH THAT ZIT-FACED COCK-SUCKER FRIEND OF YOURS, YOU GOT--
DAD, NO! WAIT! PLEASE!
I TOLD YOU, BOY!
DON'T YOU LIP ME!
SHERIFF
EEEEIIIGHH!

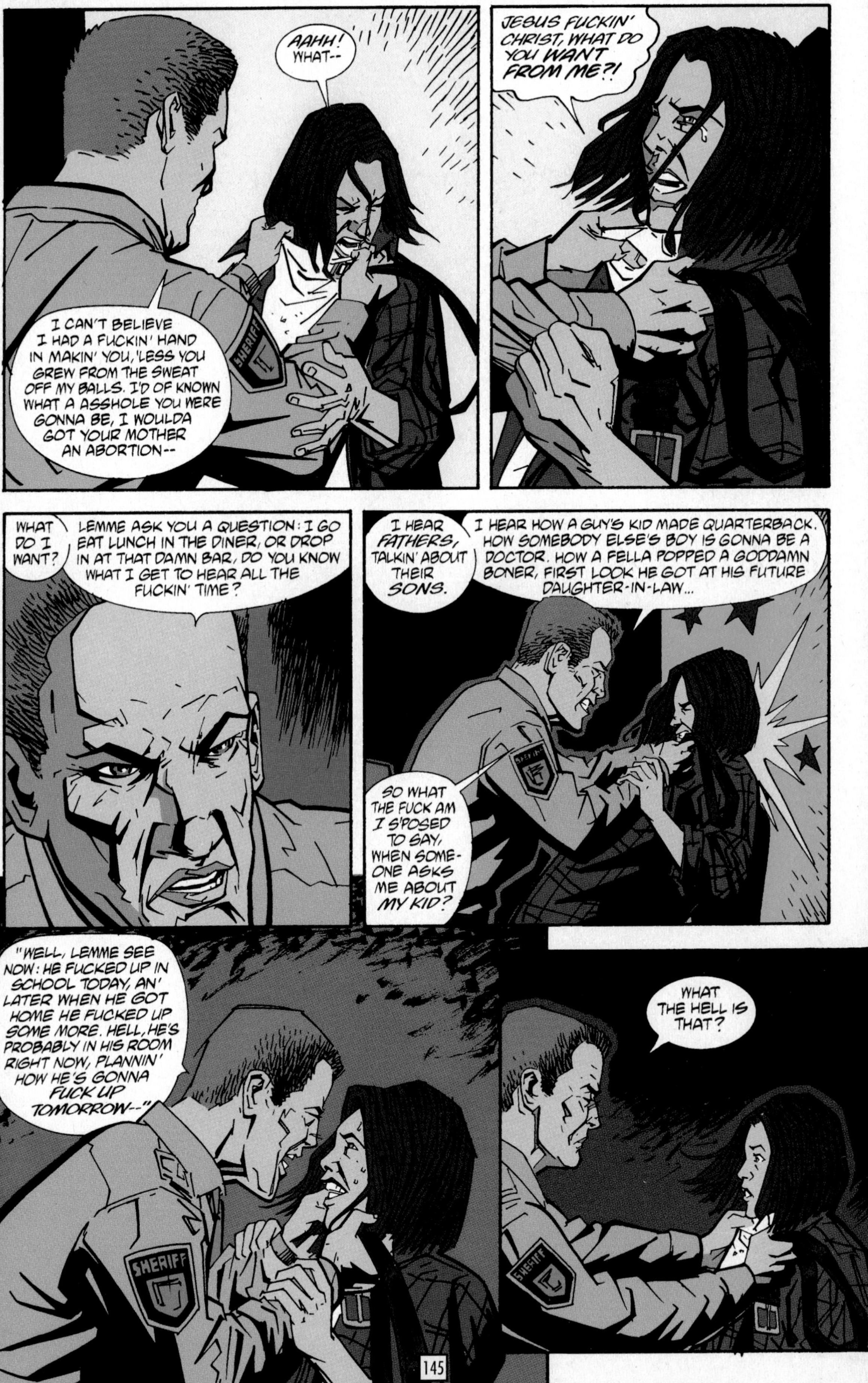
AAHH! WHAT--
I CAN'T BELIEVE I HAD A FUCKIN' HAND IN MAKIN' YOU, 'LESS YOU GREW FROM THE SWEAT OFF MY BALLS. I'D OF KNOWN WHAT A ASSHOLE YOU WERE GONNA BE, I WOULDA GOT YOUR MOTHER AN ABORTION--
SHERIFF
JESUS FUCKIN' CHRIST, WHAT DO YOU WANT FROM ME?!
WHAT DO I WANT?
LEMME ASK YOU A QUESTION: I GO EAT LUNCH IN THE DINER, OR DROP IN AT THAT DAMN BAR, DO YOU KNOW WHAT I GET TO HEAR ALL THE FUCKIN' TIME?
I HEAR FATHERS, TALKIN' ABOUT THEIR SONS.
I HEAR HOW A GUY'S KID MADE QUARTERBACK. HOW SOMEBODY ELSE'S BOY IS GONNA BE A DOCTOR. HOW A FELLA POPPED A GODDAMN BONER, FIRST LOOK HE GOT AT HIS FUTURE DAUGHTER-IN-LAW...
SO WHAT THE FUCK AM I S'POSED TO SAY, WHEN SOME-ONE ASKS ME ABOUT MY KID?
"WELL, LEMME SEE NOW: HE FUCKED UP IN SCHOOL TODAY, AN' LATER WHEN HE GOT HOME HE FUCKED UP SOME MORE. HELL, HE'S PROBABLY IN HIS ROOM RIGHT NOW, PLANNIN' HOW HE'S GONNA FUCK UP TOMORROW--"
SHERIFF
WHAT THE HELL IS THAT?
SHERIFF

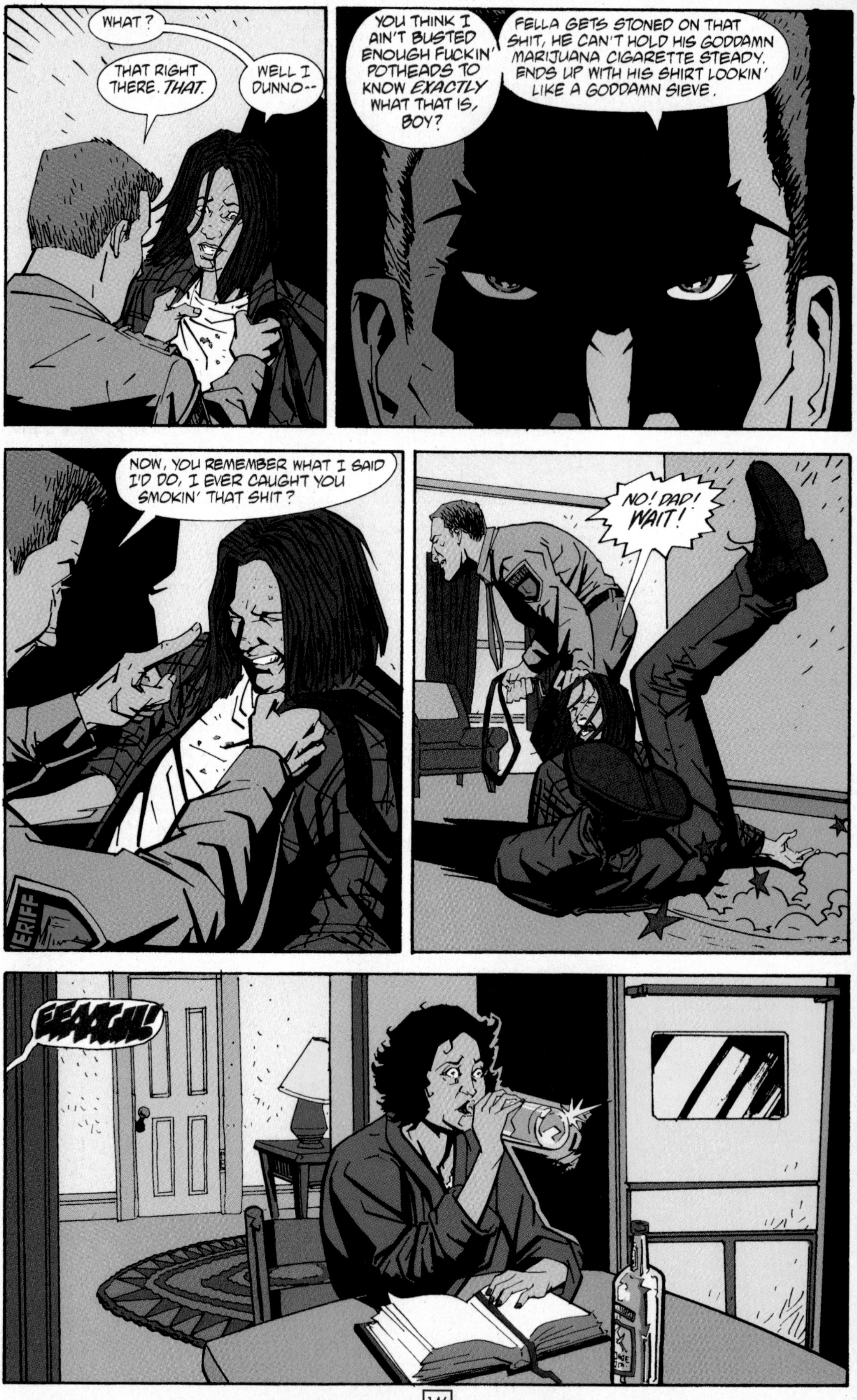
WHAT?
THAT RIGHT THERE. *THAT.*
WELL I DUNNO--
YOU THINK I AIN'T BUSTED ENOUGH FUCKIN' POTHEADS TO KNOW *EXACTLY* WHAT THAT IS, BOY?
FELLA GETS STONED ON THAT SHIT, HE CAN'T HOLD HIS GODDAMN MARIJUANA CIGARETTE STEADY. ENDS UP WITH HIS SHIRT LOOKIN' LIKE A GODDAMN SIEVE.
NOW, YOU REMEMBER WHAT I SAID I'D DO, I EVER CAUGHT YOU SMOKIN' THAT SHIT?
SHERIFF
NO! DAD! WAIT!
EEAAGH!

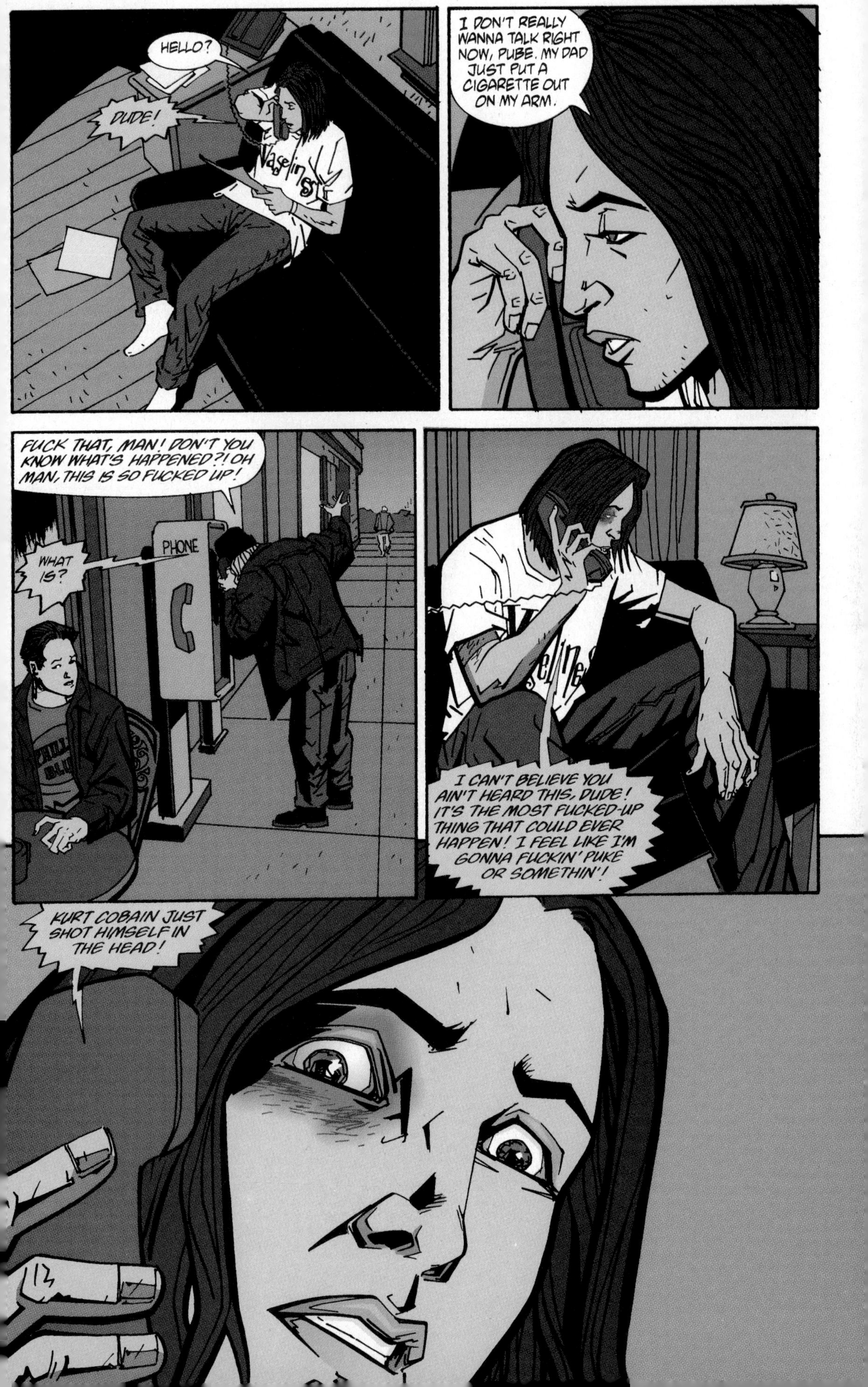
HELLO?
DUDE!
I DON'T REALLY WANNA TALK RIGHT NOW, PUBE. MY DAD JUST PUT A CIGARETTE OUT ON MY ARM.
FUCK THAT, MAN! DON'T YOU KNOW WHAT'S HAPPENED?! OH MAN, THIS IS SO FUCKED UP!
PHONE
WHAT IS?
I CAN'T BELIEVE YOU AIN'T HEARD THIS, DUDE! IT'S THE MOST FUCKED-UP THING THAT COULD EVER HAPPEN! I FEEL LIKE I'M GONNA FUCKIN' PUKE OR SOMETHIN'!
KURT COBAIN JUST SHOT HIMSELF IN THE HEAD!

4. Nevermind

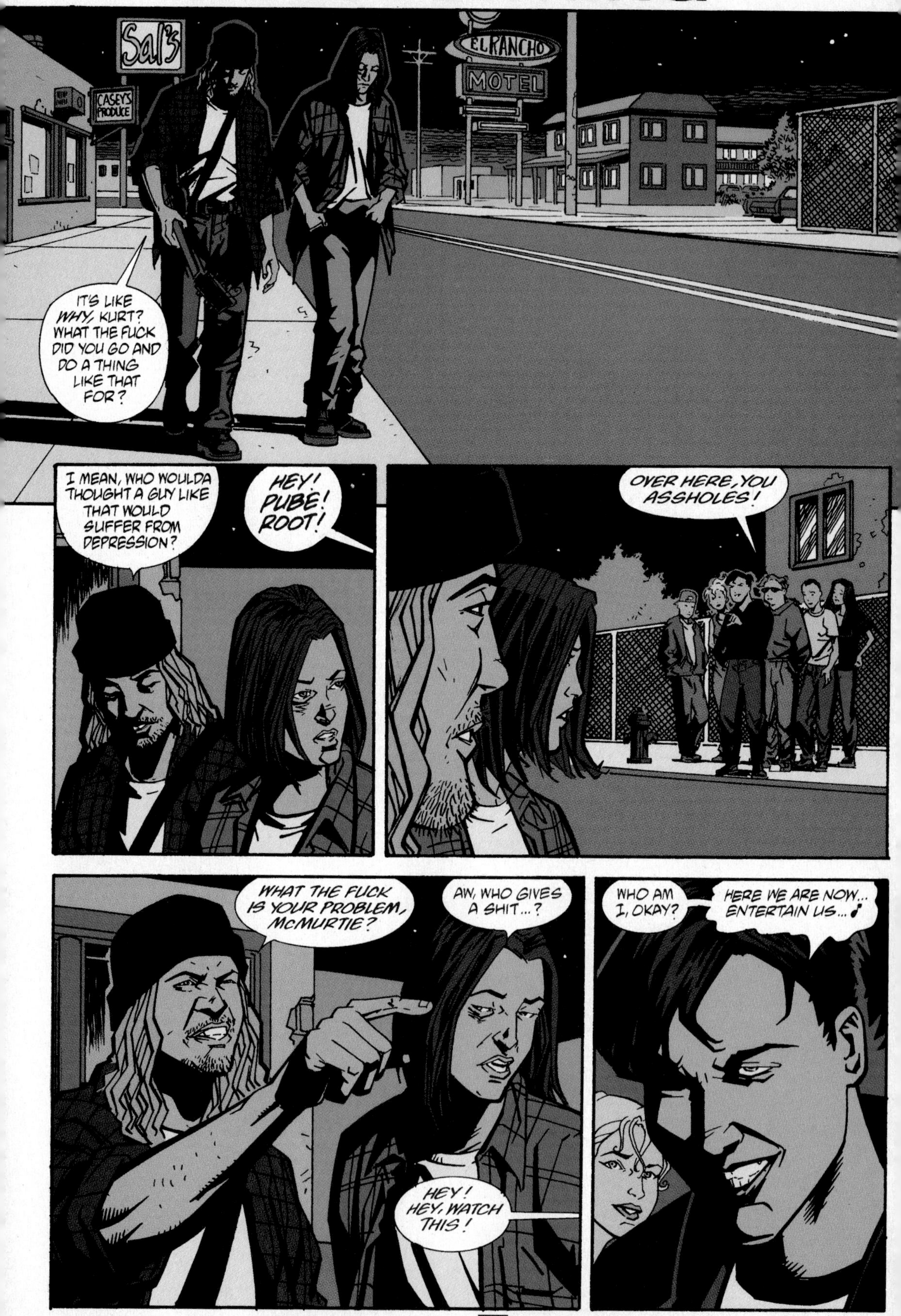
Sal's
CASEY'S PRODUCE
EL RANCHO
MOTEL
IT'S LIKE WHY, KURT? WHAT THE FUCK DID YOU GO AND DO A THING LIKE THAT FOR?
I MEAN, WHO WOULDA THOUGHT A GUY LIKE THAT WOULD SUFFER FROM DEPRESSION?
HEY! PUBE! ROOT!
OVER HERE, YOU ASSHOLES!
WHAT THE FUCK IS YOUR PROBLEM, McMURTIE?
AW, WHO GIVES A SHIT...?
HEY! HEY, WATCH THIS!
WHO AM I, OKAY?
HERE WE ARE NOW... ENTERTAIN US...♪

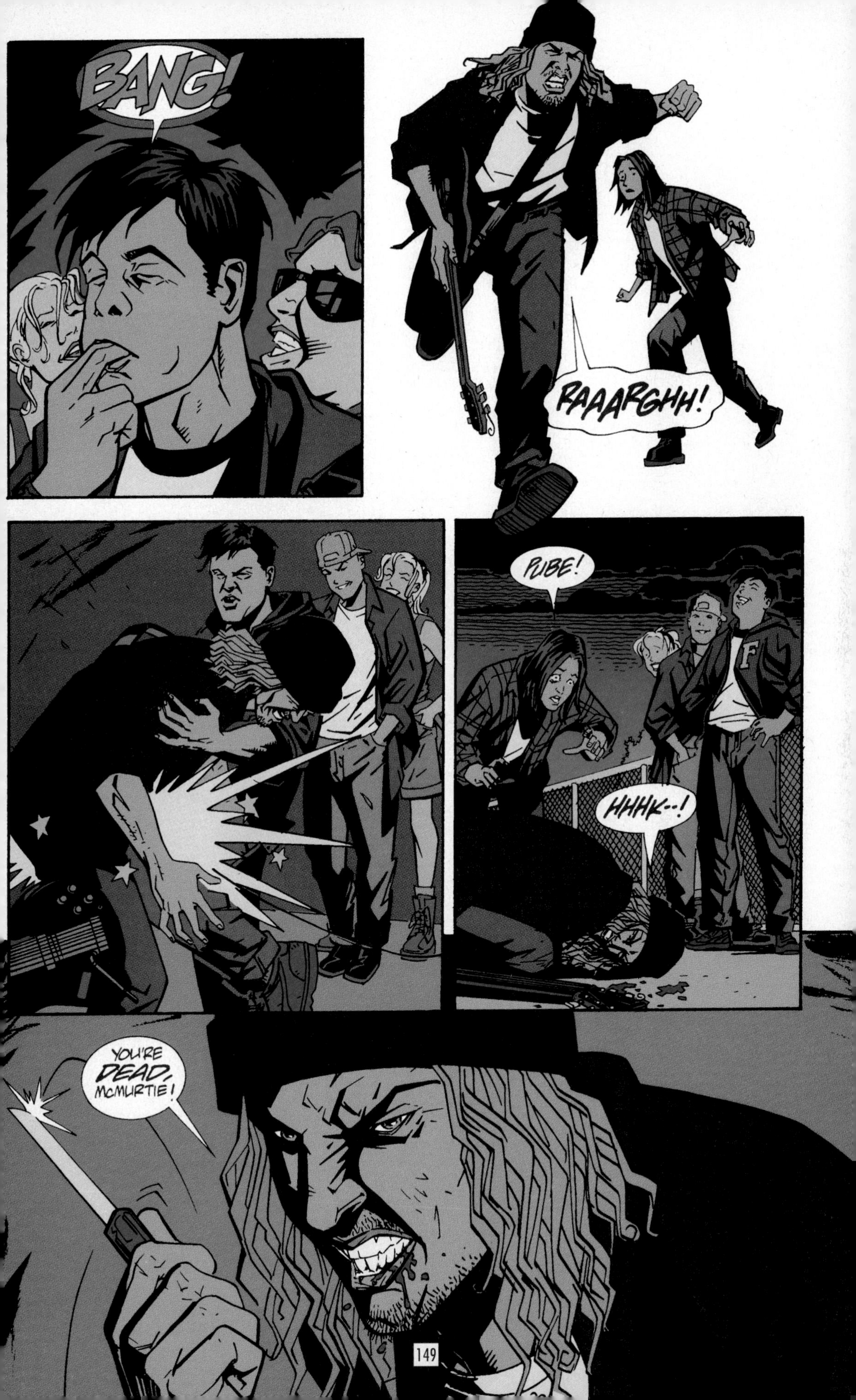
BANG!
RAAARGHH!
PUBE!
HHHK--!
YOU'RE DEAD, McMURTIE!

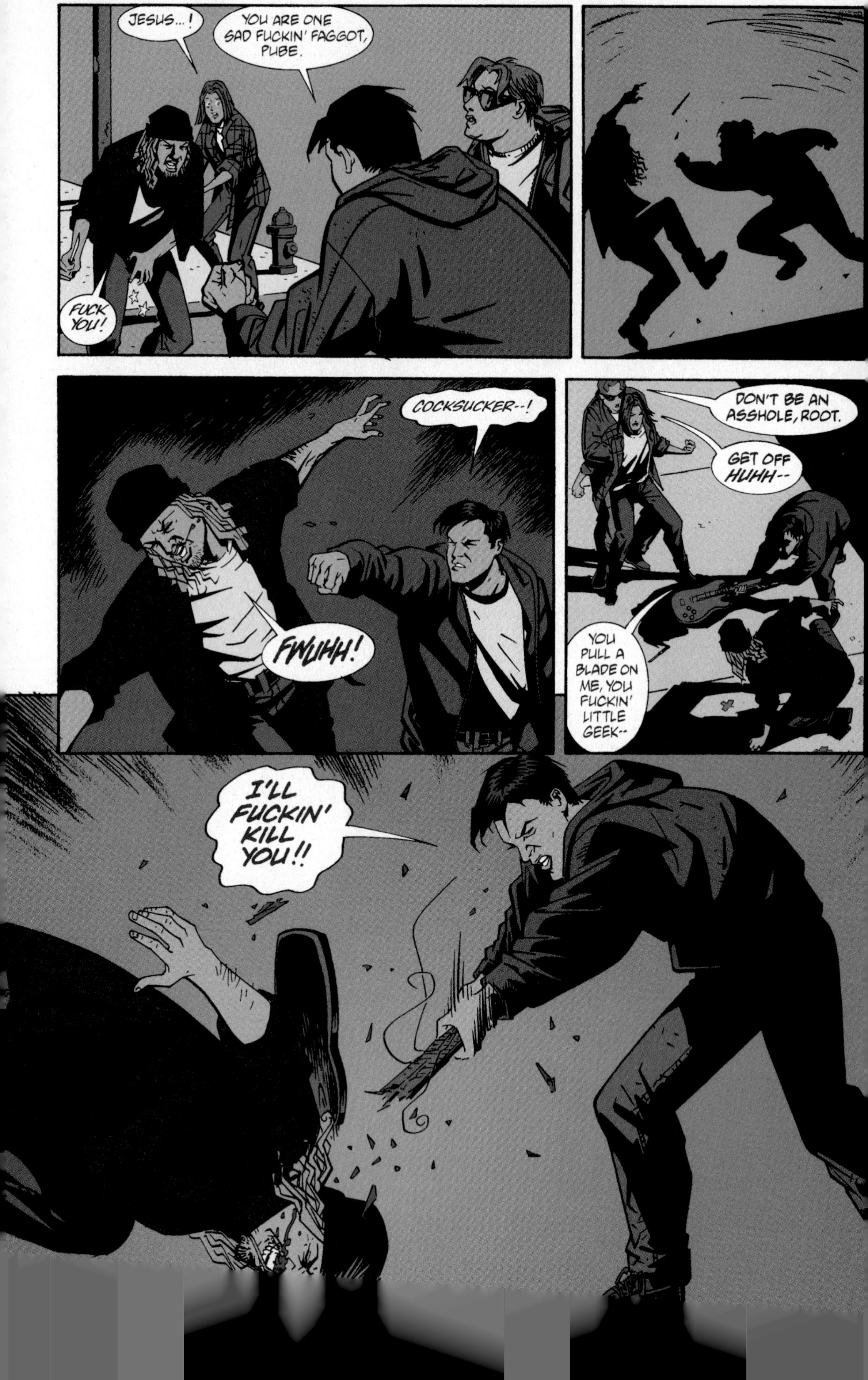

JESUS...!
YOU ARE ONE SAD FUCKIN' FAGGOT, PUBE.
FUCK YOU!
COCKSUCKER--!
FWUHH!
DON'T BE AN ASSHOLE, ROOT.
GET OFF HUHH--
YOU PULL A BLADE ON ME, YOU FUCKIN' LITTLE GEEK--
I'LL FUCKIN' KILL YOU!!

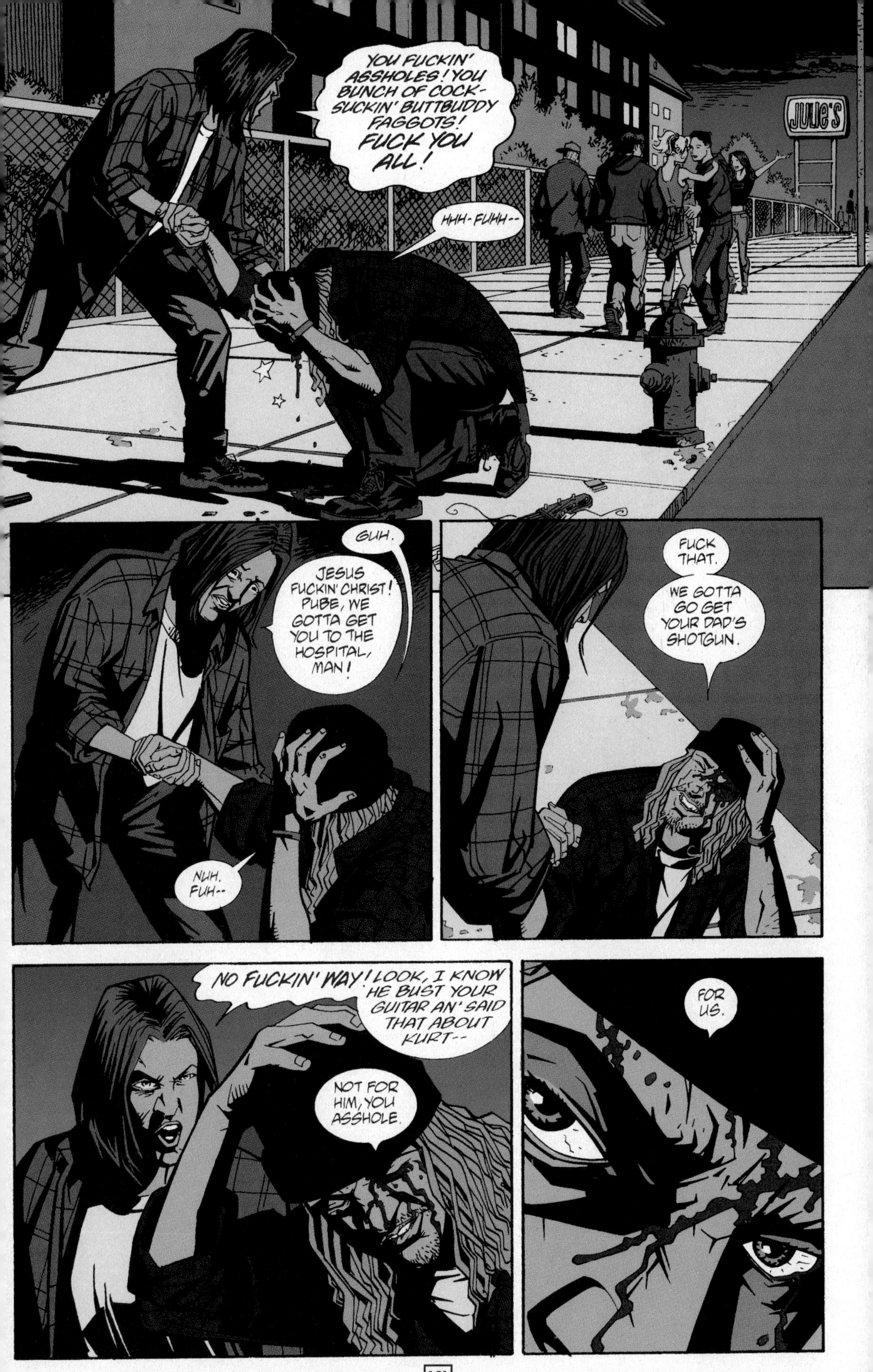

YOU FUCKIN' ASSHOLES! YOU BUNCH OF COCK-SUCKIN' BUTTBUDDY FAGGOTS! FUCK YOU ALL!
JULIE'S
HHH-FUHH--
GUH.
JESUS FUCKIN' CHRIST! PUBE, WE GOTTA GET YOU TO THE HOSPITAL, MAN!
NUH. FUH--
FUCK THAT.
WE GOTTA GO GET YOUR DAD'S SHOTGUN.
NO FUCKIN' WAY! LOOK, I KNOW HE BUST YOUR GUITAR AN' SAID THAT ABOUT KURT--
NOT FOR HIM, YOU ASSHOLE.
FOR US.

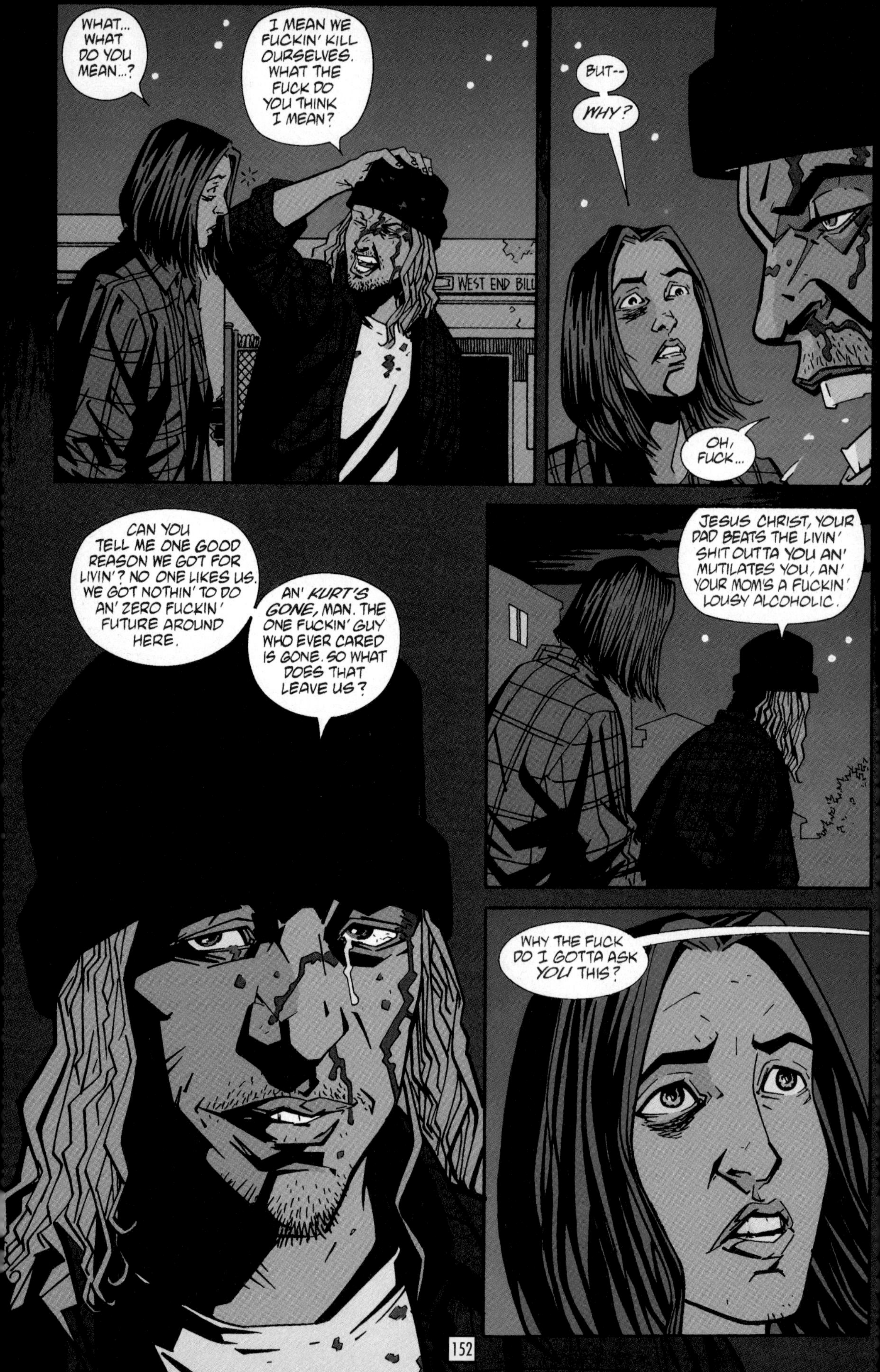
WHAT... WHAT DO YOU MEAN...?
I MEAN WE FUCKIN' KILL OURSELVES. WHAT THE FUCK DO YOU THINK I MEAN?
WEST END BILL
BUT--
WHY?
OH, FUCK...
CAN YOU TELL ME ONE GOOD REASON WE GOT FOR LIVIN'? NO ONE LIKES US. WE GOT NOTHIN' TO DO AN' ZERO FUCKIN' FUTURE AROUND HERE.
AN' KURT'S GONE, MAN. THE ONE FUCKIN' GUY WHO EVER CARED IS GONE. SO WHAT DOES THAT LEAVE US?
JESUS CHRIST, YOUR DAD BEATS THE LIVIN' SHIT OUTTA YOU AN' MUTILATES YOU, AN' YOUR MOM'S A FUCKIN' LOUSY ALCOHOLIC.
WHY THE FUCK DO I GOTTA ASK YOU THIS?

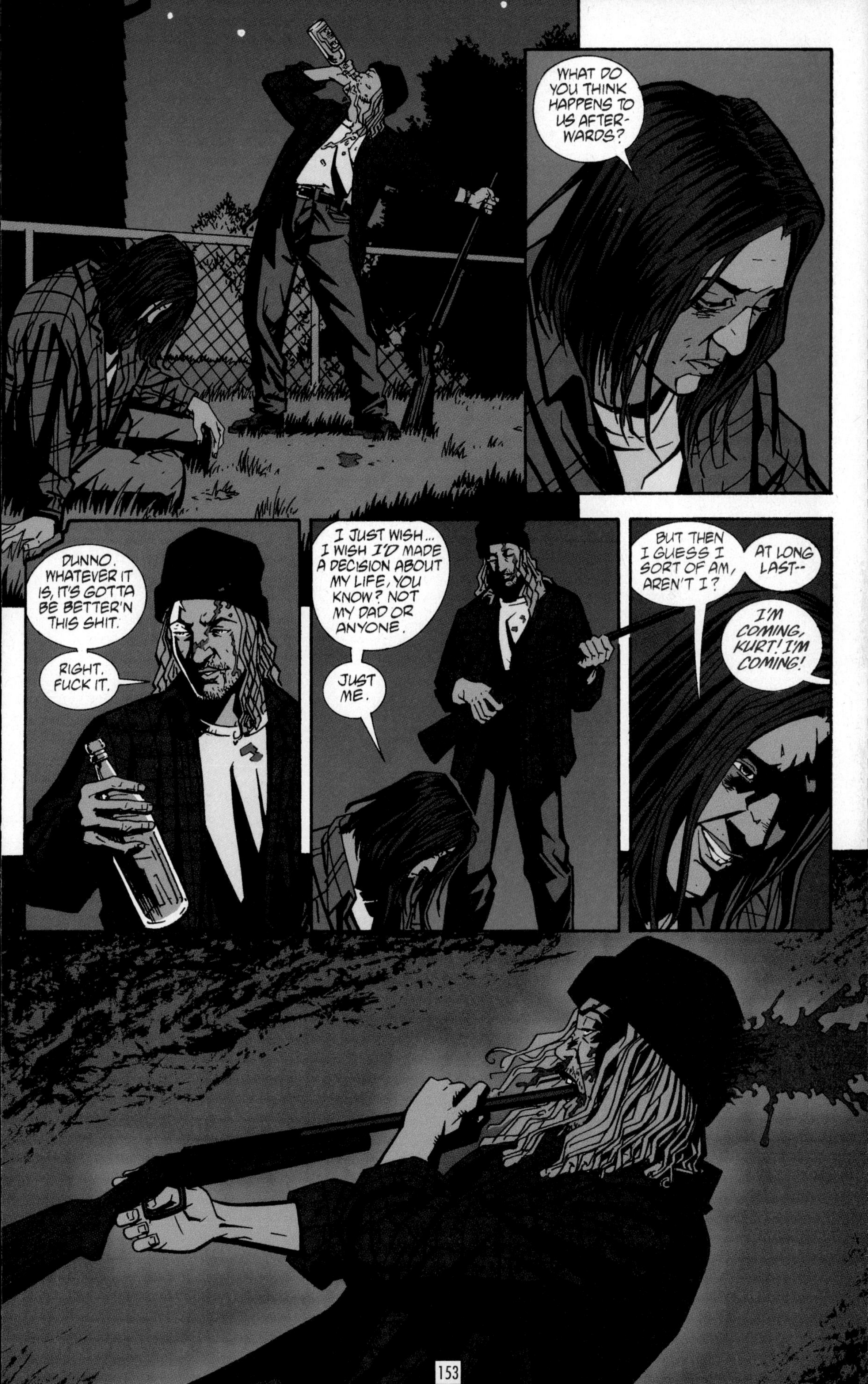
WHAT DO YOU THINK HAPPENS TO US AFTER-WARDS?
DUNNO. WHATEVER IT IS, IT'S GOTTA BE BETTER'N THIS SHIT.
RIGHT. FUCK IT.
I JUST WISH... I WISH I'D MADE A DECISION ABOUT MY LIFE, YOU KNOW? NOT MY DAD OR ANYONE.
JUST ME.
BUT THEN I GUESS I SORT OF AM, AREN'T I?
AT LONG LAST--
I'M COMING, KURT! I'M COMING!

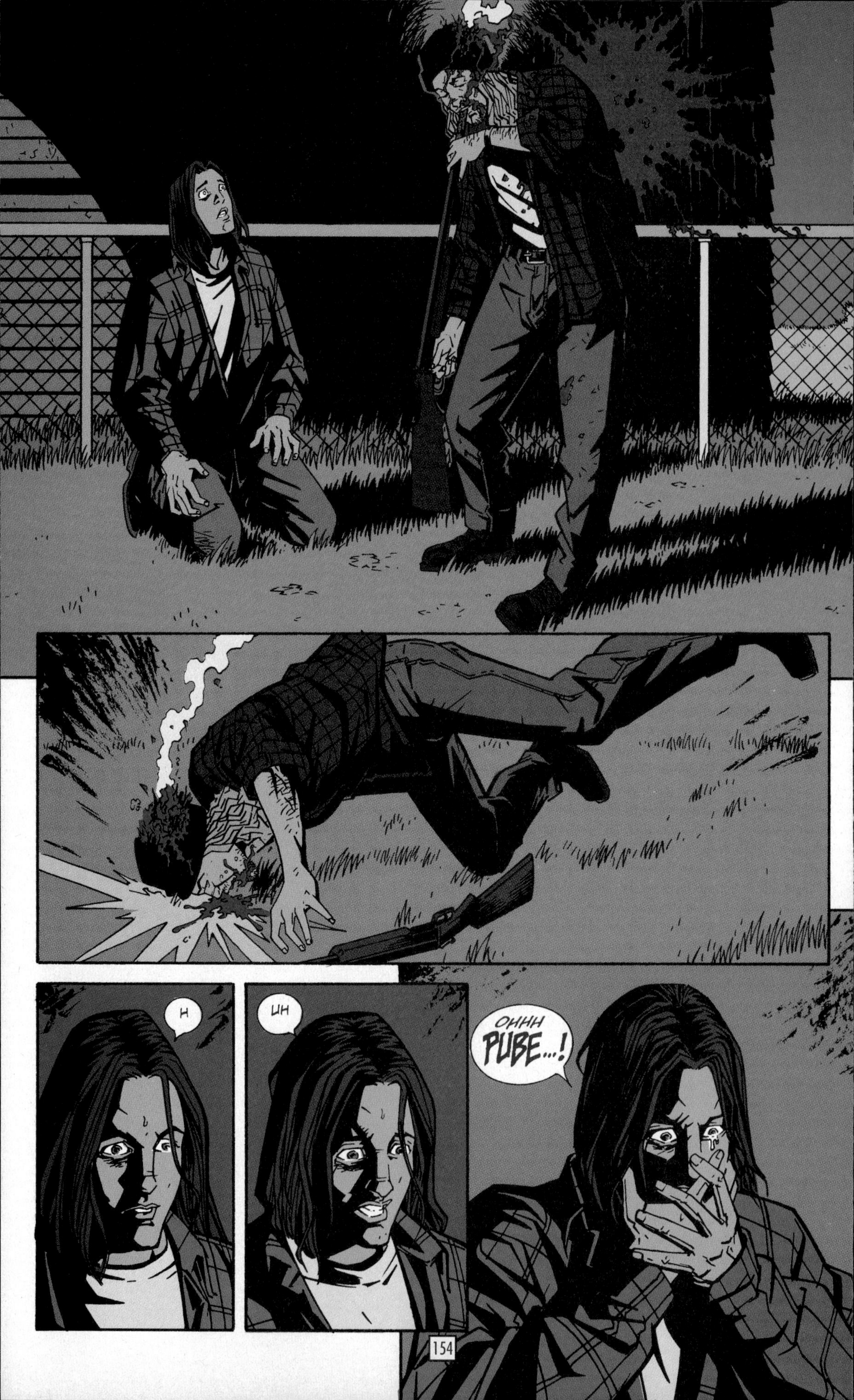
H
UH
OHHH PUBE...!

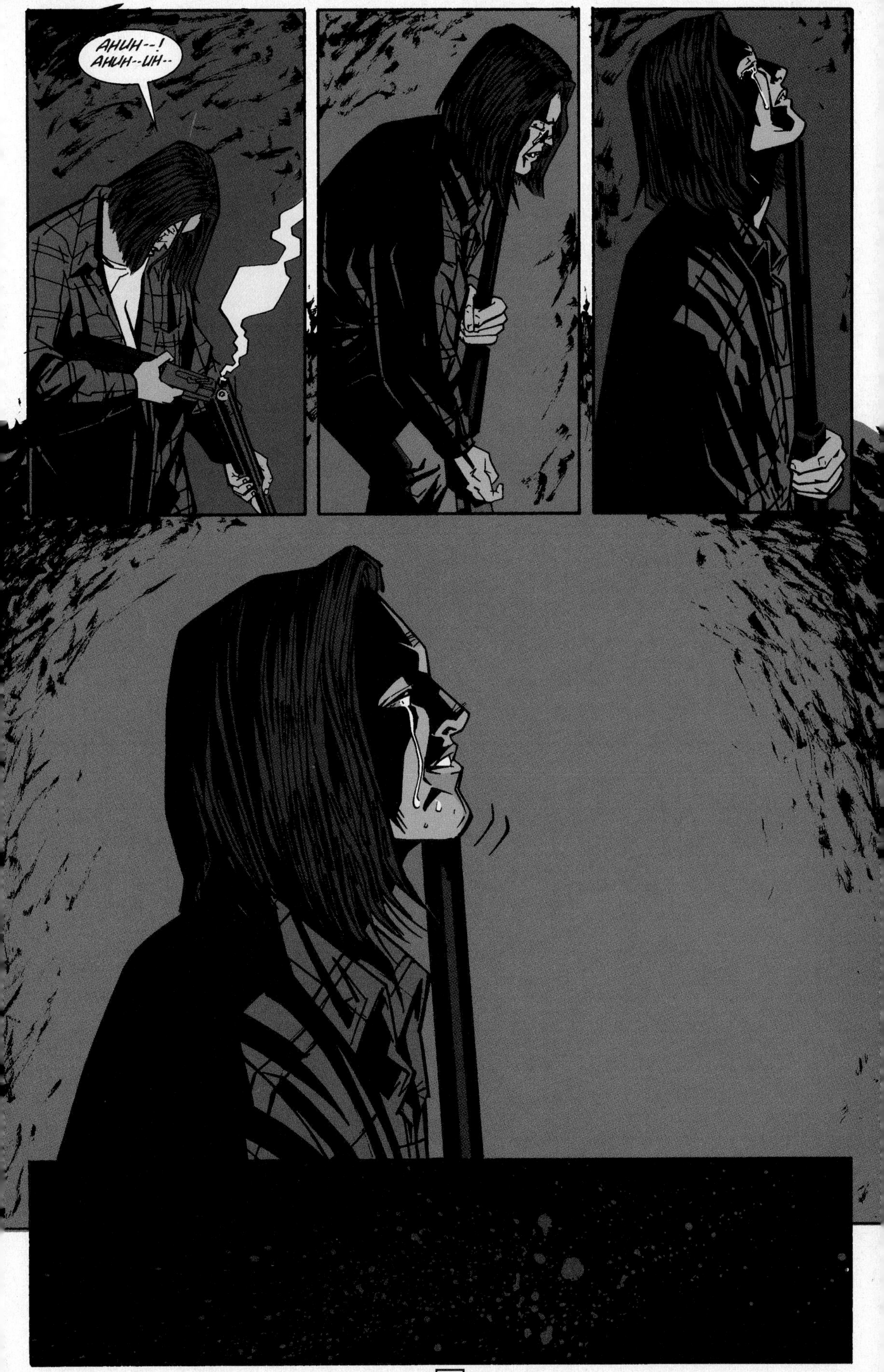
AHUH--! AHUH--UH--

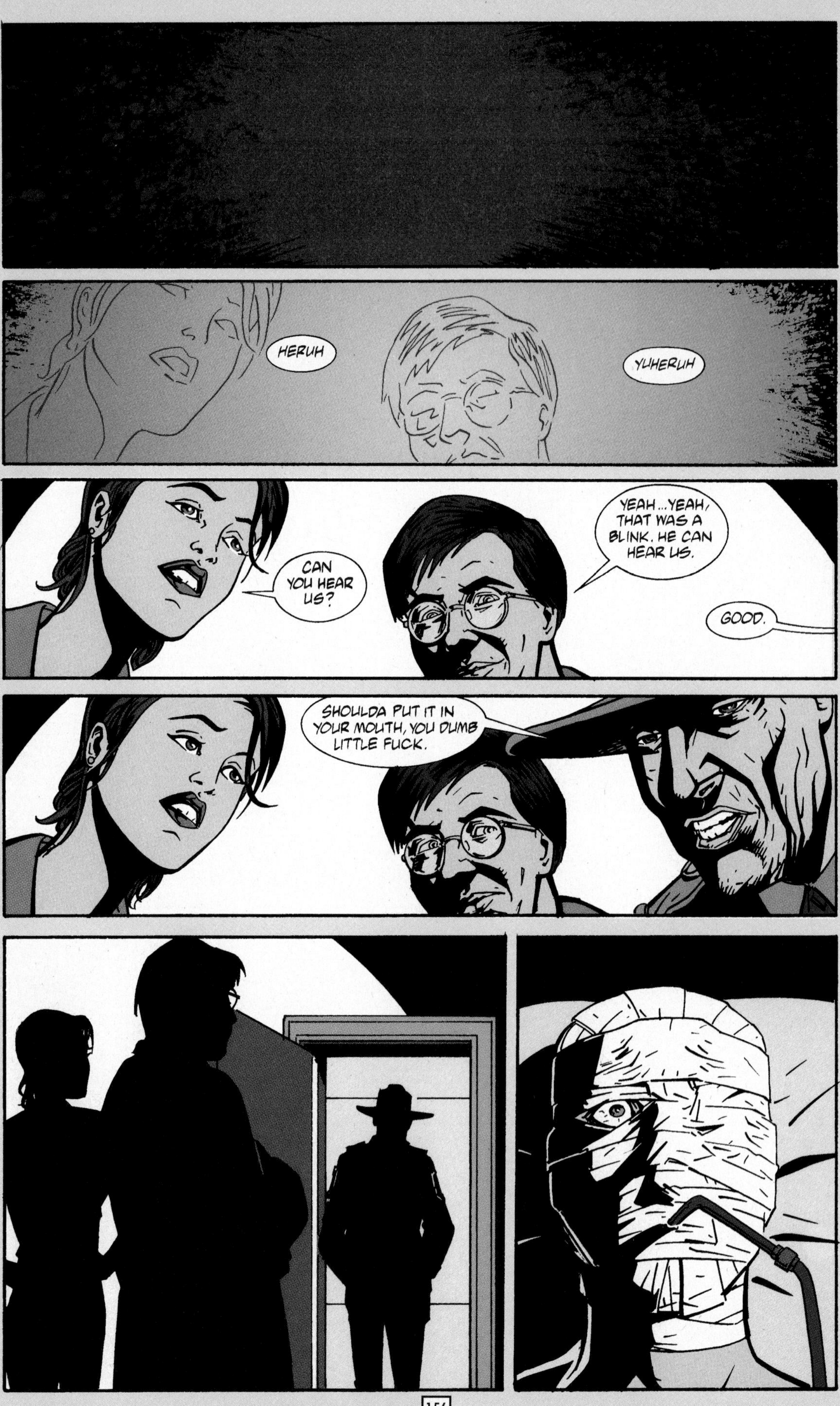
HERUH
YUHERUH
CAN YOU HEAR US?
YEAH...YEAH, THAT WAS A BLINK. HE CAN HEAR US.
GOOD.
SHOULDA PUT IT IN YOUR MOUTH, YOU DUMB LITTLE FUCK.

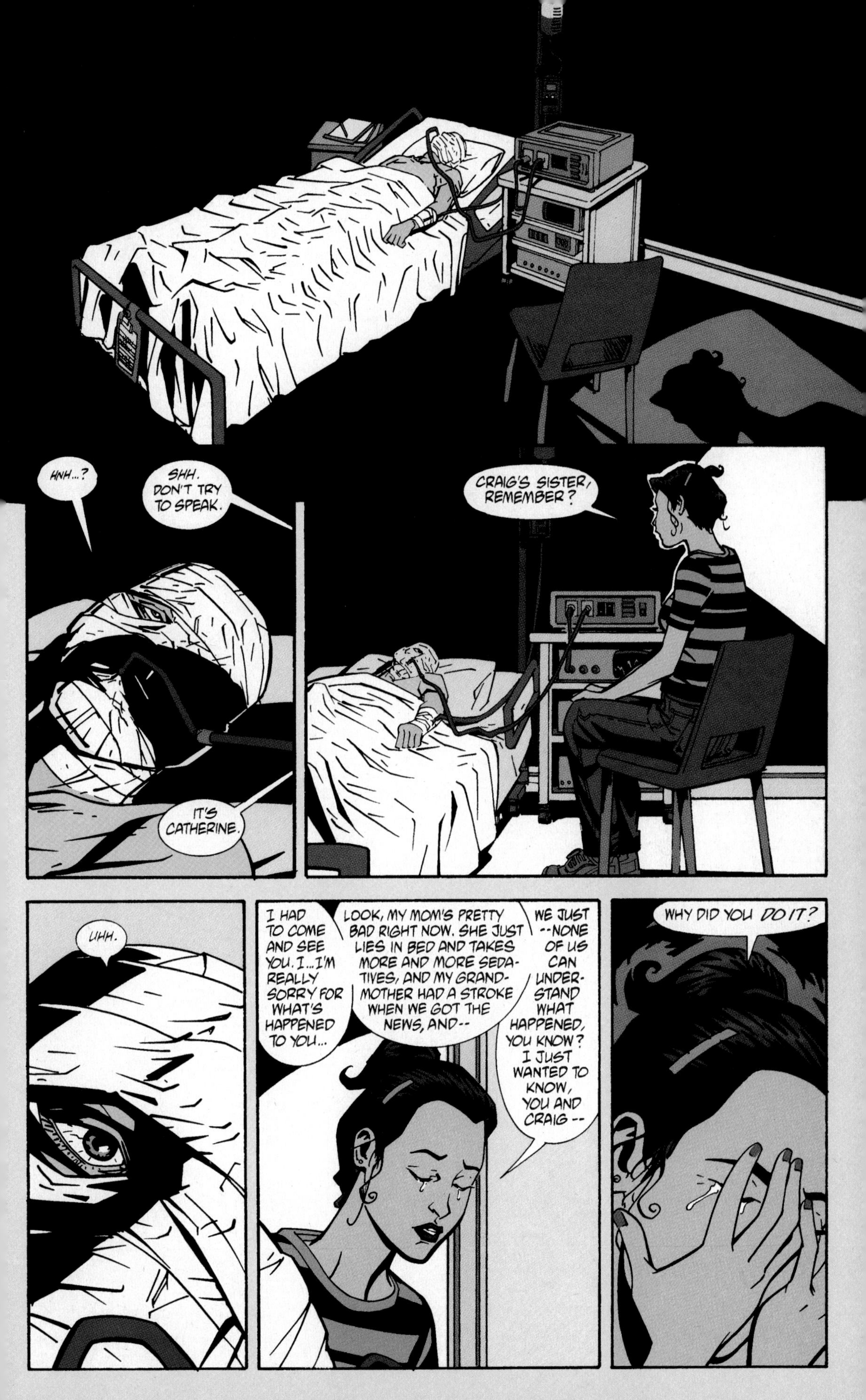

HNH...?
SHH. DON'T TRY TO SPEAK.
IT'S CATHERINE.
CRAIG'S SISTER, REMEMBER?
UHH.
I HAD TO COME AND SEE YOU. I...I'M REALLY SORRY FOR WHAT'S HAPPENED TO YOU...
LOOK, MY MOM'S PRETTY BAD RIGHT NOW. SHE JUST LIES IN BED AND TAKES MORE AND MORE SEDA-TIVES, AND MY GRAND-MOTHER HAD A STROKE WHEN WE GOT THE NEWS, AND--
WE JUST --NONE OF US CAN UNDER-STAND WHAT HAPPENED, YOU KNOW? I JUST WANTED TO KNOW, YOU AND CRAIG --
WHY DID YOU DO IT?

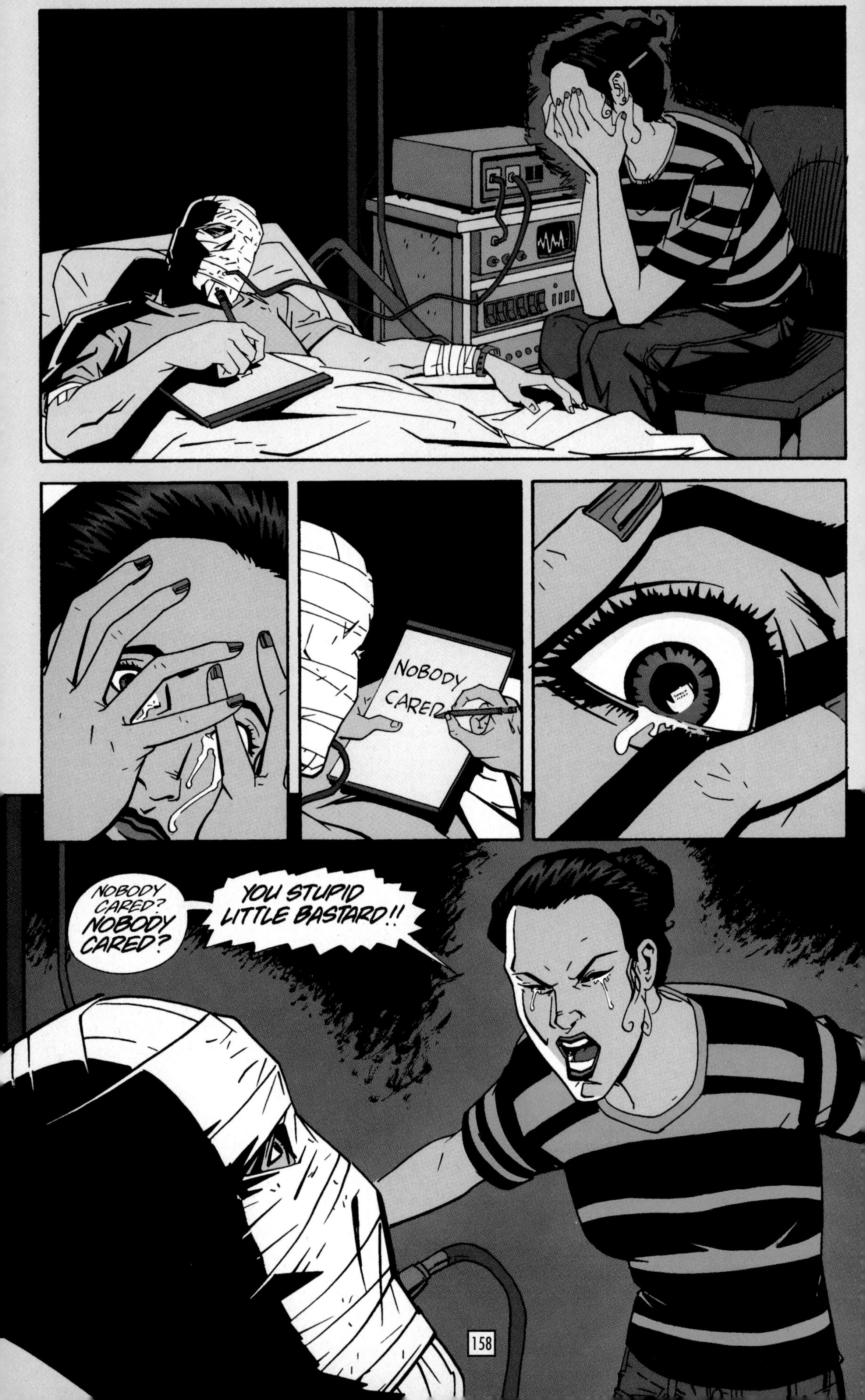

NOBODY
CARED
NOBODY CARED? NOBODY CARED?
YOU STUPID LITTLE BASTARD!!

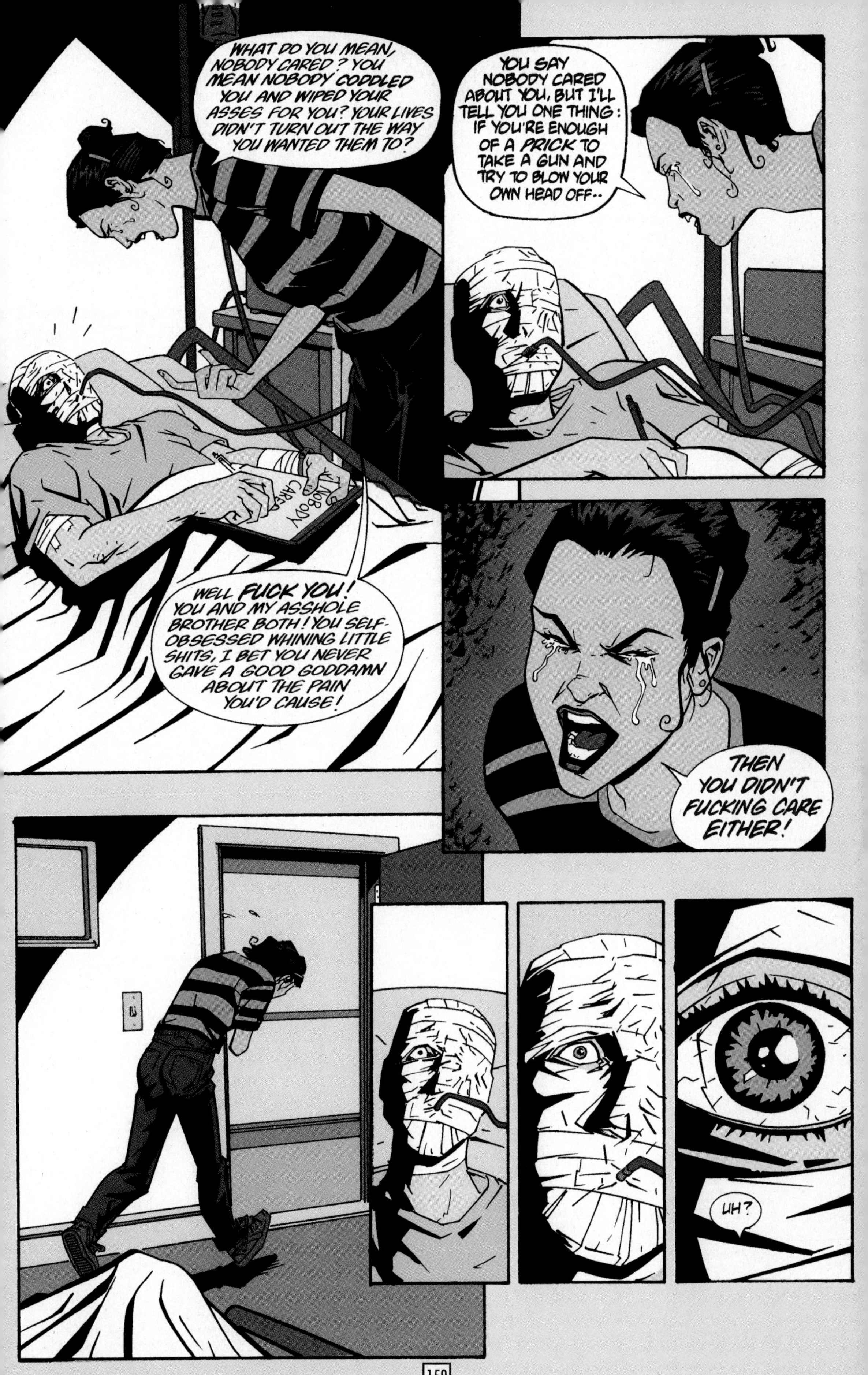
WHAT DO YOU MEAN, NOBODY CARED? YOU MEAN NOBODY CODDLED YOU AND WIPED YOUR ASSES FOR YOU? YOUR LIVES DIDN'T TURN OUT THE WAY YOU WANTED THEM TO?
YOU SAY NOBODY CARED ABOUT YOU, BUT I'LL TELL YOU ONE THING: IF YOU'RE ENOUGH OF A *PRICK* TO TAKE A GUN AND TRY TO BLOW YOUR OWN HEAD OFF..
WELL **FUCK YOU**! YOU AND MY ASSHOLE BROTHER BOTH! YOU SELF-OBSESSED WHINING LITTLE SHITS, I BET YOU NEVER GAVE A GOOD GODDAMN ABOUT THE PAIN YOU'D CAUSE!
THEN YOU DIDN'T FUCKING CARE EITHER!
UH?

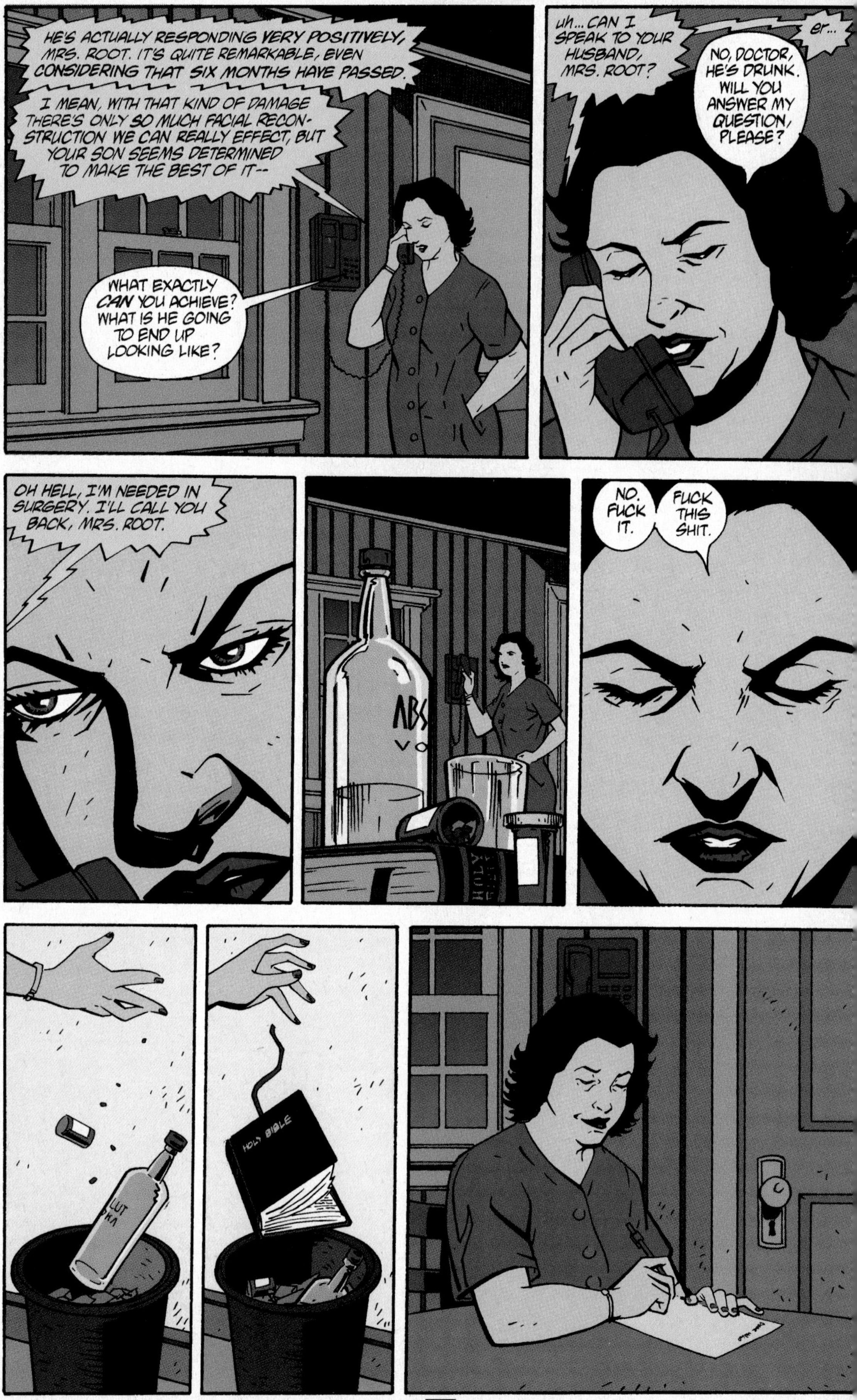
HE'S ACTUALLY RESPONDING VERY POSITIVELY, MRS. ROOT. IT'S QUITE REMARKABLE, EVEN CONSIDERING THAT SIX MONTHS HAVE PASSED.
I MEAN, WITH THAT KIND OF DAMAGE THERE'S ONLY SO MUCH FACIAL RECONSTRUCTION WE CAN REALLY EFFECT, BUT YOUR SON SEEMS DETERMINED TO MAKE THE BEST OF IT--
WHAT EXACTLY CAN YOU ACHIEVE? WHAT IS HE GOING TO END UP LOOKING LIKE?
uh... CAN I SPEAK TO YOUR HUSBAND, MRS. ROOT?
er...
NO, DOCTOR, HE'S DRUNK. WILL YOU ANSWER MY QUESTION, PLEASE?
OH HELL, I'M NEEDED IN SURGERY. I'LL CALL YOU BACK, MRS. ROOT.
NO. FUCK IT.
FUCK THIS SHIT.
HOLY BIBLE

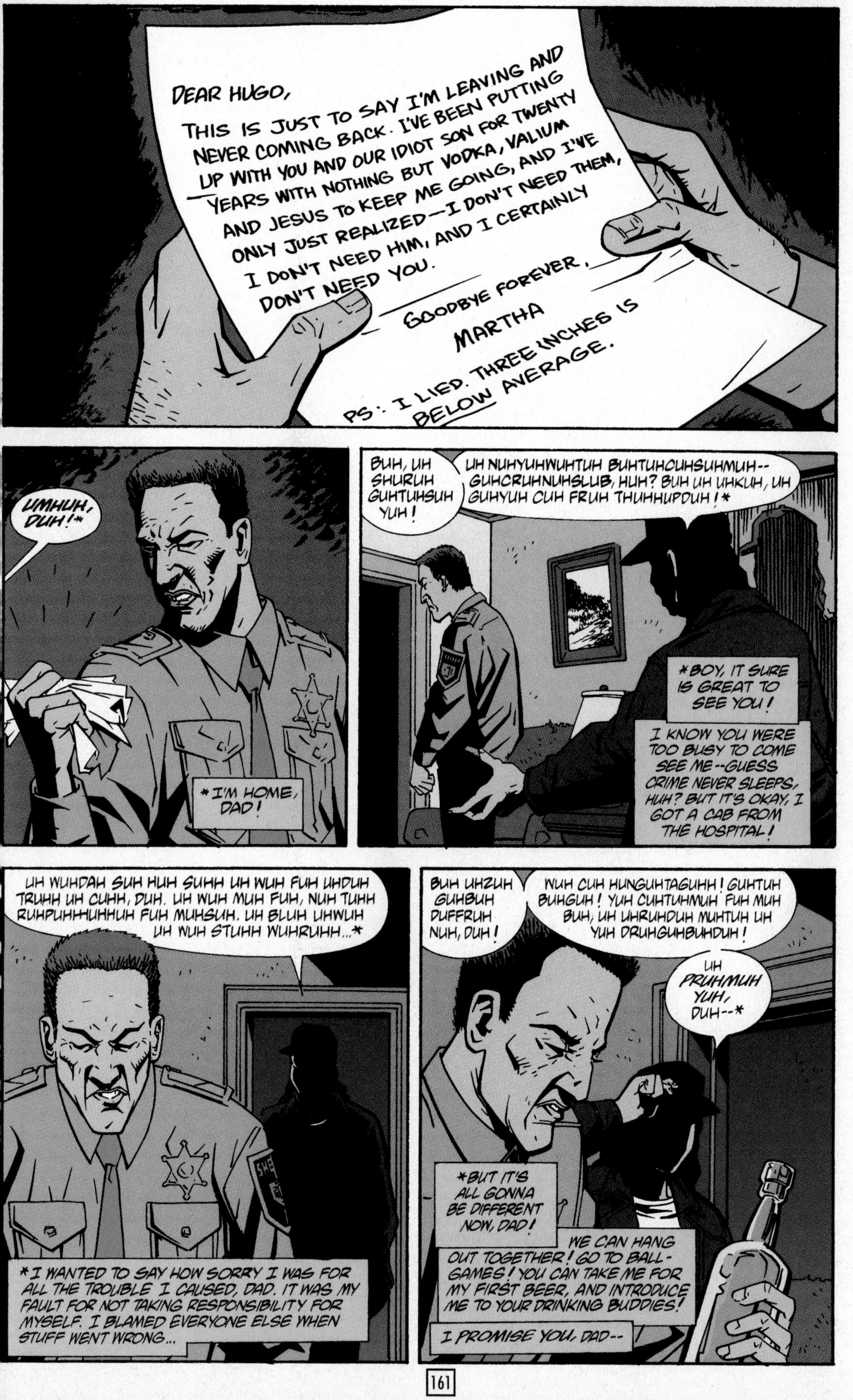
DEAR HUGO,
THIS IS JUST TO SAY I'M LEAVING AND NEVER COMING BACK. I'VE BEEN PUTTING UP WITH YOU AND OUR IDIOT SON FOR TWENTY YEARS WITH NOTHING BUT VODKA, VALIUM AND JESUS TO KEEP ME GOING, AND I'VE ONLY JUST REALIZED--I DON'T NEED THEM, I DON'T NEED HIM, AND I CERTAINLY DON'T NEED YOU.
GOODBYE FOREVER,
MARTHA
PS: I LIED. THREE INCHES IS BELOW AVERAGE.
UMHUH, DUH!*
*I'M HOME, DAD!
BUH, UH SHURUH GUHTUHSUH YUH!
UH NUHYUHWUHTUH BUHTUHCUHSUHMUH--GUHCRUHNUHSLUB, HUH? BUH UH UHKUH, UH GUHYUH CUH FRUH THUHHUPDUH!*
*BOY, IT SURE IS GREAT TO SEE YOU!
I KNOW YOU WERE TOO BUSY TO COME SEE ME--GUESS CRIME NEVER SLEEPS, HUH? BUT IT'S OKAY, I GOT A CAB FROM THE HOSPITAL!
UH WUHDAH SUH HUH SUHH UH WUH FUH UHDUH TRUHH UH CUHH, DUH. UH WUH MUH FUH, NUH TUHH RUHPUHHUHHUH FUH MUHSUH. UH BLUH UHWUH UH WUH STUHH WUHRUHH...*
*I WANTED TO SAY HOW SORRY I WAS FOR ALL THE TROUBLE I CAUSED, DAD. IT WAS MY FAULT FOR NOT TAKING RESPONSIBILITY FOR MYSELF. I BLAMED EVERYONE ELSE WHEN STUFF WENT WRONG...
BUH UHZUH GUHBUH DUFFRUH NUH, DUH!
WUH CUH HUNGUHTAGUHH! GUHTUH BUHGUH! YUH CUHTUHMUH FUH MUH BUH, UH UHRUHDUH MUHTUH UH YUH DRUHGUHBUHDUH!
UH PRUHMUH YUH, DUH--*
*BUT IT'S ALL GONNA BE DIFFERENT NOW, DAD!
WE CAN HANG OUT TOGETHER! GO TO BALL-GAMES! YOU CAN TAKE ME FOR MY FIRST BEER, AND INTRODUCE ME TO YOUR DRINKING BUDDIES!
I PROMISE YOU, DAD--

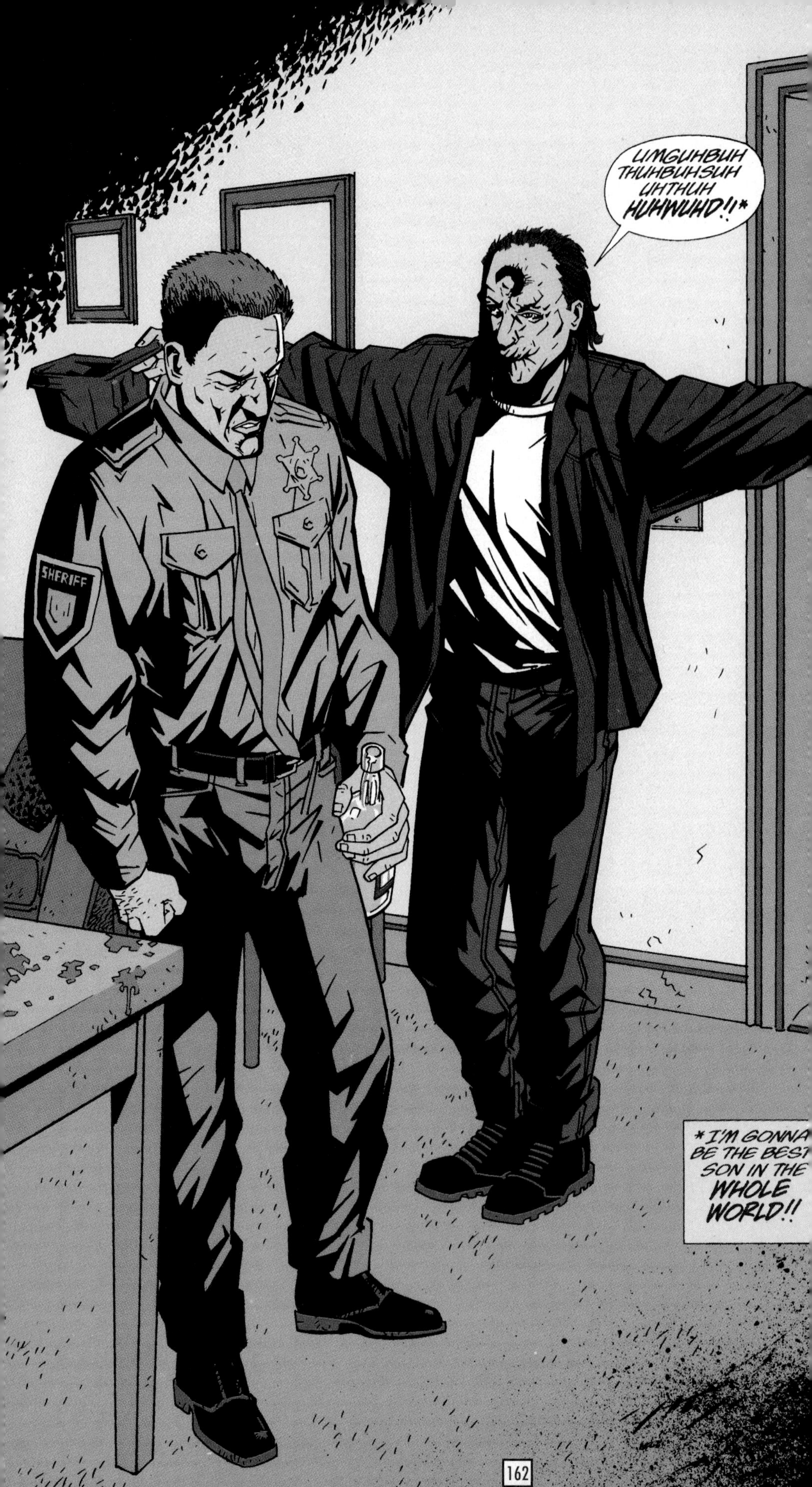
UMGUHBUH THUHBUHSUH UHTHUH HUHWUHD!!*
*I'M GONNA BE THE BEST SON IN THE WHOLE WORLD!!
SHERIFF

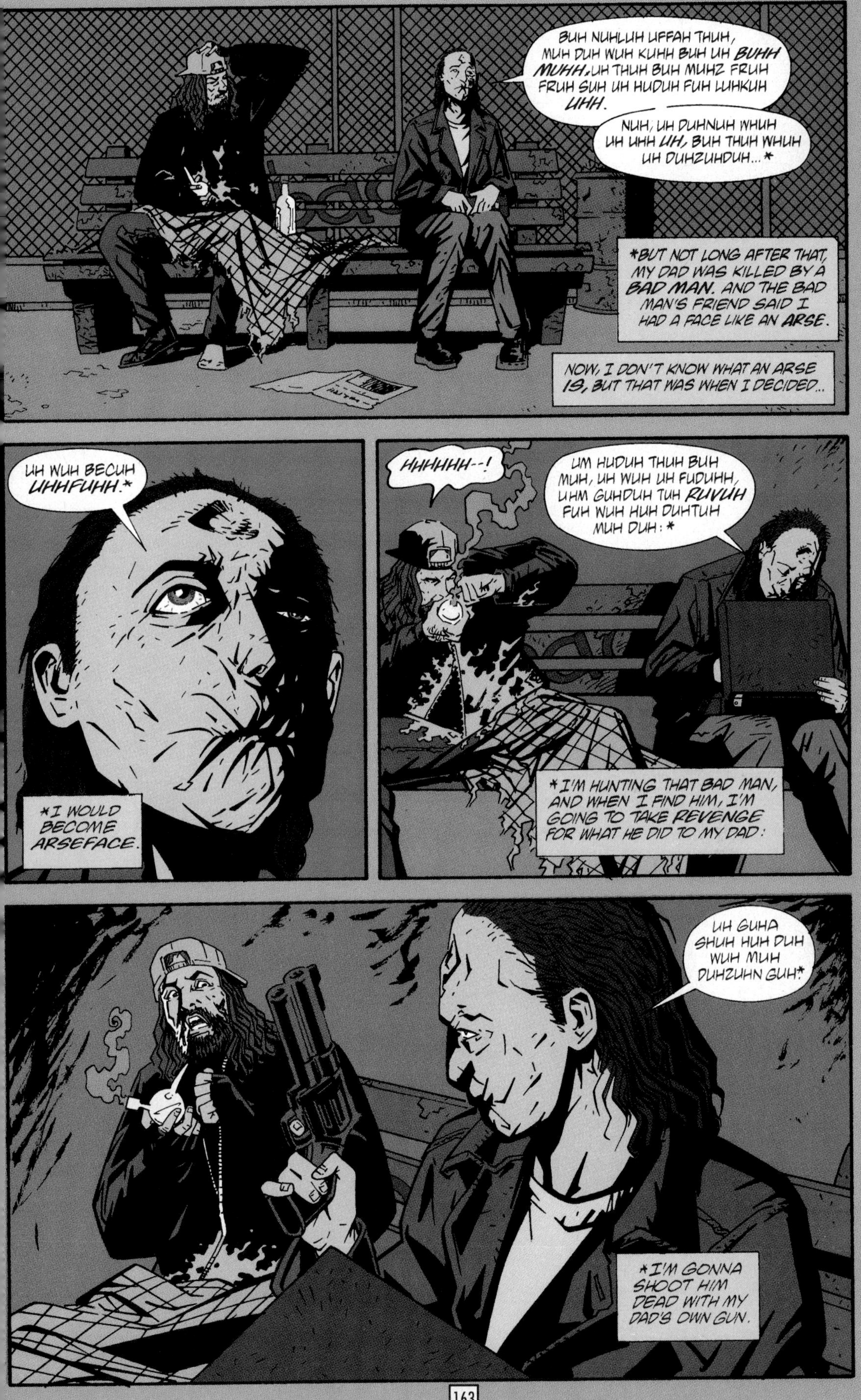
BUH NUHLUH UFFAH THUH, MUH DUH WUH KUHH BUH UH BUHH MUHH. UH THUH BUH MUHZ FRUH FRUH SUH UH HUDUH FUH LUHKUH UHH.
NUH, UH DUHNUH WHUH UH UHH UH, BUH THUH WHUH UH DUHZUHDUH...*
*BUT NOT LONG AFTER THAT, MY DAD WAS KILLED BY A BAD MAN. AND THE BAD MAN'S FRIEND SAID I HAD A FACE LIKE AN ARSE.
NOW, I DON'T KNOW WHAT AN ARSE IS, BUT THAT WAS WHEN I DECIDED...
UH WUH BECUH UHHFUHH.*
*I WOULD BECOME ARSEFACE.
HHHHHH--!
UM HUDUH THUH BUH MUH, UH WUH UH FUDUHH, UHM GUHDUH TUH RUVUH FUH WUH HUH DUHTUH MUH DUH:*
*I'M HUNTING THAT BAD MAN, AND WHEN I FIND HIM, I'M GOING TO TAKE REVENGE FOR WHAT HE DID TO MY DAD:
UH GUHA SHUH HUH DUH WUH MUH DUHZUHN GUH.*
*I'M GONNA SHOOT HIM DEAD WITH MY DAD'S OWN GUN.

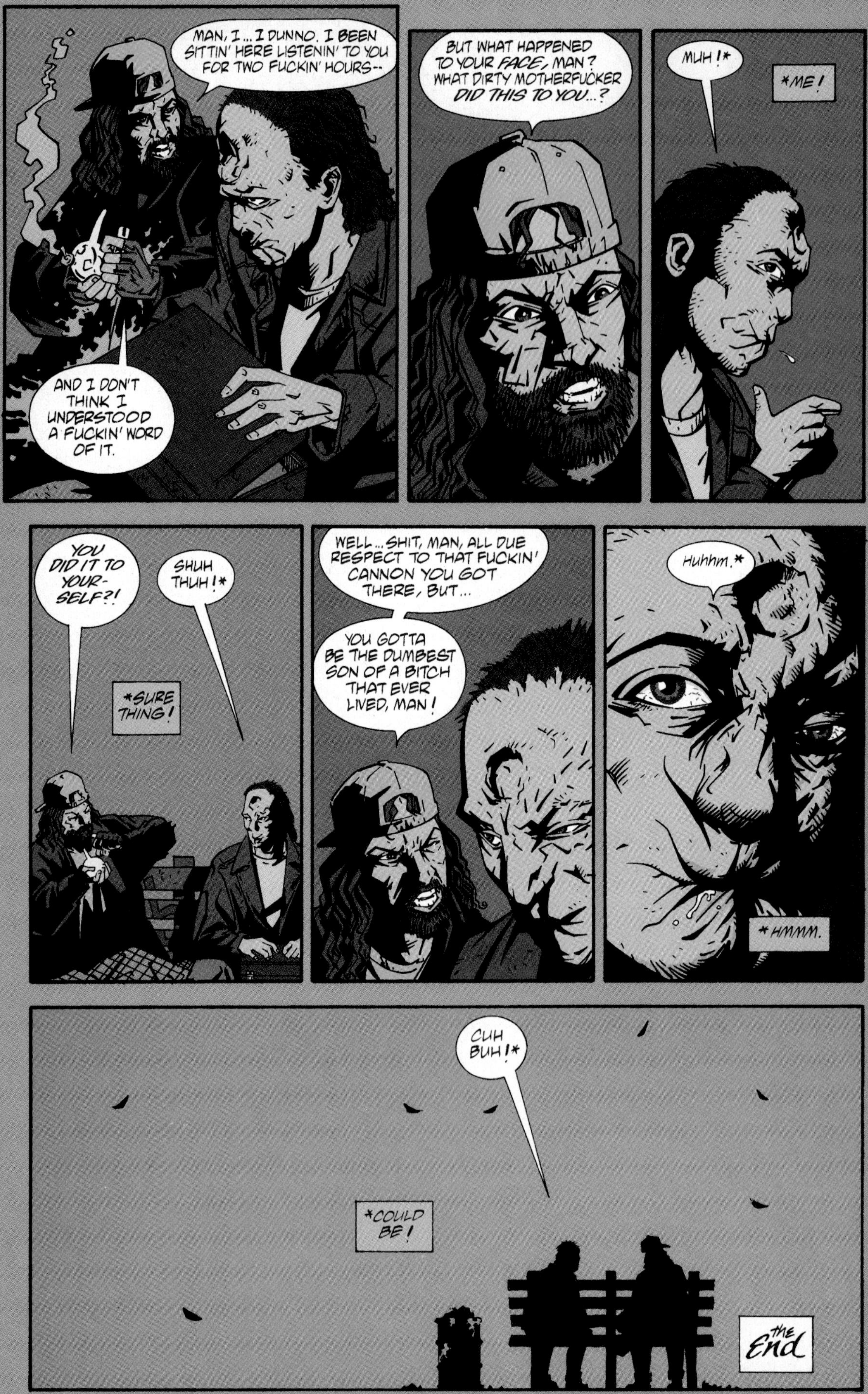
MAN, I... I DUNNO. I BEEN SITTIN' HERE LISTENIN' TO YOU FOR TWO FUCKIN' HOURS--
AND I DON'T THINK I UNDERSTOOD A FUCKIN' WORD OF IT.
BUT WHAT HAPPENED TO YOUR FACE, MAN? WHAT DIRTY MOTHERFUCKER DID THIS TO YOU...?
MUH!*
*ME!
YOU DID IT TO YOURSELF?!
SHUH THUH!*
*SURE THING!
WELL... SHIT, MAN, ALL DUE RESPECT TO THAT FUCKIN' CANNON YOU GOT THERE, BUT...
YOU GOTTA BE THE DUMBEST SON OF A BITCH THAT EVER LIVED, MAN!
Huhhm.*
*HMMM.
CUH BUH!*
*COULD BE!
the End

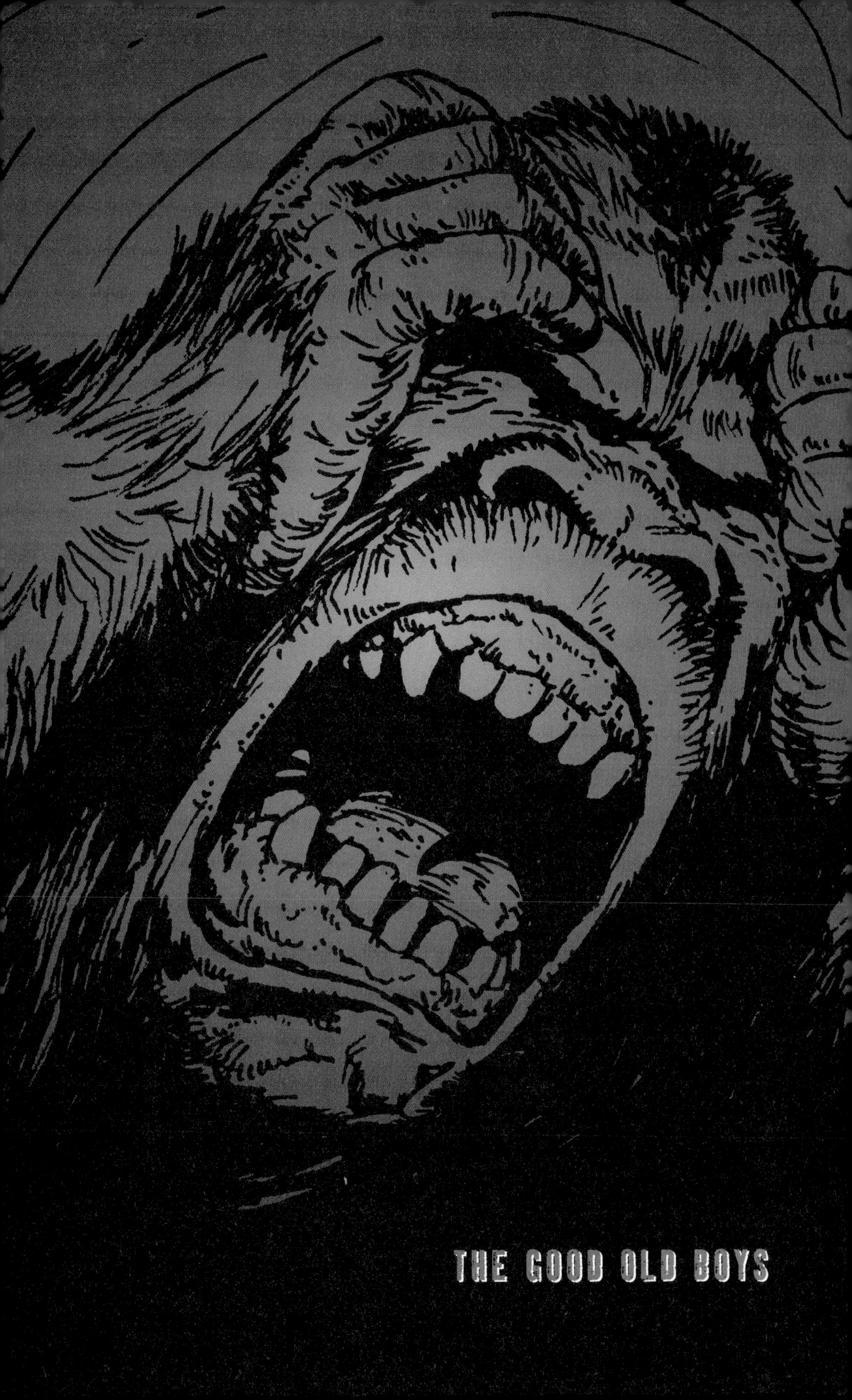

THE GOOD OLD BOYS

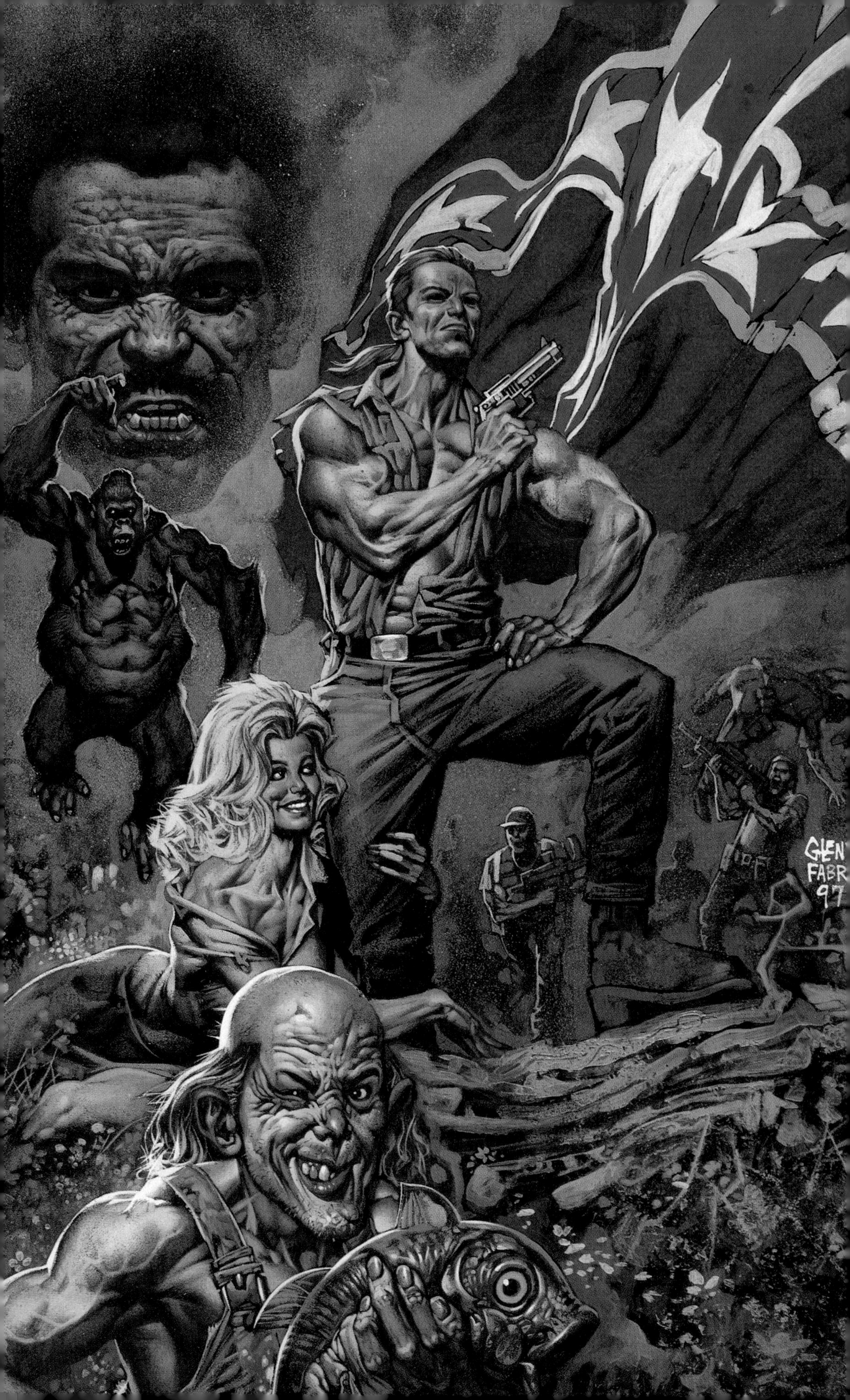
GLEN
FABR
97

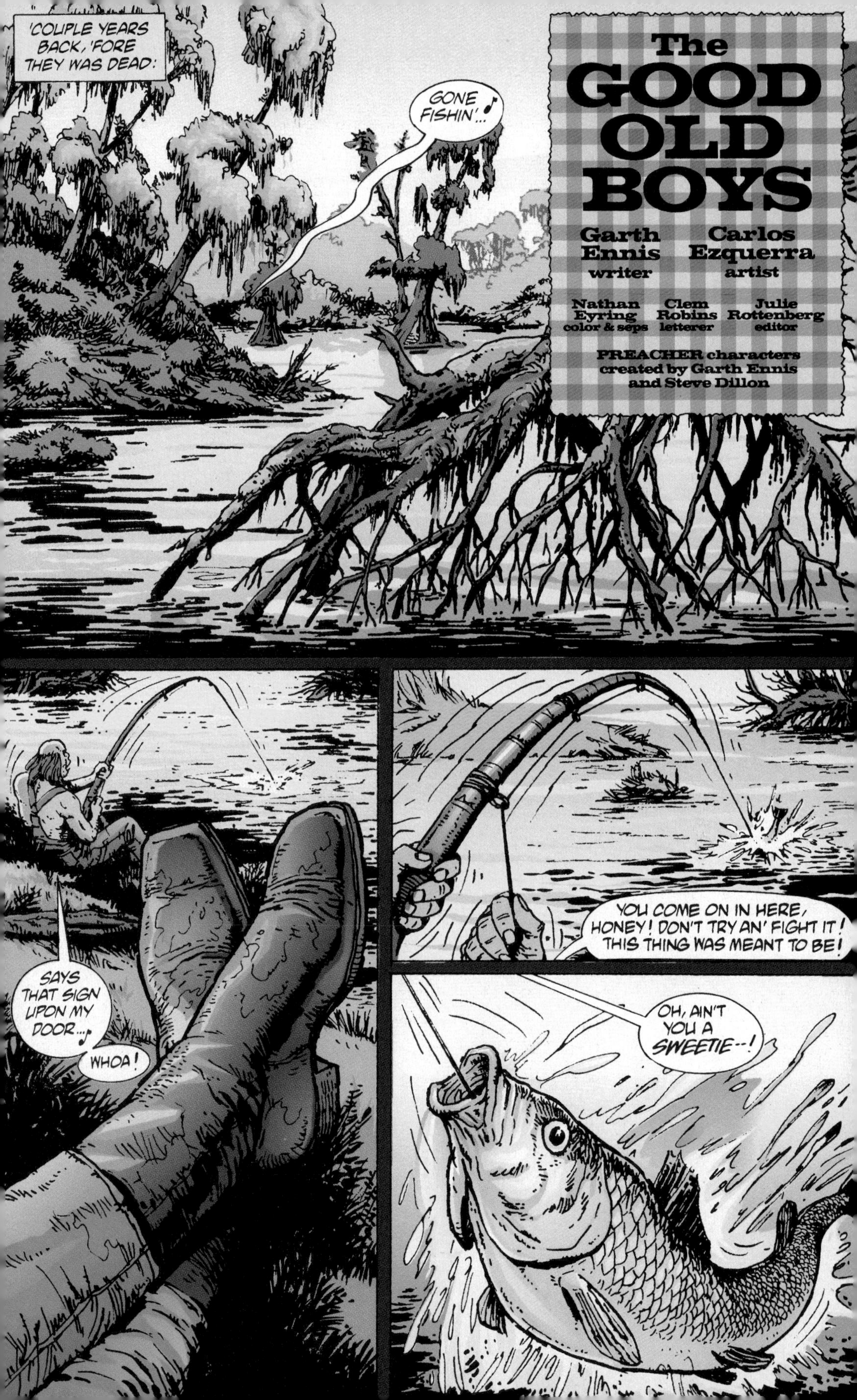
'COUPLE YEARS BACK, 'FORE THEY WAS DEAD:
GONE FISHIN'...♪
The GOOD OLD BOYS
Garth Ennis writer
Carlos Ezquerra artist
Nathan Eyring color & seps
Clem Robins letterer
Julie Rottenberg editor
PREACHER characters created by Garth Ennis and Steve Dillon
SAYS THAT SIGN UPON MY DOOR...♪
WHOA!
YOU COME ON IN HERE, HONEY! DON'T TRY AN' FIGHT IT! THIS THING WAS MEANT TO BE!
OH, AIN'T YOU A SWEETIE--!

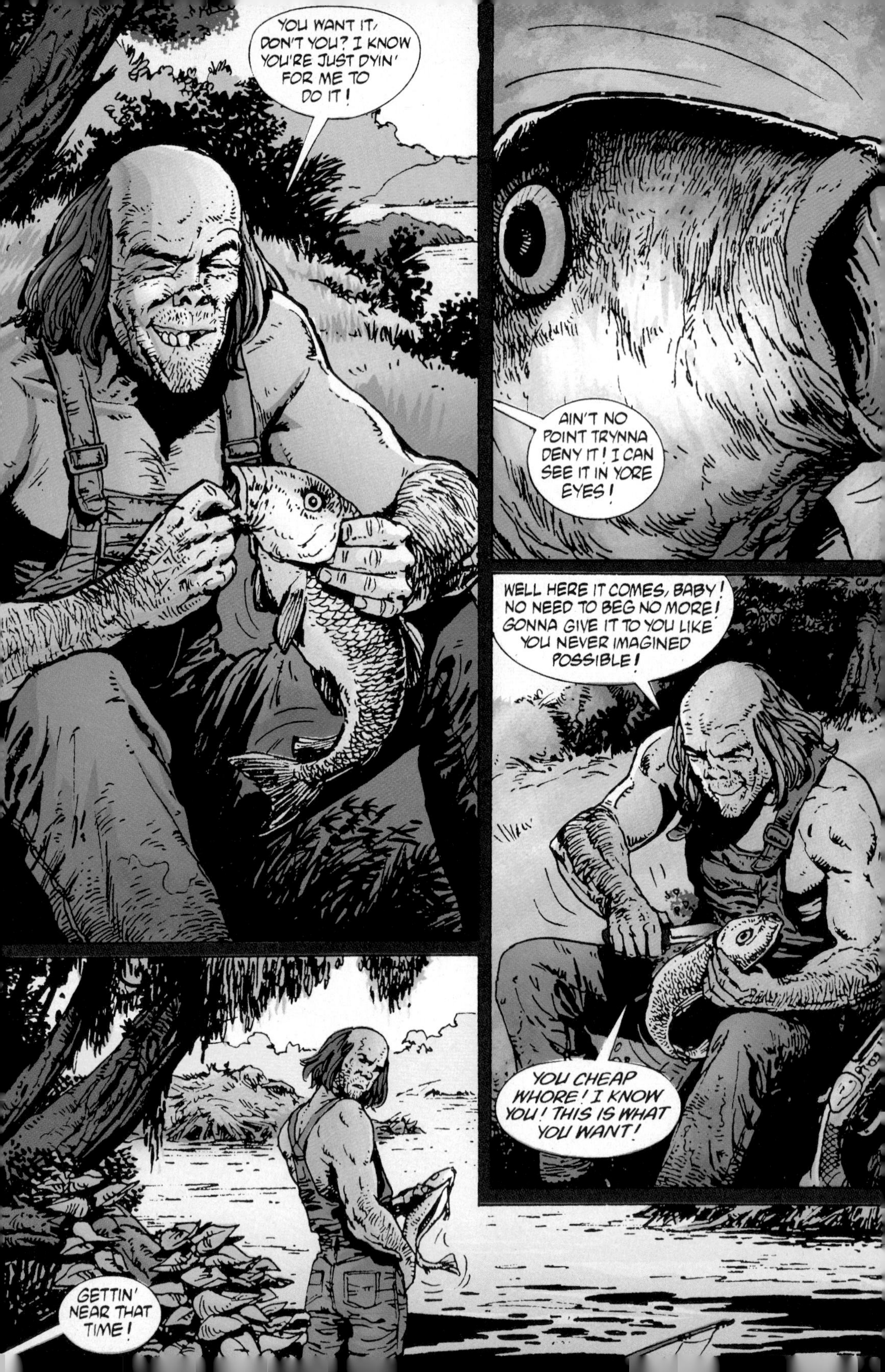
YOU WANT IT, DON'T YOU? I KNOW YOU'RE JUST DYIN' FOR ME TO DO IT!
AIN'T NO POINT TRYNNA DENY IT! I CAN SEE IT IN YORE EYES!
WELL HERE IT COMES, BABY! NO NEED TO BEG NO MORE! GONNA GIVE IT TO YOU LIKE YOU NEVER IMAGINED POSSIBLE!
YOU CHEAP WHORE! I KNOW YOU! THIS IS WHAT YOU WANT!
GETTIN' NEAR THAT TIME!

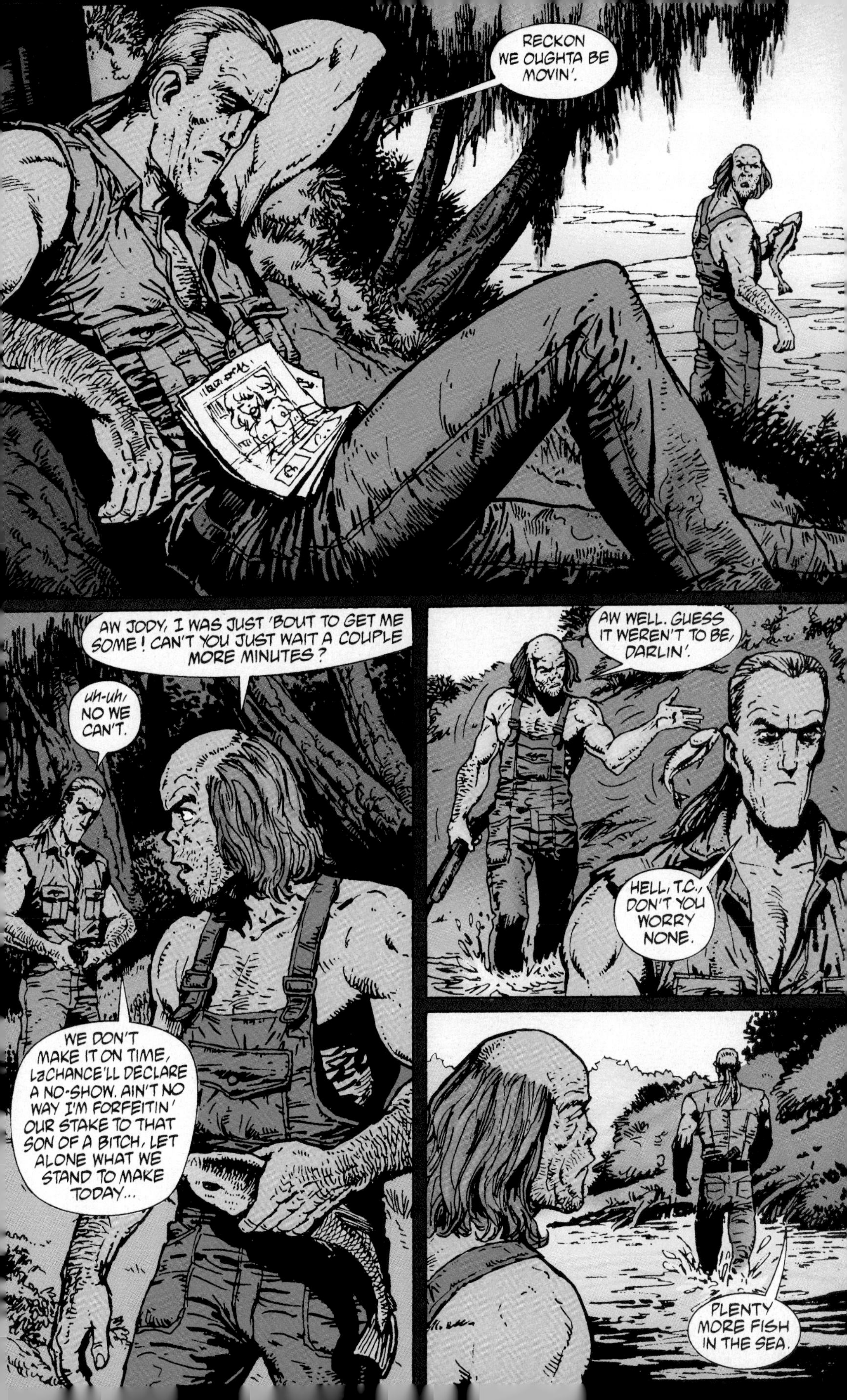
RECKON WE OUGHTA BE MOVIN'.
AW JODY, I WAS JUST 'BOUT TO GET ME SOME! CAN'T YOU JUST WAIT A COUPLE MORE MINUTES?
uh-uh, NO WE CAN'T.
WE DON'T MAKE IT ON TIME, LaCHANCE'LL DECLARE A NO-SHOW. AIN'T NO WAY I'M FORFEITIN' OUR STAKE TO THAT SON OF A BITCH, LET ALONE WHAT WE STAND TO MAKE TODAY...
AW WELL. GUESS IT WEREN'T TO BE, DARLIN'.
HELL, T.C., DON'T YOU WORRY NONE.
PLENTY MORE FISH IN THE SEA.

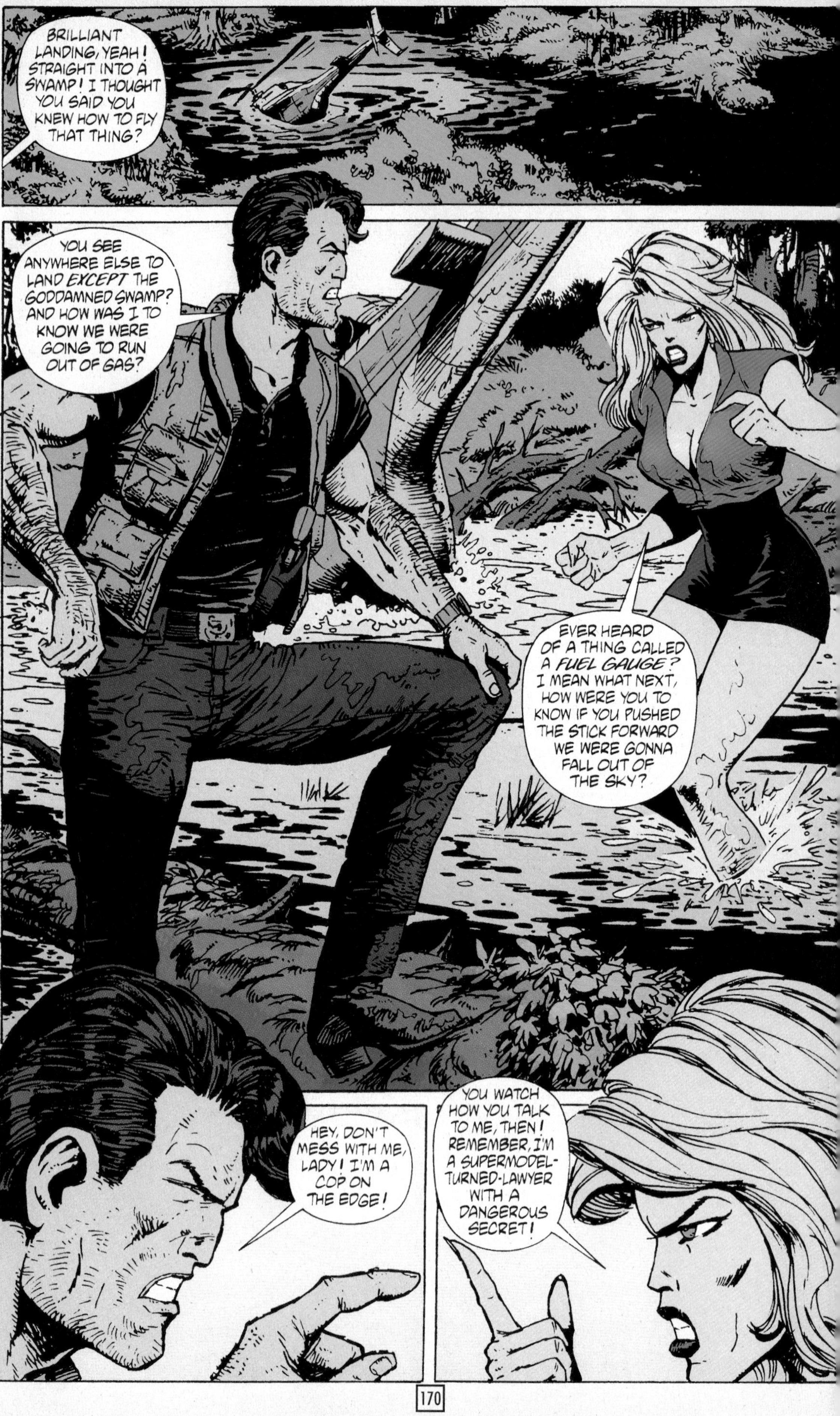
BRILLIANT LANDING, YEAH! STRAIGHT INTO A SWAMP! I THOUGHT YOU SAID YOU KNEW HOW TO FLY THAT THING?
YOU SEE ANYWHERE ELSE TO LAND *EXCEPT* THE GODDAMNED SWAMP? AND HOW WAS I TO KNOW WE WERE GOING TO RUN OUT OF GAS?
EVER HEARD OF A THING CALLED A *FUEL GAUGE*? I MEAN WHAT NEXT, HOW WERE YOU TO KNOW IF YOU PUSHED THE STICK FORWARD WE WERE GONNA FALL OUT OF THE SKY?
HEY, DON'T MESS WITH ME, LADY! I'M A COP ON THE EDGE!
YOU WATCH HOW YOU TALK TO ME, THEN! REMEMBER, I'M A SUPERMODEL-TURNED-LAWYER WITH A DANGEROUS SECRET!

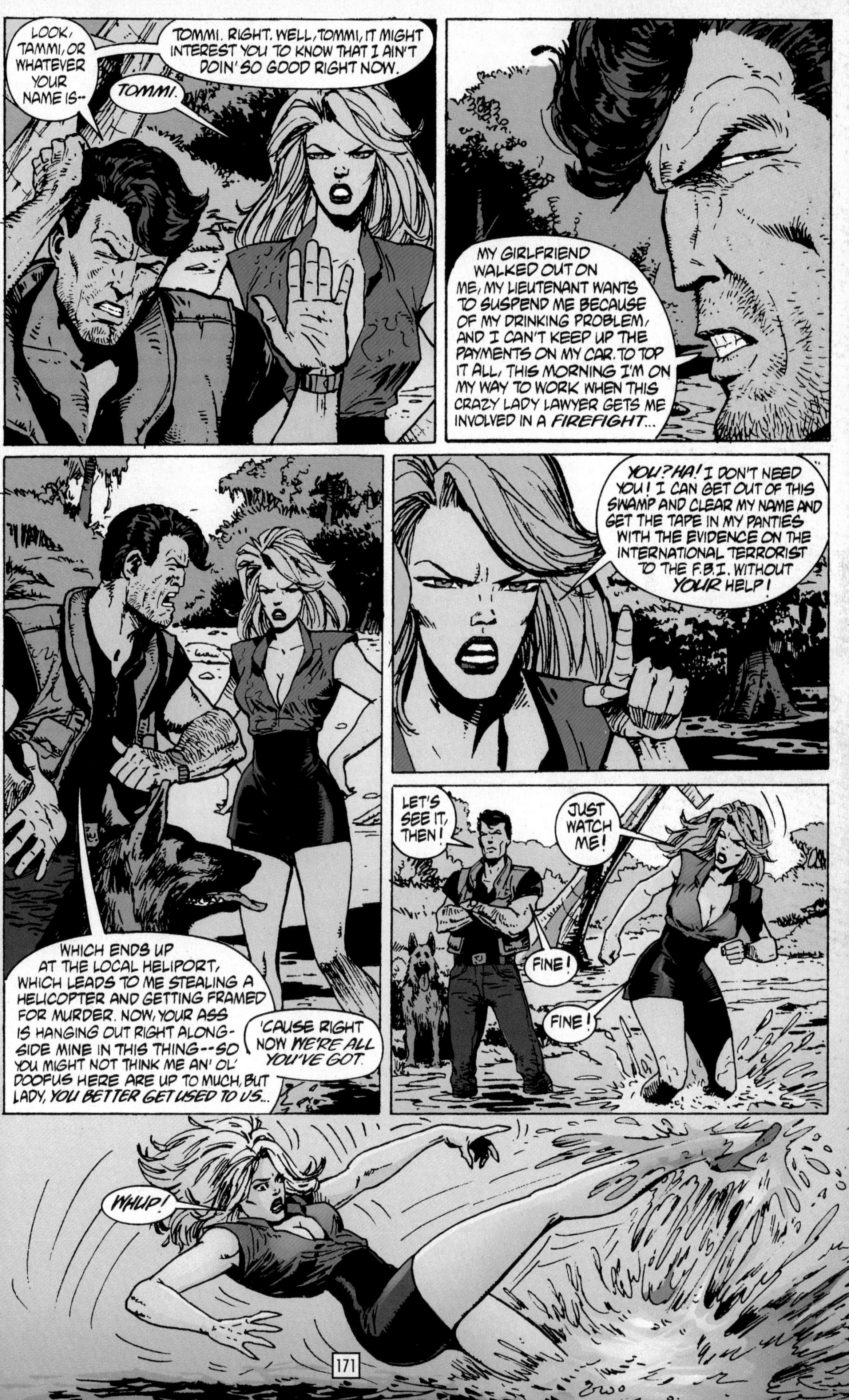
LOOK, TAMMI, OR WHATEVER YOUR NAME IS--
TOMMI.
TOMMI. RIGHT. WELL, TOMMI, IT MIGHT INTEREST YOU TO KNOW THAT I AIN'T DOIN' SO GOOD RIGHT NOW.
MY GIRLFRIEND WALKED OUT ON ME, MY LIEUTENANT WANTS TO SUSPEND ME BECAUSE OF MY DRINKING PROBLEM, AND I CAN'T KEEP UP THE PAYMENTS ON MY CAR. TO TOP IT ALL, THIS MORNING I'M ON MY WAY TO WORK WHEN THIS CRAZY LADY LAWYER GETS ME INVOLVED IN A FIREFIGHT...
WHICH ENDS UP AT THE LOCAL HELIPORT, WHICH LEADS TO ME STEALING A HELICOPTER AND GETTING FRAMED FOR MURDER. NOW, YOUR ASS IS HANGING OUT RIGHT ALONGSIDE MINE IN THIS THING--SO YOU MIGHT NOT THINK ME AN' OL' DOOFUS HERE ARE UP TO MUCH, BUT LADY, YOU BETTER GET USED TO US...
'CAUSE RIGHT NOW WE'RE ALL YOU'VE GOT.
YOU? HA! I DON'T NEED YOU! I CAN GET OUT OF THIS SWAMP AND CLEAR MY NAME AND GET THE TAPE IN MY PANTIES WITH THE EVIDENCE ON THE INTERNATIONAL TERRORIST TO THE F.B.I. WITHOUT YOUR HELP!
LET'S SEE IT, THEN!
JUST WATCH ME!
FINE!
FINE!
WHUP!

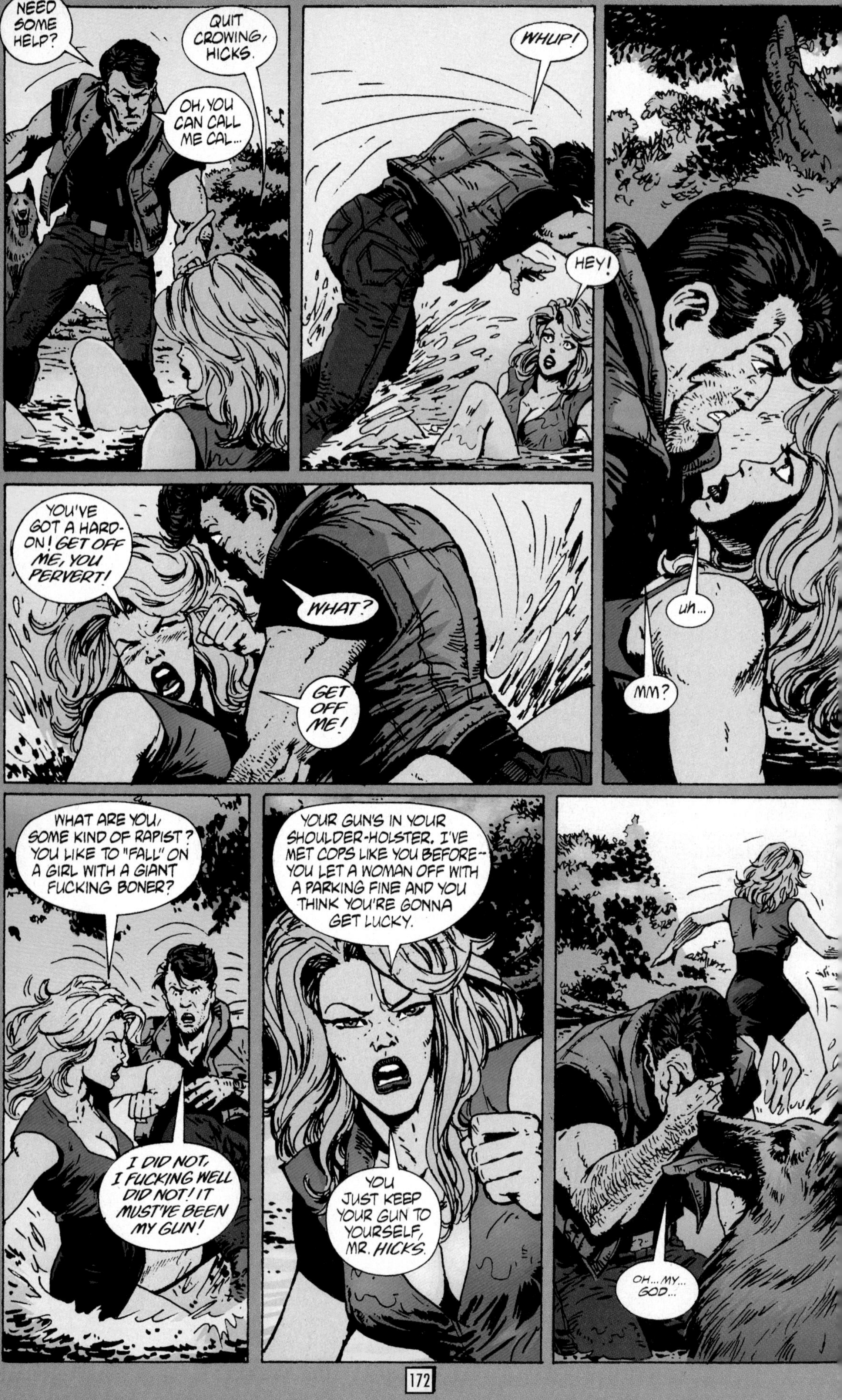
NEED SOME HELP?
QUIT CROWING, HICKS.
OH, YOU CAN CALL ME CAL...
WHUP!
HEY!
uh...
MM?
YOU'VE GOT A HARD-ON! GET OFF ME, YOU PERVERT!
WHAT?
GET OFF ME!
WHAT ARE YOU, SOME KIND OF RAPIST? YOU LIKE TO "FALL" ON A GIRL WITH A GIANT FUCKING BONER?
I DID NOT, I FUCKING WELL DID NOT! IT MUST'VE BEEN MY GUN!
YOUR GUN'S IN YOUR SHOULDER-HOLSTER. I'VE MET COPS LIKE YOU BEFORE-- YOU LET A WOMAN OFF WITH A PARKING FINE AND YOU THINK YOU'RE GONNA GET LUCKY.
YOU JUST KEEP YOUR GUN TO YOURSELF, MR. HICKS.
OH... MY... GOD...

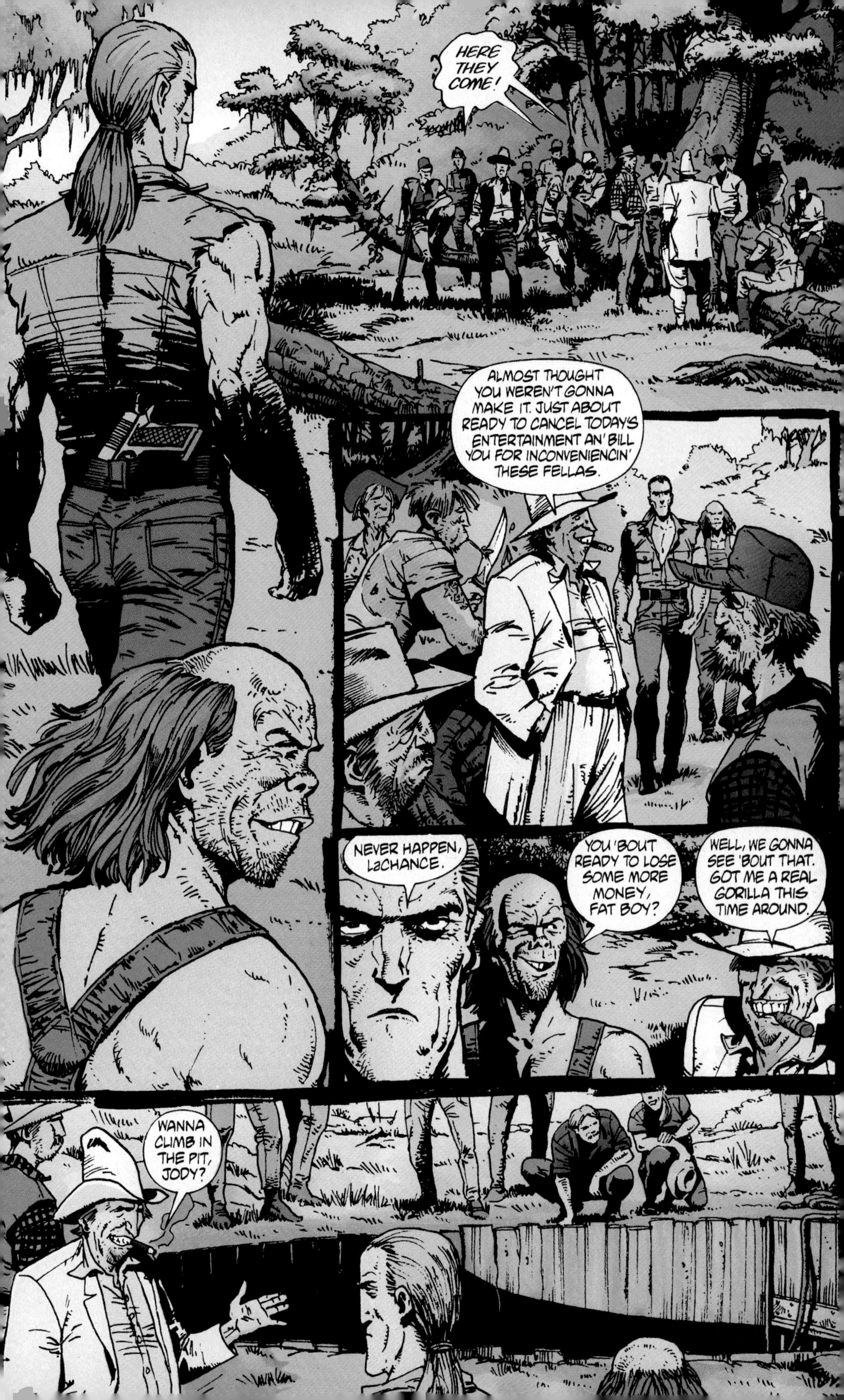
HERE THEY COME!
ALMOST THOUGHT YOU WEREN'T GONNA MAKE IT. JUST ABOUT READY TO CANCEL TODAY'S ENTERTAINMENT AN' BILL YOU FOR INCONVENIENCIN' THESE FELLAS.
NEVER HAPPEN, LaCHANCE.
YOU 'BOUT READY TO LOSE SOME MORE MONEY, FAT BOY?
WELL, WE GONNA SEE 'BOUT THAT. GOT ME A REAL GORILLA THIS TIME AROUND.
WANNA CLIMB IN THE PIT, JODY?

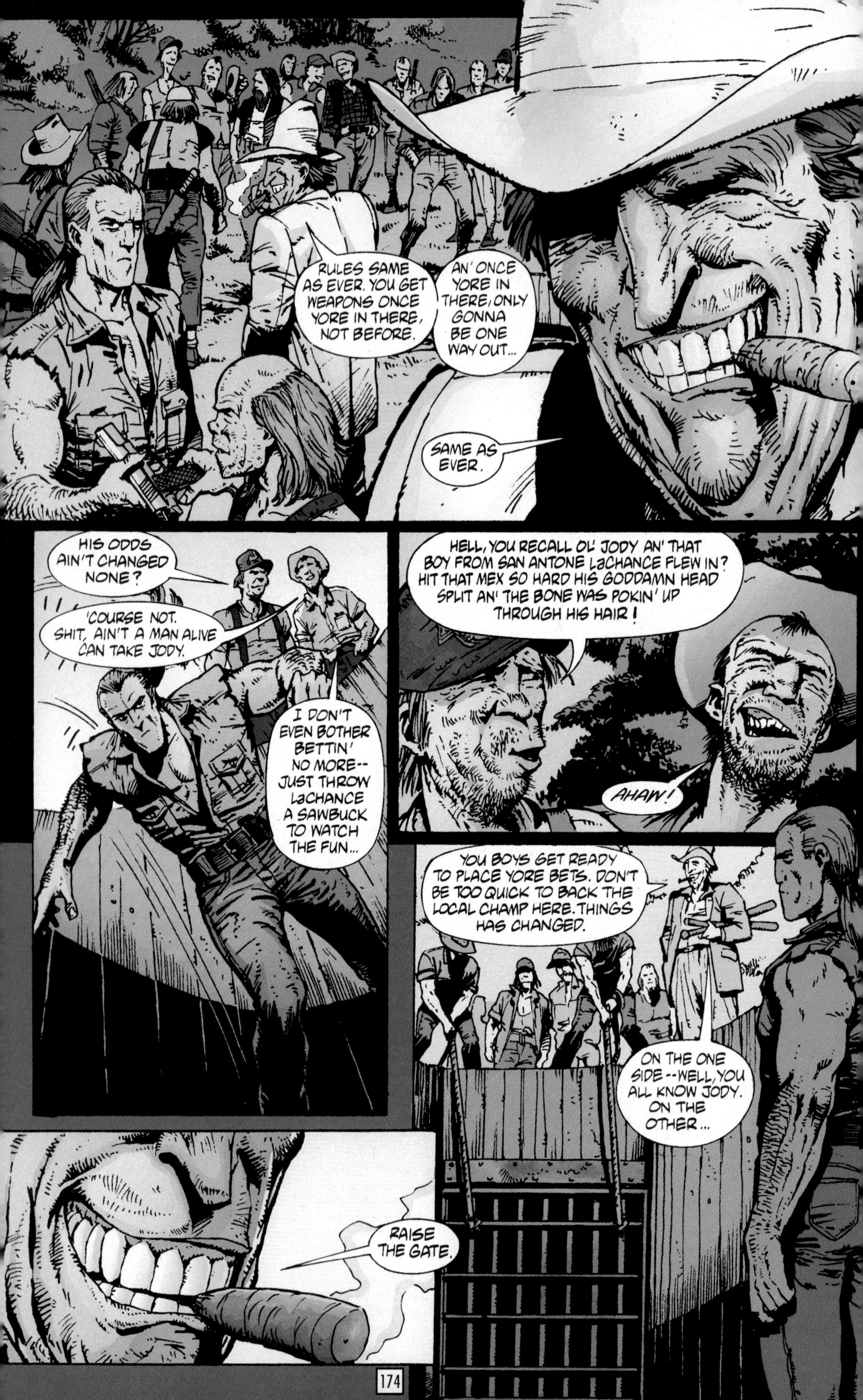
RULES SAME AS EVER. YOU GET WEAPONS ONCE YORE IN THERE, NOT BEFORE.
AN' ONCE YORE IN THERE, ONLY GONNA BE ONE WAY OUT...
SAME AS EVER.
HIS ODDS AIN'T CHANGED NONE?
'COURSE NOT. SHIT, AIN'T A MAN ALIVE CAN TAKE JODY.
I DON'T EVEN BOTHER BETTIN' NO MORE--JUST THROW LaCHANCE A SAWBUCK TO WATCH THE FUN...
HELL, YOU RECALL OL' JODY AN' THAT BOY FROM SAN ANTONE LaCHANCE FLEW IN? HIT THAT MEX SO HARD HIS GODDAMN HEAD SPLIT AN' THE BONE WAS POKIN' UP THROUGH HIS HAIR!
AHAW!
YOU BOYS GET READY TO PLACE YORE BETS. DON'T BE TOO QUICK TO BACK THE LOCAL CHAMP HERE. THINGS HAS CHANGED.
ON THE ONE SIDE--WELL, YOU ALL KNOW JODY. ON THE OTHER...
RAISE THE GATE.

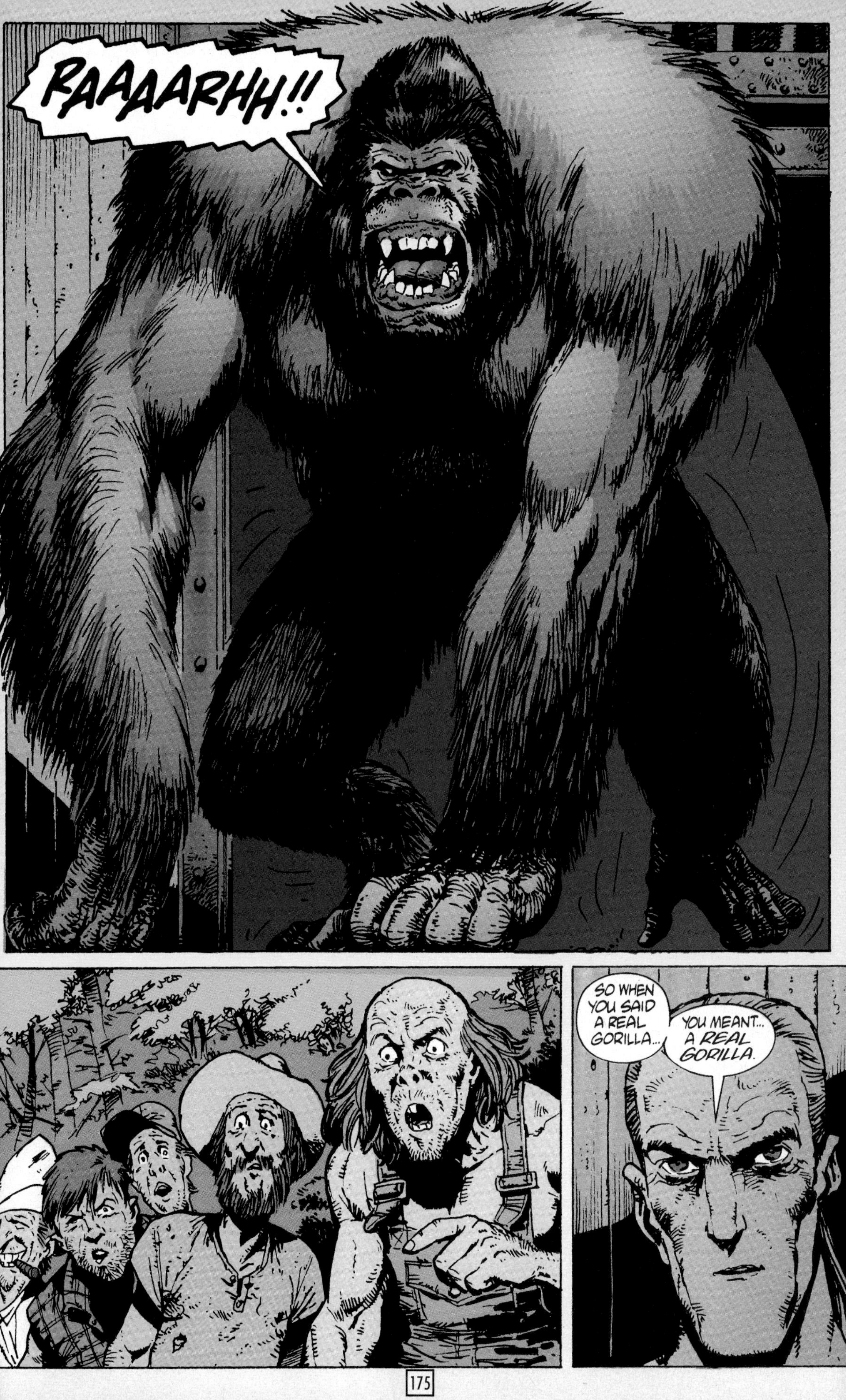
RAAAARHH!!
SO WHEN YOU SAID A REAL GORILLA...
YOU MEANT... A REAL GORILLA.

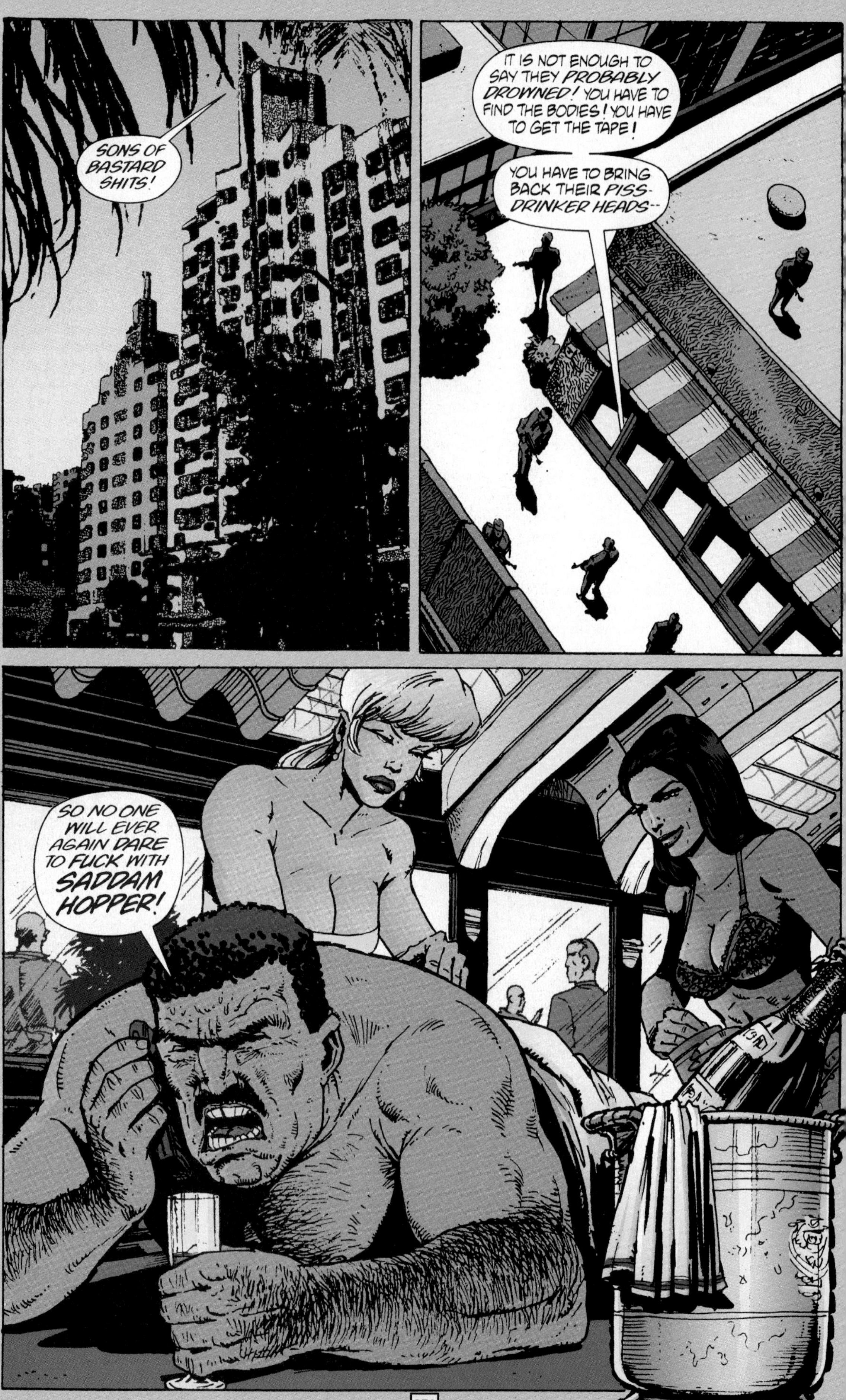
SONS OF BASTARD SHITS!
IT IS NOT ENOUGH TO SAY THEY PROBABLY DROWNED! YOU HAVE TO FIND THE BODIES! YOU HAVE TO GET THE TAPE!
YOU HAVE TO BRING BACK THEIR PISS-DRINKER HEADS--
SO NO ONE WILL EVER AGAIN DARE TO FUCK WITH SADDAM HOPPER!

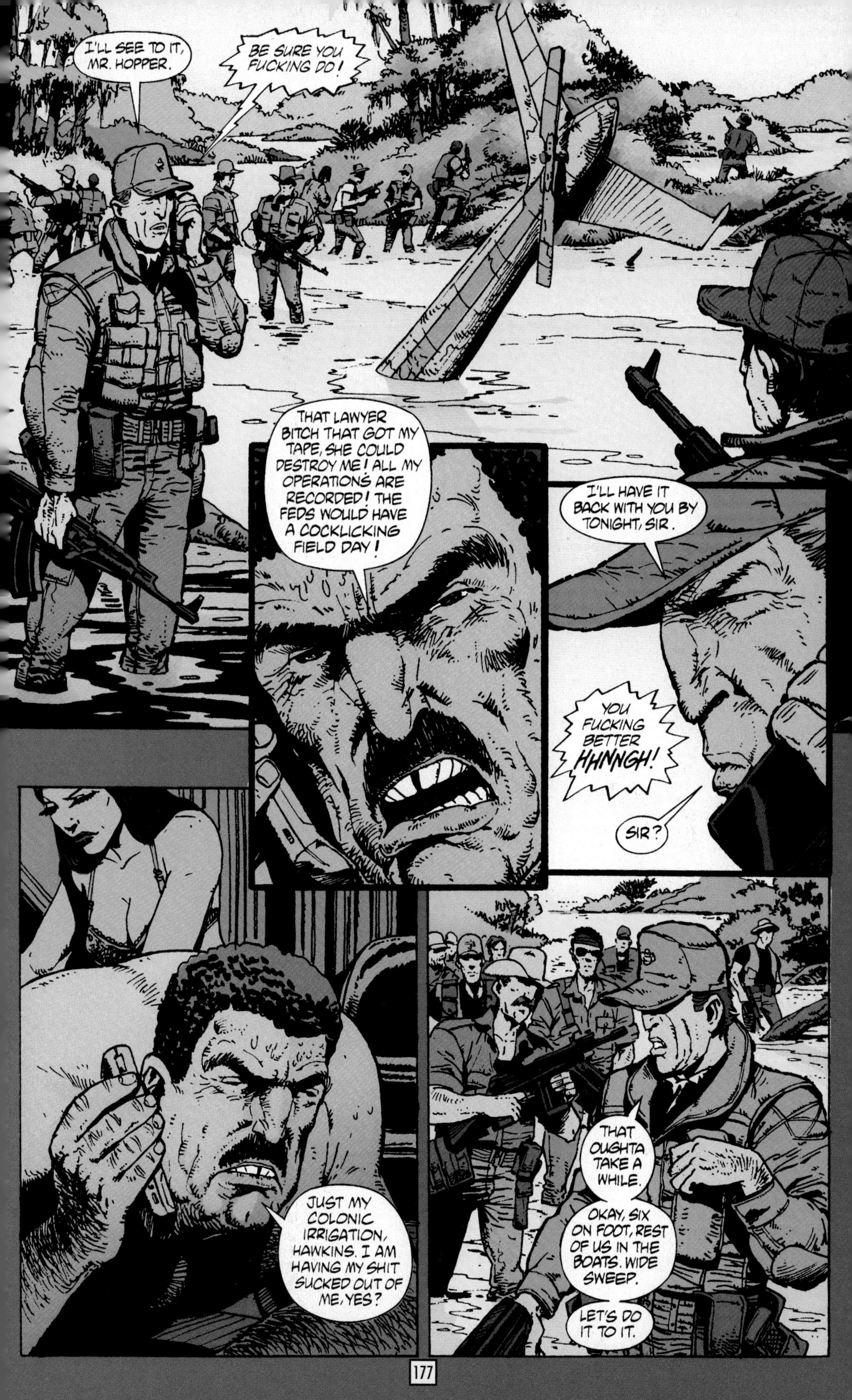

I'LL SEE TO IT, MR. HOPPER.
BE SURE YOU FUCKING DO!
THAT LAWYER BITCH THAT GOT MY TAPE, SHE COULD DESTROY ME! ALL MY OPERATIONS ARE RECORDED! THE FEDS WOULD HAVE A COCKLICKING FIELD DAY!
I'LL HAVE IT BACK WITH YOU BY TONIGHT, SIR.
YOU FUCKING BETTER HHNNGH!
SIR?
JUST MY COLONIC IRRIGATION, HAWKINS. I AM HAVING MY SHIT SUCKED OUT OF ME, YES?
THAT OUGHTA TAKE A WHILE.
OKAY, SIX ON FOOT, REST OF US IN THE BOATS. WIDE SWEEP.
LET'S DO IT TO IT.

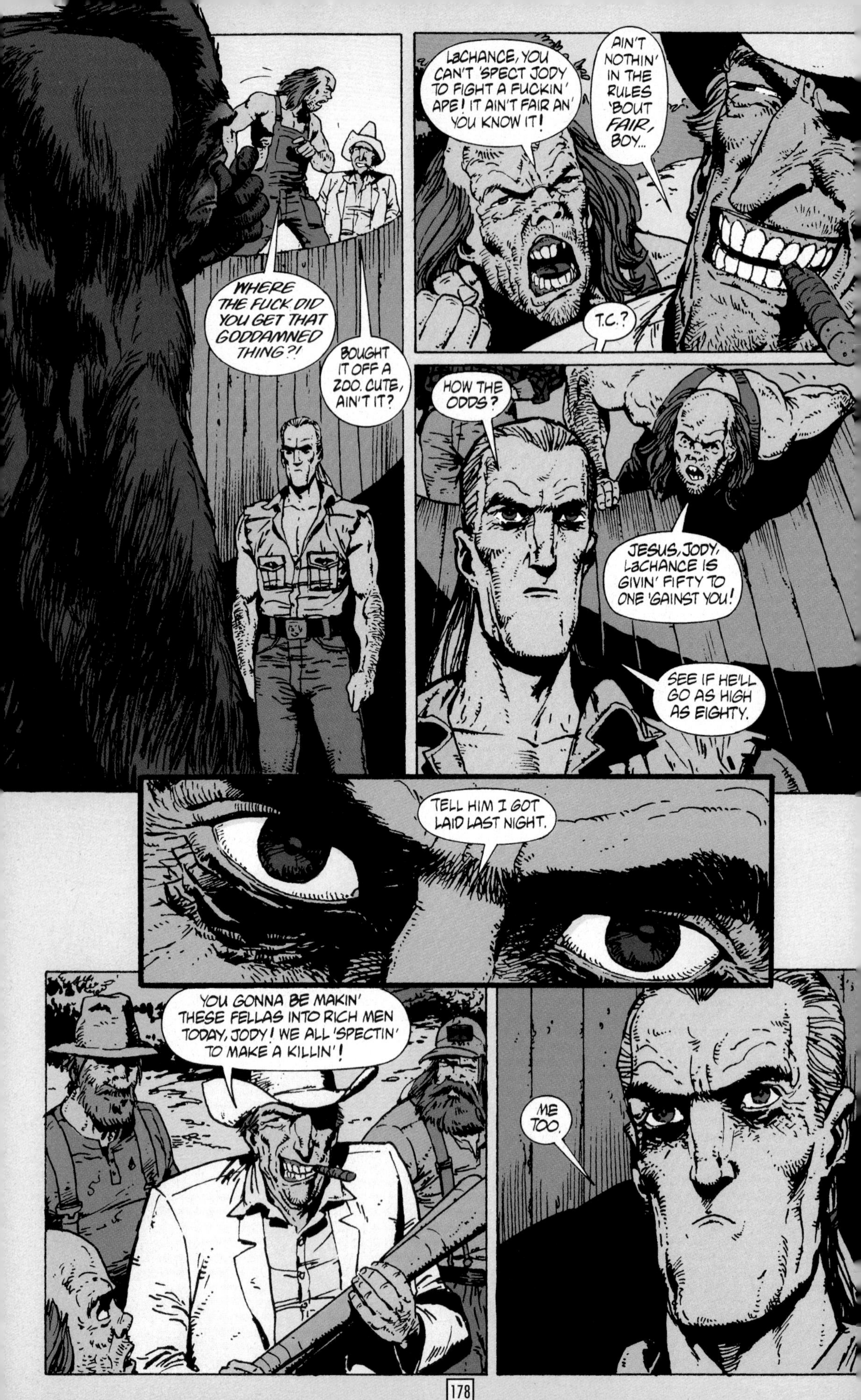
WHERE THE FUCK DID YOU GET THAT GODDAMNED THING?!
BOUGHT IT OFF A ZOO. CUTE, AIN'T IT?
LaCHANCE, YOU CAN'T 'SPECT JODY TO FIGHT A FUCKIN' APE! IT AIN'T FAIR AN' YOU KNOW IT!
AIN'T NOTHIN' IN THE RULES 'BOUT FAIR, BOY...
T.C.?
HOW THE ODDS?
JESUS, JODY, LaCHANCE IS GIVIN' FIFTY TO ONE 'GAINST YOU!
SEE IF HE'LL GO AS HIGH AS EIGHTY.
TELL HIM I GOT LAID LAST NIGHT.
YOU GONNA BE MAKIN' THESE FELLAS INTO RICH MEN TODAY, JODY! WE ALL 'SPECTIN' TO MAKE A KILLIN'!
ME TOO.

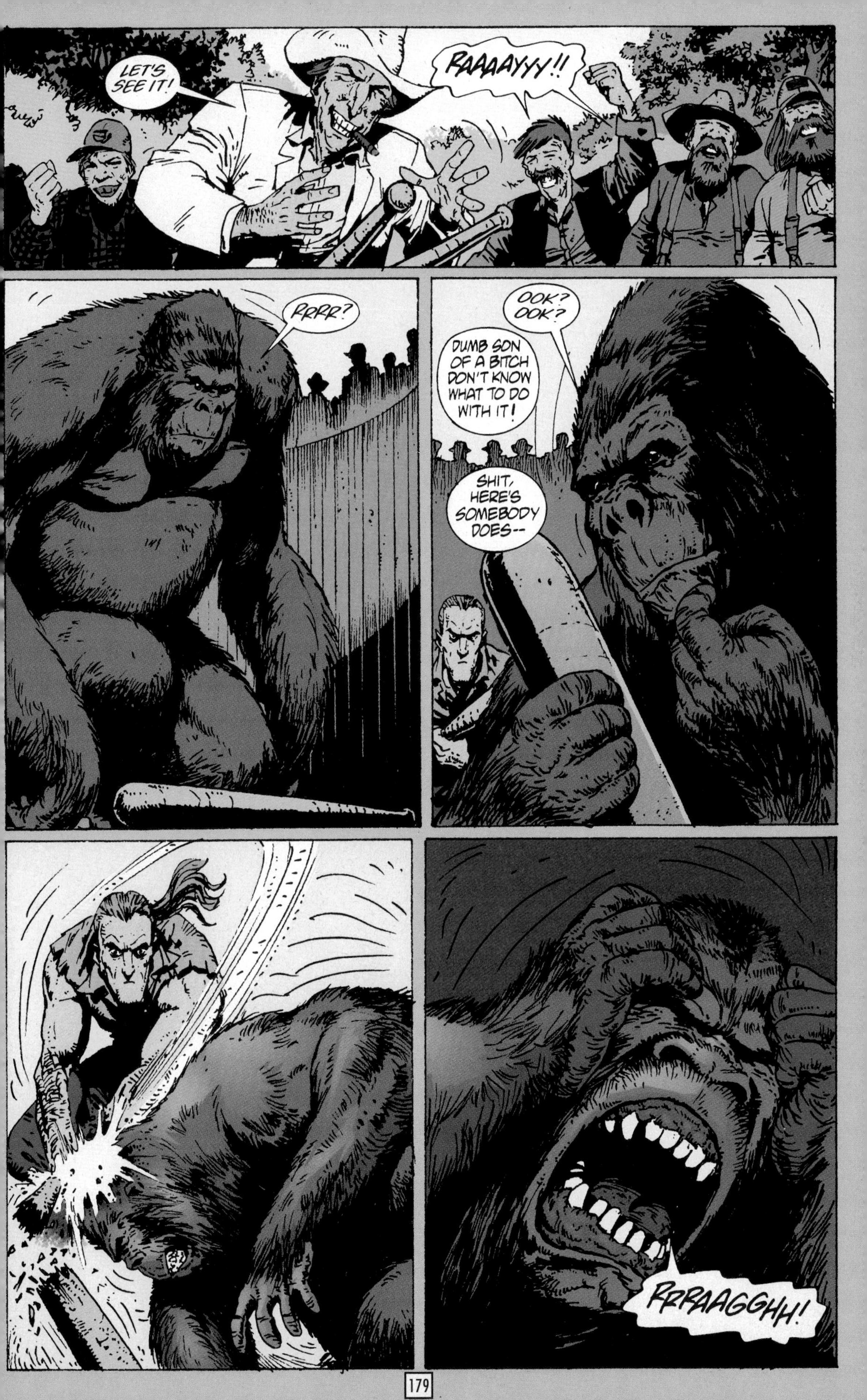
LET'S SEE IT!
RAAAAYYY!!
RRRR?
OOK? OOK?
DUMB SON OF A BITCH DON'T KNOW WHAT TO DO WITH IT!
SHIT, HERE'S SOMEBODY DOES--
RRRAAGGHH!

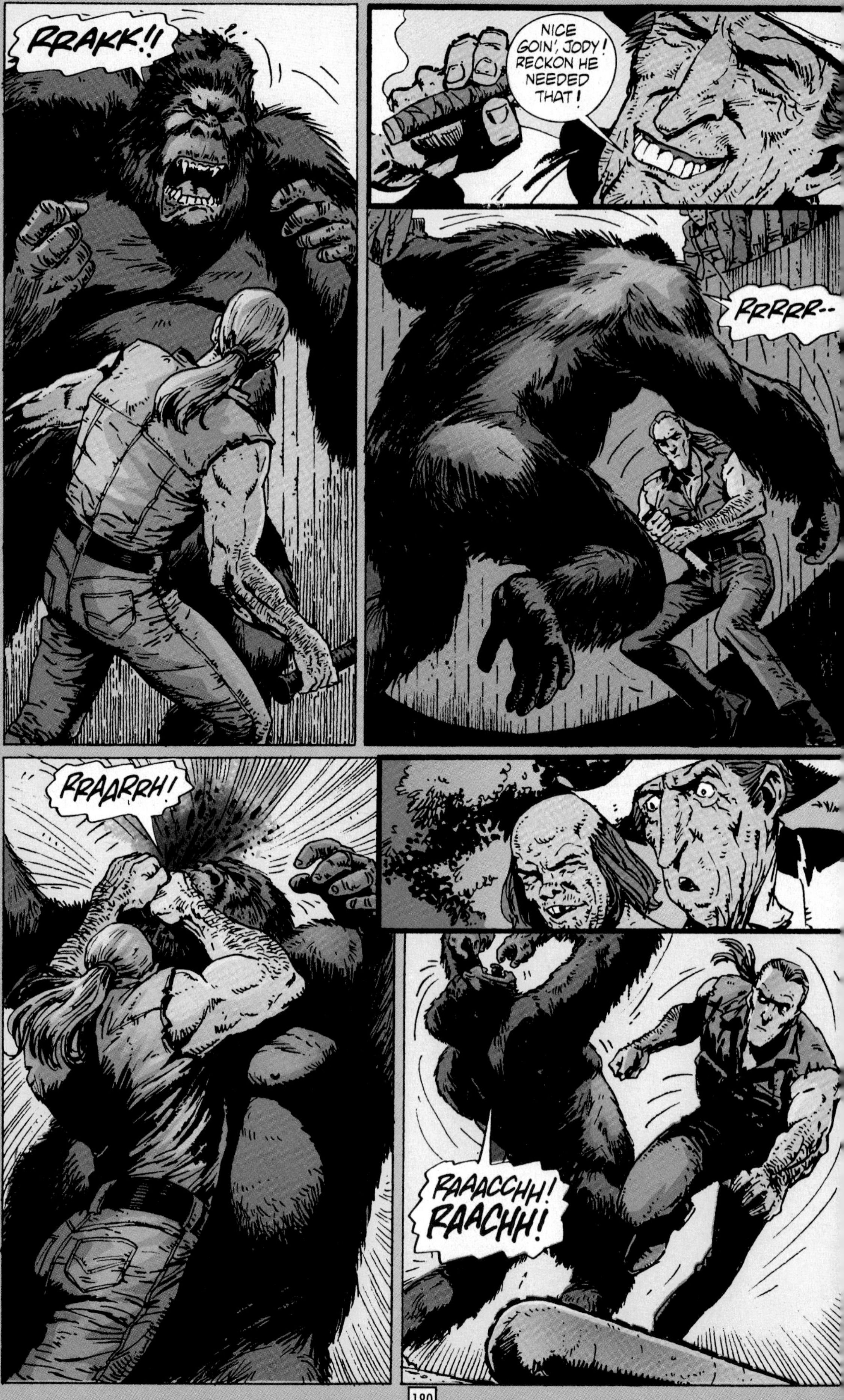
RRAKK!!
NICE GOIN', JODY! RECKON HE NEEDED THAT!
RRRRR--
RRAARRH!
RAAACCHH! RAACHH!

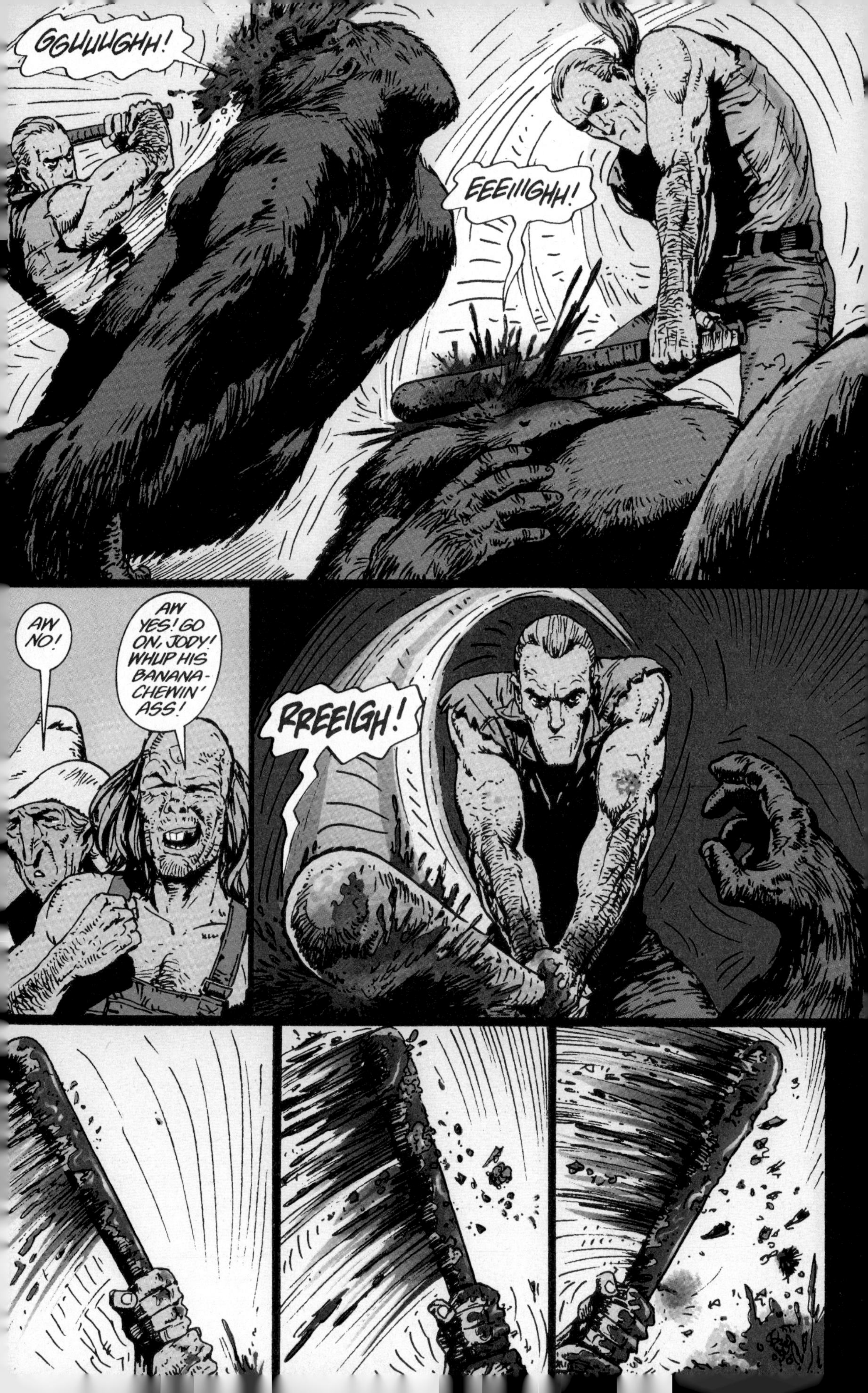
GGUUUUGHH!
EEEIIIGHH!
AW NO!
AW YES! GO ON, JODY! WHUP HIS BANANA-CHEWIN' ASS!
RREEIGH!

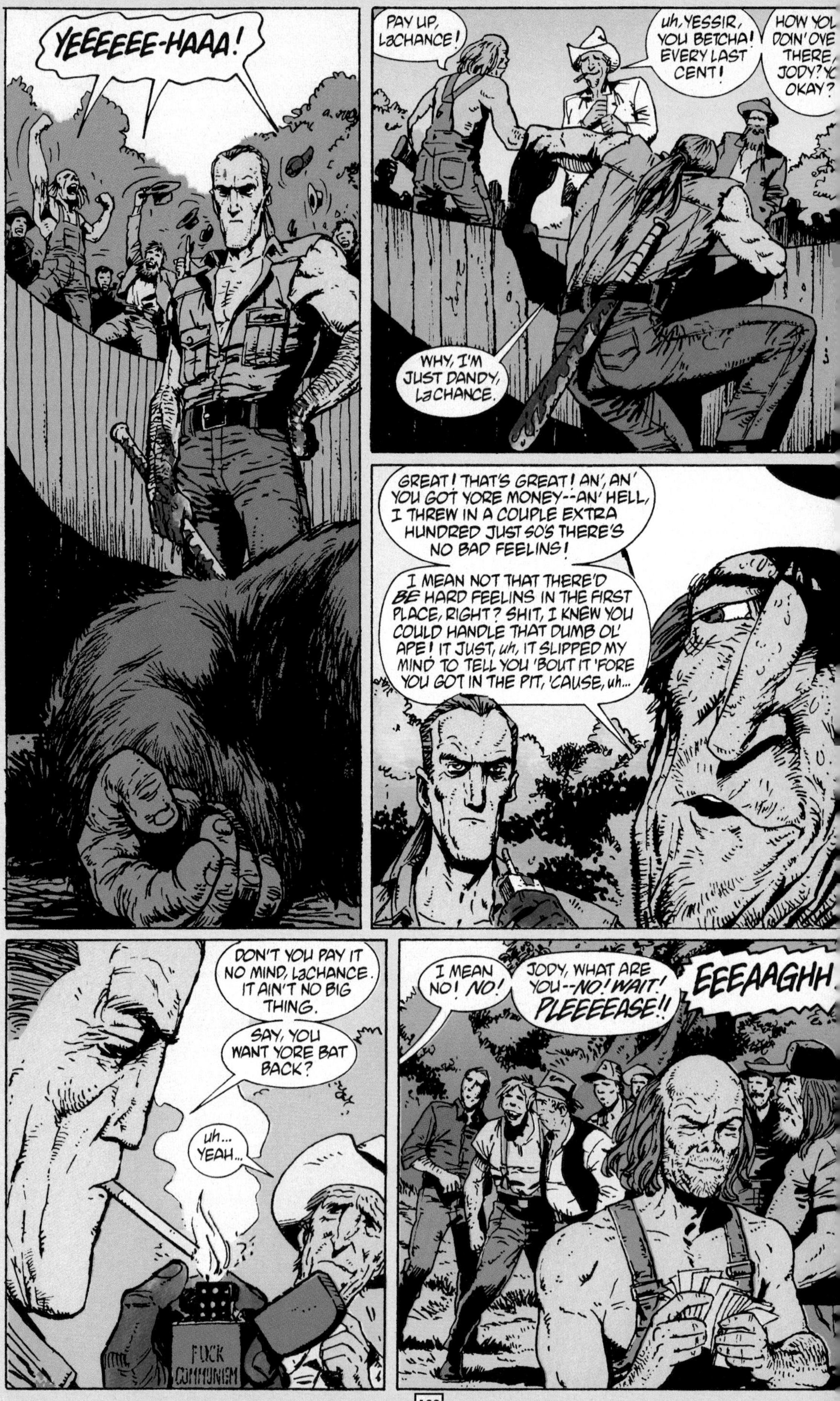
YEEEEEE-HAAA!
PAY UP, LaCHANCE!
uh, YESSIR, YOU BETCHA! EVERY LAST CENT!
HOW YOU DOIN' OVE THERE, JODY? YO OKAY?
WHY, I'M JUST DANDY, LaCHANCE.
GREAT! THAT'S GREAT! AN', AN' YOU GOT YORE MONEY--AN' HELL, I THREW IN A COUPLE EXTRA HUNDRED JUST SO'S THERE'S NO BAD FEELINS!
I MEAN NOT THAT THERE'D BE HARD FEELINS IN THE FIRST PLACE, RIGHT? SHIT, I KNEW YOU COULD HANDLE THAT DUMB OL' APE! IT JUST, uh, IT SLIPPED MY MIND TO TELL YOU 'BOUT IT 'FORE YOU GOT IN THE PIT, 'CAUSE, uh...
DON'T YOU PAY IT NO MIND, LaCHANCE. IT AIN'T NO BIG THING.
SAY, YOU WANT YORE BAT BACK?
uh... YEAH...
FUCK COMMUNISM
I MEAN NO! NO!
JODY, WHAT ARE YOU--NO! WAIT! PLEEEEASE!!
EEEAAGHH

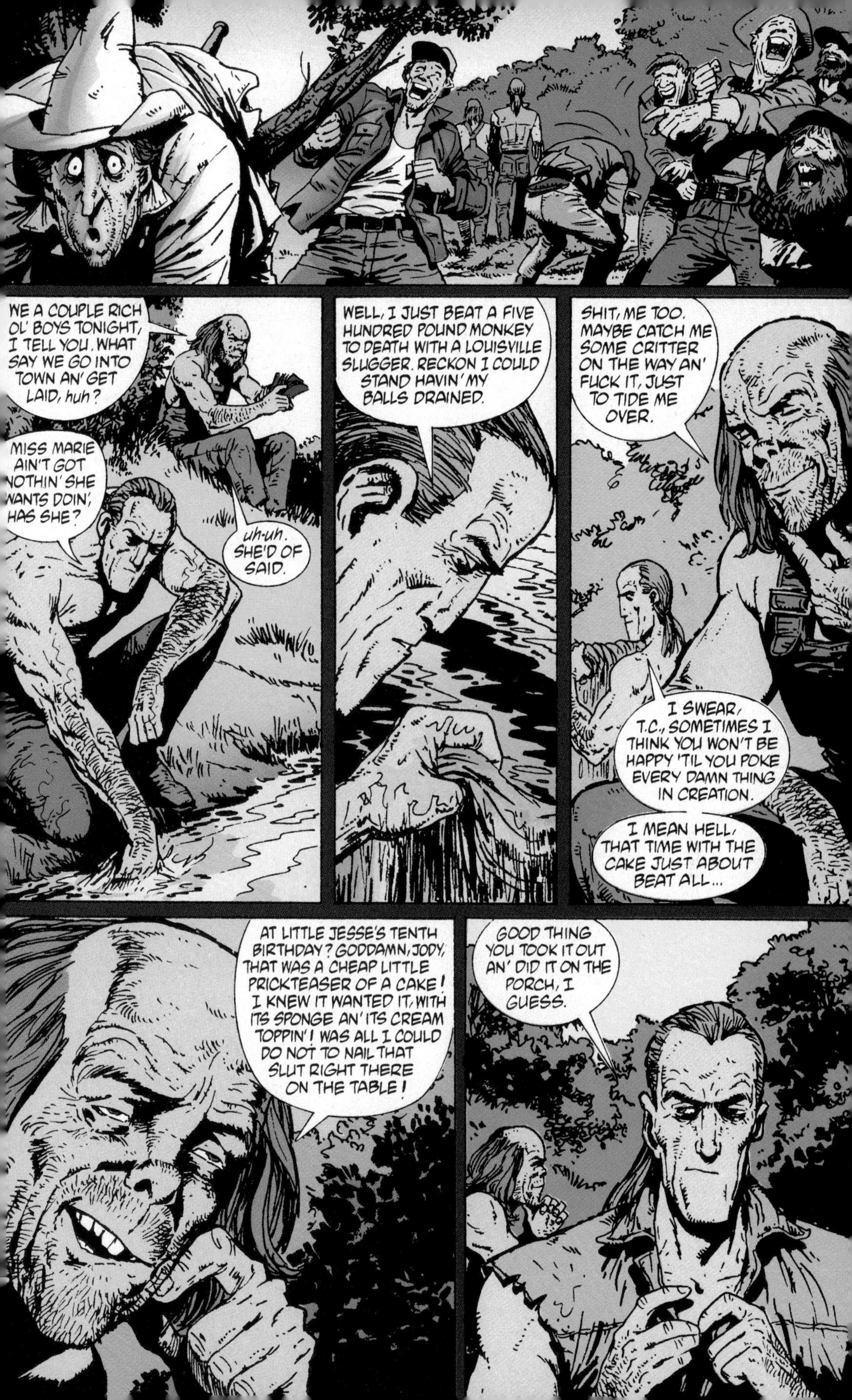
WE A COUPLE RICH OL' BOYS TONIGHT, I TELL YOU. WHAT SAY WE GO INTO TOWN AN' GET LAID, huh?
MISS MARIE AIN'T GOT NOTHIN' SHE WANTS DOIN', HAS SHE?
uh-uh. SHE'D OF SAID.
WELL, I JUST BEAT A FIVE HUNDRED POUND MONKEY TO DEATH WITH A LOUISVILLE SLUGGER. RECKON I COULD STAND HAVIN' MY BALLS DRAINED.
SHIT, ME TOO. MAYBE CATCH ME SOME CRITTER ON THE WAY AN' FUCK IT, JUST TO TIDE ME OVER.
I SWEAR, T.C., SOMETIMES I THINK YOU WON'T BE HAPPY 'TIL YOU POKE EVERY DAMN THING IN CREATION.
I MEAN HELL, THAT TIME WITH THE CAKE JUST ABOUT BEAT ALL...
AT LITTLE JESSE'S TENTH BIRTHDAY? GODDAMN, JODY, THAT WAS A CHEAP LITTLE PRICKTEASER OF A CAKE! I KNEW IT WANTED IT, WITH ITS SPONGE AN' ITS CREAM TOPPIN'! WAS ALL I COULD DO NOT TO NAIL THAT SLUT RIGHT THERE ON THE TABLE!
GOOD THING YOU TOOK IT OUT AN' DID IT ON THE PORCH, I GUESS.

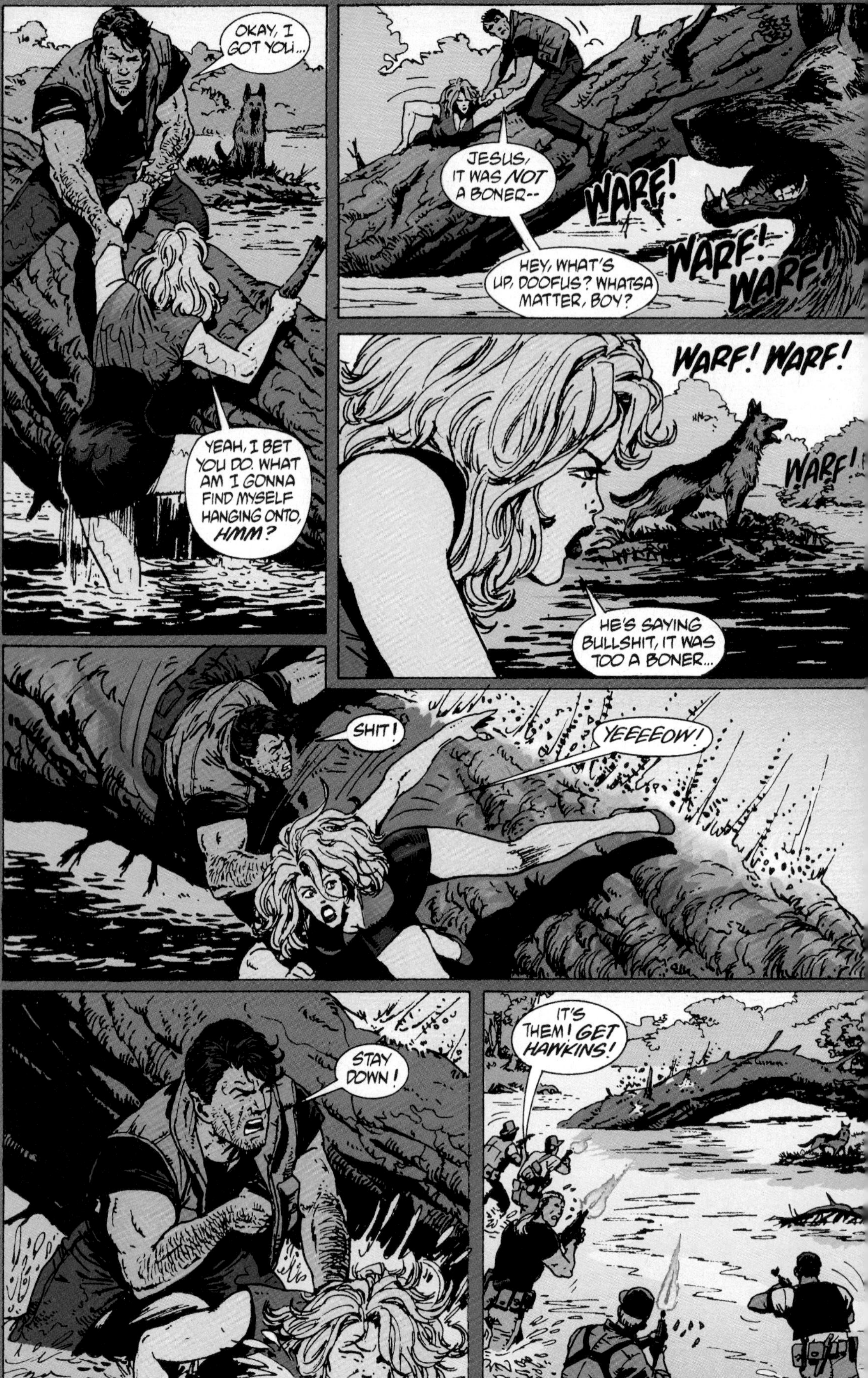
OKAY, I GOT YOU...
YEAH, I BET YOU DO. WHAT AM I GONNA FIND MYSELF HANGING ONTO, HMM?
JESUS, IT WAS NOT A BONER--
WARF!
HEY, WHAT'S UP, DOOFUS? WHATSA MATTER, BOY?
WARF!
WARF!
WARF! WARF!
WARF!
HE'S SAYING BULLSHIT, IT WAS TOO A BONER...
SHIT!
YEEEEOW!
STAY DOWN!
IT'S THEM! GET HAWKINS!

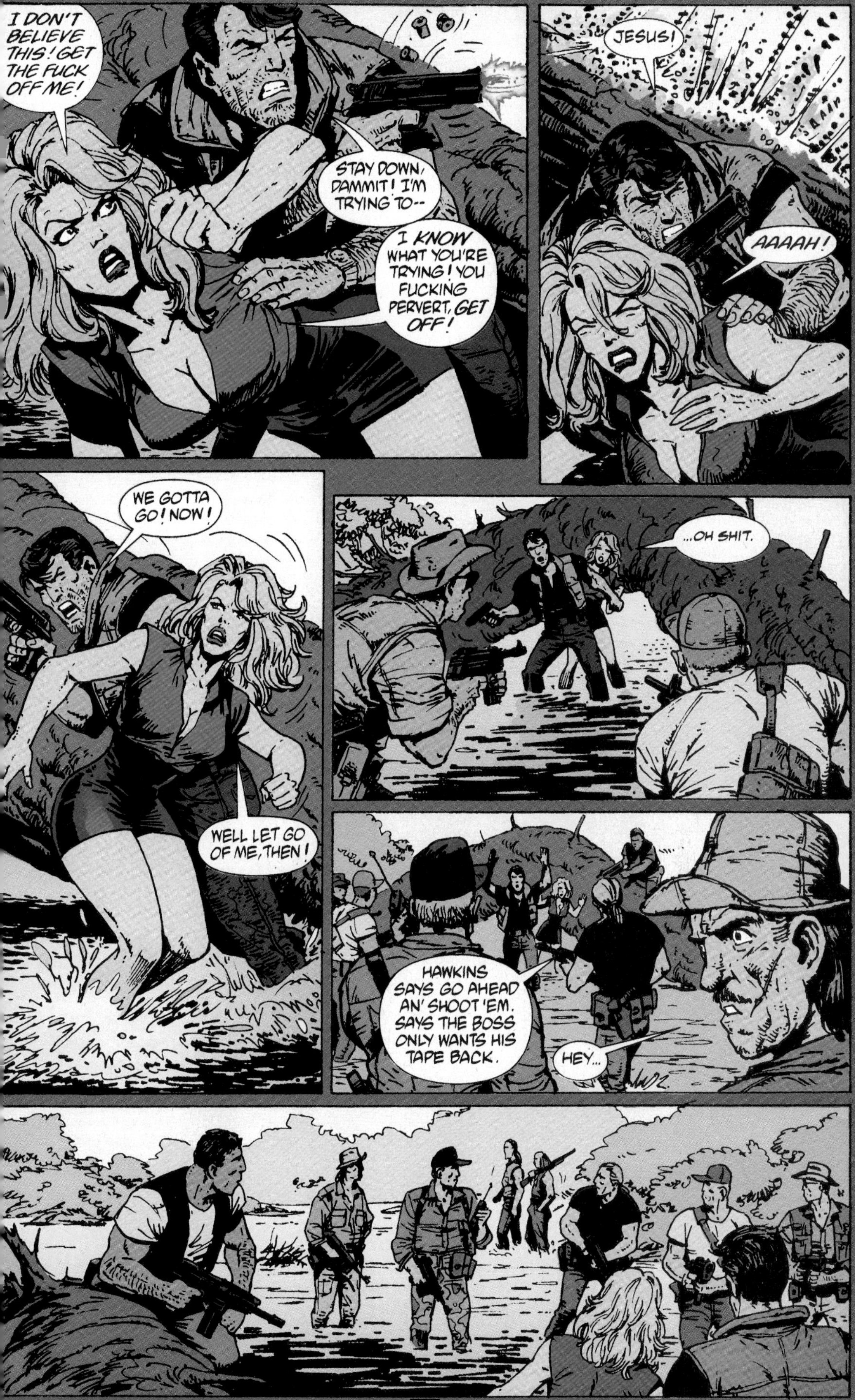
I DON'T BELIEVE THIS! GET THE FUCK OFF ME!
STAY DOWN, DAMMIT! I'M TRYING TO--
I KNOW WHAT YOU'RE TRYING! YOU FUCKING PERVERT, GET OFF!
JESUS!
AAAAH!
WE GOTTA GO! NOW!
WELL LET GO OF ME, THEN!
...OH SHIT.
HAWKINS SAYS GO AHEAD AN' SHOOT 'EM. SAYS THE BOSS ONLY WANTS HIS TAPE BACK.
HEY...

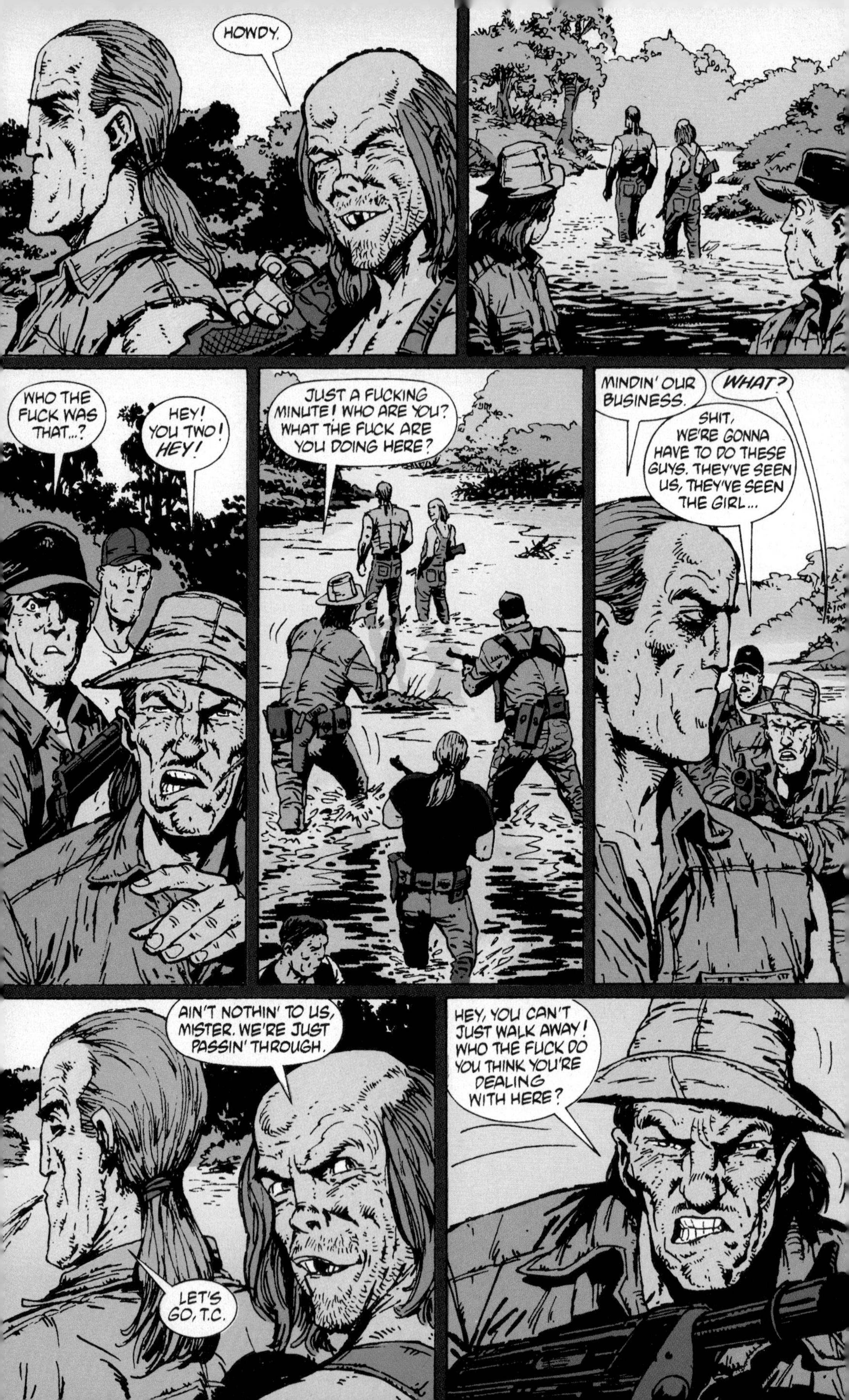
HOWDY.
WHO THE FUCK WAS THAT...?
HEY! YOU TWO! HEY!
JUST A FUCKING MINUTE! WHO ARE YOU? WHAT THE FUCK ARE YOU DOING HERE?
MINDIN' OUR BUSINESS.
WHAT?
SHIT, WE'RE GONNA HAVE TO DO THESE GUYS. THEY'VE SEEN US, THEY'VE SEEN THE GIRL...
AIN'T NOTHIN' TO US, MISTER. WE'RE JUST PASSIN' THROUGH.
LET'S GO, T.C.
HEY, YOU CAN'T JUST WALK AWAY! WHO THE FUCK DO YOU THINK YOU'RE DEALING WITH HERE?

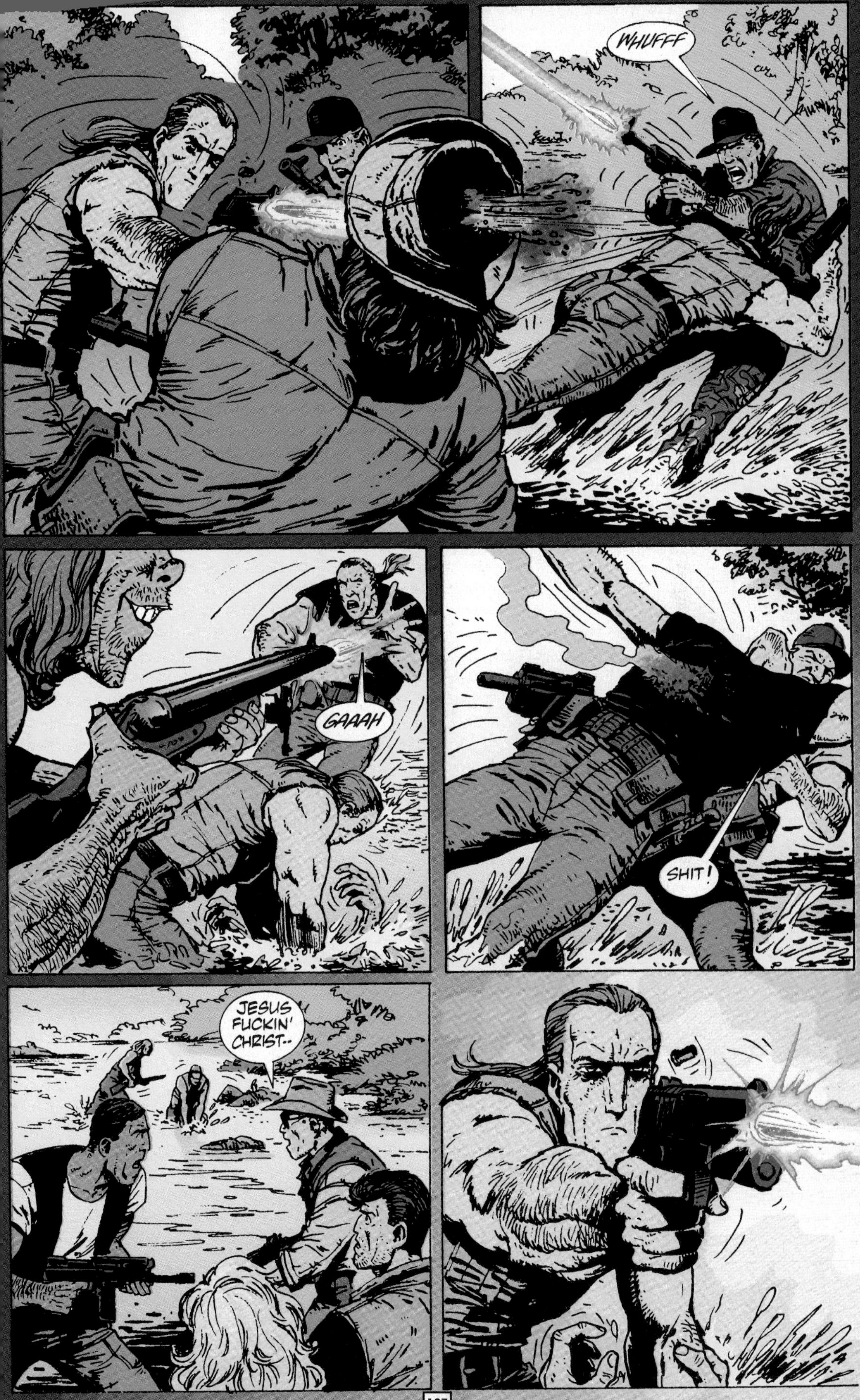
WHUFFF
GAAAH
SHIT!
JESUS FUCKIN' CHRIST--

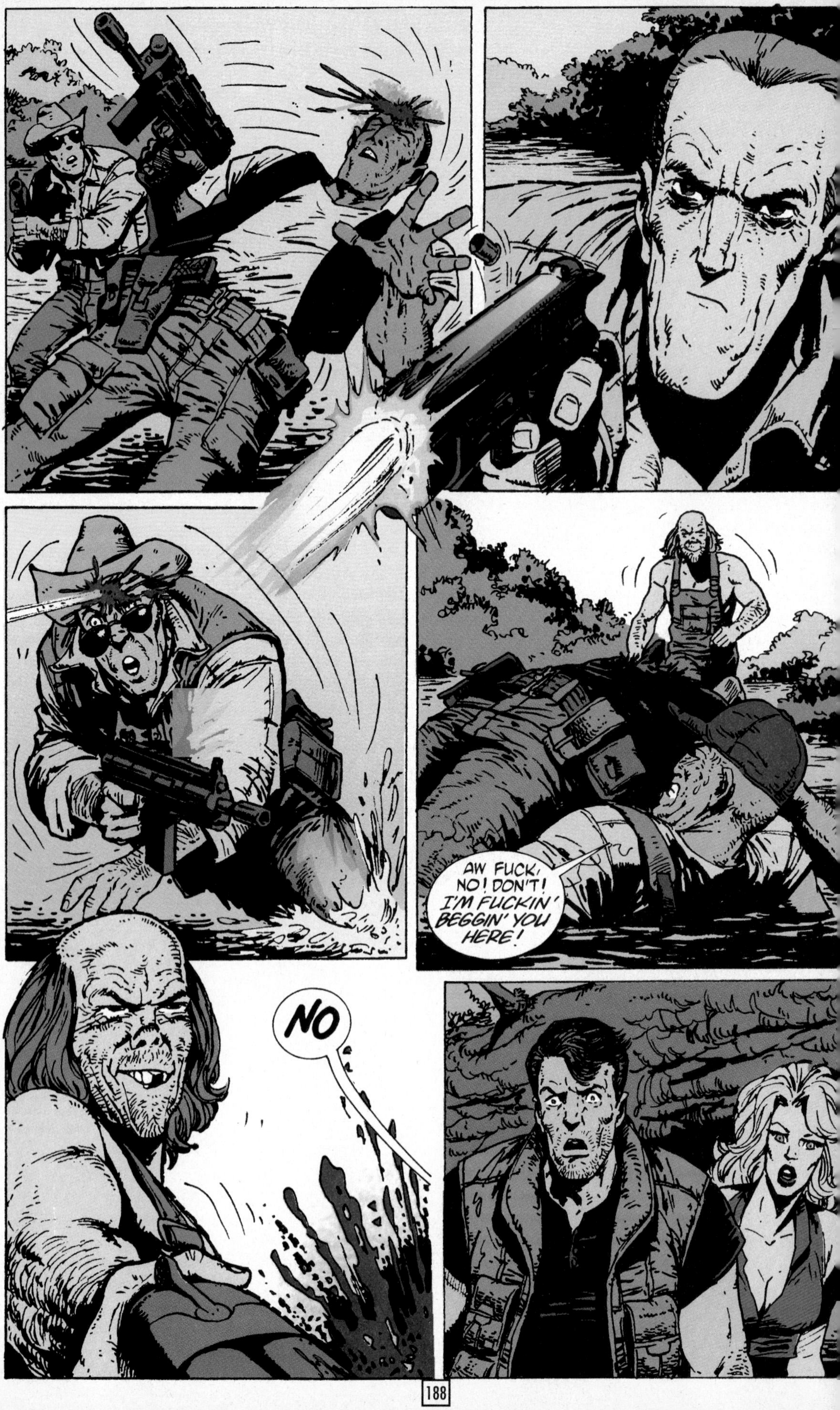
AW FUCK, NO! DON'T! I'M FUCKIN' BEGGIN' YOU HERE!
NO

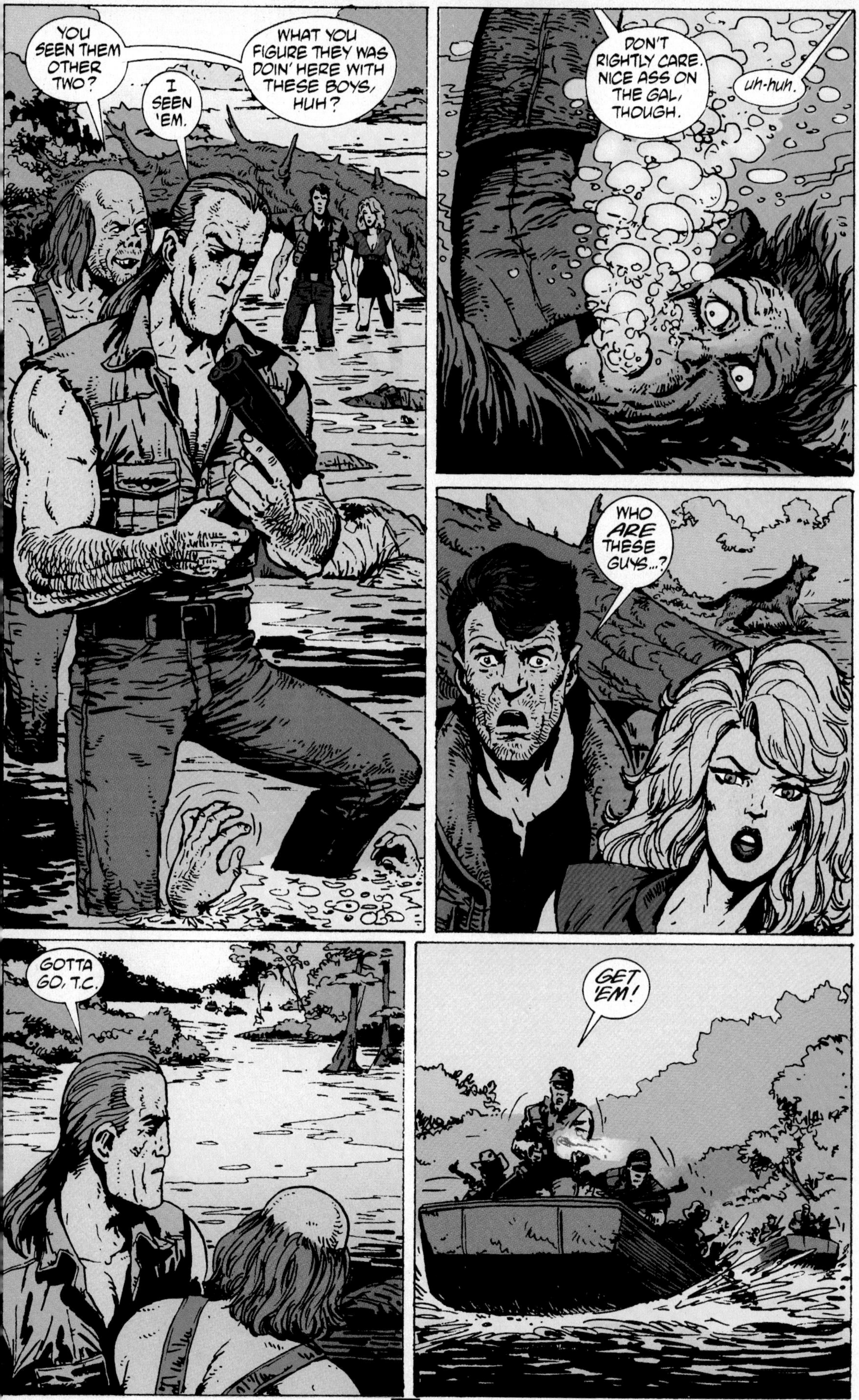
YOU SEEN THEM OTHER TWO?
WHAT YOU FIGURE THEY WAS DOIN' HERE WITH THESE BOYS, HUH?
I SEEN 'EM.
DON'T RIGHTLY CARE. NICE ASS ON THE GAL, THOUGH.
uh-huh.
WHO ARE THESE GUYS...?
GOTTA GO, T.C.
GET 'EM!

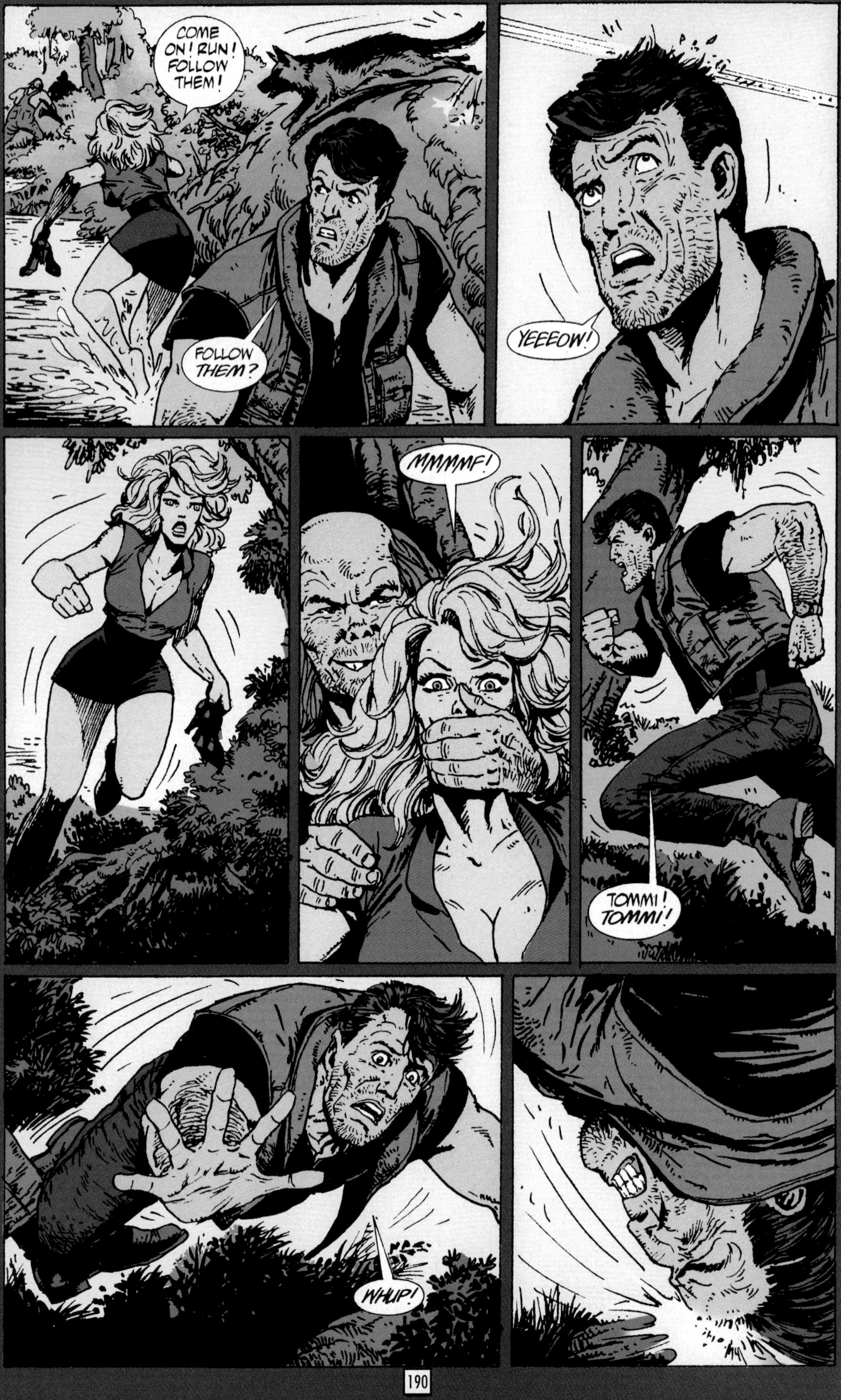
COME ON! RUN! FOLLOW THEM!
FOLLOW THEM?
YEEEOW!
MMMMF!
TOMMI! TOMMI!
WHUP!

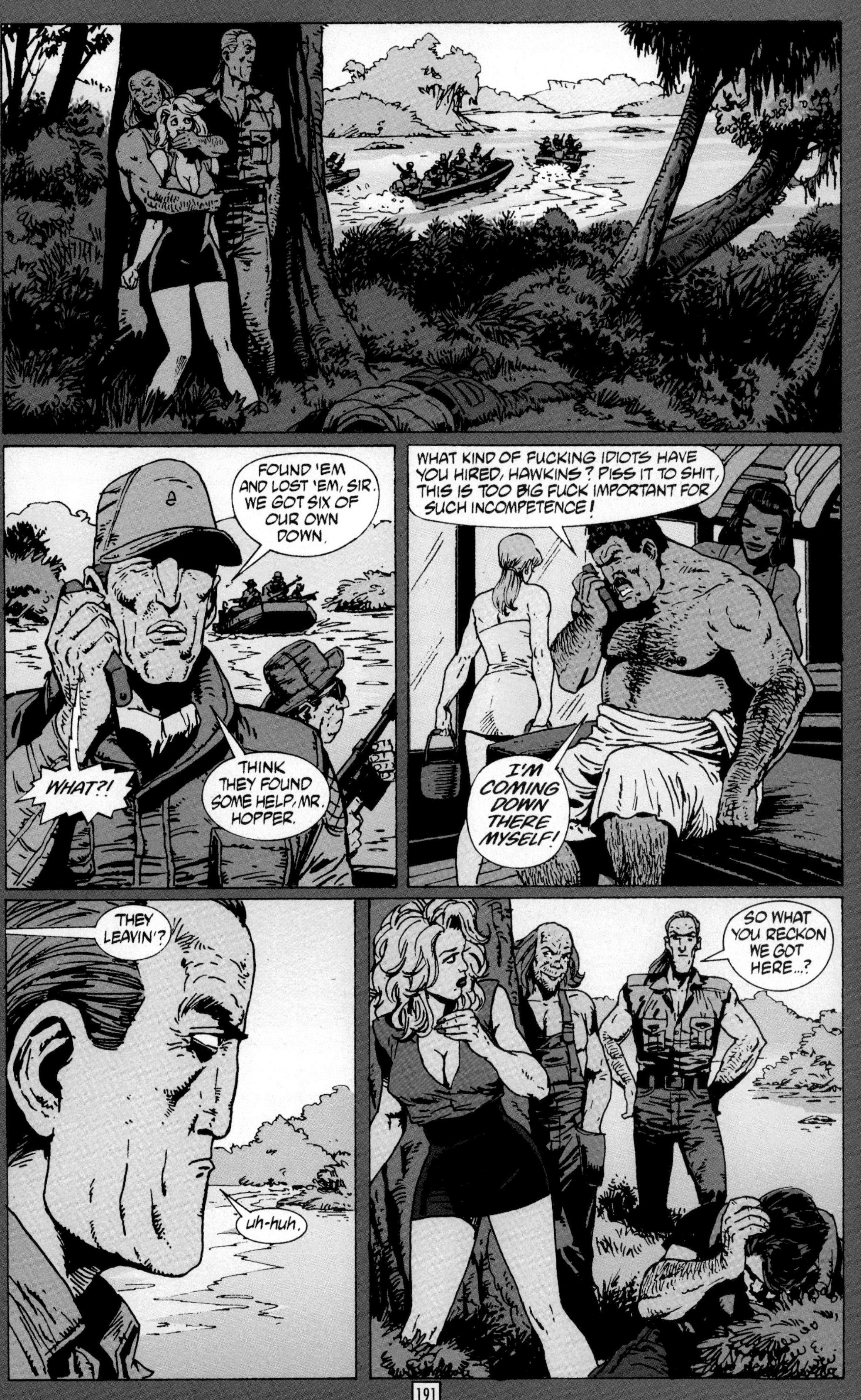
FOUND 'EM AND LOST 'EM, SIR. WE GOT SIX OF OUR OWN DOWN.
WHAT?!
THINK THEY FOUND SOME HELP, MR. HOPPER.
WHAT KIND OF FUCKING IDIOTS HAVE YOU HIRED, HAWKINS? PISS IT TO SHIT, THIS IS TOO BIG FUCK IMPORTANT FOR SUCH INCOMPETENCE!
I'M COMING DOWN THERE MYSELF!
THEY LEAVIN'?
uh-huh.
SO WHAT YOU RECKON WE GOT HERE...?

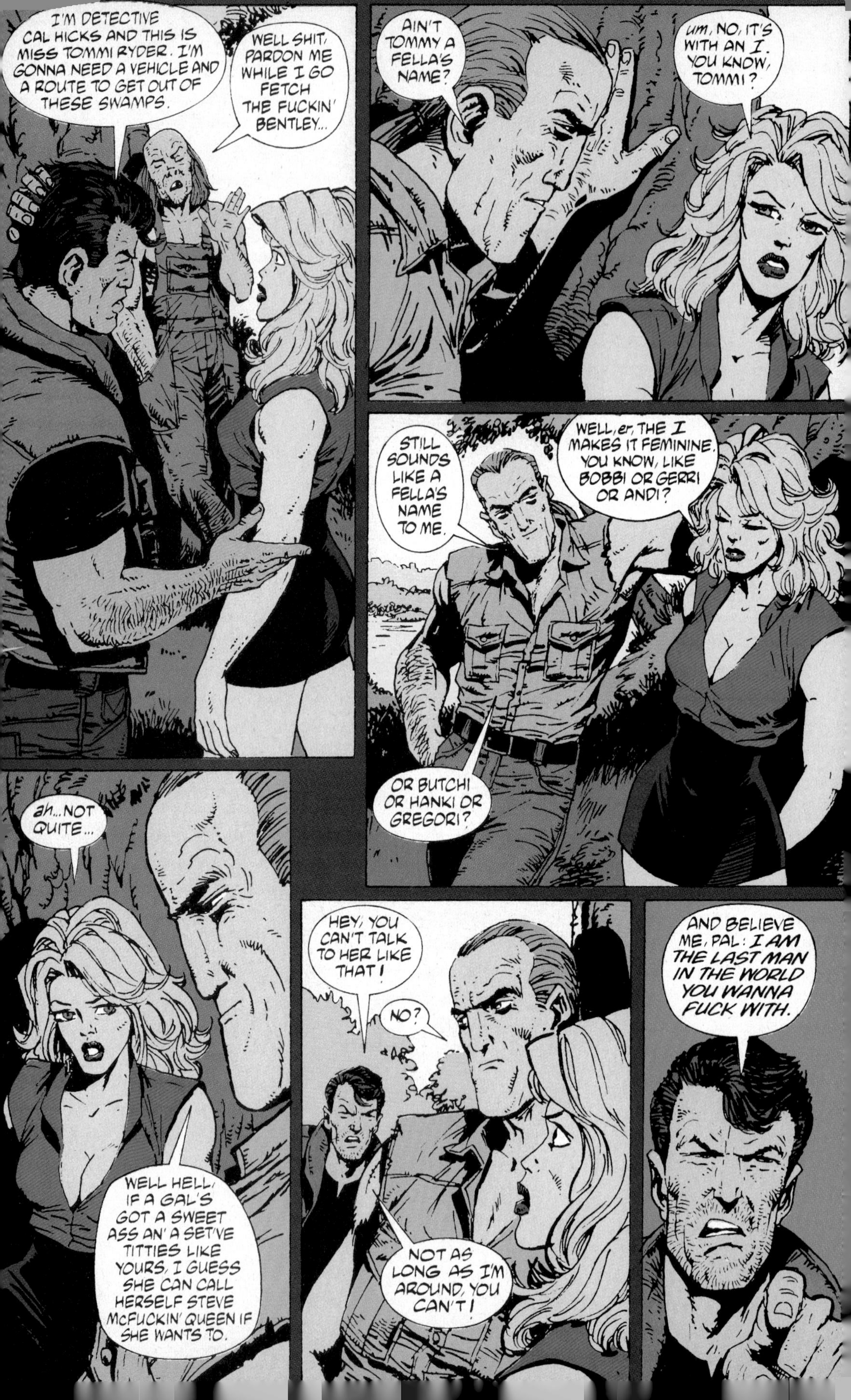

I'M DETECTIVE CAL HICKS AND THIS IS MISS TOMMI RYDER. I'M GONNA NEED A VEHICLE AND A ROUTE TO GET OUT OF THESE SWAMPS.
WELL SHIT, PARDON ME WHILE I GO FETCH THE FUCKIN' BENTLEY...
AIN'T TOMMY A FELLA'S NAME?
um, NO, IT'S WITH AN I. YOU KNOW, TOMMI?
STILL SOUNDS LIKE A FELLA'S NAME TO ME.
WELL, er, THE I MAKES IT FEMININE. YOU KNOW, LIKE BOBBI OR GERRI OR ANDI?
OR BUTCHI OR HANKI OR GREGORI?
ah... NOT QUITE...
WELL HELL, IF A GAL'S GOT A SWEET ASS AN' A SET'VE TITTIES LIKE YOURS, I GUESS SHE CAN CALL HERSELF STEVE McFUCKIN' QUEEN IF SHE WANTS TO.
HEY, YOU CAN'T TALK TO HER LIKE THAT!
NO?
NOT AS LONG AS I'M AROUND, YOU CAN'T!
AND BELIEVE ME, PAL: I AM THE LAST MAN IN THE WORLD YOU WANNA FUCK WITH.

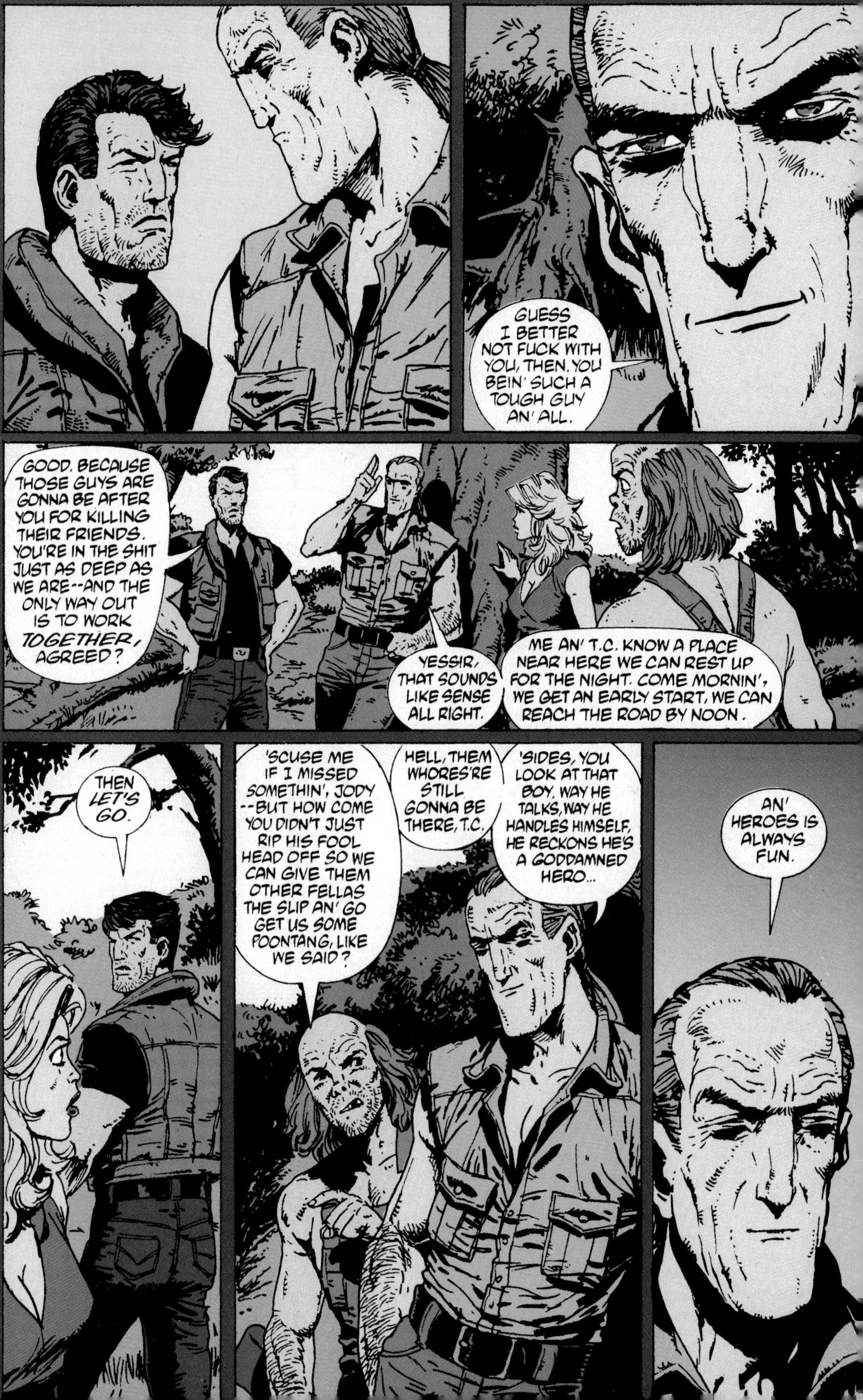
GUESS I BETTER NOT FUCK WITH YOU, THEN. YOU BEIN' SUCH A TOUGH GUY AN' ALL.
GOOD. BECAUSE THOSE GUYS ARE GONNA BE AFTER YOU FOR KILLING THEIR FRIENDS. YOU'RE IN THE SHIT JUST AS DEEP AS WE ARE--AND THE ONLY WAY OUT IS TO WORK *TOGETHER*, AGREED?
YESSIR, THAT SOUNDS LIKE SENSE ALL RIGHT.
ME AN' T.C. KNOW A PLACE NEAR HERE WE CAN REST UP FOR THE NIGHT. COME MORNIN', WE GET AN EARLY START, WE CAN REACH THE ROAD BY NOON.
THEN *LET'S GO*.
'SCUSE ME IF I MISSED SOMETHIN', JODY --BUT HOW COME YOU DIDN'T JUST RIP HIS FOOL HEAD OFF SO WE CAN GIVE THEM OTHER FELLAS THE SLIP AN' GO GET US SOME POONTANG, LIKE WE SAID?
HELL, THEM WHORES'RE STILL GONNA BE THERE, T.C.
'SIDES, YOU LOOK AT THAT BOY. WAY HE TALKS, WAY HE HANDLES HIMSELF, HE RECKONS HE'S A GODDAMNED HERO...
AN' HEROES IS ALWAYS FUN.

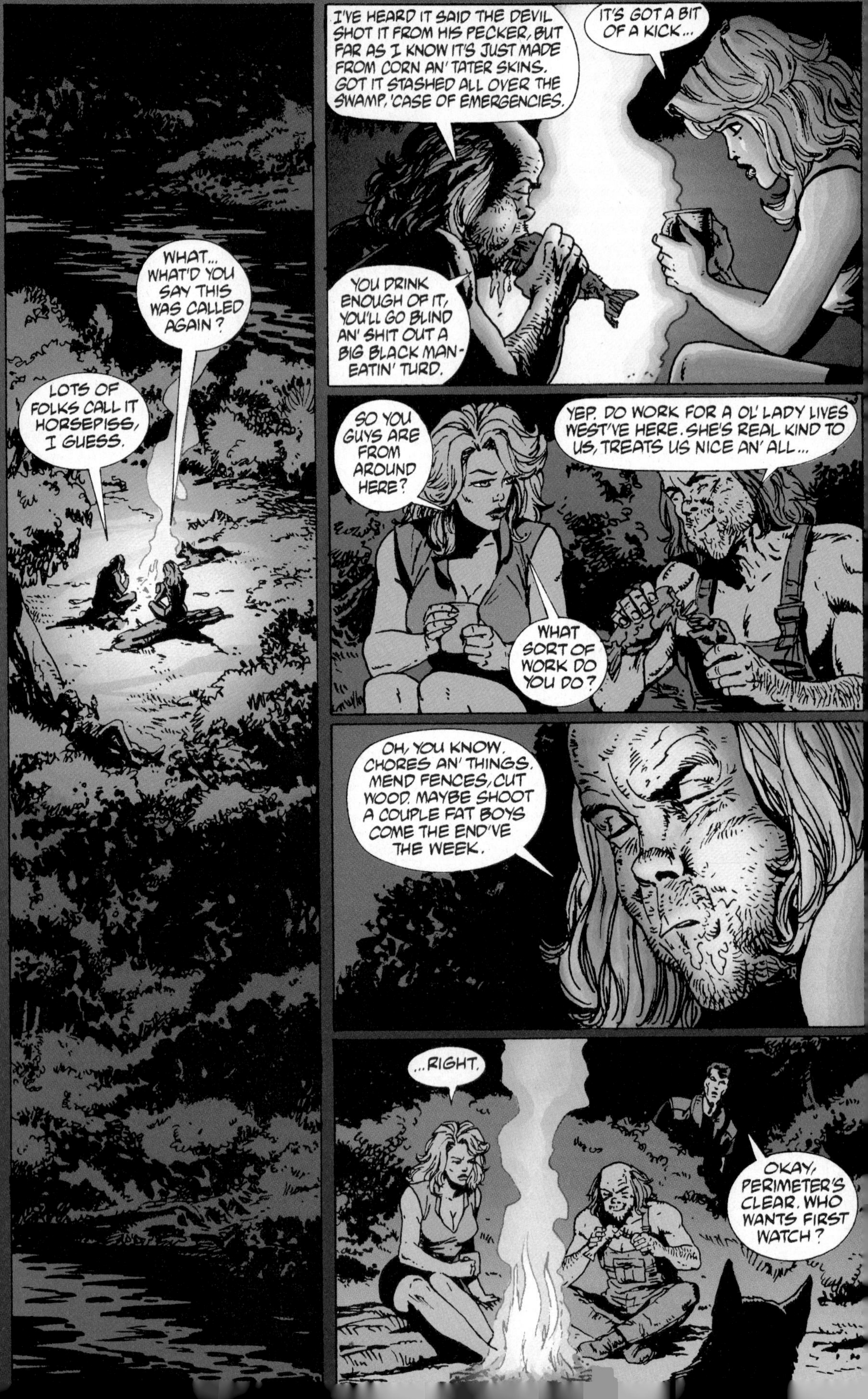

WHAT... WHAT'D YOU SAY THIS WAS CALLED AGAIN?
LOTS OF FOLKS CALL IT HORSEPISS, I GUESS.
I'VE HEARD IT SAID THE DEVIL SHOT IT FROM HIS PECKER, BUT FAR AS I KNOW IT'S JUST MADE FROM CORN AN' TATER SKINS. GOT IT STASHED ALL OVER THE SWAMP, 'CASE OF EMERGENCIES.
IT'S GOT A BIT OF A KICK...
YOU DRINK ENOUGH OF IT, YOU'LL GO BLIND AN' SHIT OUT A BIG BLACK MAN-EATIN' TURD.
SO YOU GUYS ARE FROM AROUND HERE?
YEP. DO WORK FOR A OL' LADY LIVES WEST'VE HERE. SHE'S REAL KIND TO US, TREATS US NICE AN' ALL...
WHAT SORT OF WORK DO YOU DO?
OH, YOU KNOW. CHORES AN' THINGS. MEND FENCES, CUT WOOD. MAYBE SHOOT A COUPLE FAT BOYS COME THE END'VE THE WEEK.
...RIGHT.
OKAY, PERIMETER'S CLEAR. WHO WANTS FIRST WATCH?

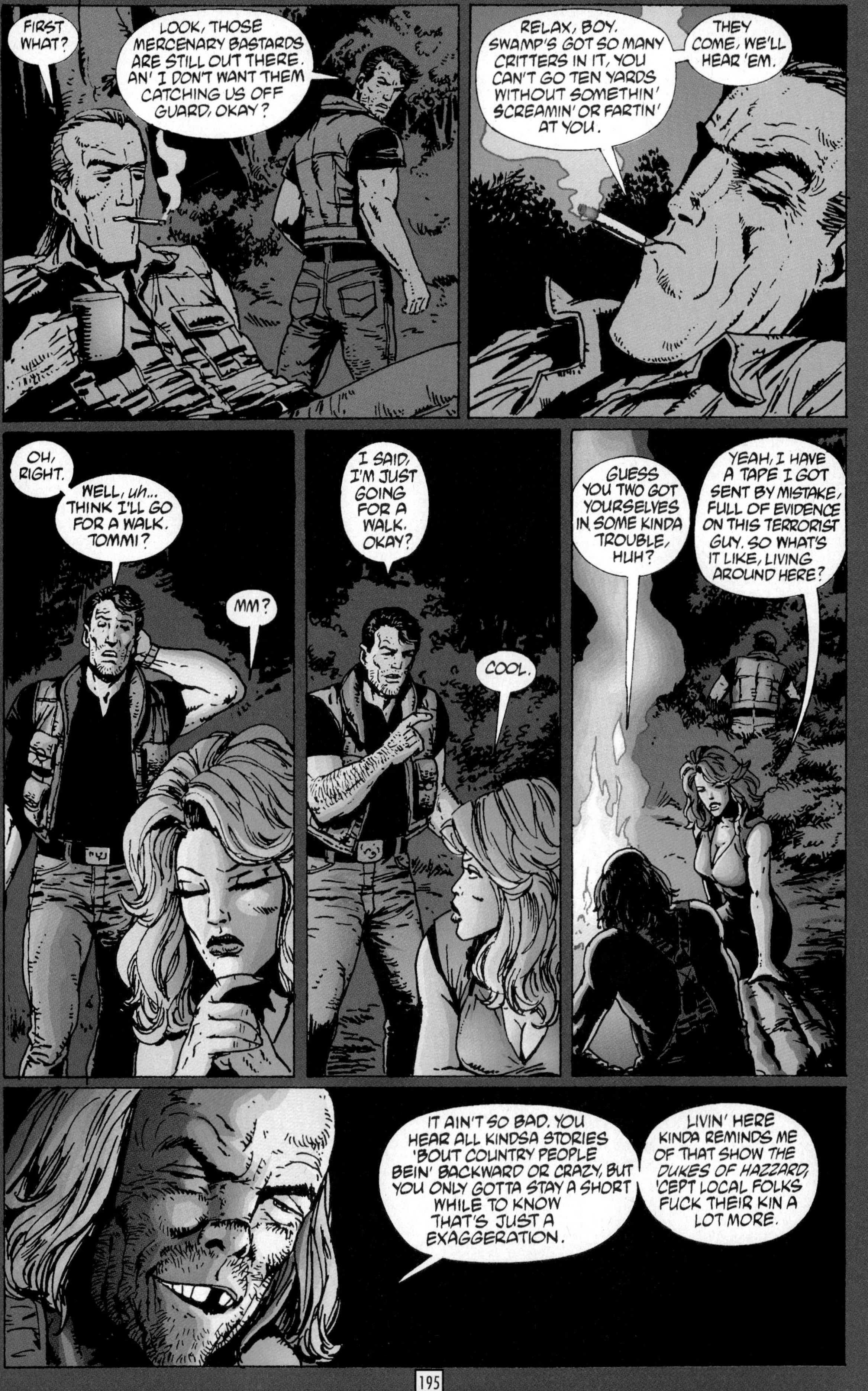
FIRST WHAT?
LOOK, THOSE MERCENARY BASTARDS ARE STILL OUT THERE. AN' I DON'T WANT THEM CATCHING US OFF GUARD, OKAY?
RELAX, BOY. SWAMP'S GOT SO MANY CRITTERS IN IT, YOU CAN'T GO TEN YARDS WITHOUT SOMETHIN' SCREAMIN' OR FARTIN' AT YOU.
THEY COME, WE'LL HEAR 'EM.
OH, RIGHT.
WELL, uh... THINK I'LL GO FOR A WALK. TOMMI?
MM?
I SAID, I'M JUST GOING FOR A WALK. OKAY?
COOL.
GUESS YOU TWO GOT YOURSELVES IN SOME KINDA TROUBLE, HUH?
YEAH, I HAVE A TAPE I GOT SENT BY MISTAKE, FULL OF EVIDENCE ON THIS TERRORIST GUY. SO WHAT'S IT LIKE, LIVING AROUND HERE?
IT AIN'T SO BAD. YOU HEAR ALL KINDSA STORIES 'BOUT COUNTRY PEOPLE BEIN' BACKWARD OR CRAZY, BUT YOU ONLY GOTTA STAY A SHORT WHILE TO KNOW THAT'S JUST A EXAGGERATION.
LIVIN' HERE KINDA REMINDS ME OF THAT SHOW THE *DUKES OF HAZZARD*, 'CEPT LOCAL FOLKS FUCK THEIR KIN A LOT MORE.

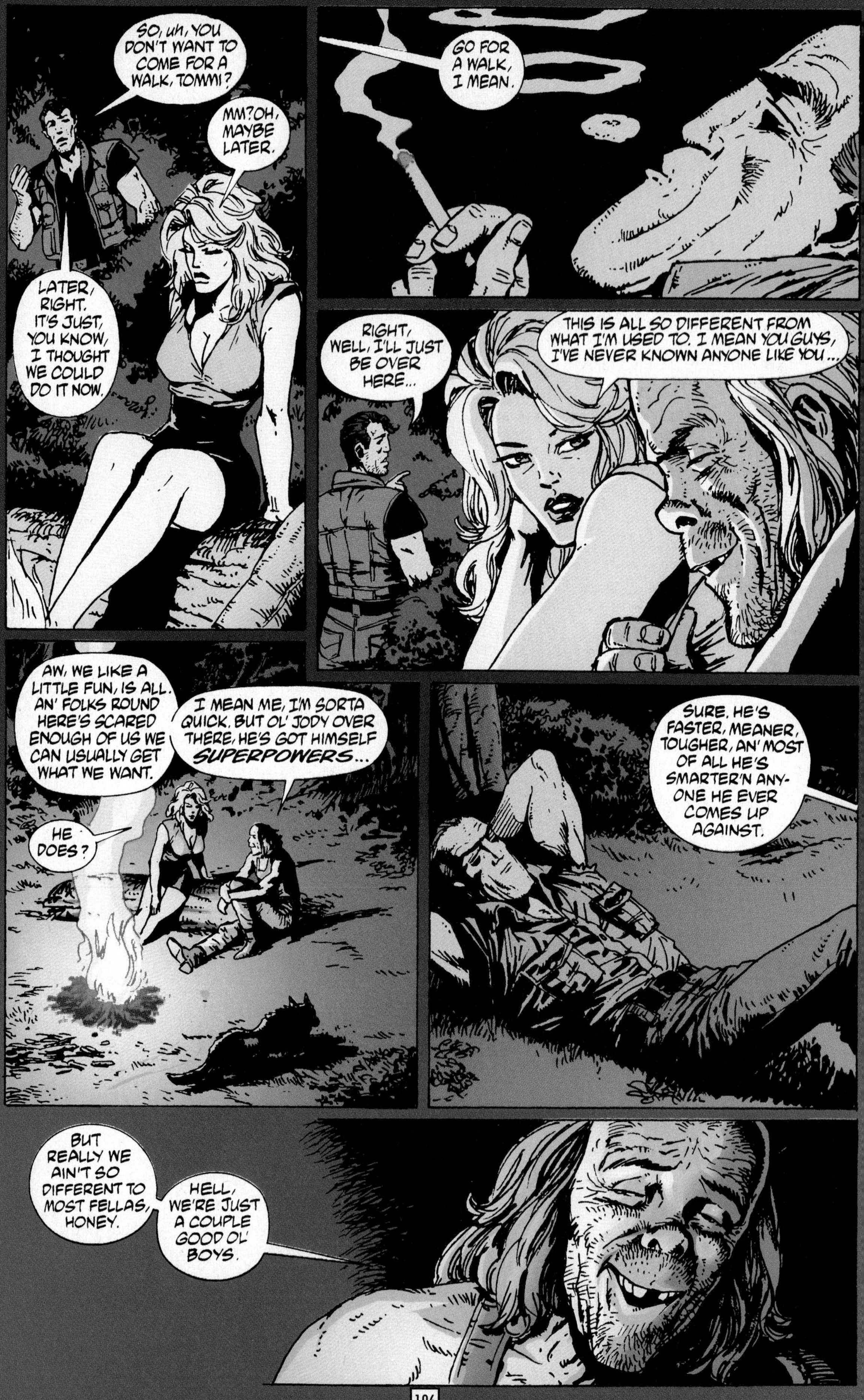

SO, uh, YOU DON'T WANT TO COME FOR A WALK, TOMMI?
MM? OH, MAYBE LATER.
LATER, RIGHT. IT'S JUST, YOU KNOW, I THOUGHT WE COULD DO IT NOW.
GO FOR A WALK, I MEAN.
RIGHT, WELL, I'LL JUST BE OVER HERE...
THIS IS ALL SO DIFFERENT FROM WHAT I'M USED TO. I MEAN YOU GUYS, I'VE NEVER KNOWN ANYONE LIKE YOU...
AW, WE LIKE A LITTLE FUN, IS ALL. AN' FOLKS ROUND HERE'S SCARED ENOUGH OF US WE CAN USUALLY GET WHAT WE WANT.
I MEAN ME, I'M SORTA QUICK. BUT OL' JODY OVER THERE, HE'S GOT HIMSELF SUPERPOWERS...
HE DOES?
SURE. HE'S FASTER, MEANER, TOUGHER, AN' MOST OF ALL HE'S SMARTER'N ANY-ONE HE EVER COMES UP AGAINST.
BUT REALLY WE AIN'T SO DIFFERENT TO MOST FELLAS, HONEY.
HELL, WE'RE JUST A COUPLE GOOD OL' BOYS.

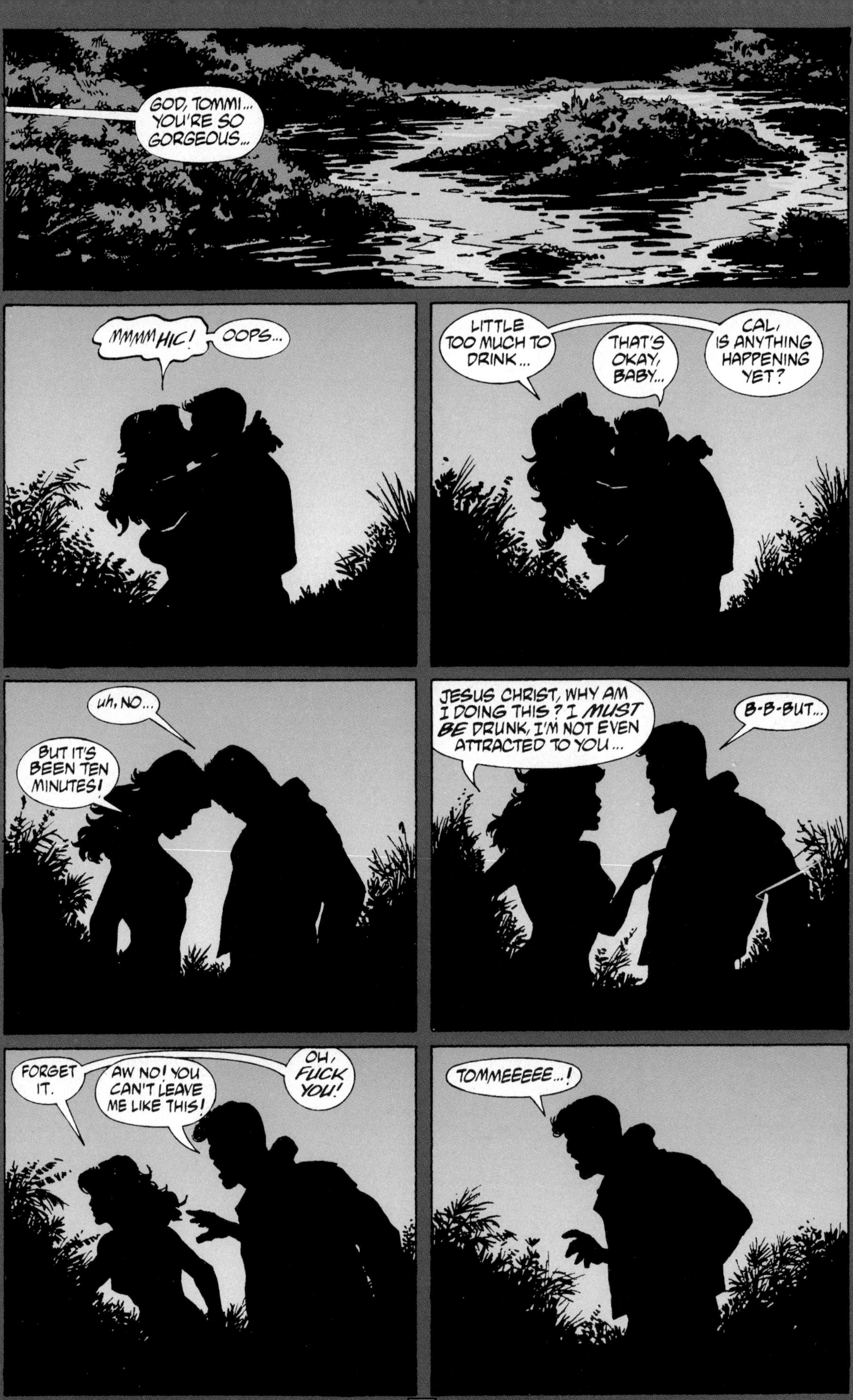
GOD, TOMMI... YOU'RE SO GORGEOUS...
MMMM HIC!
OOPS...
LITTLE TOO MUCH TO DRINK...
THAT'S OKAY, BABY...
CAL, IS ANYTHING HAPPENING YET?
uh, NO...
BUT IT'S BEEN TEN MINUTES!
JESUS CHRIST, WHY AM I DOING THIS? I MUST BE DRUNK, I'M NOT EVEN ATTRACTED TO YOU...
B-B-BUT...
FORGET IT.
AW NO! YOU CAN'T LEAVE ME LIKE THIS!
OH, FUCK YOU!
TOMMEEEEE...!

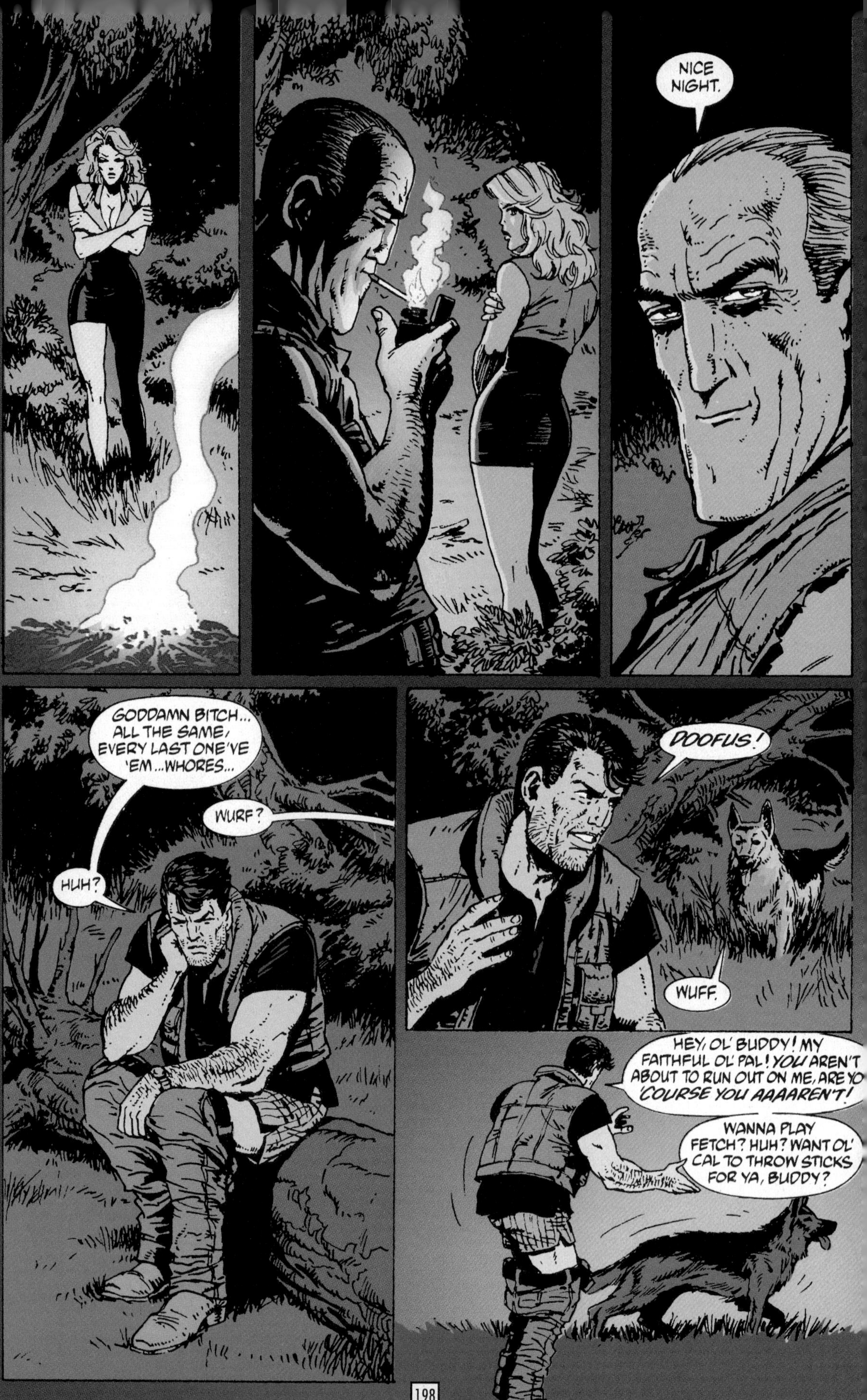
NICE NIGHT.
GODDAMN BITCH... ALL THE SAME, EVERY LAST ONE'VE 'EM...WHORES...
WURF?
HUH?
DOOFUS!
WUFF.
HEY, OL' BUDDY! MY FAITHFUL OL' PAL! YOU AREN'T ABOUT TO RUN OUT ON ME, ARE YO 'COURSE YOU AAAAREN'T!
WANNA PLAY FETCH? HUH? WANT OL' CAL TO THROW STICKS FOR YA, BUDDY?

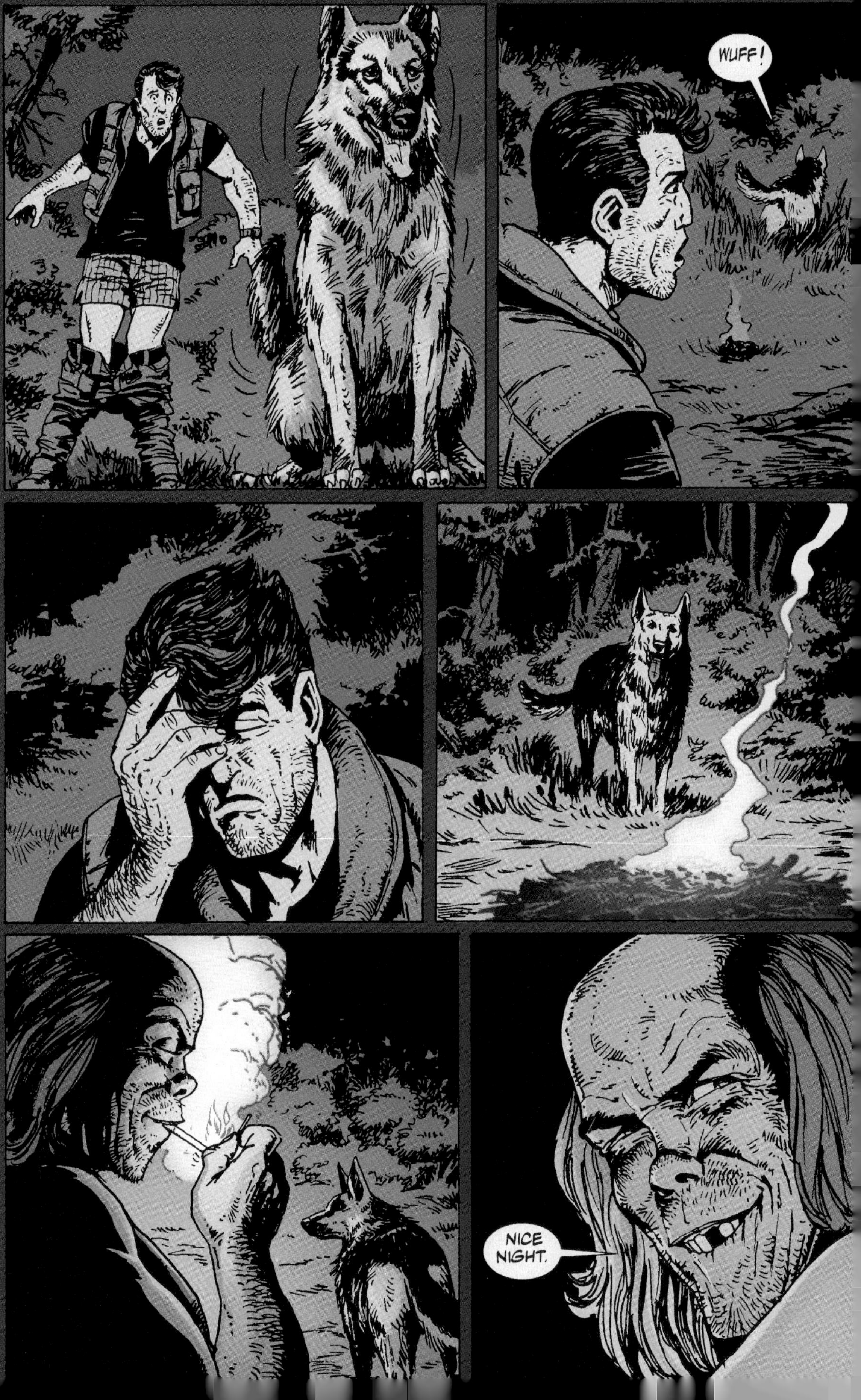
WUFF!
NICE NIGHT.

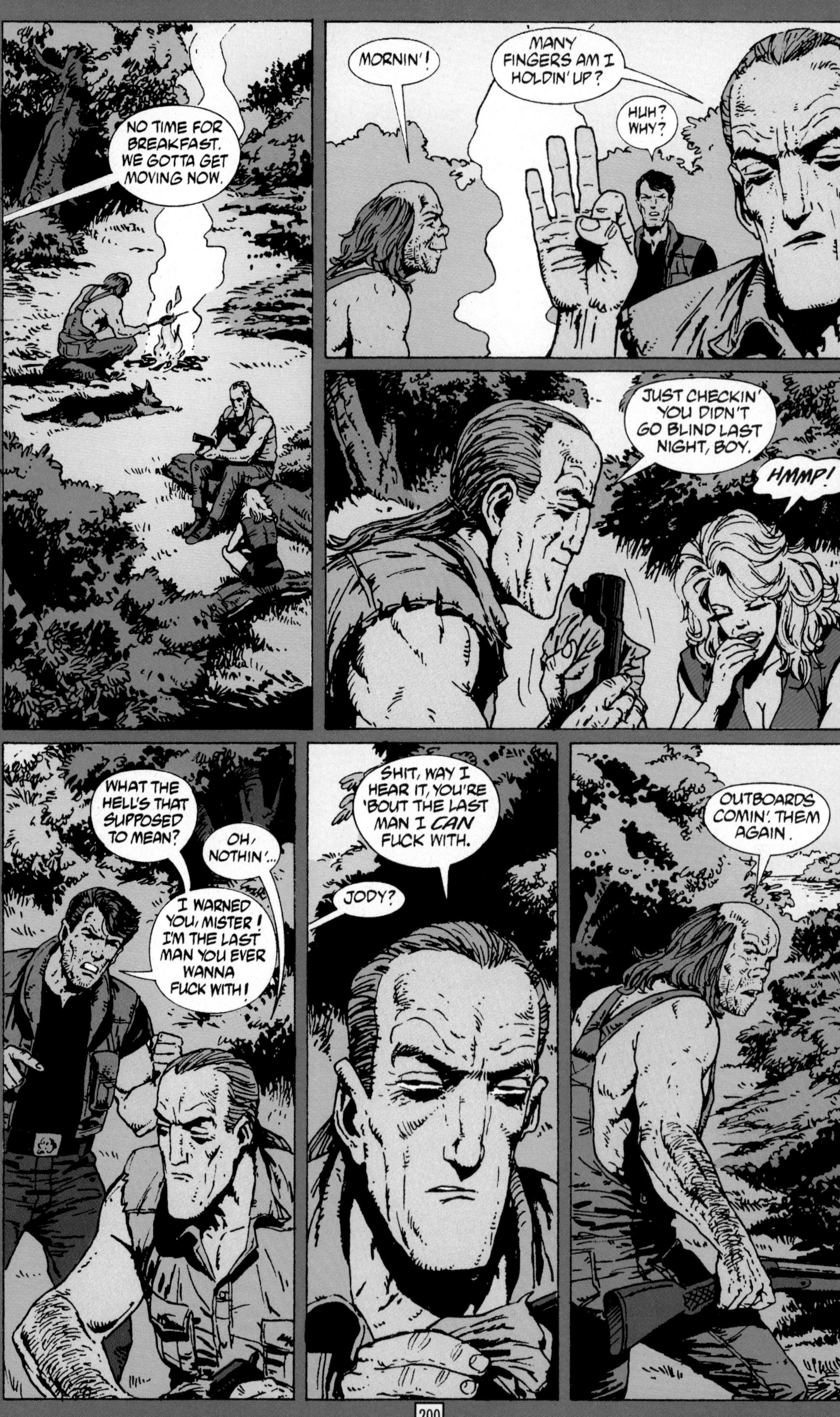

NO TIME FOR BREAKFAST. WE GOTTA GET MOVING NOW.
MORNIN'!
MANY FINGERS AM I HOLDIN' UP?
HUH? WHY?
JUST CHECKIN' YOU DIDN'T GO BLIND LAST NIGHT, BOY.
HMMP!
WHAT THE HELL'S THAT SUPPOSED TO MEAN?
OH, NOTHIN'...
I WARNED YOU, MISTER! I'M THE LAST MAN YOU EVER WANNA FUCK WITH!
JODY?
SHIT, WAY I HEAR IT, YOU'RE 'BOUT THE LAST MAN I CAN FUCK WITH.
OUTBOARDS COMIN'. THEM AGAIN.

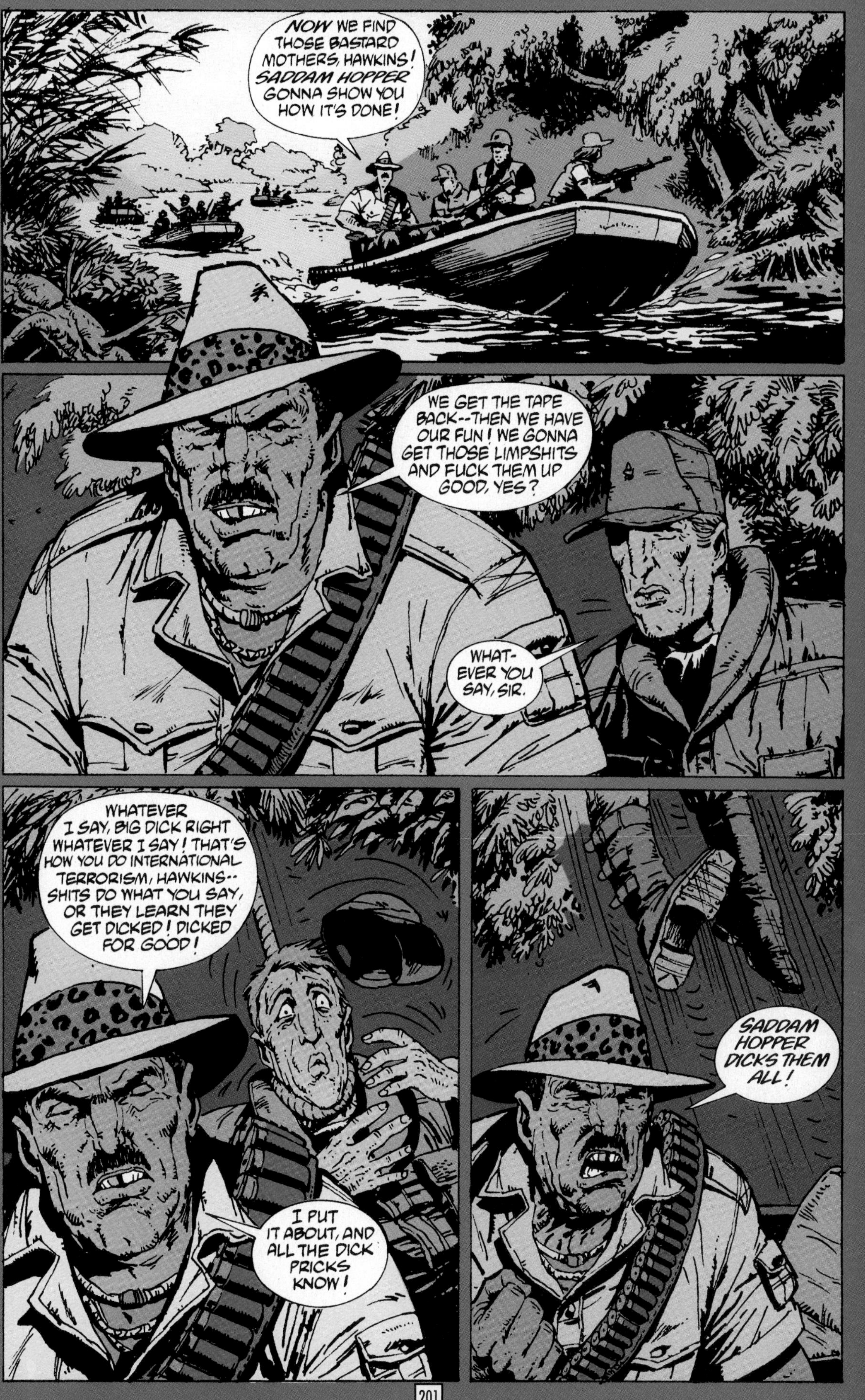

NOW WE FIND THOSE BASTARD MOTHERS, HAWKINS! SADDAM HOPPER GONNA SHOW YOU HOW IT'S DONE!
WE GET THE TAPE BACK--THEN WE HAVE OUR FUN! WE GONNA GET THOSE LIMPSHITS AND FUCK THEM UP GOOD, YES?
WHAT-EVER YOU SAY, SIR.
WHATEVER I SAY, BIG DICK RIGHT WHATEVER I SAY! THAT'S HOW YOU DO INTERNATIONAL TERRORISM, HAWKINS-- SHITS DO WHAT YOU SAY, OR THEY LEARN THEY GET DICKED! DICKED FOR GOOD!
I PUT IT ABOUT, AND ALL THE DICK PRICKS KNOW!
SADDAM HOPPER DICKS THEM ALL!

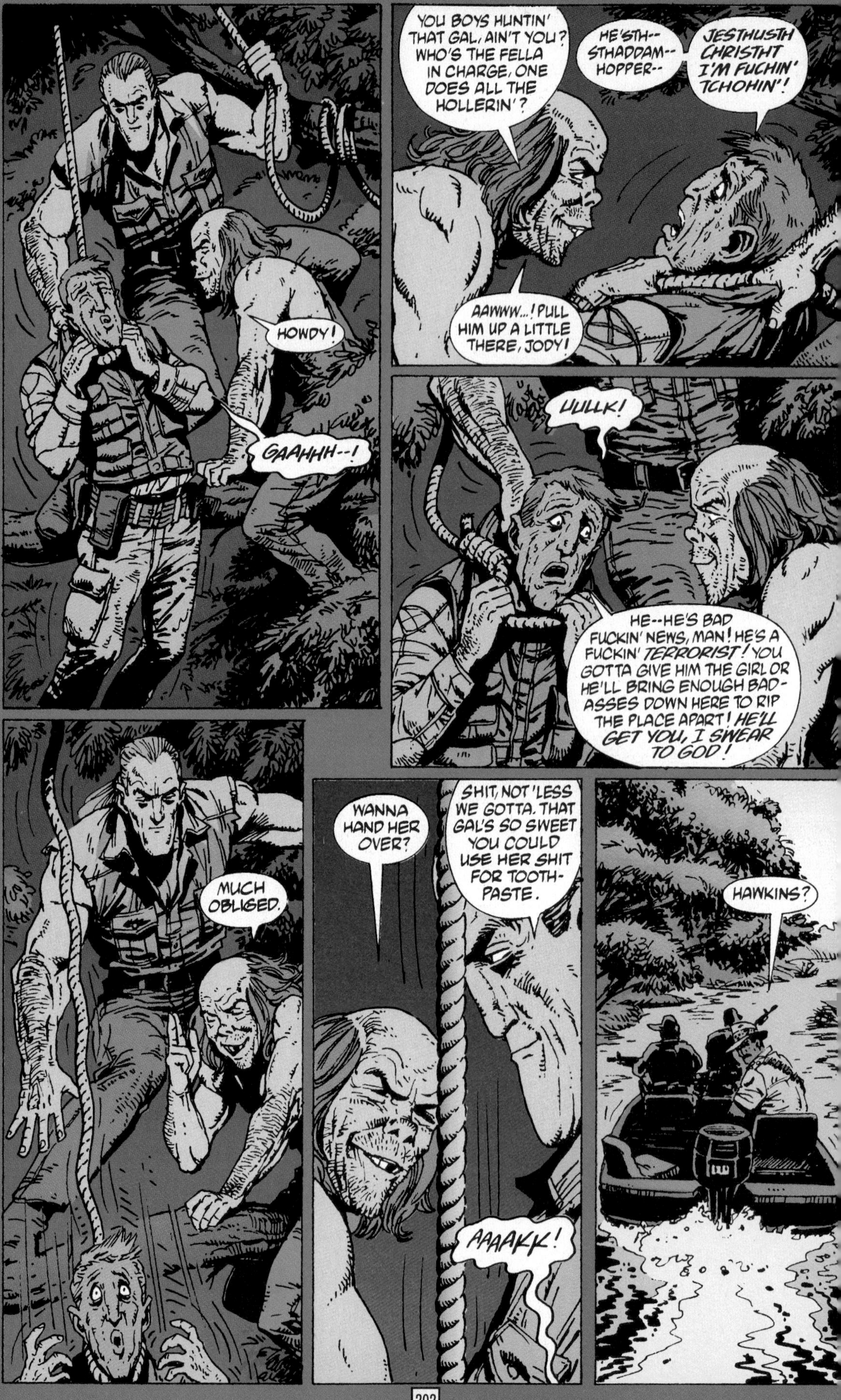
HOWDY!
GAAHHH--!
YOU BOYS HUNTIN' THAT GAL, AIN'T YOU? WHO'S THE FELLA IN CHARGE, ONE DOES ALL THE HOLLERIN'?
HE'STH--STHADDAM--HOPPER--
JESTHUSTH CHRISTHT I'M FUCHIN' TCHOHIN'!
AAWWW...! PULL HIM UP A LITTLE THERE, JODY!
UULLK!
HE--HE'S BAD FUCKIN' NEWS, MAN! HE'S A FUCKIN' TERRORIST! YOU GOTTA GIVE HIM THE GIRL OR HE'LL BRING ENOUGH BAD-ASSES DOWN HERE TO RIP THE PLACE APART! HE'LL GET YOU, I SWEAR TO GOD!
MUCH OBLIGED.
WANNA HAND HER OVER?
SHIT, NOT 'LESS WE GOTTA. THAT GAL'S SO SWEET YOU COULD USE HER SHIT FOR TOOTH-PASTE.
AAAKK!
HAWKINS?

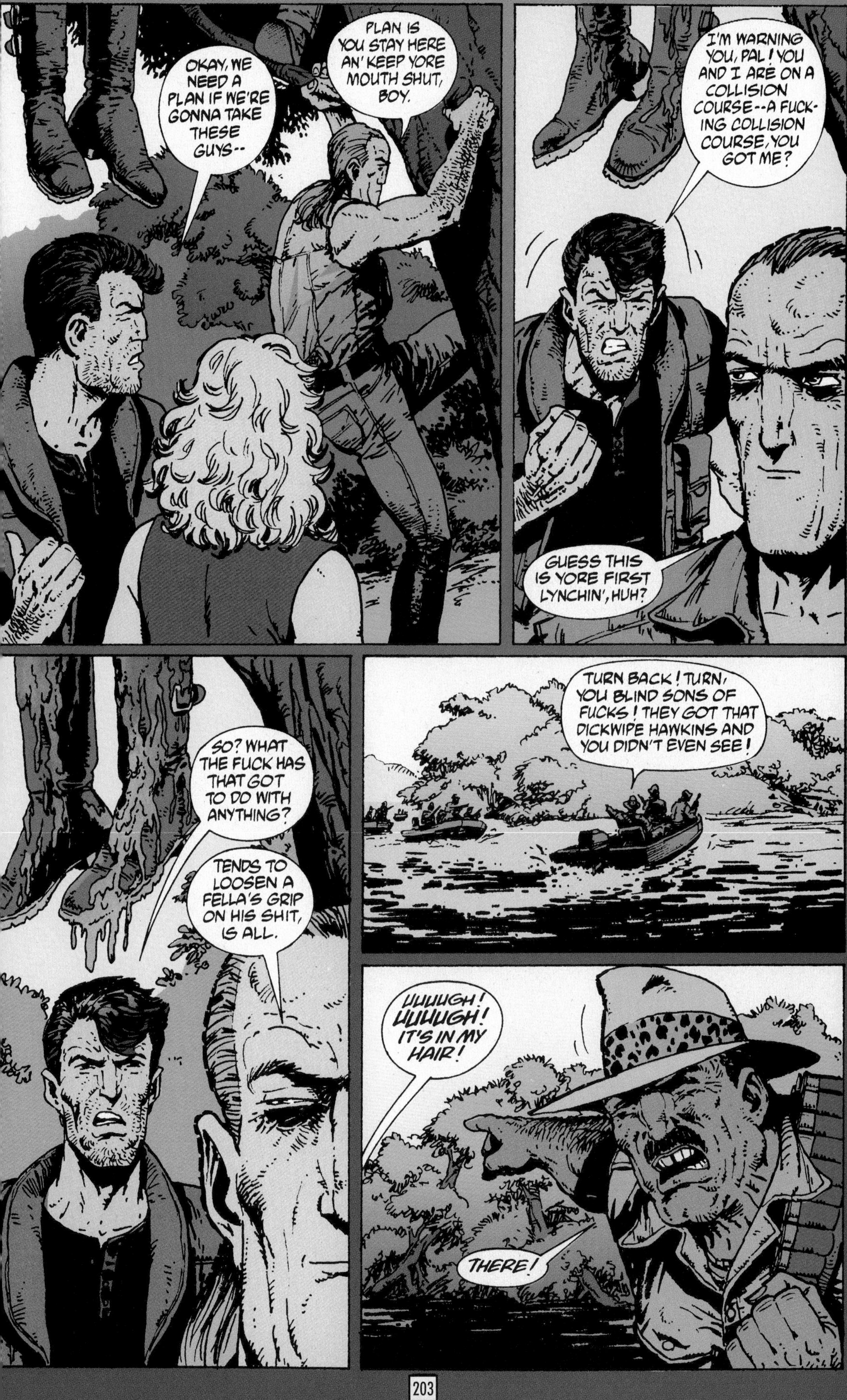
OKAY, WE NEED A PLAN IF WE'RE GONNA TAKE THESE GUYS--
PLAN IS YOU STAY HERE AN' KEEP YORE MOUTH SHUT, BOY.
I'M WARNING YOU, PAL! YOU AND I ARE ON A COLLISION COURSE--A FUCKING COLLISION COURSE, YOU GOT ME?
GUESS THIS IS YORE FIRST LYNCHIN', HUH?
SO? WHAT THE FUCK HAS THAT GOT TO DO WITH ANYTHING?
TENDS TO LOOSEN A FELLA'S GRIP ON HIS SHIT, IS ALL.
TURN BACK! TURN, YOU BLIND SONS OF FUCKS! THEY GOT THAT DICKWIPE HAWKINS AND YOU DIDN'T EVEN SEE!
UUUUGH! UUUUGH! IT'S IN MY HAIR!
THERE!

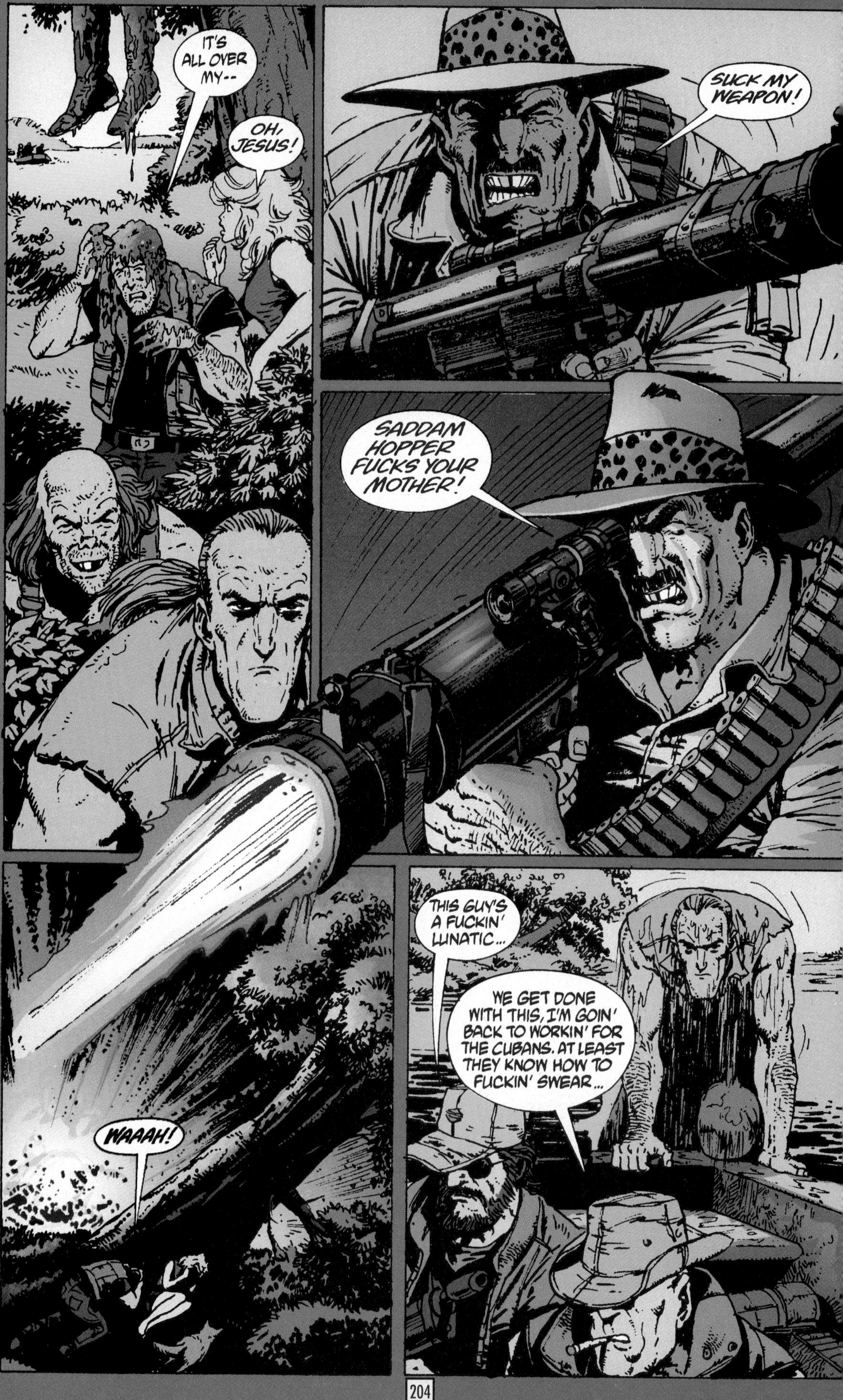
IT'S ALL OVER MY--
OH, JESUS!
SUCK MY WEAPON!
SADDAM HOPPER FUCKS YOUR MOTHER!
WAAAH!
THIS GUY'S A FUCKIN' LUNATIC...
WE GET DONE WITH THIS, I'M GOIN' BACK TO WORKIN' FOR THE CUBANS. AT LEAST THEY KNOW HOW TO FUCKIN' SWEAR...

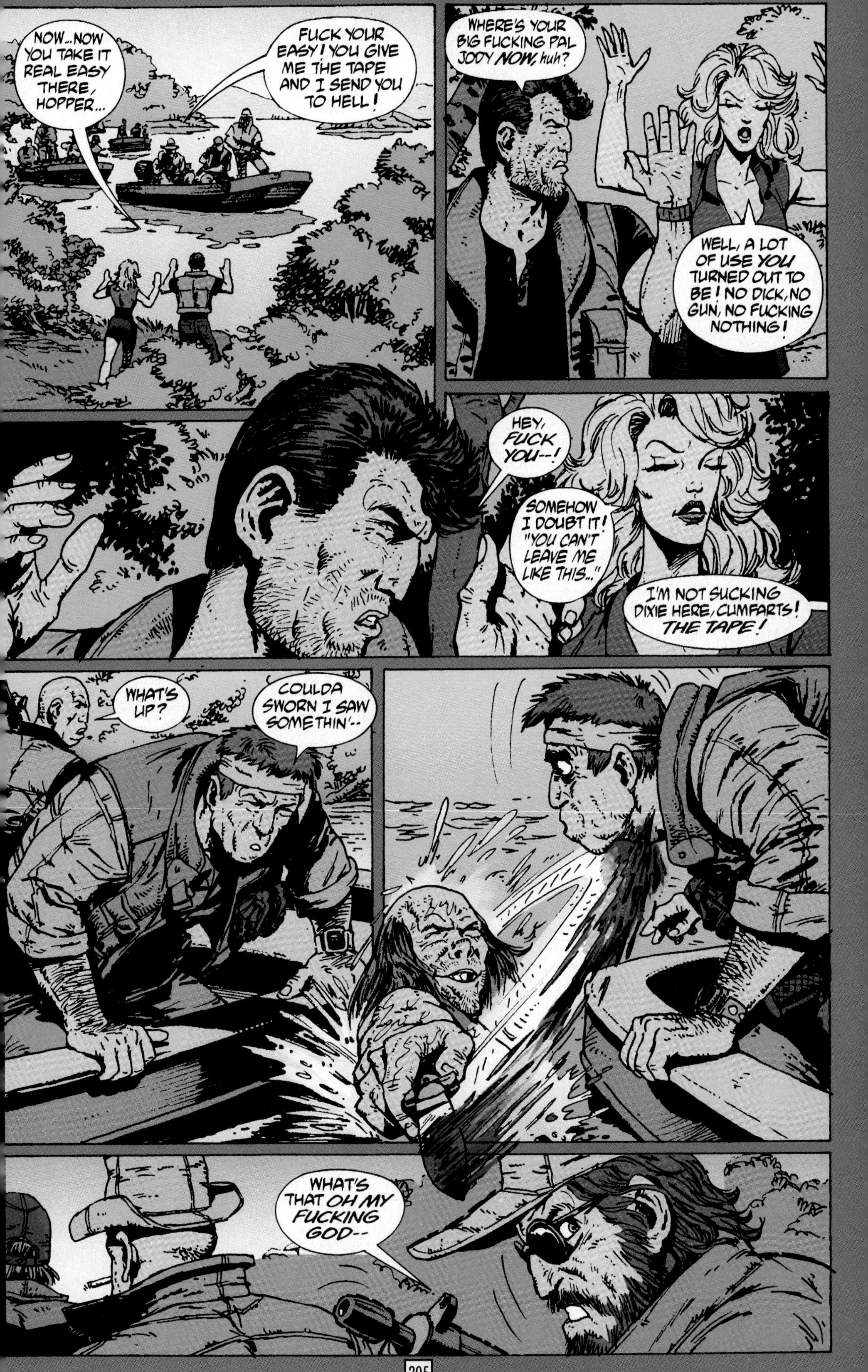

NOW...NOW YOU TAKE IT REAL EASY THERE, HOPPER...
FUCK YOUR EASY! YOU GIVE ME THE TAPE AND I SEND YOU TO HELL!
WHERE'S YOUR BIG FUCKING PAL JODY NOW, huh?
WELL, A LOT OF USE YOU TURNED OUT TO BE! NO DICK, NO GUN, NO FUCKING NOTHING!
HEY, FUCK YOU--!
SOMEHOW I DOUBT IT! "YOU CAN'T LEAVE ME LIKE THIS.."
I'M NOT SUCKING DIXIE HERE, CUMFARTS! THE TAPE!
WHAT'S UP?
COULDA SWORN I SAW SOMETHIN'--
WHAT'S THAT OH MY FUCKING GOD--

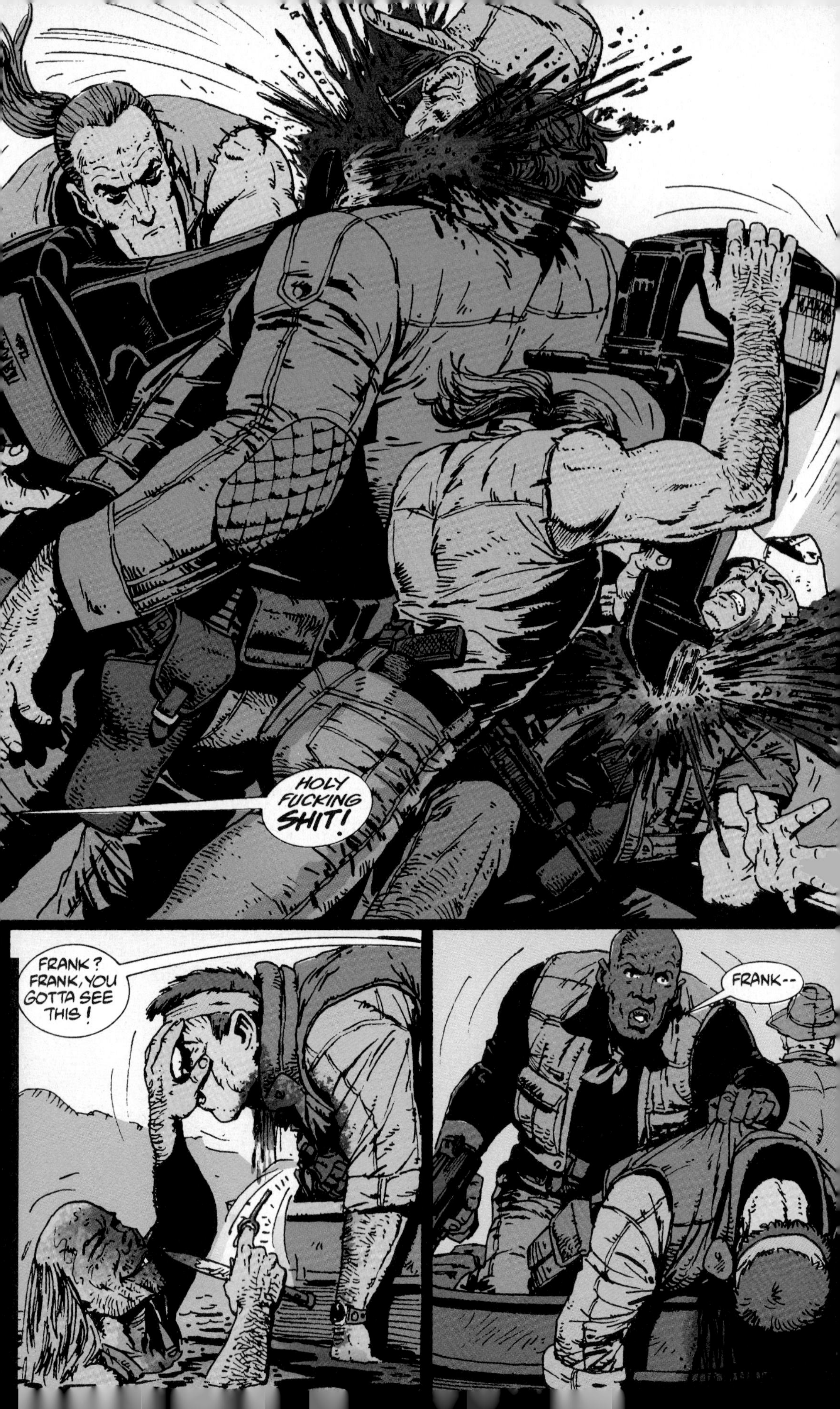
HOLY FUCKING SHIT!
FRANK? FRANK, YOU GOTTA SEE THIS!
FRANK--

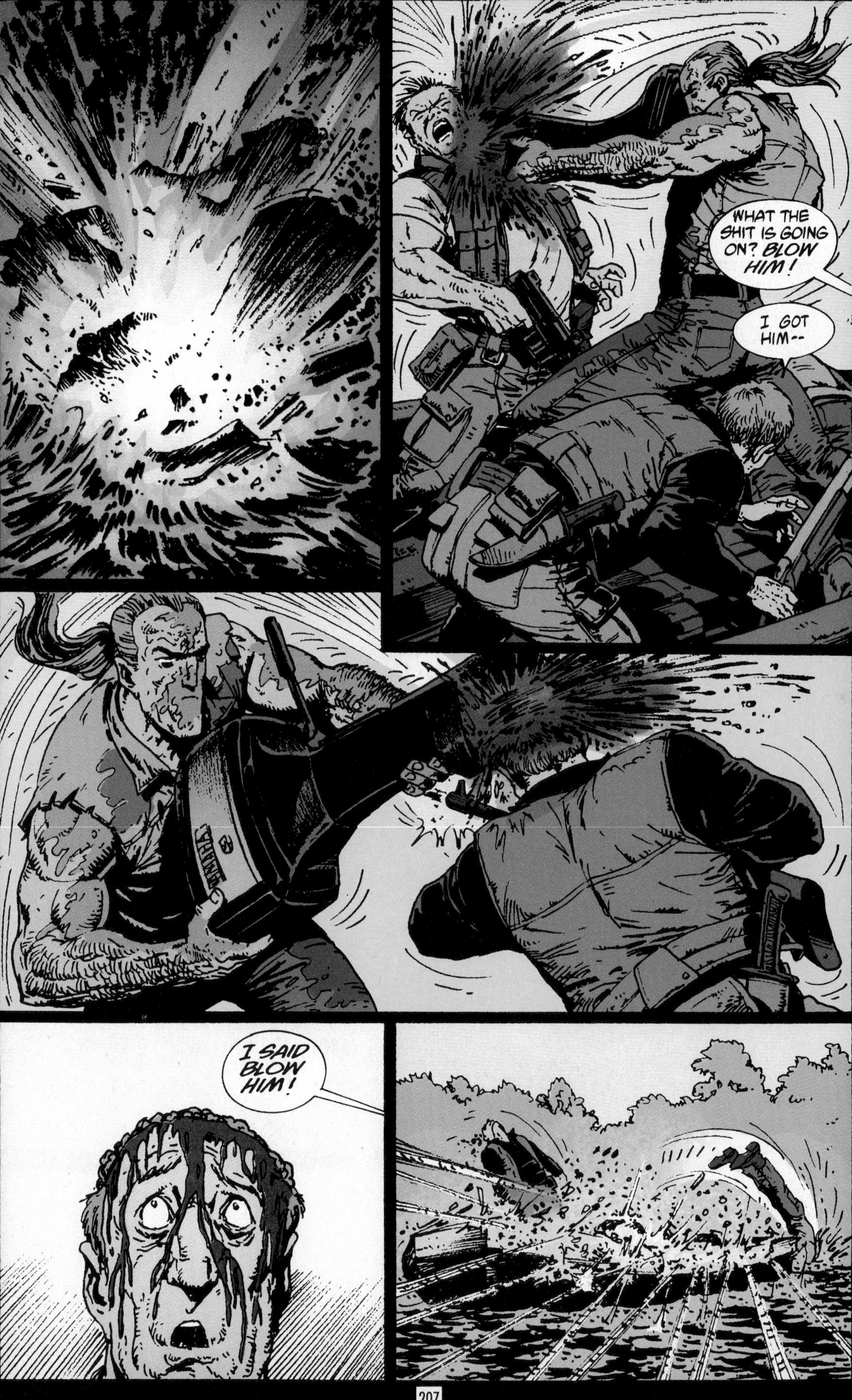
WHAT THE SHIT IS GOING ON? BLOW HIM!
I GOT HIM--
I SAID BLOW HIM!

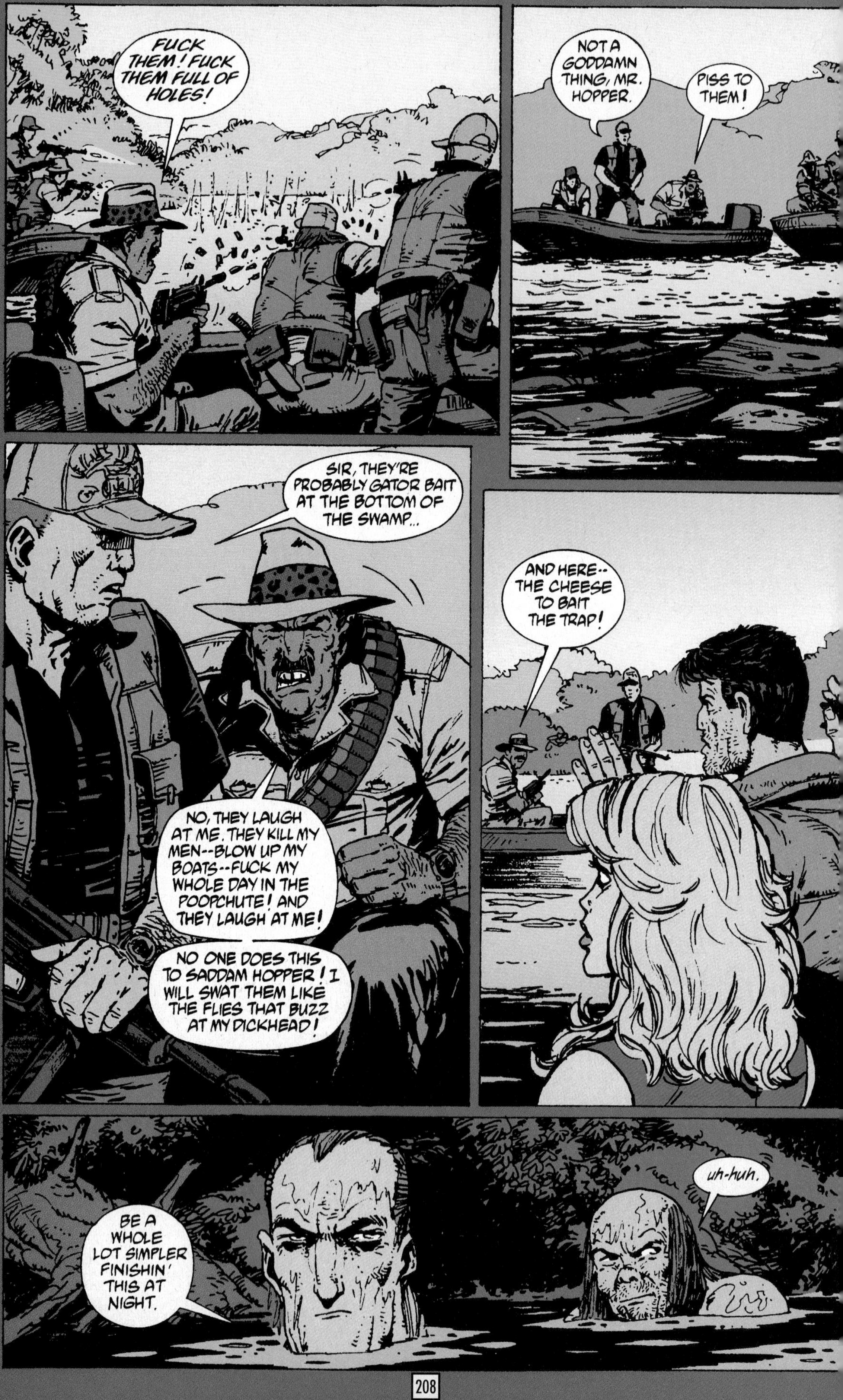
FUCK THEM! FUCK THEM FULL OF HOLES!
NOT A GODDAMN THING, MR. HOPPER.
PISS TO THEM!
SIR, THEY'RE PROBABLY GATOR BAIT AT THE BOTTOM OF THE SWAMP...
NO, THEY LAUGH AT ME. THEY KILL MY MEN--BLOW UP MY BOATS--FUCK MY WHOLE DAY IN THE POOPCHUTE! AND THEY LAUGH AT ME!
NO ONE DOES THIS TO SADDAM HOPPER! I WILL SWAT THEM LIKE THE FLIES THAT BUZZ AT MY DICKHEAD!
AND HERE-- THE CHEESE TO BAIT THE TRAP!
BE A WHOLE LOT SIMPLER FINISHIN' THIS AT NIGHT.
uh-huh.

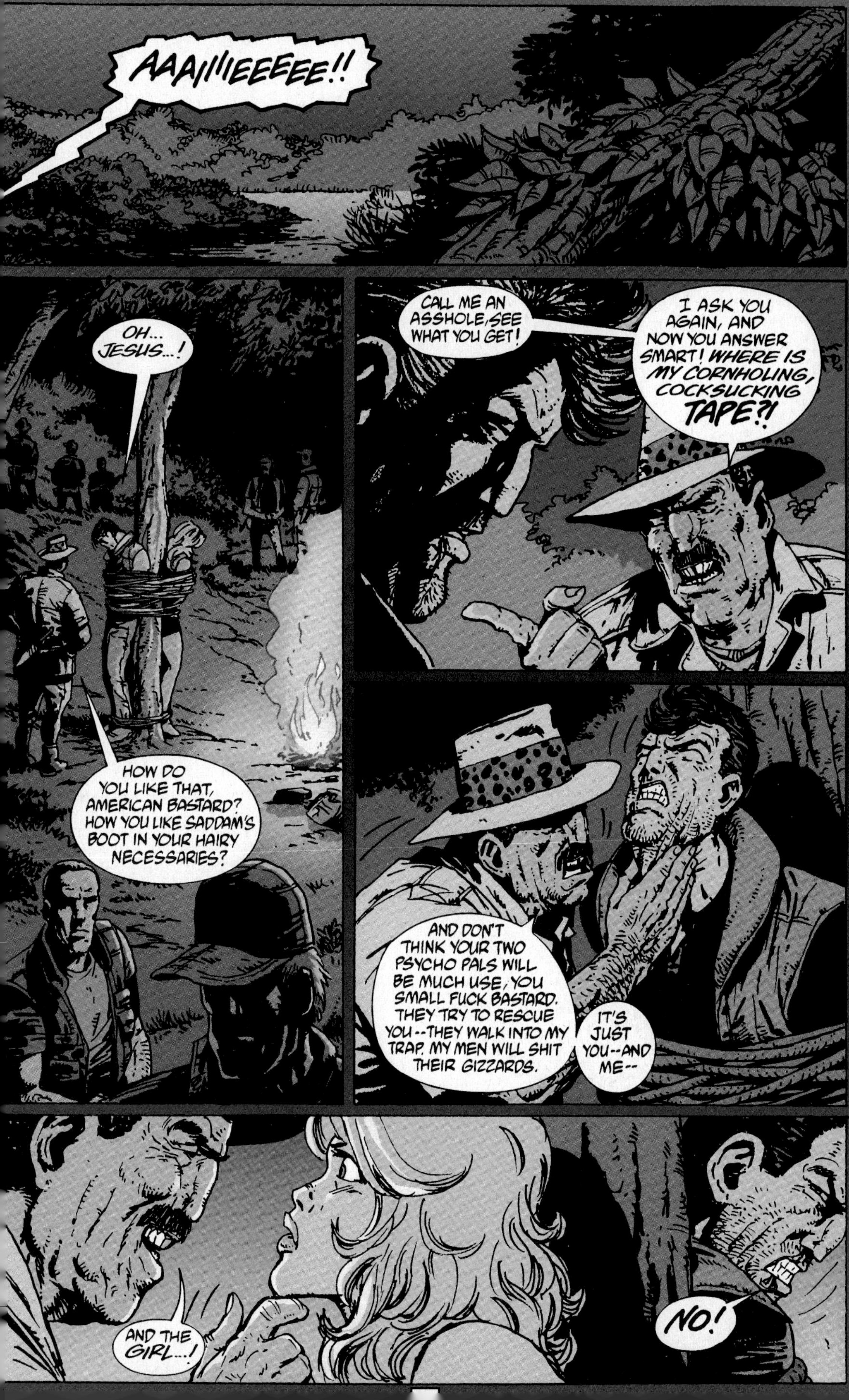

AAAIIIIEEEEEE!!
OH... JESUS...!
HOW DO YOU LIKE THAT, AMERICAN BASTARD? HOW YOU LIKE SADDAM'S BOOT IN YOUR HAIRY NECESSARIES?
CALL ME AN ASSHOLE, SEE WHAT YOU GET!
I ASK YOU AGAIN, AND NOW YOU ANSWER SMART! WHERE IS MY CORNHOLING, COCKSUCKING TAPE?!
AND DON'T THINK YOUR TWO PSYCHO PALS WILL BE MUCH USE, YOU SMALL FUCK BASTARD. THEY TRY TO RESCUE YOU--THEY WALK INTO MY TRAP. MY MEN WILL SHIT THEIR GIZZARDS.
IT'S JUST YOU--AND ME--
AND THE GIRL...!
NO!

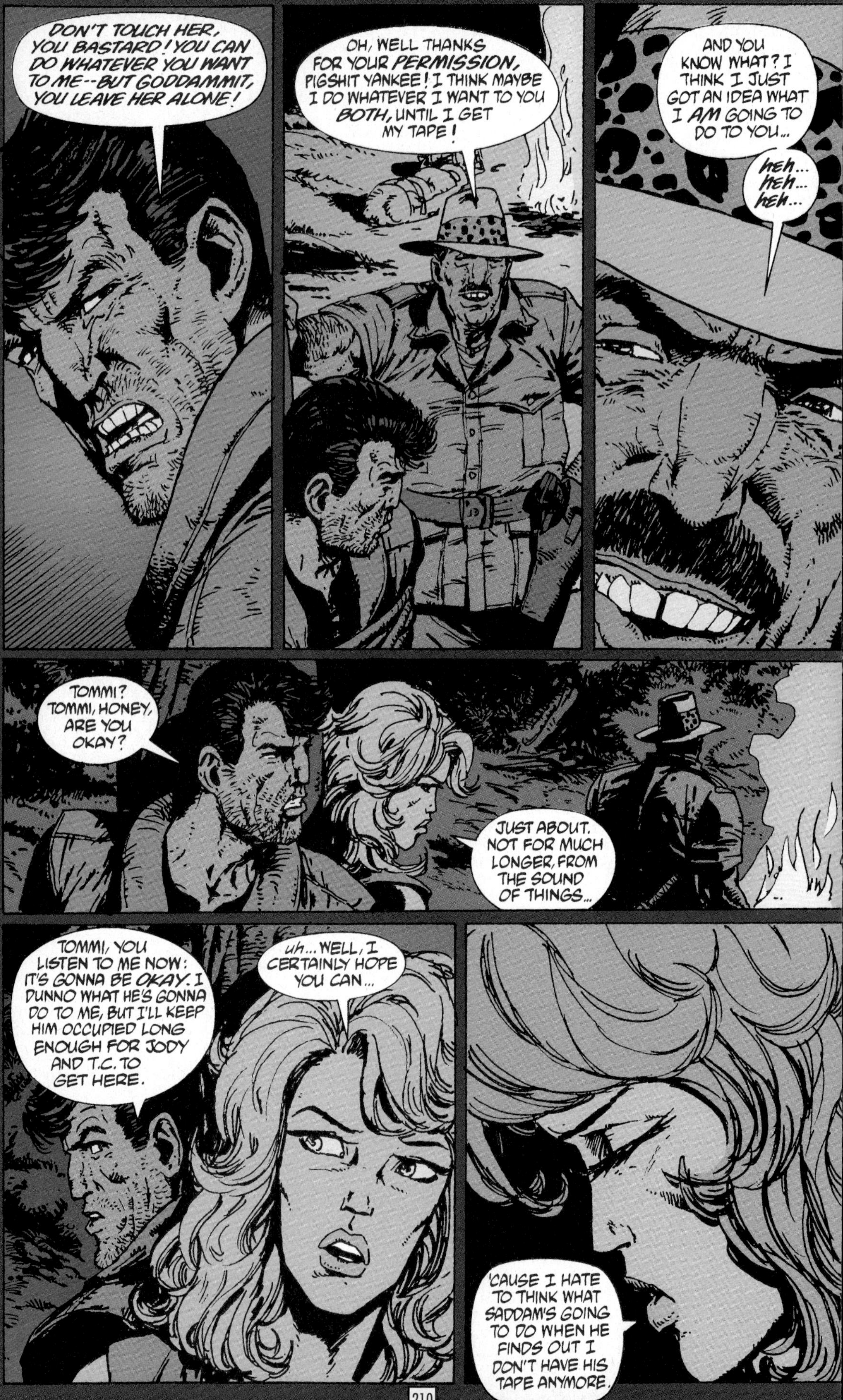
DON'T TOUCH HER, YOU BASTARD! YOU CAN DO WHATEVER YOU WANT TO ME--BUT GODDAMMIT, YOU LEAVE HER ALONE!
OH, WELL THANKS FOR YOUR PERMISSION, PIGSHIT YANKEE! I THINK MAYBE I DO WHATEVER I WANT TO YOU BOTH, UNTIL I GET MY TAPE!
AND YOU KNOW WHAT? I THINK I JUST GOT AN IDEA WHAT I AM GOING TO DO TO YOU...
heh... heh... heh...
TOMMI? TOMMI, HONEY, ARE YOU OKAY?
JUST ABOUT. NOT FOR MUCH LONGER, FROM THE SOUND OF THINGS...
TOMMI, YOU LISTEN TO ME NOW: IT'S GONNA BE OKAY. I DUNNO WHAT HE'S GONNA DO TO ME, BUT I'LL KEEP HIM OCCUPIED LONG ENOUGH FOR JODY AND T.C. TO GET HERE.
uh... WELL, I CERTAINLY HOPE YOU CAN...
'CAUSE I HATE TO THINK WHAT SADDAM'S GOING TO DO WHEN HE FINDS OUT I DON'T HAVE HIS TAPE ANYMORE.

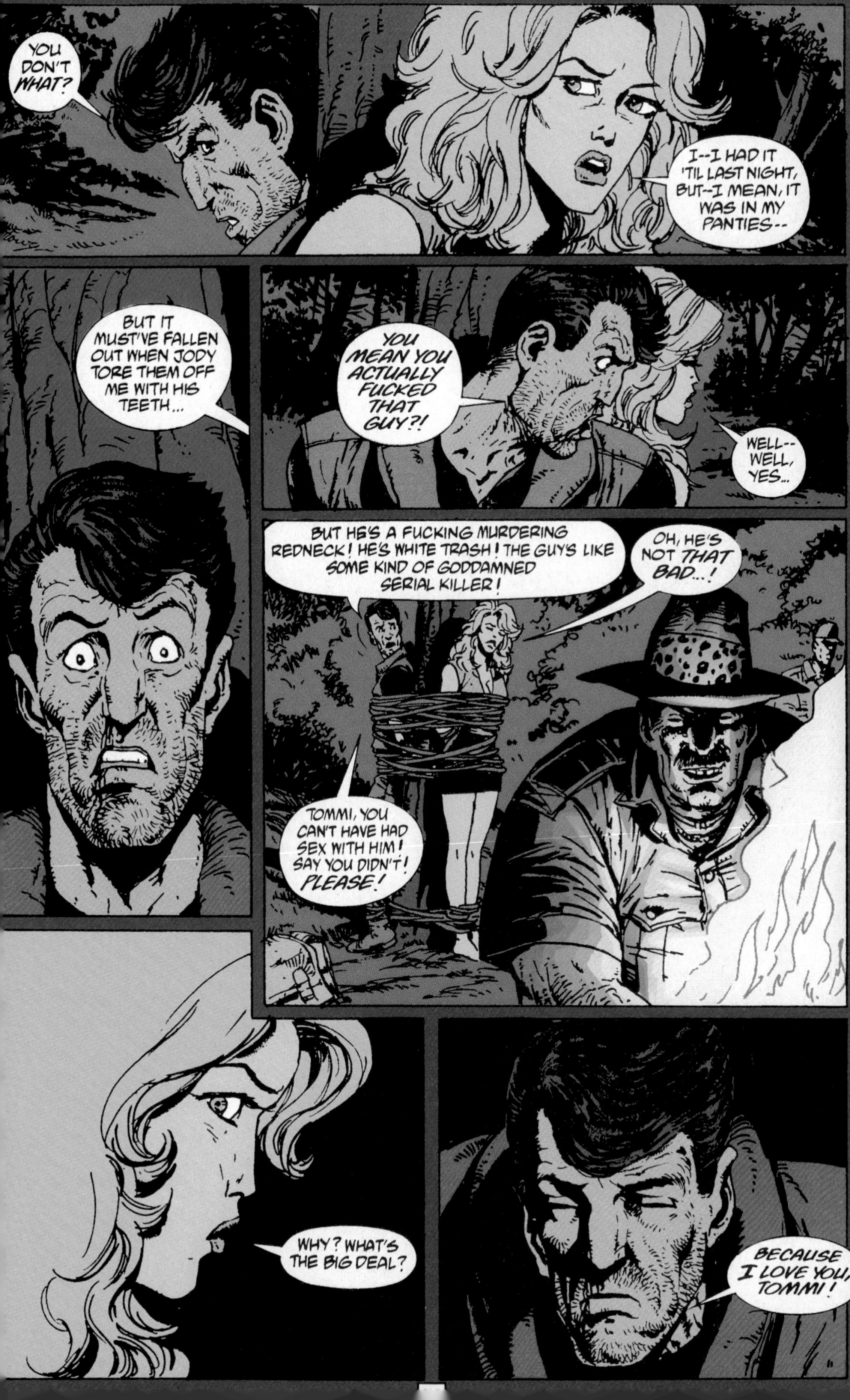
YOU DON'T WHAT?
I--I HAD IT 'TIL LAST NIGHT, BUT--I MEAN, IT WAS IN MY PANTIES--
BUT IT MUST'VE FALLEN OUT WHEN JODY TORE THEM OFF ME WITH HIS TEETH...
YOU MEAN YOU ACTUALLY FUCKED THAT GUY?!
WELL-- WELL, YES...
BUT HE'S A FUCKING MURDERING REDNECK! HE'S WHITE TRASH! THE GUY'S LIKE SOME KIND OF GODDAMNED SERIAL KILLER!
OH, HE'S NOT THAT BAD...!
TOMMI, YOU CAN'T HAVE HAD SEX WITH HIM! SAY YOU DIDN'T! PLEASE!
WHY? WHAT'S THE BIG DEAL?
BECAUSE I LOVE YOU, TOMMI!

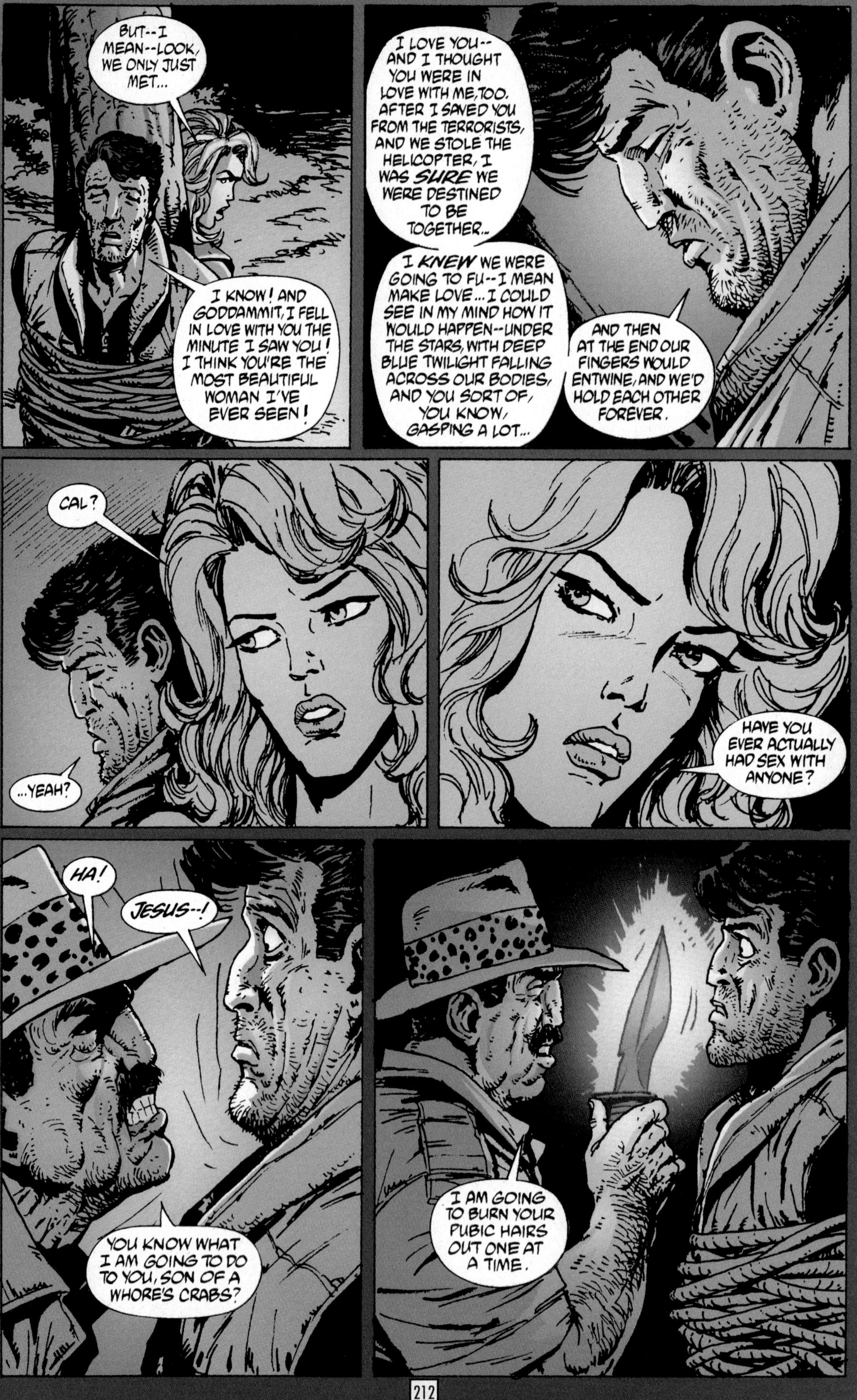
BUT--I MEAN--LOOK, WE ONLY JUST MET...
I KNOW! AND GODDAMMIT, I FELL IN LOVE WITH YOU THE MINUTE I SAW YOU! I THINK YOU'RE THE MOST BEAUTIFUL WOMAN I'VE EVER SEEN!
I LOVE YOU-- AND I THOUGHT YOU WERE IN LOVE WITH ME, TOO. AFTER I SAVED YOU FROM THE TERRORISTS, AND WE STOLE THE HELICOPTER, I WAS *SURE* WE WERE DESTINED TO BE TOGETHER...
I *KNEW* WE WERE GOING TO FU--I MEAN MAKE LOVE... I COULD SEE IN MY MIND HOW IT WOULD HAPPEN--UNDER THE STARS, WITH DEEP BLUE TWILIGHT FALLING ACROSS OUR BODIES, AND YOU SORT OF, YOU KNOW, GASPING A LOT...
AND THEN AT THE END OUR FINGERS WOULD ENTWINE, AND WE'D HOLD EACH OTHER FOREVER.
CAL?
...YEAH?
HAVE YOU EVER ACTUALLY HAD SEX WITH ANYONE?
HA!
JESUS--!
YOU KNOW WHAT I AM GOING TO DO TO YOU, SON OF A WHORE'S CRABS?
I AM GOING TO BURN YOUR PUBIC HAIRS OUT ONE AT A TIME.

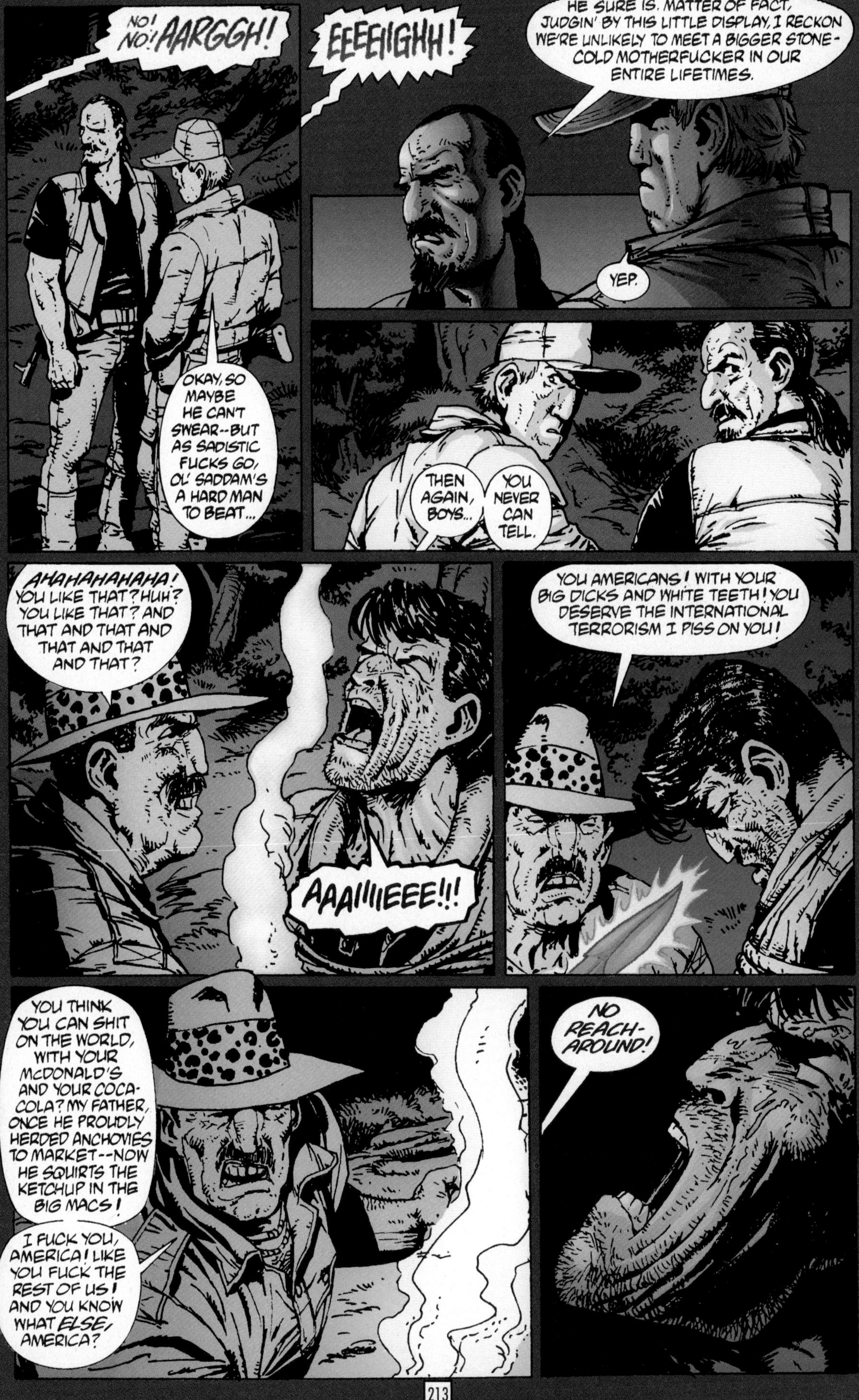
NO! NO! AARGGH!
EEEEIIGHH!
HE SURE IS. MATTER OF FACT, JUDGIN' BY THIS LITTLE DISPLAY, I RECKON WE'RE UNLIKELY TO MEET A BIGGER STONE-COLD MOTHERFUCKER IN OUR ENTIRE LIFETIMES.
YEP.
OKAY, SO MAYBE HE CAN'T SWEAR--BUT AS SADISTIC FUCKS GO, OL' SADDAM'S A HARD MAN TO BEAT...
THEN AGAIN, BOYS...
YOU NEVER CAN TELL.
AHAHAHAHAHA! YOU LIKE THAT? HUH? YOU LIKE THAT? AND THAT AND THAT AND THAT AND THAT AND THAT?
AAAIIIIEEE!!!
YOU AMERICANS! WITH YOUR BIG DICKS AND WHITE TEETH! YOU DESERVE THE INTERNATIONAL TERRORISM I PISS ON YOU!
YOU THINK YOU CAN SHIT ON THE WORLD, WITH YOUR McDONALD'S AND YOUR COCA-COLA? MY FATHER, ONCE HE PROUDLY HERDED ANCHOVIES TO MARKET--NOW HE SQUIRTS THE KETCHUP IN THE BIG MACS!
I FUCK YOU, AMERICA! LIKE YOU FUCK THE REST OF US! AND YOU KNOW WHAT ELSE, AMERICA?
NO REACH-AROUND!

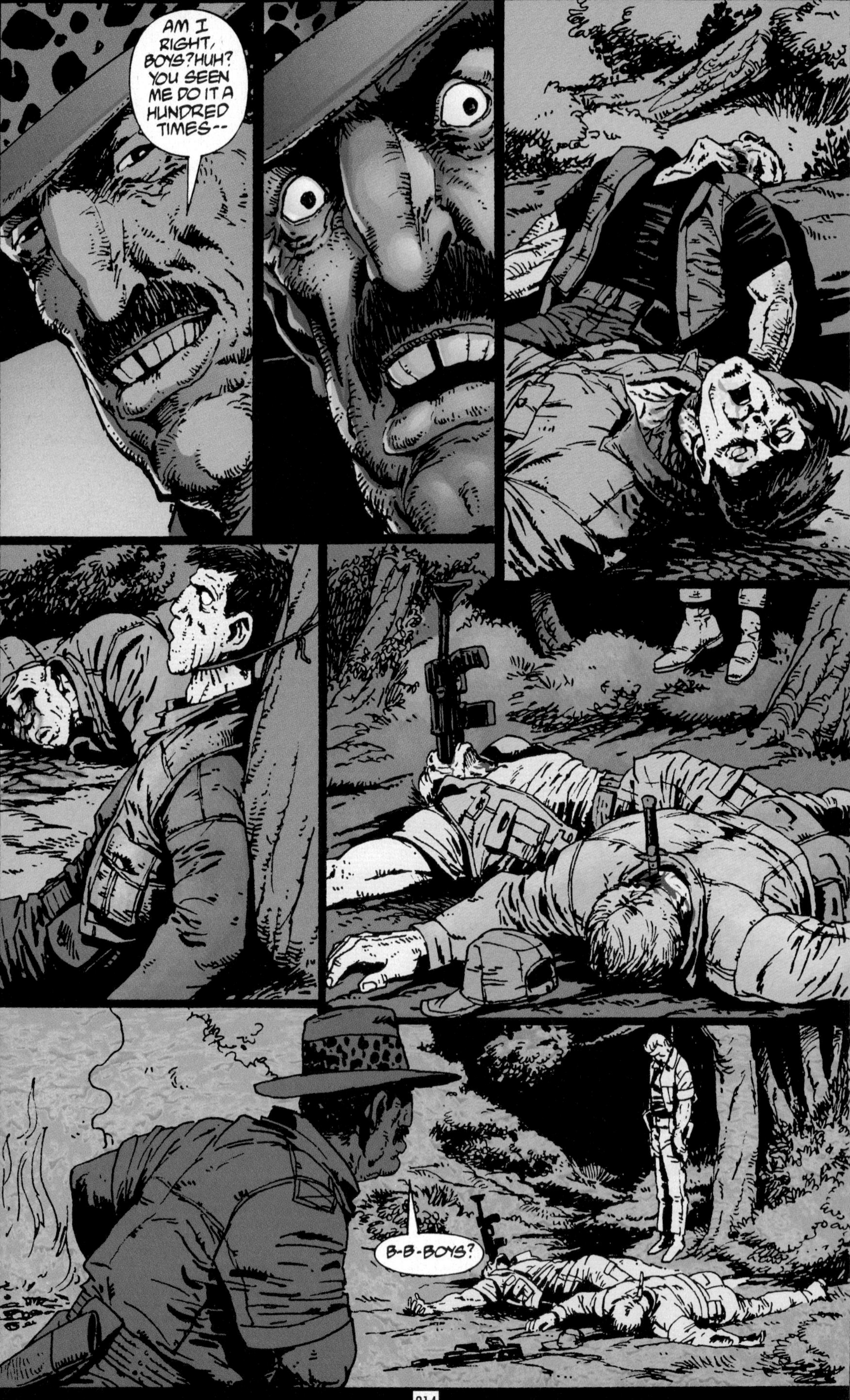
AM I RIGHT, BOYS? HUH? YOU SEEN ME DO IT A HUNDRED TIMES--
B-B-BOYS?

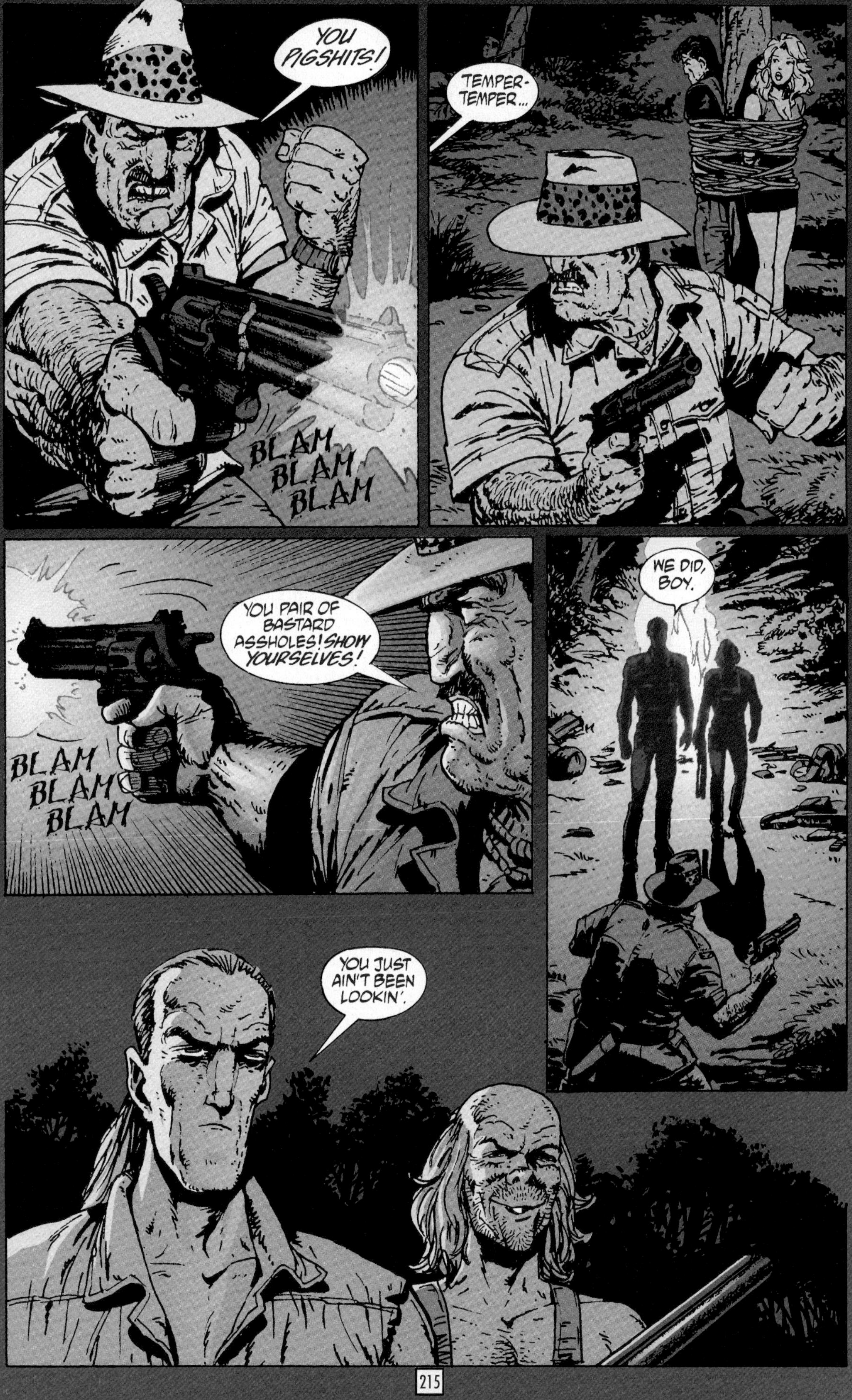
YOU PIGSHITS!
BLAM BLAM BLAM
TEMPER-TEMPER...
YOU PAIR OF BASTARD ASSHOLES! SHOW YOURSELVES!
BLAM BLAM BLAM
WE DID, BOY.
YOU JUST AIN'T BEEN LOOKIN'.

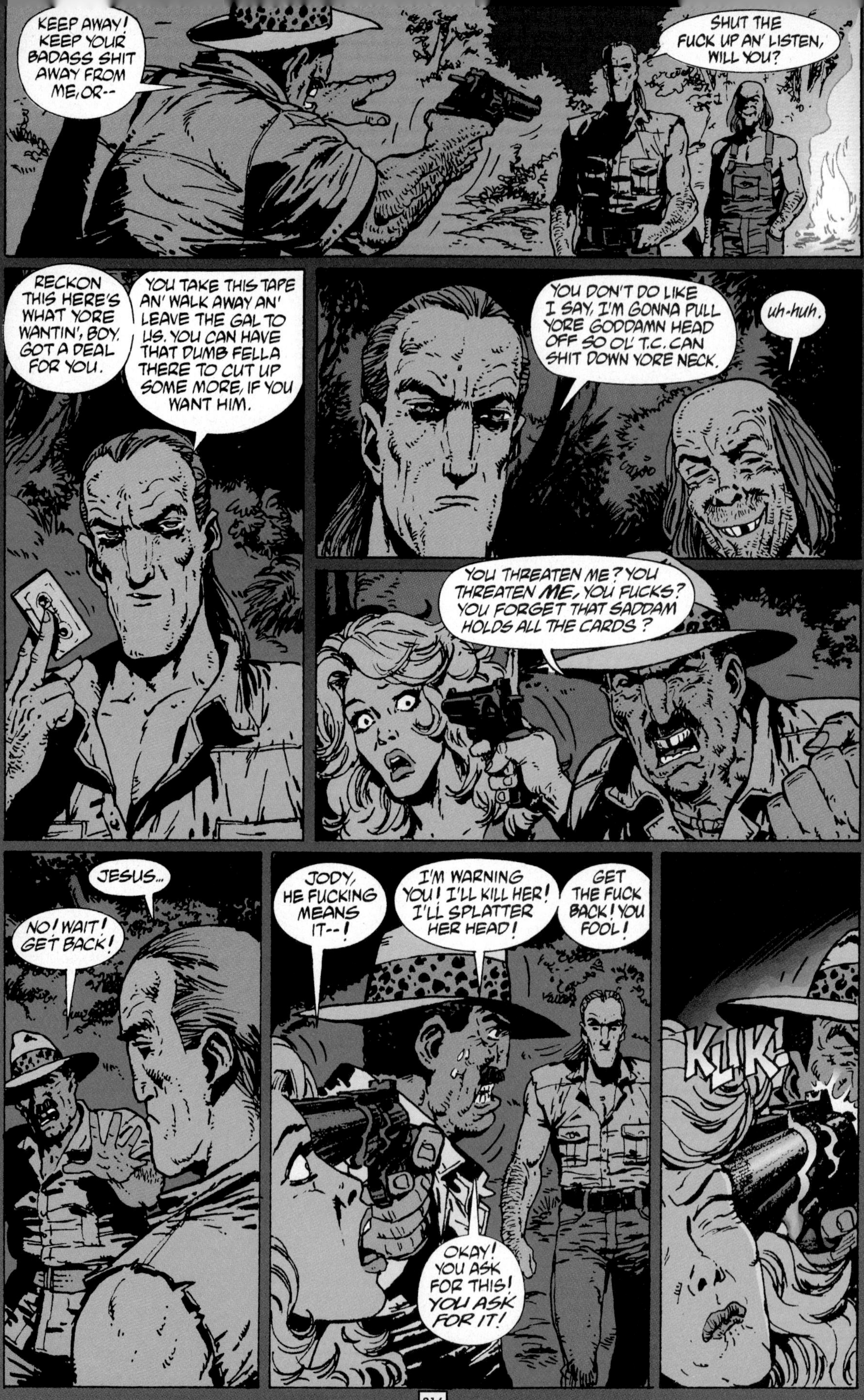
KEEP AWAY! KEEP YOUR BADASS SHIT AWAY FROM ME, OR--
SHUT THE FUCK UP AN' LISTEN, WILL YOU?
RECKON THIS HERE'S WHAT YORE WANTIN', BOY. GOT A DEAL FOR YOU.
YOU TAKE THIS TAPE AN' WALK AWAY AN' LEAVE THE GAL TO US. YOU CAN HAVE THAT DUMB FELLA THERE TO CUT UP SOME MORE, IF YOU WANT HIM.
YOU DON'T DO LIKE I SAY, I'M GONNA PULL YORE GODDAMN HEAD OFF SO OL' T.C. CAN SHIT DOWN YORE NECK.
uh-huh.
YOU THREATEN ME? YOU THREATEN ME, YOU FUCKS? YOU FORGET THAT SADDAM HOLDS ALL THE CARDS?
JESUS...
NO! WAIT! GET BACK!
JODY, HE FUCKING MEANS IT--!
I'M WARNING YOU! I'LL KILL HER! I'LL SPLATTER HER HEAD!
GET THE FUCK BACK! YOU FOOL!
OKAY! YOU ASK FOR THIS! YOU ASK FOR IT!
KLIK!

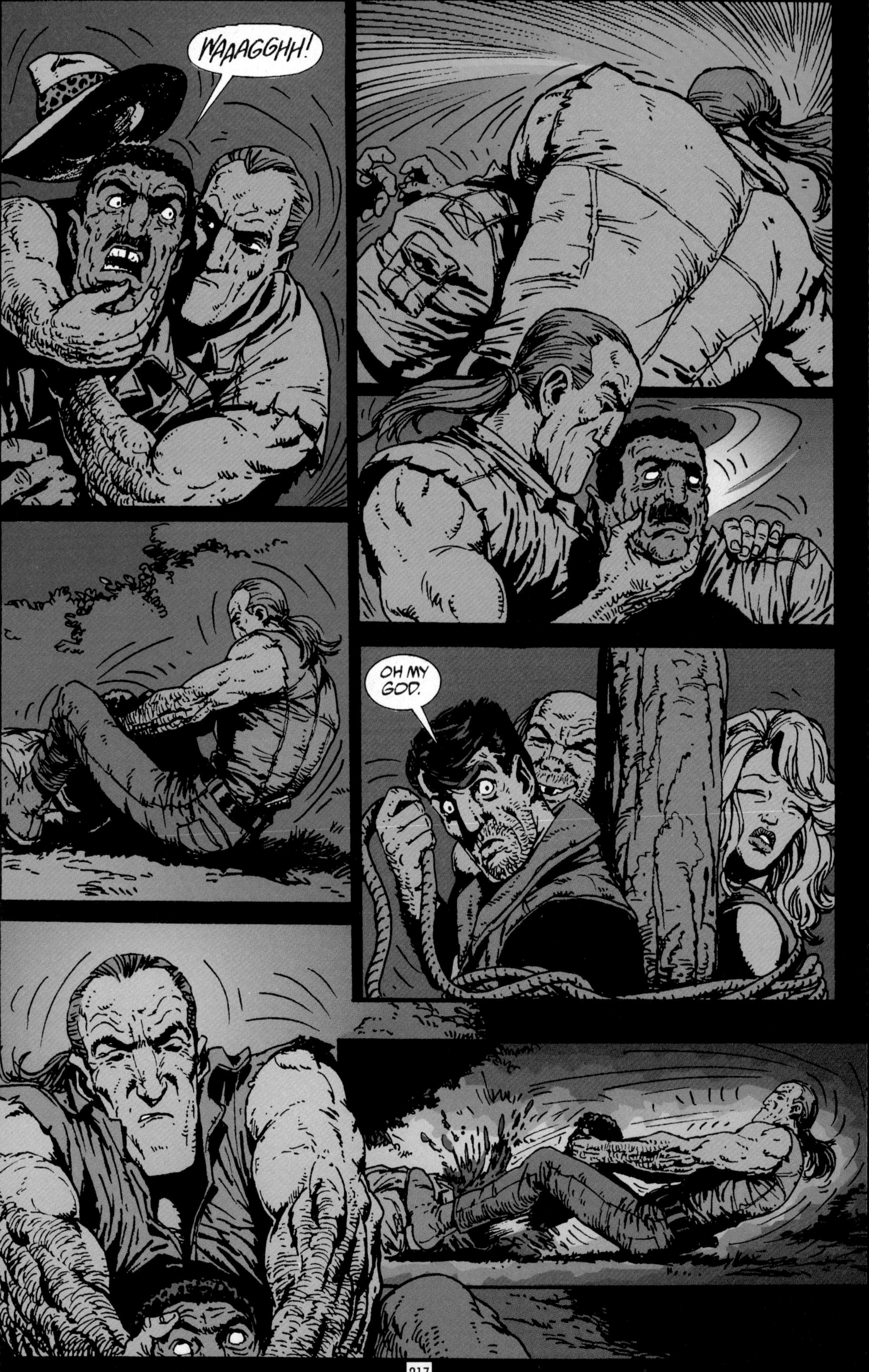
WAAAGGHH!
OH MY GOD.

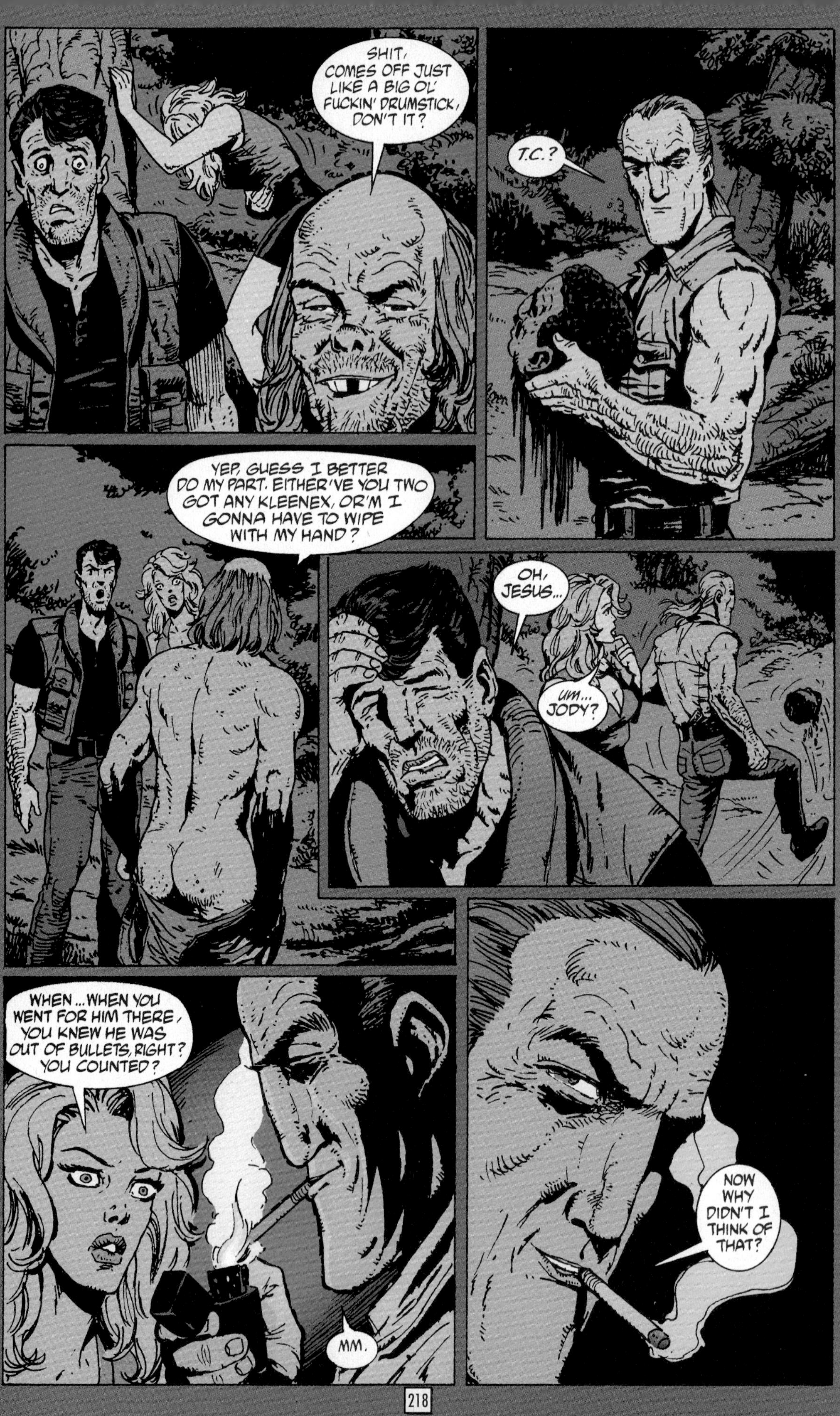
SHIT, COMES OFF JUST LIKE A BIG OL' FUCKIN' DRUMSTICK, DON'T IT?
T.C.?
YEP, GUESS I BETTER DO MY PART. EITHER'VE YOU TWO GOT ANY KLEENEX, OR'M I GONNA HAVE TO WIPE WITH MY HAND?
OH, JESUS...
UM... JODY?
WHEN ...WHEN YOU WENT FOR HIM THERE, YOU KNEW HE WAS OUT OF BULLETS, RIGHT? YOU COUNTED?
MM.
NOW WHY DIDN'T I THINK OF THAT?

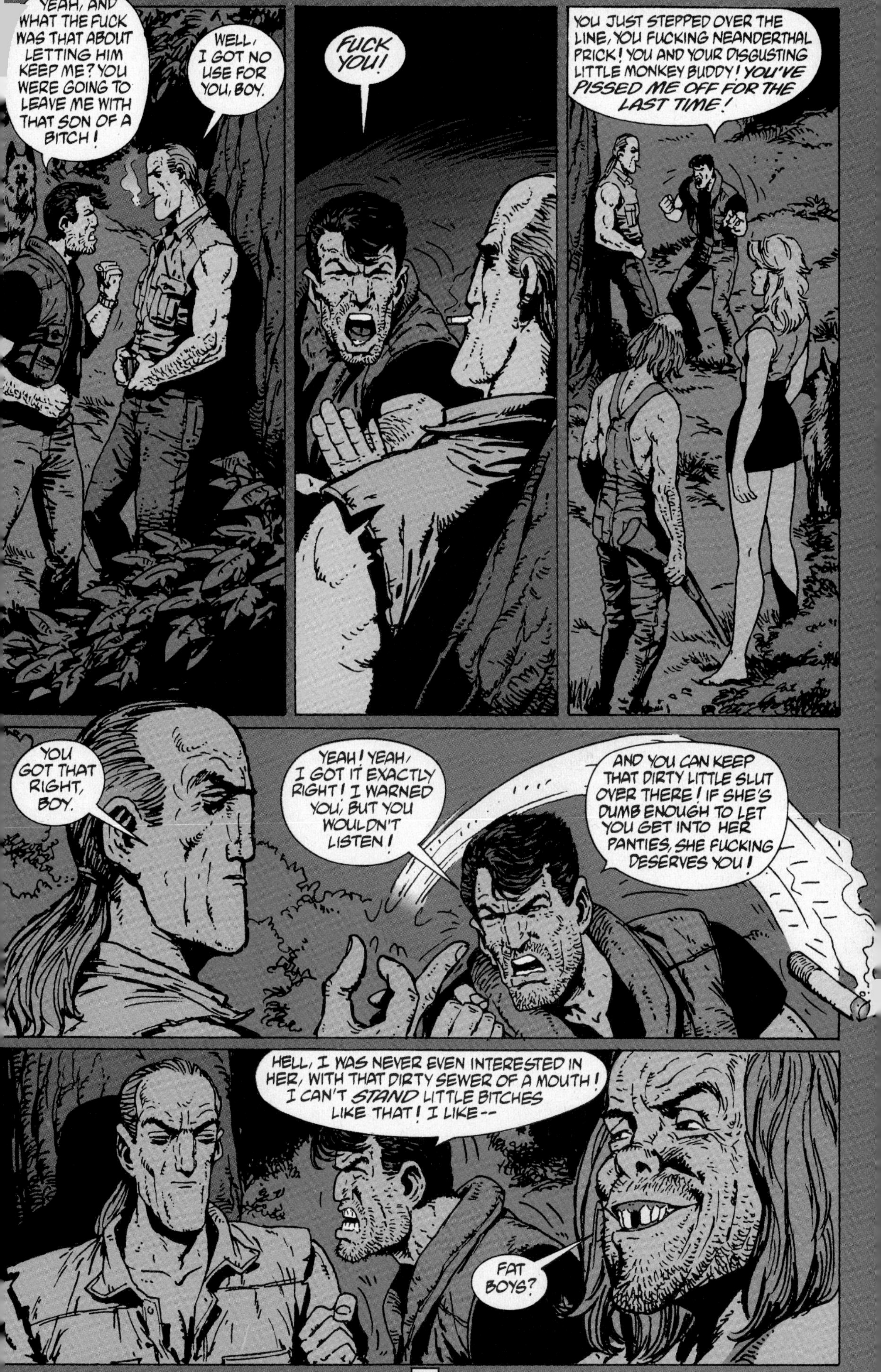
YEAH, AND WHAT THE FUCK WAS THAT ABOUT LETTING HIM KEEP ME? YOU WERE GOING TO LEAVE ME WITH THAT SON OF A BITCH!
WELL, I GOT NO USE FOR YOU, BOY.
FUCK YOU!
YOU JUST STEPPED OVER THE LINE, YOU FUCKING NEANDERTHAL PRICK! YOU AND YOUR DISGUSTING LITTLE MONKEY BUDDY! YOU'VE PISSED ME OFF FOR THE LAST TIME!
YOU GOT THAT RIGHT, BOY.
YEAH! YEAH, I GOT IT EXACTLY RIGHT! I WARNED YOU, BUT YOU WOULDN'T LISTEN!
AND YOU CAN KEEP THAT DIRTY LITTLE SLUT OVER THERE! IF SHE'S DUMB ENOUGH TO LET YOU GET INTO HER PANTIES, SHE FUCKING DESERVES YOU!
HELL, I WAS NEVER EVEN INTERESTED IN HER, WITH THAT DIRTY SEWER OF A MOUTH! I CAN'T STAND LITTLE BITCHES LIKE THAT! I LIKE--
FAT BOYS?

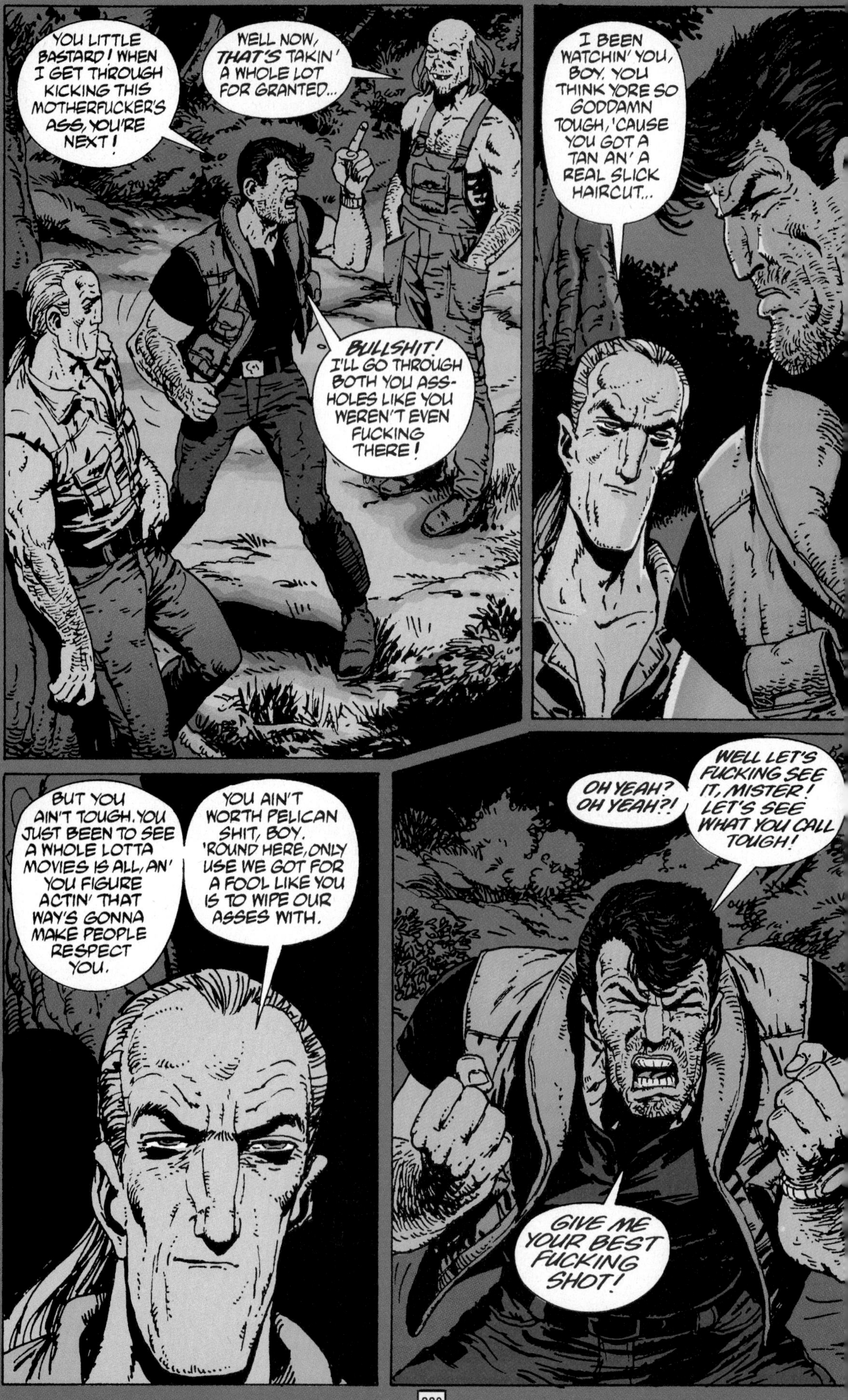
YOU LITTLE BASTARD! WHEN I GET THROUGH KICKING THIS MOTHERFUCKER'S ASS, YOU'RE NEXT!
WELL NOW, THAT'S TAKIN' A WHOLE LOT FOR GRANTED...
BULLSHIT! I'LL GO THROUGH BOTH YOU ASS-HOLES LIKE YOU WEREN'T EVEN FUCKING THERE!
I BEEN WATCHIN' YOU, BOY. YOU THINK YORE SO GODDAMN TOUGH, 'CAUSE YOU GOT A TAN AN' A REAL SLICK HAIRCUT...
BUT YOU AIN'T TOUGH. YOU JUST BEEN TO SEE A WHOLE LOTTA MOVIES IS ALL, AN' YOU FIGURE ACTIN' THAT WAY'S GONNA MAKE PEOPLE RESPECT YOU.
YOU AIN'T WORTH PELICAN SHIT, BOY. 'ROUND HERE, ONLY USE WE GOT FOR A FOOL LIKE YOU IS TO WIPE OUR ASSES WITH.
OH YEAH? OH YEAH?!
WELL LET'S FUCKING SEE IT, MISTER! LET'S SEE WHAT YOU CALL TOUGH!
GIVE ME YOUR BEST FUCKING SHOT!

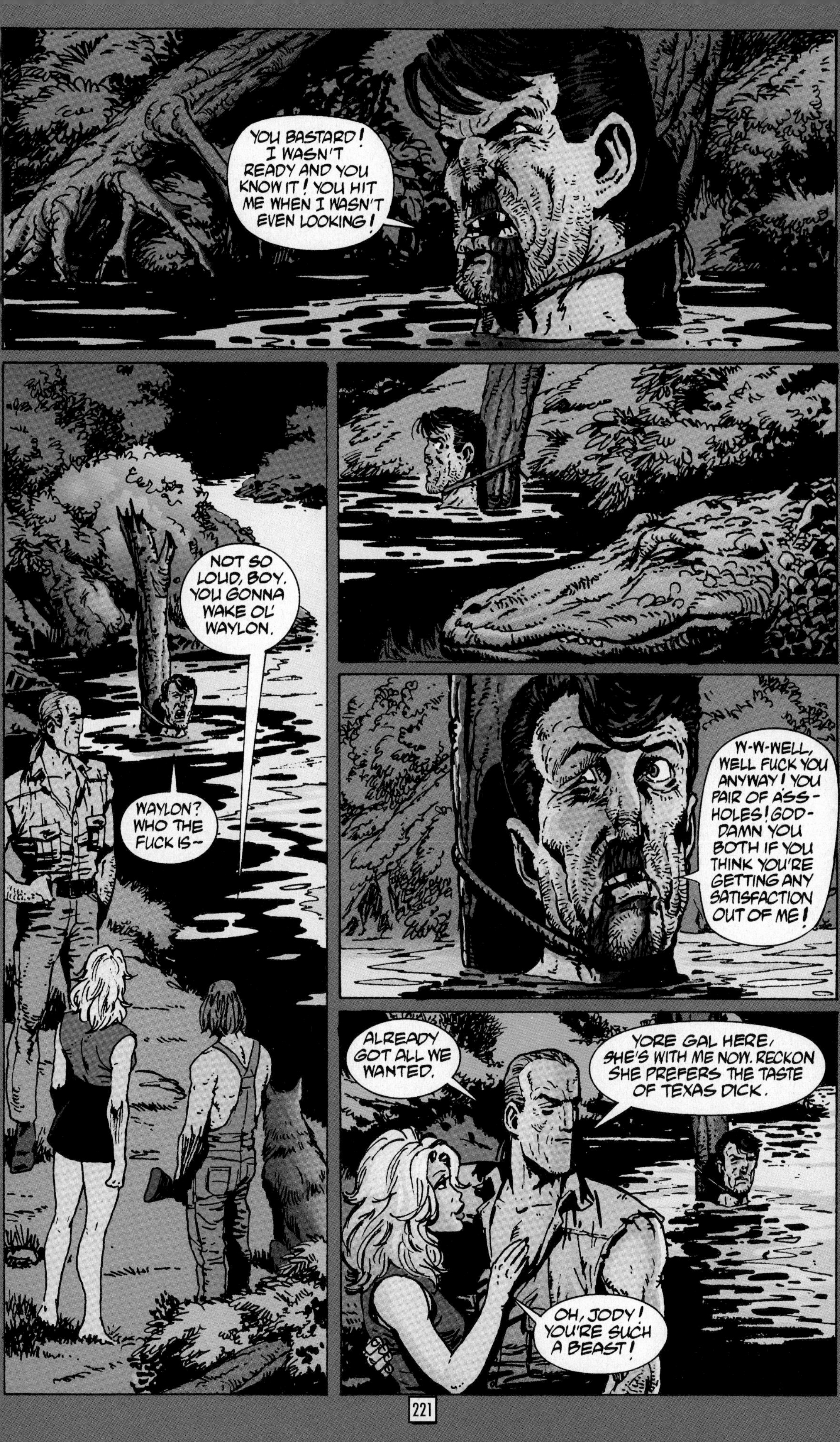
YOU BASTARD! I WASN'T READY AND YOU KNOW IT! YOU HIT ME WHEN I WASN'T EVEN LOOKING!
NOT SO LOUD, BOY. YOU GONNA WAKE OL' WAYLON.
WAYLON? WHO THE FUCK IS--
W-W-WELL, WELL FUCK YOU ANYWAY! YOU PAIR OF ASS-HOLES! GOD-DAMN YOU BOTH IF YOU THINK YOU'RE GETTING ANY SATISFACTION OUT OF ME!
ALREADY GOT ALL WE WANTED.
YORE GAL HERE, SHE'S WITH ME NOW. RECKON SHE PREFERS THE TASTE OF TEXAS DICK.
OH, JODY! YOU'RE SUCH A BEAST!

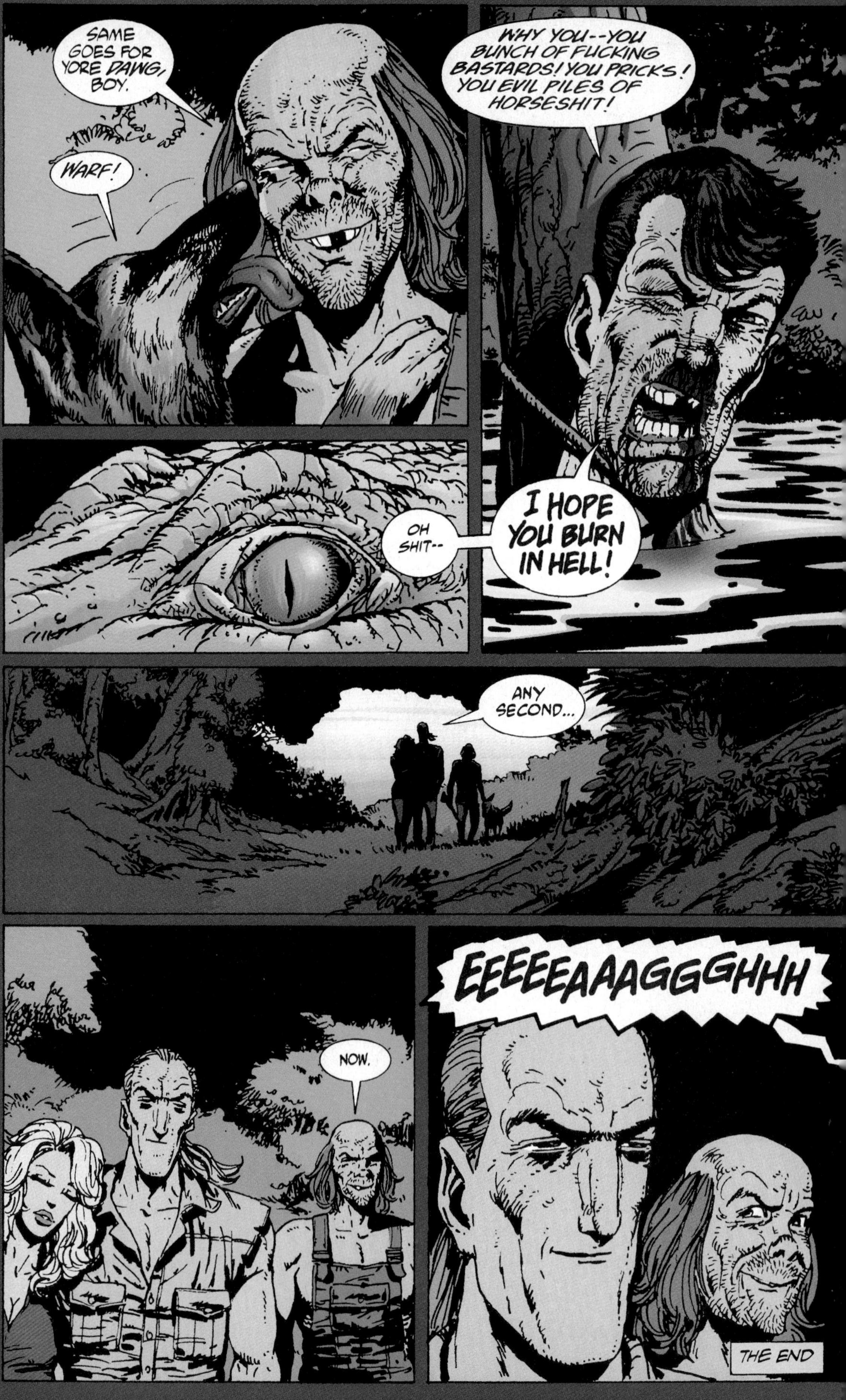
SAME GOES FOR YORE DAWG, BOY.
WARF!
WHY YOU--YOU BUNCH OF FUCKING BASTARDS! YOU PRICKS! YOU EVIL PILES OF HORSESHIT!
I HOPE YOU BURN IN HELL!
OH SHIT--
ANY SECOND...
NOW.
EEEEEAAAGGGHHH
THE END

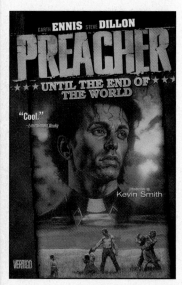
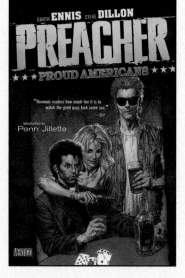
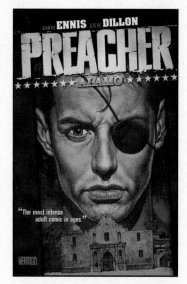

AND DON'T MISS THESE OTHER TITLES BY **GARTH ENNIS**

ADVENTURES IN THE RIFLE BRIGADE

VERTIGO
Adventures in the
Rifle Brigade
GARTH ENNIS
CARLOS EZQUERRA

WITH CARLOS EZQUERRA

WAR STORIES

GARTH ENNIS
WAR
STORIES
VOL. 1
CHRIS WESTON
GARY ERSKINE
JOHN HIGGINS
DAVE GIBBONS
DAVID LLOYD

WITH CHRIS WESTON, GARY ERSKINE, JOHN HIGGINS, DAVE GIBBONS AND DAVID LLOYD

GODDESS

VERTIGO
GODDESS
Garth
Ennis
Phil
Winslade

WITH PHIL WINSLADE

ALL TITLES ARE SUGGESTED FOR MATURE READERS.

PRIDE & JOY

VERTIGO
GARTH ENNIS
JOHN HIGGINS
PRIDE
& JOY

WITH JOHN HIGGINS

TRUE FAITH

VERTIGO
TRUE
FAITH
GARTH
ENNIS
WARREN
PLEECE

WITH WARREN PLEECE

UNKNOWN SOLDIER

VERTIGO
UNKNOWN
SOLDIER
BY GARTH ENNIS
& KILIAN PLUNKETT

WITH KILIAN PLUNKETT

SEARCH THE GRAPHIC NOVELS SECTION OF

www.VERTIGOCOMICS.com

FOR ART AND INFORMATION ON ALL OF OUR BOOKS!

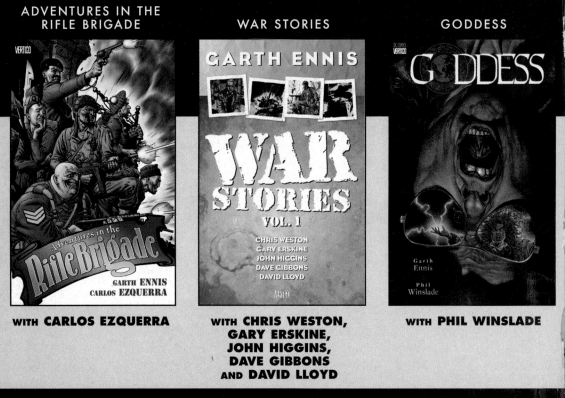

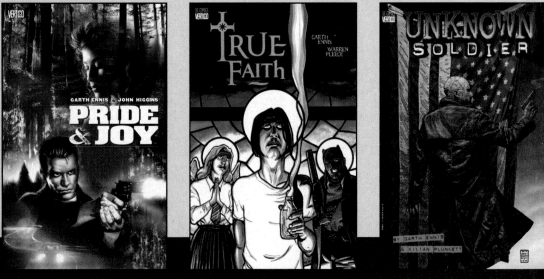